Administrative Philosophy

Titles of Related Interest

Evers & Lakomski/*Knowing Educational Administration*

Evers & Lakomski/*Exploring Administrative Coherentist Applications and Critical Debates*

Macpherson/*Educative Accountability Policies for Educational Institutions and Systems: Research, Theory and Practices in Educational Administration*

Administrative Philosophy

*Values and Motivations in
Administrative Life*

by

Christopher Hodgkinson
University of Victoria

Pergamon

U.K.   Elsevier Science Ltd, The Boulevard, Langford Lane, Kidlington, Oxford
            OX5 1GB, U.K.
U.S.A.   Elsevier Science Inc., 660 White Plains Road, Tarrytown, New York
            10591-5153, U.S.A.
JAPAN   Elsevier Science Japan, Higashi Azabu 1-chome Building 4F, 1-9-15
            Higashi Azabu, Mingto-ku, Tokyo 106, Japan.

First edition 1996

Library of Congress Cataloging in Publication Data
Hodgkinson, Christopher.
Administrative philosophy: values and motivations in administrative
life/by Christopher Hodgkinson —1st ed.
p. cm.
Includes index.
1. Management—Philosophy. 2. Power (Social sciences)—Philosophy.
3. Organizational behavior—Philosophy. I. Title.
HD38.H62 1966
658.4'001—dc920   96-13519
                                                                  CIP

British Library Cataloguing in Publication Data
A catalogue record for this book is available from the British Library.

ISBN 0 08 041924 0

Printed in Great Britain by Redwood Books Ltd, Trowbridge, Wilts

Contents

Preface

The experience of administering and of being administered is not exotic. It is the common lot of humanity. So common and so all-embracing—from the mother who is the first administrator to the estate executor who is the last—that one wonders why it has not attracted more philosophical attention. This book is an effort at redressing such inattentiveness.

Not that there has not been a plenitude of administrative studies—one could easily maintain that there has been a superfluity. Yet in all this surfeit something fundamental may have become lost. That which is missing, or at least neglected, could be called in Kantian terms, practical reason, or more simply: the *wisdom* of the administrative art. In other words, its philosophy. It is passing strange that a species of human activity which affects all of us all of the time seems so easily to elude philosophical scrutiny. At least to the point that while there are within the general rubric of philosophy proper such established subdisciplines as philosophy of law, philosophy of religion, and even philosophy of sport (not to mention science, language, and economics) yet there is no comparable discipline of either philosophy of administration or philosophy of leadership.

It is to be noted that all such established philosophical endeavours seek to do at least two things: to clarify the central concepts of their particular language games; and to illuminate the central issues, the polemic, of their respective domains. The philosophy of administration expounded here would no less but it also has a distinctive and perhaps more ambitious emphasis: to contribute to general as well as merely administrative axiology by a special consideration of the nature of value. Values, morals, and ethics intrude into every interstice of organizational life. The business of leadership is praxis: values-in-practice; values-in-action; values a priori; values a posteriori. Confusion about values, at every level from the individual to the cultural, has become a defining characteristic of the postmodern world.

This enquiry into the nature of people, power, and organizations is in four parts. The first and last of these deal respectively with the conjunction and disjunction of philosophy and administration while the two middle parts deal with the meat of the matter: hierarchy, power, values, and interests. By conjunction is meant the union, as in the Platonic ideal, of philosopher and administrator; by disjunction the degeneration and decadence of this idealism in the realistic condition. A motivation for the enquiry, and its guiding presumption, was that it does not seem possible to issue, or even presume, a clean bill of health for the administrative and organizational world of the late second and early third millennia. Why is this so? Why do things go wrong? Why is dishonour a more tenable norm than honour? How does the evil get done?

It is in attempting to answer such questions that administrative philosophy finds its proper place in the scheme of things. True (and this is surely part of the problem) that place may be denied by the busy administrator and the time-stressed executive—the man or woman of affairs—but as the text will contend, such an administrator is less of a leader and more of a manager, a factotum. This book is for leaders and for those who aspire to leadership. Such leaders practise philosophy *of* administration rather than philosophy *and* administration. This last: administration on the one hand and philosophy on the other, is an arbitrary divorce. Though academically convenient it tends to a loss of connection between theory and practice, a failing which, rightly understood, philosophy *of* administration would remedy.

Something else must be said. Given that administration is an imperfect and suspect art any critique of it must nevertheless allow that it can also be construed as the ultimate of art forms—it paints after all with human pigment on the canvas of history. And any such critique must take into account the legacy and endowment of all past collective effort and cooperative evolution. In this light it becomes possible to utter a philosophical Yea-saying, an affirmation and endorsement of the administrative calling. But such a response cannot be unsophisticated, uninformed, naive. It implies at the least a fund of passion large enough to overcome, with clear eyes, the forces of negativity and pathology that beset the organizational leader. Truly, their name is legion. Thus, at the end of the day, one can only assert the joy of leadership in the joy of overcoming which I would wish to show must be, *de profundis*, a *self*-overcoming.

A NOTE ON THE PROPOSITIONS

At the conclusion of all but the final chapter the reader will find a consecutive series of numbered propositions. These constitute a sort of second text or subtext to the main body and are cast in summative, aphoristic, and occasionally provocative form. This propositional logic is intended to serve a number of purposes.

It may be used simply as a recapitulation of essential content in each chapter. It can be used as a stimulus to reflection by the practising administrator. Or it can be treated as an invitation to sceptical re-examination of one's own presuppositions and administrative world-view. In their most ambitious aspect the propositions attempt to constitute *in toto* the general structural logic of fact and value in administration. The justification for such a claim would rest upon their contingent nature for each proposition is open to falsification and valid only until refutation. Finally, the propositions may be used as a pedagogical tool or device in the teaching of administrative theory and at their very best may serve as bolts to be hurled against the natural armour of the administrative soul.

What the propositions are *not*, however, is any sort of orthodoxy or dogmata. On the contrary they should provide an incentive towards the development of examined values and, consequently, heterogeneous philosophies on the part of individual practitioners.

If an author is entitled to something like, let us say, a fond and earnest hope, then let mine be that any such truly Socratic effort on the part of our leaders, each acting uniquely, will of itself enrich the overall reality of administrative philosophy and thence, at not too many removes, the quality of life for everyone.

Christopher Hodgkinson
Victoria, Canada
1996

I
CONJUNCTIONS

He who sees the inaction that is in action,
and the action that is in inaction, is wise indeed.
Bhagavad Gita Ch. IV

Chapter 1
Philosophy and Administration

Administration is inescapable. We live our lives in organizations. We are born into organizations called the family and the nation state. We die as members of these same organizations. And between birth and death we are relentlessly administered and administering.

Man is a social animal. An organizational animal. Aristotle declared that a man who lived alone would have to be either a god or a beast, and he was right. Even mystics and hermits, feral autistic children, psychopaths and misanthropics are dependent for their very existence, and their expression of that existence, upon a sustaining society and a supportive fabric of organization and administration. We are born into families, educated in school, and live out our adult lives in, by, and through a complex of organizations. Modern bureaucracy affects and embraces all levels of cooperative association from the purely familial up to the global influences of nation states, multi-national corporations and international systems of administration. Each of us is a member not only of a national entity but also of a multiplicity of lesser organizations. And among all these there is usually one specific organization (or at most a very few) upon which we depend for our economic livelihood and our social status. It is not excessive to say then that we are utterly administration-dependent.

This dependency means that the class of specialists known variously as managers, administrators, leaders, executives, officials, and functionaries has a profound significance for the quality of human life. The expertise of this class is administration, and it follows that if philosophy is a humanism it can never divorce itself from the subject-matter of administration. The administrative profession, let us use the world loosely for now, has existed since the first discovery of cooperative efficacy and, from that primeval moment has created those basic disjunctions which have persisted throughout history in the distinctions between ruler and ruled, governors and governed, leaders and led. This division, however expressed, implies and entails two aspects: first a body of practice, knowledge, and theory which we can tentatively label as administration and, second, a body of reflection, analysis, and critique of administration which for the moment we can call administrative philosophy. Philosophy of administration is thus the reflective aspect of man's oldest cooperative activity. But, as we shall see, it is not merely social action recollected in tranquility but an

3

informing process of praxis that helps shape and determine the very nature of organizational behaviour. Administrative philosophy has proximate and ultimate ends. The former seeks to clarify, organize, synthesize, and illuminate the knowledge about organization and administration which does exist. The latter to provide a hermeneutic and propadeutic for the improvement of collective life.

Given these ends and the extent of the historical record one might expect that the literature of this discipline would be voluminous indeed. Yet this is not the case. On the contrary the work in philosophy of administration *per se* is slight, and indeed almost negligible in terms of quantity, when compared with such disciplinary subsets as, say, philosophy of science, philosophy of religion, even philosophy of sport.[1] Works of political theory abound, of course, as do analyses of bureaucracy and social psychology but the general tendency, with rare and notable exceptions, is to disjunction rather than conjunction of bodies of knowledge; to a separation of value and fact, and to an abdication of wisdom in favour of knowledge, especially in technologized or empiricized forms.

The pages that follow are an attempt to reverse this tendency; to synthesize as well as analyse. In the end philosophy must be synoptic, conjunctive, and benevolent even if, towards this end, it must pass through phases that are analytic, disjunctive, and distressing. This enterprise of uniting philosophy and administration is not without hazard. It demands, above all, a passionate commitment to truth-seeking; to following ruthlessly wherever that value leads. As a Renaissance philosopher of administration once remarked, "... if some of our rulers were to be confronted by a strict philosopher, or indeed anyone at all who openly and candidly might wish to show them the awesome face of true virtue, teach them a good way of life and how a good prince should conduct himself, I am sure that as soon as he appeared they would loath him as if he were a serpent or mock at him as if he were dirt.[2]

PROPOSITIONS, REALITY, AND LOGIC

Just as war is too serious a matter to be left to the generals so the business of administration is too serious an activity to be left either to social scientists on the reflective side or to the administrators themselves on the active side. The former conduces to the unsynthesized and endless inquiry of quantitative methodology and is often circumscribed by the strictures and limits of that form of social conditioning known as political correctness.[3] The latter is susceptible to pragmatic indifference, self-justification, or an infinity of follies and fallacies which we shall later discuss and explore in some detail.

At this point it is useful to discriminate between philosophy and social science (sometimes "human science"). Numerically it seems not unreasonable to say that philosophers of administration are in short supply while the "scientists" of administration are legion. In consequence there is large and ever-growing literature of administrative science which has been referred to by one eminent authority as a "weak and tasteless synthetic brew" of scientific administration, human relations, and systems theory.[4] This corpus of empirical study forms a large and useful body of knowledge that lays some claim to the honorific term science, though quasi-science or proto-science might be more exact. Yet at its very best it is not philosophy. The value elements that pervade administration tend to be elided, bracketed-out, suspended, ignored, or otherwise given short shrift by the scientists of administration. Philosophy on the other hand, to give but one example, is properly represented in modern literature in the work of Barnard.[5] He expresses profound concerns about problems of morality, of purpose; about the being or character of administrators themselves, in a way which is in stark opposition to that of even his own protégé, the Nobelist H. A. Simon.

The intent of this book is a restoration of balance. Most fervently one wishes for the raising of philosophical consciousness, of *value* consciousness, on the part of administrators themselves. Beyond that one wishes for a restoration of dialogue between humanists and philosophers as well as between administrators and practitioners. As Sir Karl Popper maintained, we are all practising philosophers because we all subscribe to philosophical theories and act on them.[6] But we do so badly. Unconsciously and uncritically. Therefore our task must be to become aware of our determining philosophies and to critique them. To Socrates' dictum that the unexamined life was not worth living should now be added an addendum: the unexamined value is not worth holding.

Any conscious philosophical scheme entails subscription to certain propositions. The term *proposition* is crucial. It will be used in a special sense in this book and, from time to time, a proposition as such will be enunciated in order to condense or crystallize a level of meaning in succinct form. Now meaning can refer to a variety of realities, some of which are amenable to scientific methodology and some of which are not. Hence a proposition in our sense is not necessarily a scientifically verifiable or testable truth. Nor even a logical necessity since some propositions will go beyond logic as well as beyond science. Let me illustrate this point.

Reality is not a simple, unambiguous term. It is at the very least triplex, if not multiplex. Thus, in the empirical domain of science, that deterministic world of cause and effect (let's leave quantum mechanics aside for the moment), of quantities and measurable relationships and replicable experimentation it is possible to declare some propositions that have the force of law. These propositions are predictive and verifiable such as $E = mc^2$; or electrical current is directly proportional to voltage and inversely proportional to resistance; or a falling object accelerates at 32 feet per second squared. Hard science is in the business of discovering such lawful propositions and the more it can come up with the better for us. If, that is, we accept the non-scientific proposition "Knowledge is power."

Then there is the reality appropriate to social science. This, it so happens, is the stuff and furniture of administrative experience. Here there are some predictabilities: If I fail to pay my staff they will probably cease to contribute their services. But certainties are fewer and indeterminacies loom larger. A proposition such as $B = f(P, E)$: Behaviour is a function of personality and environment, or the Fiedler/Argyris proposition that in organizational contexts the factor of personality is a fixed variable,[7] are softer and mushier if not entirely vacuous as statements of law. In this domain of reality there are degrees of freedom and only partial determination of events. The domain of social inter-action (which pervades and subsumes organizational behaviour) is in part imponderable and the propositions of this language are always hypothetical to some degree. Nevertheless, there are regularities in human behaviour and the more verified or unfalsified propositions that social science can deliver the more we can lay claim to a knowledge base for administrative philosophy.

Lastly, but perhaps more accurately one should say firstly, there is the reality of direct human experience. This reality is where we live our lives and it is termed variously the subjective, the phenomenological, the psychological, the social psychological, the life-world; the regions bounded by the horizons of conscious-ness. This reality is primal; it includes the parameters of pain, pleasure, emo-tion, and motivation. It contains elements of voluntarism, of choice, intention, will which render it intractably indeterminate and yet—if atomic insularity or solipsism is not to be countenanced, if indeed "no man is an island"—then this type of reality converges and intertwines with the factual and the social realities of natural and human science. The intersubjectivity of language enables us to enunciate propositions at this level of reality also. Such propositions differ from those of the other realities in that they are not scientific in either the certain or the probabilistic sense but instead are linguistic assertions of a philosophical nature whose function is to induce connotations and provoke changes in the received level of understanding. They could therefore be called pedagogical aphorisms or pedagogisms. Readers bring to these propositions their own value biases and presumptions, their own epistemology, and their own wealth of experience, knowledge, and insight. From the interaction of life-worlds implicit in the formulation and transmissions of such administrative propositions there emerges the possibility and the potential of an authentic legitimate qualitative philosophy of administration. Propositions of the last kind will occur, therefore, throughout this book. The first of such propositions is:

1. Administration is philosophy-in-action

Neither of the key terms in this proposition has as yet been defined but already it will be understood that administration is a very *general* activity and it is "philo-sophical" at least in the sense that it has something to do with the formulation of purposes, especially that collective purpose which applies to organizations.

This first and basic proposition is also a three-fold conjunction. It unites the three elements: administration itself, philosophy, and action. Each of these terms needs definition, clarification and explication. Our first concern is naturally with the concept of administration, the subject of the proposition and our basic subject matter, but, since this will be treated in depth later (Part II, Chapter 2) it will suffice for now if we acknowledge a certain necessary distinction between administration and management. The former subsumes the latter and together they form a spectrum of experiences, behaviours, and actions which range from the subjective and valuational to the objective and mechanical. Along this spectrum administration refers to the more qualitative and "political" aspects while management refers to the more quantitative and "practical"; it being understood that both aspects combine within the executive role. In short, administration is a generalism.

It is that set of activities, otherwise known as policy making, which determines the ends (and their implicit means) of a collectivity or organization. And, whether consciously recognized as such or not, this activity of forming purposes, for oneself or others is the doing of philosophy. Purpose grounded in or emergent from philosophy is at the heart of administrative process and, in the last analysis, organizations represent *fasces* or bundles of values (ends, purposes, goals, aims) held together by an integument of administrative will and managerial skill. In this pure sense they could be considered fascistic. Intellectual comprehension and general understanding of this complex organizational value system may in fact be confused, opaque, or even mistaken. The system itself may be differentially perceived within and without the organization. Nevertheless, the prerogative of administration remains that of formulating, re-formulating, and modulating purpose and value throughout the life-history of the organization. Administrators are specialists in generalism.

One must note the dynamic quality of this "philosophy", this generalist speciality. It is never absolute, never permanent. It is rather emergent, dialectical, ever in the process of interpretation. It was one of Nietzsche's most trenchant insights, now a cardinal tenet of postmodernism, that "There are no facts, only interpretations." Administration is the art of interpretation of organizational reality.

Philosophy and the Academy

The term philosophy is somewhat forbidding in modern times. While etymologically it may be defined quite simply as the love of wisdom the educated organization man is also sensitive to the fact that it has been appropriated by the academy. And it is not lost upon him that academicians, theorists, and professional philosophers (the last a concept that Wittgenstein would call a contradiction in terms)[8] have been, on the historical record, singularly ineffective, or else downright dangerous, in the arts of governance and the practical affairs of men. Yet this merely accentuates the need for clarity about what philosophy means. It has many senses. So many that we must isolate from amongst them those that serve our special purpose and invest Proposition 1 with meaning.

Let us return to the classical interpretation: love of wisdom. The point that may be overlooked here is a conflict with contemporary egalitarian norms and democratic ethos. Philosophy in this ancient sense is intrinsically elitist. It does not require any Derridean deconstruction to remark that while all men may be presumed to love wisdom all are differentially wise and the mark of the philosopher is *his* claim to some kind of extra purchase upon this value of wisdom. Perhaps because of this disjunction between elitism (the claim to wisdom) and democratic egalitarianism (all men have an equal claim) few, if any, professional philosophers overtly purport nowadays to be wise.[9] Instead, humbler pretensions towards expertise in this, that, or the other speciality or subspeciality are the general academic norm.

Nevertheless the lure of wisdom as a vague compound of goodness and cleverness persists. Certainly the value is germane to administration and governance. Executives and leaders, especially in the political ring, seek to establish their intimacy with this quality. Indeed they would not hesitate to appropriate it as a personal, characterological attribute. Other things being equal the organization will wish to appoint the "wisest" men or women to its administrative offices, though this desire is likely to be couched in terms neither of philosophy nor wisdom but rather of such qualities as a sophistication, credibility, know-how, cleverness, common sense, integrity, and vision.

Administrators ought therefore to be wisdom-seekers. Socrates declared that the unexamined life was not worth living. We shall extend this dictum later to "The unexamined value is not worth holding", and more immediately "Unexamined administration is not worth doing."

But philosophy in this sense is more classical than academic. This interpretation is still placed on philosophy by the unschooled and by those unexposed to academic niceties or pedantries. Such usage is not to be despised. On the contrary the meaning of practical wisdom or wise and good administration is central to the more specific definition developed later. Nevertheless, the academic understanding of philosophy deserves a closer examination, even by the practical and pragmatic man of action.

Ontology

As a discipline of study philosophy is technically and conventionally divided into ontology, epistemology, and axiology. Ontology or metaphysics deals with the nature of reality or being. Its guiding question is, What is real? At one extreme this can yield answers such as, Brahman (God) is real, everything else is unreal.[10] Since all human experiences occur in a mind, the exact relationship of which to brain and neural circuitry has not been scientifically (i.e. objectively) determined, the option of absolute subjective idealism exists. On the other hand, at the other extreme, realism (materialism) expounds an empirical universe in which consciousness (and human experience) is a mere side-effect of evolution, an epiphenomenon. As may be imagined, between these extremes are located a rich variety of ontologies each with its own exegesis and attendant belief system. Some of these bear directly upon organization and administration and will merit our attention later. The metaphysical side of philosophy thus described, *tout court,* may seem very remote at first glance from the world of administrative action yet, if only because religion and ontology share common ground (in fact they are symbiotic on each other) it can easily be appreciated that this branch of philosophy affects action through the person of the administrator. A man is a belief system.

> A man consists of the faith that is in him.
> Whatever his faith is, he is.[11]

An executive's behaviour pattern may be a function of his belief system regardless of whether the associated value complex, or the ontological structure, is conscious and articulated or unconscious, unexamined, unarticulated. Metaphysical assumptions in fact often determine the level and scope of an administrator's commitment and directly influence his actual and perceived integrity. So metaphysics and theory of mind must enter into any accounting of the overall complex of motivation, interests, and values. It could be said, for example, that the main ontological concern for administration lies in the disjunction: Are humans different from the rest of the animal kingdom in kind, or only in degree?[12] The position taken upon this question is a determinant of administrative philosophy and, thereby, upon philosophy-in-action.

Administrators possess models-of-man. These are judgements of man-in-the-world by which they form their way of organizational life. Whether these implicit or explicit commitments to world-views, religions, or ideologies are correlated with administrative success or whether, say, men or women with strong religious beliefs are disproportionately represented (or underrepresented) in the higher levels of organizational hierarchy are questions for empirical investigation, for sociology not philosophy. But the philosophical linkage between ontology and value systems generally is sufficiently obvious that the subject cannot be summarily dismissed as irrelevant, either to administrative philosophy *per se* or to the practice of administration and governance.

Epistemology

Epistemology, in contrast to metaphysics, is at once of interest and relevance to administrators in that its control questions are "What is true?" and "How do you know?" Both are questions of daily executive concern. While Pontius Pilate could be dismissive about the former no modern executive can afford to be cavalier about either. Epistemology or knowledge about knowing has led to the development of highly technical systems of logic as well as to the broad disciplinary developments of psychology and social psychology. All of these knowledge contributions are vital for policy making, policy analysis, and policy implementation.[13] Furthermore, it goes without saying that computerology now forms an important part of the infrastructure of any management science. Truth and logic are components of systematic rationality and rationality itself is a value premise so deeply and powerfully entrenched that it enters unconsciously into all administrative thought processes. Thus, no one sets out to manage illogically or irrationally, any more than one would set out to manage inefficiently, or to the perceived detriment of the organization's welfare.

Logic is not only a subset of formal philosophy, it is the executive's basic and most fundamental tool. It enters into his work through the weighing and assessing of arguments, policies, proposals, and presentations—the executive is continuously obliged to monitor for fallacies and errors in projects, schemes, and plans. It could be easily argued that the difference between a more competent and a less competent manager/administrator is a function of logical capacity and logical acuity. A whole armamentarium of critical faculties and skills is thus crucial to the executive task. And it follows that academics would surely be worth their weight in executive gold if they could but guarantee some means of sharpening and strengthening the logical faculties. A guarantee that, unfortunately, is neither present nor forthcoming.

Yet logic itself is neither singular nor simple. More recently, theoretical circles in administration[14] have become interested in advanced and complex logics which challenge the conventional assumptions about organizational reality and perception. Questions are raised about the truth of organizational life and its amenability to law, prediction, and linear rationality. What are the deep inconsistencies in organizational behaviour? Questions about the ontology and epistemology of power have had far reaching ramifications for the practice of administration, notably, for example, in the radical feminist and pluralist movements. Questions such as these are rooted in epistemology (How do we know what we think we know?) but they also lead into the farthest reaches of individual and collective psychology.

Axiology

The last, and for us the greatest, division of formal philosophy is axiology. This is the study of value, ethics, and aesthetics guided by the radical questions, What is good?, What is right? What is elegant or beautiful? These questions directly fund the moral art of administration and will constitute the central burden of this text. They will be treated in detail later and it will be shown that value is the very essence of the administrative art form.

For now it can be conceded that the emergence of values, their realization through cooperative action, the resolution of their conflict in administrative process, their debate and containment within the organizational political arena and its surrounding environment—all this is an hourly and daily preoccupation of executive experience.

Of course, the reflective, analytical function epitomized by formal philosophy is at the other extreme from the daily combat, the tactical decision making, the rough and tumble, and the affective realities of organizational action. Nevertheless, whatever academic philosophy can do by way of explicating the nature and sources of ethics, or by way of synthesis of the findings of social and behavioural science concerning the nature of values, is of direct relevance to administration. That so little communication occurs between these two realms of discourse is a matter both for curiosity and regret.[15]

Unreflective action is degenerative. It is entropic.

For administrators philosophy also means *policy*. That is, the formulation and implementation of policy—policy making. Policy making cannot occur *tabula rasa*. Each policymaker arrives at the table already prejudiced and predisposed. Any myth of impartiality is akin to the illusion of scientific objectivity. Any decision entails values and any single decision maker embodies an a priori value complex. When policy is being formed or, in other words, when organizational philosophy is being established, what happens is that a factual scenario is *re*-presented to the policy makers with more or less logical consistency and empirical accuracy. Included in this representation, explicitly or tacitly, is a projection of hypothetical future states of affairs. This is then subjugated to the value considerations of the policy making administrators. That is, to their desires, wills, and intentions. Thus, through complex and subtle processes, as well as simple and direct mechanisms, agendas conflict and interact, and via dialogue, dialectic, and power the purposes, aims, objectives, and goals of the organization come to be formulated. An actual organizational value complex evolves which, regardless of the formulation or verbalization or rhetoric in which it is couched, becomes the mundane, quotidian philosophy that is translated into the realities and events of the workaday world through managerial processes.

PHILOSOPHY AND ACTION

The previous discussion shows that the concept of philosophy is protean and elusive. It ranges from love of wisdom to the intricacies of the technical divisions of an academic discipline. Yet all of this range of meaning has some relevance to administration and to the practical business of policy making. In this book, however, we shall seek to simplify by adopting a dualistic interpretation of the term. In this interpretation the domain of philosophy is divided into two parts: logic and value. The former deals with matters of fact, structures, coherence and consistency, causal chains and explanatory systems and sequences. It encompasses, for example, our knowledge of organization and methods, systems theory, and bureaucratic analysis. The latter deals with all matters of value from the ethical and moral, through the valuational, to all the complexities of motivation. It would thus embrace all the infra- and supra-rational elements revealed by or known from depth study of the human psyche. Together these two divisions; the logical–empirical and the valuational–intentional, establish the field of administrative philosophy. They constitute the foundations of philosophy-in-action.

PHILOSOPHY AND PRACTICE

While the case has now been made for the sheer relevance of philosophy to administration a disturbing question lingers. The pragmatic administrator may simply ask, Why do philosophy? If administration is philosophy-in-action anyway, why not let the philosophy take care of itself? Or, more precisely, let the philosophical elements take care of themselves. The question applies not solely to practitioners but also to theorists, and most especially to professors of organizational and administrative theory. In ordinary language the word philosophy suffers from a host of not entirely undeserved negative connotations. It stands over against and in opposition to, the active milieu of organizations, the practicalities and constraints, the hurly-burly of the "real world". Why engage in academic gymnastics and speculation? Why not simply assume that the history of everyday life will write its own philosophical record, which can then, after the fact, be perused *ad nauseam* by the professional pundits. Why seek a more conscious approach to what is already over-complex and incomprehensible in all its variables and interactions demanding of action *now*? Why not rest upon the institutionalized methods that have evolved and become approved since time immemorial: bureaucratic rationality, *savoir faire*, intuition, common sense?

But above all, what is to be gained? The practitioner is a very busy man. The theorist also is very busy; there are a host of empirical questions before him and these include the question whether there even exists a body of knowledge in the field that would permit of any synthetic or philosophical treatment.

In short, what is the pay-off?

Before attempting to answer this last question it is advisable to consider the a-philosophical or anti-philosophical views of some eminent administrative authorities. Positivists in particular, and behaviourists generally, are satisfied to consider administrative process as the negotiation of means-ends chains wherein the ends are given or derived from elsewhere (that is, from somewhere "outside" administration) and the function of the executive is merely to satisfice such means-ends consummation subject to the metavaluational criteria of efficiency and effectiveness.[16] The organization is a bus and the administrator its driver.[17] Philosophy, policy, is *ultra vires*; outside the ambit of the manager or executive.

Adherents of this viewpoint and, to a less extent, the mass of administrative–managerial functionaries who are for getting things done (not theirs to question why...) are impressed by the classic distinction celebrated in the literature as the politics–administration dichotomy.[18] Cases in point are abundant and common to both democratic and totalitarian systems. After a prolonged period of imprisonment Albert Speer, a superlatively successful but a-philosophical administrator, said to have single-handedly extended the duration of World War II by almost two years, was eventually moved to philosophical and ethical misgivings about his past administrative performance.[19] But none of these latter-day regrets were evident at the peak of his activity. Contemplation and action were then effectively divorced. Indeed at that time he might well have considered any such reflections as inhibitory, debilitating, and counter-productive. Not to mention, for a patriotic citizen, their constituting a potential threat to the war effort. Analagous are those administrators everywhere who are generally preoccupied with organizational techniques, technology, and tactics. They may regard any philosophical reflection as at best luxurious and distracting, or at worst a downright impediment to efficiency and effectiveness that could become destructive and demoralizing, a threat to their central interest which is job security.

The underlying rationale in this general antagonism to philosophy may be that a centipede who indulges in too much self-analysis might have difficulty in walking. But it is perhaps neither unkind nor untrue to suggest that there is also a sort of anti-intellectualism that runs with the pragmatic spirit of men of action.[20] Whatever the reason, the fact remains that the philosophy of administration often has to overcome distrust, dislike, suspicion, and on occasion contempt. How is this to be done?

The main counter-argument to administrative philosophy has already been stated. It is that intellectualizing may prove detrimental to pragmatic managerial efficiency and effectiveness once means are discriminated from ends. Knowing why or asking why is seen to inhibit know-how and can-do.

We shall show that this charge is fallacious and unwarranted. It rests on a deficient understanding of administrative reality and a total misunderstanding of the logic of value. Values can only be analytically divorced from fact. Fact and value always appear together as do substance and quality. Likewise, ends cannot be truly divorced from means without damage to the synthetic philosophical fabric—that is, the meaning of the whole—despite the apparent but delusory ease with which this can seem to be done by pragmatists, positivists, and activists. True there is a time for thought and a different time for action, but with administration defined and understood as philosophy-in-action the maxim, He who hesitates is lost, no longer obtains. He who does not hesitate is lost.

As for the question of pay-off let us defer the answer until we have considered briefly two further contingent aspects of philosophy of administration: its relationship to society and to the individual.

PHILOSOPHY AND SOCIETY

Administrative action is like the throwing of a stone into a pool of water. Ripples move outward from the centre of impact while the impact itself is constrained and limited by the geometry and physics of the medium. Any chains of cause and effect initiated by an administrator are similarly modulated and tempered by the organizational and socio-cultural environment. Administration always occurs in a context that is political, economic, social, and cultural. The administrator must constantly look outwards as well as inwards. Therefore administrative philosophy has a global dimension, it cannot be delimited just to organizational behaviour or experience. Its parameters include explicitly and implicitly social, political, ideological and cultural concerns. And therefore, social critique.

It is useful here to discriminate between social (organizational) behaviour, experience, and understanding. Social behaviour is a matter for the empiricist record; it is amenable to statistical method and positivist interpretation. Political scientists, polling specialists, sexologists (e.g. Professor Kinsey),[21] advertising and media consultants, actuaries, biologists, and medical information specialists all practise legitimately in this mode of reality. On the other hand social experience is also and inevitably a matter of subjectivity. Another level of reality is engaged and this reality in its turn depends upon understanding or interpretation. This movement from behaviour to experience and its understanding through interpretation is exhibited in the method expounded by Max Weber "the observation and theoretical interpretation of the subjective 'states of mind' of actors", what Weber famously referred to as *Verstehen* or "understanding".[22] Once again we are reminded of Nietzsche's declaration, "There are no facts, only interpretations."

This approach to social or collective truth or knowledge has been referred to as the "interpretive turn" in social science and can be illustrated in sociology by the work of Goffmann, Geertz, and Giddens.[23] In administrative philosophy we need to note especially the work of T. B. Greenfield,[24] while in philosophy proper the sources of the interpretive turn can be traced *inter alia* to Heidegger, Husserl, and Gadamer. In the extremes the subjectivist position is clearly stated by Sergiovanni: "there is no separate reality in organizational behaviour and administrative functioning. Objectivity and truth are evasive and no order exists beyond that which is created in the minds of persons and that which is imposed upon the organization by persons."[25]

This mentalist approach is taken one step farther by Evers and Lakomski who subscribe to an ontology of mind–brain identity "... while we do not deny the existence of inner phenomena as causing human behaviour, it is not intentions which do the causal work but fine-grained, neuro-physiological mechanisms. Intentions, as referred to in ordinary talk, are more fruitfully conceived as 'promissory notes' for these underlying mechanisms which, unlike the former are, and will be identifiable by our best science." This assertion in itself would appear to be a "promissory note" for positivistic science but, ignoring the distraction of the mind–body problem it serves to confirm the wisdom that socio-cultural reality, the environment of administrative praxis, is firstly a matter for interpretation (logic) and, second, a matter for judgement and critique (value); neither of which branches of administrative philosophy are amenable to natural science methodology or *Naturwissenschaften* in Dilthey's terminology.[26] In brief, social reality and organizational reality are phenomenological constructs. What is perceived to be, *is*—but perception itself is a complex product of values, logic, and intersubjectivity.

Given that social order, as represented in political structures and complex organizations, is open to interpretation and judgement by the administrative philosopher it is understandable that major challenges have been launched against the status quo, most notably by the Marxists and neo-Marxists, the so-called school of Critical Theory, and more latterly by a number of postmodernist French philosophers whose ranks include Derrida, Foucault, and Lyotard.[27] It would be difficult, not to say tedious, to attempt any synopsis of these voluminous writings but they exhibit common themes of administrative concern, for example: domination-oppression, the use of power to this end as disguised or hidden in language, and rationality as a means of domination, especially administrative–managerial–technical control through systems of hierarchy, interest, dramaturgy and bureaucracy. The status quo of social order and arrangement is interpreted as malignant. Power corrupts and has corrupted the forms of life and organization in which humanity works out its collective destiny. The postmodern critics are also, by and large, heavily pessimistic in their prognoses. They have by their lights diagnosed the disease but, in the aftermath of the demise of classical Marxism, they offer little by way of cure. It may be noted too that their criticisms rely heavily, *pace* Freud, upon the assumption of an unconscious substratum in human affairs and hence they derive their warrant to ascribe unconscious intentions and motivations to social actors. The philosopher of administration in considering their interpretations will have already observed the reality shift that has occurred in their discourse. In modern science only the observable is taken as real, that is, only data observable by the senses or by the extension of senses through technological instrumentation. All else is at worst discarded, at best discounted. The postmoderns, however, deal with a level of reality which, by this canon, is non-scientific. Verstehen, inference, imputation, interpretation, introspection and intuition are the typical modes of research. The differing realities dealt with by natural and social science need not, however, deter the philosopher of administration but clearly they impose greater demands for subtlety in the dialectics of value and logic that go to make up administrative understanding.

Social debate, sociological theory, social science, critique, dialectic, social consciousness, social conscience, social "sense" of wisdom—none of these can be divorced from any coherent philosophy of administration. Neither can they be eliminated from administrative practice for administration *is* social and the sum of administration shapes society, culture, and the quality of life.

PHILOSOPHY AND THE INDIVIDUAL

Philosophy can raise its voice about social issues. Often it sees itself charged with the responsibility to do so. In times ancient and modern, philosophers have become irritants to the holders of power and in 399 BC Socrates was made to take his life for an offence of administrative philosophy. Countless others through the ages, from Sir Thomas More to the faceless heroes and heroines who resisted and dissented from totalitarianism, have followed in his train. But whether the philosophically resisting voice is at all efficacious, or whether it is merely a prophetic crying in the wilderness is another question. Marx was perhaps the first amongst moderns to call for philosophers to become administrators; to move from observation to transformation. His manifesto to philosophers declared that the time had come to cease observing history and to begin to change it. Even here, despite the dubious record of nearly a century of Marxist praxis the concept of philosophy-in-action remains potent.

Given this potency and the historical record it is all the more peculiar that we should then encounter a strange aberration in the literature of administration. It is true that the literature is replete with empirical studies of administrative personality attributes, most notably in connection with the trait theory of leadership.[28] But these traits, by and large, refer to the *characteristics* of administrators rather than to their *character*. Indeed, the distinction between characteristics and character is an important one for administrative philosophy for our database is heavily weighted towards the former. In a recent survey of a hundred years of leadership research Van Fleet and Yukl trace the historical movement from personal characteristics through behavioural studies and situational emphases to present times in which they regard the state of affairs as analogous to the multiplex bewilderment of modern particle physics.[29] Looking forward to the future they likewise only approach *character* indirectly and tentatively through the concepts of transformational and charismatic leadership.[30]

On the other hand the problem of character is also approached obliquely through the focus of a concern with ethics and morality. In this way insights into character occasionally surface. Consider this quotation from a classic work in public administration:

> Highly mobile individuals—with very strong personal ambitions—gravitate into positions of power. In order to mount the ladder of hierarchical success it is often necessary to take actions or make decisions of a somewhat cold-blooded kind. One must "go to lunch with the right people." Sometimes friends must be by-passed. Occasionally someone must be fired who badly needs his job. Yearnings and aspirations of incapable people must sometimes be disregarded. Most persons, except those who have strong personal ambitions or unusually strong attachments to a goal, find such behaviour difficult. Consequently, many highly mobile people climb upward in organizational hierarchies by a kind of self-selection.[31]

The quote is perennially valid but it still reveals an empirical bias towards such externalized concepts as "goal orientation" and "ambition" the psychologized analogies of which appear in constructs such as N-Ach or "need for achievement". The tendency is to avoid internal explanations dealing with the value-intentional composition of the actor or, in plain terms, moral character.

The ancients had the reverse preoccupation, favouring philosophy over its daughter psychology, and generally arriving at a pessimistic view of administrative man. The *character* of the administrator or ruler or governor tended to be defined by such qualities as power-seeking, success-achievement orientation, ruthlessness, aggressivity and, in general, immorality or amorality. Machiavelli delivers the classic exposition of this philosophical orientation.[32] His *realpolitische* treatment endorses a suspension of conventional morality. In an earlier work I was moved to declare that there might be, within political administration at least, a "democracy of great men in which Hitler and Churchill, Ignatius Loyola and Lucrezia Borgia are coeval. They all share the common property of skill in the administration of men. Theirs is the confraternity of administrative elitism, the freemasonry of power."[33] The passage of time and the historical record serve only to confirm this judgement. Scott Fitzgerald once said that the rich were another country. Perhaps, *mutatis mutandis*, the same sort of observation can be made of at least some administrators.

Yet, curiously, the modern literature tends to depict the administrator, *pace* Simon, as a moral cipher, an ethical or valuational neuter. The administrator, by and large, is cast as organizational agent and since the organization itself not only goes uncriticized but is tacitly assumed to be benevolent it follows that the administrator in turn is benevolent at best or morally neutral at worst. That the agent may have self interests more than potent enough to subvert or pervert even a truly benevolent organization is simply overlooked.

The reasons for the contemporary shift from character to characteristics may be attributed to many factors, including an emergent profession with a journal literature struggling for academic and scientific respectability, large and entrenched vested career interests, a socio-political culture of value relativism and pluralism in which bland formulations and political correctness inhibit or prohibit the scrutiny of personal morality and perhaps the tender-minded conviction that human nature is essentially good and we are all honourable men. Yet as early as the counter-cultural evolution of the 1960s La Porte had attributed this disinterest in the moral side of administration to an eroding ethos and to the decline of philosophical consciousness in administrative studies.[34] That decline has persisted and today the philosophy of administration is at a nadir, not to be sure facing extinction because, contrariwise, moral concerns in the subsets of administration, especially business and political administration, have intensified—but facing impotence and confusion as an embryonic discipline. While professional philosophers have long since succumbed to the incestuous sterilities of academicism, social scientists flounder in a welter of information overload, and administrators themselves have taken an anti-intellectualist stance, resorting to pragmatism, positivism, or scepticism about the "pay-off" from any philosophical effort. It is to this pay-off question that we must now return.

PHILOSOPHY AND POWER

Administration is first and last about power, power over others and later, we shall come to see, power over oneself. This makes it at one and the same time the oldest, the noblest, and the basest of callings. Part art, part science, but always grounded in the humanities, its sheer potential for good and evil is so obvious that one can only wonder why philosophers and administrators do not talk to each other, do not take each other seriously, hold each other in contempt even, and fail again and again to realize their grand conjunction.

The simplest and most persuasive reason for that conjunction is that administrators make decisions about others, about people. They affect directly and forcefully that quality of human life first in the workplace and hence and thereafter in every place. This is the more so because our society is increasingly organizational. Max Weber, whose prophetic insights have proven to be so much more accurate than those of Karl Marx, foresaw the inexorable growth of bureaucracy in the public and private sectors of developed nations.[35] Our lives are increasingly (never decreasingly) affected and governed by ever larger and more complex organizations, the archetype of which is the modern nation state with its bureau-technological apparatus.

The present era has been characterized variously as postliberal, postindustrial, and postmodern by, respectively, Sir Geoffrey Vickers, Peter Drucker, and Alvin Gouldner.[36] It could also be considered post-Christian in that any unifying ideology or commitment to traditional Judeo-Christian values has been diffused, refracted, and weakened under the impress of secular humanism, liberalism, narcissistic or hedonic materialism, and heterogeneous pluralism or multi-culturalism. Consistent with this loss of firm philosophical footing in the shifting sands of postmodern value there are the factual aspects of environmental change: massive growth of large-scale corporations often with a multi-national dimension; a world economy segmented into articulated trading blocs; complex and proliferating bureaucracies at all levels of government; a technological explosion that has erected an information culture upon a silicon infrastructure; regulated capitalism and welfare statism: *in toto* an organizational society that depends for its functioning upon the skills of administrators and managers.

In this kind of society the fundamental relationship for the individual is his organizational affiliation. From this the individual derives not merely livelihood and status but often identity. He, or she, may be dependent upon the organizational relationship for a self-concept and a sense of being and worth. Without it there is the threat of anomie, alienation, despair. A man without an organizational role is a sort of outcast or pariah, a discard or reject from the complex web and weave of the network of organizational structures that serve to establish identity, meaning, and purpose in life. Each of these elements takes on even greater importance when basic economic life-support is in any event guaranteed by the umbrella organization of the nation state. The State will not let one starve or die from want of medical care but only organizations can gratify those desires that take survival as a prerequisite. And all of this entails an intensification of organizational and administrative power.

In feudal times this power was contained, inhibited, or regulated by ideology and consensus. People knew where they stood and were resigned to their station in life. Philosophy functioned as a civilizing and liberalizing force; a foundation for the status quo and an inspiration for incremental evolution and the occasional radical change. In our own neo-feudal times no such consensus exists, there is no clearly emergent consensus about the values that ought to guide administrative behaviour in a world of competing interests and factions. Thomas has shown that even within the British school of administrative thought, a school traditionally committed to unifying ethics and management science, no coherent philosophy has developed. On the contrary, modern developments such as systems theory, operations research, group dynamics, and personnel psychology have lent an emphasis to the quasi-scientific aspects of administrative thought at the expense of ethical, valuational, or philosophical considerations. Means have overshadowed ends and there has set in a sort of anaesthesia of the administrative soul.[37]

It can of course be said that there is nothing new in all of this with respect to power. It is an essential element of organizational logic that individual desires be suppressed where necessary through subordination to the cooperative endeavour. Ends have always justified means. Power is a condition of any administration.

All this is true but it elides the problem of large-scale complex organizational, technological, and bureaucratic power. Neo-feudal power is power raised in its order of magnitude and in inverse relationship to the power of the organizational member. The scope for individual alienation within and without organizations has been exponential in proportion to the growth in complexity of structures and the distancing of individual role from organizational purpose. Often that purpose cannot even be stated or, if stated, is so far removed from truth or clarity or reality that it is effectively meaningless.

It is potential for psychological distancing which is so distinctively modern. Combined with an excess and overload of information provided through technological means the trend towards superficiality and anomie is exacerbated. The modern citizen's sense of impotence is enhanced in a world of image manipulation and sound bites; the perception of inability to modify or affect social, political, or organization action is intensified. And within organizations the member low upon the hierarchy is similarly affected. Consequently and concomitantly the scope for organizational malevolence, witting or unwitting, expands to where the central administrative question becomes intensely value-philosophical: How can men administer each other so as to minimize the evil done by organizations?

This is also a question of meaning or purpose. Technology and modern organization are committed to the metavalues of efficiency and effectiveness but while they raise productivity they leach away meaning. Philosophy is the countervailing force. By analysis and synthesis, by description and prescription, by questioning and critique, by scrutiny and overriding devotion to truth philosophy seeks meaning: the restoration of old meanings and the establishment of new ones. The function of administrative philosophy is to take on these tasks, not in the armchair, but at the level of organizations and administrative practice.

Such work will not appeal to all executives and leaders. It will be resisted. Occasionally, but rarely, it will be embraced. Consider for example the following questions extracted from the curriculum of an elite Japanese school of administration and deemed to be of the most central importance for future leadership in that nation.[38] What is the nature of man? What is involved in an organizational system based on the true nature of man? What is the true vision of leaders? How should we view the social responsibility of enterprises? How to get "the right man in the right place?" How, in other words, to use power intelligently and benevolently?

Or again, in America it has been persuasively argued in business administration that "... the philosophical task must precede action. And if philosophers will not become managers, it is certain that managers must become philosophers."[39] A sentiment which we would wish to amend by saying that the task is continuous, not only preceding action but abiding throughout and certainly evaluating after. That task is the subject of this book. In it we seek to provide aid and understanding primarily through a technique of value analysis but also through critical examination of the various aspects of administrative process. No grand philosophy or overarching ideology is expounded; the aim is comprehension, clarification, understanding, and an analytical contribution that will serve the individual synthesis of working philosophies of administration. To the extent that that is accomplished it can be said that philosophy itself is power or even, power *over* power. And for administration, power is pay-off.

THE GRAND CONJUNCTION

Let us continue to vex the question, Why philosophy of administration? Ought it to be somehow within the administrator's curriculum? and Why should practitioners take any philosophical pains anyway?

Authorities have given a variety of answers to these questions. Dimock says succinctly that "At bottom our professional life is meaningless unless each one works through to a philosophy which sees human dignity and significance as the essential criteria."[40] And, more fully:

> We have swung so far in the direction of science, however, that it would be healthy for us now to realize that administration is essentially one of the humanities. Administration is, or at least ought to be, wedded to subjects such as philosophy, literature, history, and art, and not merely to engineering, finance, and structure...

Administration is administrators. Administrators become increasingly human and philosophical, capable of planning ongoing programs which meet human needs and aspirations, when they are unified by areas of knowledge and skill which stress man's humanity and his philosophical insights."[41]

Ordway Tead gave the justification that, "If we would seek clear purposes we require a philosophy, or rather the search is part of the philosophizing. And this is true also of long-range corporate objectives, of the selective gratifications of personal needs, of finding the adequate scope for individual creativity, of interrelating a single corporate organization into a national (and presently an international) economy." And Chester Barnard in the closing lines of his classic declared; "I believe that the expansion of cooperation and the development of the individual are mutually dependent realities, and that a due proportion or balance between them is a necessary condition of human welfare. Because it is subjective with respect both to a society as a whole and to the individual, what this proportion is I believe science cannot say. It is a question for philosophy and religion."[42] All of these assertions and propositions are seeking to establish a merger of philosophy and administration in what might be called a grand conjunction.

Administration is the applied art of power; its artisans are people. Nothing could be more human than the attempt to cooperatively change the world. Yet the results can be inhuman, bereft of any tincture of the humane. We do not need macrocataclysms of history, gulags and genocides to teach us this; we know it daily at the microlevel of organizational life; we know it in our hearts and minds if not yet in our wills. This is why administrators must learn to do philosophy for themselves and not leave it to be done by others by default. Least of all must they abdicate their philosophical prerogatives or seek to become neutered functionaries. On the contrary, practitioners and theorists alike must work to forge the grand conjunction.

VALUES, INTEREST, AND POWER

To sum up, this chapter has dealt with philosophy as it applies to the art and proto-science of administration and management. To this end philosophy was treated as a wisdom endeavour divisible into the basic components of logic and values. Logic describes the power structures and functions of administration while values analyses and prescribes the affective interest dimensions of administrative discourse.

Philosophy and policy have always been conjoined and the linkage with governance has been the focus of intense thought and intellection throughout the ages, from Plato's *Republic* to Marx's *Das Kapital*. Nevertheless the modern evolution of academic disciplines and the general development of the history of ideas have blurred or confused the connection between philosophy and administration to the point where the concept of philosophy of administration urgently demands clarification.

Numerous trends and factors have contributed to this condition and to frustration of the grand conjunction between these realms of discourse called for by Socrates and his heirs down through the ages of the Western tradition. These inhibitions include a disinterest by academic philosophy in practical affairs and administrative realities; a reciprocal suspicion and distrust from the side of administrators; reinforcement of quantitative, pragmatic, empirical, and quantitative research emphases in related fields through the advent of computerization and microchip technology; cultural developments antagonistic to critical inquiry; postmodern rationalism and bureaucratization; legalism and politicization; and, above all, profound confusion about the nature and function of value in individual, social, and organizational life.

In this book we shall seek to clarify and elucidate the elements of value and logic that apply to administration. This will require a comprehensive understanding of the workings of organizations and their administration and leadership. It will also require an in-depth analysis of the problems of value, interest, and power. We shall work towards a general theory of these elements as a basis for *praxis*, or practitioner-initiated value-imbued systems of action. The justification for any such theoretical endeavour lies in the potential reward for the practitioner. In Part II we shall examine hierarchy and power, in Part III values, interests, and power, and in Part IV the disjunctions that frustrate conjunction. Underlying this exposition, for both reader and writer, is the presumption that knowledge, understanding, and comprehension are in some sense power and that power itself is in some sense desirable. This broad presumption is hypothetical; it remains to be tested. But we take as articles of faith that the vocation of administration is in essence deeply *humane*, and that "the proper study of mankind is man."[43]

PROPOSITIONS

1. Administration is philosophy-in-action
2. Administration is a generalism
3. Administrators are specialists in generalism
4. Administrators possess models-of-man. These are judgements of man-in-the-world by which they form their way of organizational life.
5. The boundary between a psychology and a philosophy of administration is fluid. Intention and commitment are central terms for both.
6. The main philosophical need in administration is for value sophistication. But this entails logical critique.
7. Administrators must learn how to listen to the philosophers and the philosophers must learn how to speak to administrators. Unreflective action is degenerative. It is entropic.
8. The administrator cannot help being a philosopher-in-action but can help the quality of that philosophy.
9. Reflective analysis and critique is the way in which the administrator does philosophy. His subjects are himself, his organization, and the world.
10. In the first analysis, a philosophy of administration must be constrained by culture and ideology; in the last analysis it must go beyond these.
11. Philosophy begins in the dirt.
12. Administrative philosophy seeks to convert practice into praxis.
13. To do philosophy is the right of all but the special obligation of the administrator.

II
HIERARCHY AND POWER

Straight lines exist in the mind,
not in a bent world

Chapter 2
Organization and Administrative Theory

The first proposition states that administration is philosophy-in-action. We have now some concept of the predicate of this proposition but have not yet considered its subject. What *is* administration? In seeking the answer to this question an immediate discrimination must be made between two divergent sets of activities and experiences. This leads to a robust distinction.[1]

ADMINISTRATION AND MANAGEMENT

Although semantic usage varies,[2] an important conceptual difference exists between the terms administration and management. Each concept is itself complex and will not yield to precise definition but their scope can be shown in a figure (Figure 2.1).

These dimensions of action and experience are illustrative rather than comprehensive. They do not exhaust the manifold complexity of the administration–management spectrum.[3] In general, however, it can be said that by administration we mean those aspects dealing with the more value-laden issues and the human component of organizational life and by management we mean those aspects that are more routine, material, programmatic, and amenable to quantitative methods.

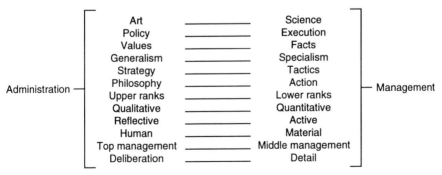

Figure 2.1   Differentiating Aspects of Administration/Management.

Once this distinction is agreed it is of course a matter of semantic convenience as to the terminology chosen and indeed conventions vary in a somewhat curious and confusing manner. In Great Britain, for example, there is today a tendency to regard management as the higher status function despite the title of the Royal Institute of Public Administration and the superior ranking of the administrative grade to that of the managerial grade in the British Civil Service. The usage chosen in this book is generally consistent with American terminology, especially as that refers to successive political administrations but it is interesting that Barnard himself avoided the problem by referring instead to executives or, alternatively, to leaders.[4] Generally then administration is the broad art of determining organizational goals and motivating towards them while management is the ancillary, auxiliary, and subordinate science of specifying and implementing means towards the achievement of the same goals. Administration is ends-oriented, management means-oriented. The pure administrator would be a philosopher, the pure manager a technologist, the pure non-administrative worker a technician or, perhaps better still, a robot. But there is no purity in the reality of administration/management and the distinction is often blurred in practice, sometimes deliberately so.

The concept of administration subsumes management. The former systematically generates and includes the latter as a logical subset. Furthermore neither set of functions can exist in practice in discrete isolation from each other. In general the distinction, though robust, is one of emphasis and the overall set of processes permeate the entire organization to which they apply. All organization members of whatever rank will from time to time find themselves engaged in administrative acts (e.g. pondering whether to quit or seek promotion) while the most exalted of executives will be compelled to perform some (and often many) managerial tasks.

Let it be noted too that although administration is hierarchically and systemically superior and prior to management this does not entail a value judgement. It is not to say that the one is somehow "better" than the other. To make a value judgement, criteria must be specified. Thus, on the criterion of survival, it might be said that management is better (more vital, essential) than administration since organizations can persist longer without administration than they can without management. (An example would be the nation state that is ill-served at the political level but well served by its bureaucracy.)

In the long run, of course, no organization can survive without administration and this reality perhaps explains the general tendency to accord the higher status to the broader set of functions, a distinction revealed in the military usage of the rank of general and the terms general staff and field officers.

The usefulness of the distinction has to do with the understanding of organizational functions. The more one is involved with behaviours that bear on the ends, aims, and purposes of the organization the more one is engaged in administration. Likewise, the more general the value component in decision making and the more it affects *interests*, the more administrative and the less managerial such decision making becomes.

As organizational means become specified they give rise to technology and to techniques of management. Management may thus legitimately become increasingly specialized and organization specific. Administration in contrast refers to a broad commonality of problems and strategies. That it is a generalism is shown by the way in which at the highest systemic levels administrators pass easily from one complex organization to another. The general becomes a university president and ministers of state move from portfolio to portfolio or criss-cross the lines of public and private sector enterprise. Conversely, a factory manager would not normally pass easily into the role of school superintendent or college dean.

The distinction also alerts us to the fact that, in principle, anyone can do administration. Not anyone, either in principle or practice, can do management. Administration is the province of the amateur and Anglo-Saxon constitutional theory insists that, in political administration, the professional expert or manager should be "on tap and not on top". Familial organizations also rarely see any problem in assigning administrative roles on the nepotistic qualification of kinship, the assumption being perhaps that managerial expertise is always available for hire. We shall return to this issue of qualification later in discussing the professional character of modern administration. Meanwhile, in the hard world outside of academic distinctions, managers will continue to persist in intrusion into the administrative ambit while administrators will often persist in withdrawing from responsibilities that are rightly theirs by a "retreat into management".

Administration is typically divided into adjectival subsets: hospital administration, police administration, political, military, educational, business, and public administration. Does it therefore make sense, or is it legitimate, to consider administration as a *general* class of activities when in fact the between-organization differences (hospital vs. police force) or within-organization differences (department head vs. school superintendent) are so obvious and significant? In other words, is administration so context-determined that the proper study should be not of administration *per se* but of management in the appropriate subset?

This question was dealt with in the opening issue of *Administrative Science Quarterly* by Professor Litchfield.[5] His major proposition, subscribed to in this book, was that administration and administrative processes occur in substantially the same generalized form in industrial, commercial, educational, military, and hospital organizations. And to these can be added civil services and governmental bureaucracies generally. To my knowledge that proposition has never been refuted since it was first set forth as a postulate for a theory of administration and it can be maintained that, whatever the status of administration as a clearly discernible profession, it refers to a class of acts, among which decision making is salient but not exclusively definitive, which can be conventionally prescribed by organizational context but which are not restricted or determined in essential nature by any given set of organizational boundaries. In other words, administration is a generalism.

Of course organizational contexts are important. They modify, modulate, and determine the style and scope of administrative acts. They prescribe the subject matter of administration and assign boundaries. They may also, in interesting ways, determine the administrative quality or form-of-life:[6] one might expect, for example, a sub-unit of a complex bureaucracy with a clearly defined mission to be more managerial and less administrative than, say, a large university with vague and imprecise goals. Again, a peacetime military may in its higher echelons be perforce more administrative than it would be in a wartime context. In all contexts, however, and at all times administrative subsystems will be in place whose general functions will be similar while the managerial subsystems in the hierarchy will be more differential and specialized according to their organizational contexts.

What then of leadership? This term is commonly associated with administration. Sometimes it is identified with it. Sometimes the two terms are contrasted. It will be argued in Chapter 4 that administration is leadership and leadership is administration. Leadership pervades organizations and is intrinsic to their structure. Indeed structures can be designed so as to substitute for human leadership acts and decisions.[7] When leadership is identified with administration it can be understood as the effecting of policy, values, and philosophy through collective action. It is the moving of men towards goals through organization and it can be done well, badly, or indifferently.

The mix of administration–management–leadership, that is to say, the mix of value and fact in action will naturally vary, in complex and sometimes imponderable ways, with process, situational contingency, personality, and role but however routinized, homeostatic, and even robotic an organizational role may be it will still be occupied by a human actor and the role itself will be integral to the organization. In time of crisis or special contingency its leadership potential may be intensified. The petty bureaucrat faced with a "whistle blowing" dilemma, the resentful worker presented with an opportunity for sabotage, the isolated soldier in heat of battle—all may have to make exquisitely difficult value judgements that crystallize into leadership acts of crucial administrative importance.

The distinction between administration and management has also been treated, in public administration especially, as the difference between policy and implementation. This discrimination may be more fully comprehended if we consider a model of the overall administration process. The general logic should then become clear.

ADMINISTRATIVE PROCESS

A taxonomy of administrative process is given in Figure 2.2.

The process of administration is a seamless web but its initial or first stage can be clearly identified as philosophy. It is at this stage that the central intrinsic *idea* or *raison d'être* of the organization is conceived. The means by which this is done are essentially philosophical or intellectual: imagination, intuition, inspiration, speculation, hypothesis, argument, dialectic, synthesis, analysis, logic, rhetoric, introspection, value analysis, and value clarification. In other words the primal activity is one of ideas. And ideas must be expressed in words so, in the beginning is the word. But these words must be ordered in logic if communication is to

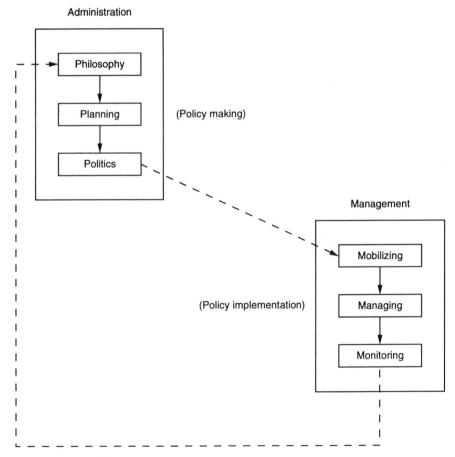

Figure 2.2   Administration/Management.

occur. They cannot remain in a single head. There must be a rational (or even on occasion an irrational) *plan*. Planning is the translation of organizational values into a project-for-action.

Once the plan is formulated—a process often vaguely referred to as policy making—it yet remains at the abstract level of ideas and has only a *potential* for action. To translate that potential *into* action requires political process. This means that people (together with their interests) must be engaged and motivated towards the organizational ends. Moreover, *power* or resources must be commanded and bent to those same ends. Commitments must be made, interests traded and aligned, contracts signed, legal obstacles removed or overcome—all this is the domain of politics. While still at this people-level of process the material and human resources necessary for the realization of the plan must be mobilized or organized or ordered. And here a shift occurs towards the managerial end of the spectrum. It now becomes possible and necessary to contemplate actual material change.

Once workers and technical staff are engaged and motivated a movement begins whereby events occur under the aegis of the organizational plan not merely in the realm of ideas or people's psychology but also in the real world of *things*. The material order of the universe is changed in the direction of the organizational philosophy. Goods and services are created, work is done, energy expended. These temporal events and their attendant resources need *managing*. The phase of management refers to the establishment, control, and adjustment of routines. The daily work of the professional, technical, and worker staff has to be structured and organized. Often an element of motivation of human resources and clientele also enters into this phase and merges it to some extent with the preceding process of mobilizing.

Finally, there is the business of monitoring or control, a phase that includes formal supervision, accounting, auditing, reporting and evaluation.[8] The ultimate object of process here is to discuss the extent to which the philosophy (policy) has in fact been actualized or the degree of discrepancy that exists. This feeds back to the philosophy stage of process and completes the dynamic cycle of policy making—administration/policy implementation–management. It is to be understood that this total process covering the general field of administration and leadership is an ideal type. In practice, phases can be omitted or elided but in principle the model is dynamic, recurrent, and continuous with the cycle repeating and overlapping with other cycles in the same pattern as it is initiated at various points in the organizational history. The movement is always in the same direction: from ideas to things, from the abstract to the concrete, and always via the mediation of people. It represents the triumph of the intellectual over the material through the phenomenon of action. Therefore the central problem of administration is always that of motivation of action or, more precisely, the reconciliation of the interests of individual organization members or clients with the collective interest of the organization.

An examination of Figure 2.2 will reveal also how central to administrative process is the business of decision making. Policies themselves are decisions writ large and they entail a cascade of subordinate decision making to effect their implementation. But decisions, as we shall see, are inextricably interwoven with values. Nor should it be surprising that there is a value pervasion of administrative process when that process is a complex interrelation and interaction of ideas, human interests, and the world of objective reality. Administration is distinctive, however, in that it is political, it is an enterprise dependent upon power in which decisions are made for and about others and in which a primary concern is with the acquisition, the establishment, the maintenance, and the enhancement of power and authority; functions which must continuously be re-asserted and legitimated through the concepts of organizational purpose and commitment.

If morality is interpreted as a concern for others then it would follow that administration is a peculiarly moral activity. It is contestable whether administration is a profession in the conventional sense but perhaps we can at this point allow that it is an occupation under its own sort of cloud. It has in the past and present appealed to the amoral, the immoral, and even the anti-moral and it has its own esoteric literature of the left-hand path which later we must regard more closely.[9]

Perhaps it is this very feature of administration that has led to numerous modern attempts at ignoring or bypassing the problem of value. One could trace a line from the emergency of modern bureaucratic theory in the work of Max Weber to the systems approach of modern management with its rational planning models and techniques such as planning, programming, and budgeting systems (PPBS), management by objectives (MBO), OR, OM, and programme evaluation and review technique (PERT). All such emergent quasi-philosophies of administration are imbued with the spirit of rationalistic positivism.[10] They tend to avoid value issues integral to the executive function. This tendency is intimately associated with the growth and development to near dominant proportions in modern times of science, applied science and technology. The *reductio ad absurdum* would be the administrator as pure technologist with values and ethics provided by some *deus ex machina* such as the "will of the people" or the "will of the owners as expressed through their board of directors". Thus the administrator is diminished to managerial factotum and a value antisepsis is achieved which in theory defines reality but in truth constitutes a sort of hypocrisy—the homage paid by would-be virtue to as-is vice. The real world of administration is intrinsically political, value-saturated, and interest-fraught; it cannot take as its model the natural sciences, themselves no longer considered by themselves to be value-immaculate.

ADMINISTRATIVE THEORY

The process and practice of administration are as old as mankind but the emergence of any coherent body of theory about them is a relatively modern phenomenon. Contemporary literature is now voluminous and can be treated only summarily here[11] but the general dialectic of its development can be thought of as a classical thesis and a humanistic antithesis.

The Classical Approach

The spirit of early twentieth century administrative thought is well illustrated in the work of Frederick W. Taylor in America, Henri Fayol in France, and Max Weber in Germany. Each viewed the field of study from differing standpoints and both Taylor and Fayol shared a rationalist logic and a mechanistic view of organization. Taylor is still eminent for his attempts to create a science of productive effort and his text, the *Principles of Scientific Management* remains a corner-stone classic for students of the field.[12] His method was inductive, pragmatic, and empiricist and from his philosophical bedrock there emerges the principle that there *must* be "one best way of doing any specific task". The power of this principle is hard to overestimate and it led inevitably to time and motion study, to the treatment of workers as machines, and finally, one might say, to the end-states of automation and robotics. One should note however that in Taylor's time, pre-1914, there could have been little vision of high technology or the productive capacity and potential of contemporary industry. The microchip was still a long way off.

Henri Fayol,[13] like his American contemporary, was a highly successful practical administrator. His approach was, however, more deductive and took the form of rational analyses and taxonomies of organizational structure and function. His legacy includes the organization chart and the rubrics Planning, Organizing, Staffing, Directing, Coordinating, Record-keeping, and Budgeting (POSDCORB) which he viewed as the definitive components of administrative process. Again organization is a mechanism that can be engineered and administration is logically a species of engineering.

Max Weber differs from his more specifically administrative–managerial contemporaries Taylor and Fayol in that he can be fairly classed as one of the greatest scholars and thinkers of modern times; on a par with other Germanic shapers of modern thought such as Karl Marx, Sigmund Freud, and Albert Einstein. Although a polymathic professor his contribution to administrative ideas lies in his general theories of authority, power, and bureaucracy.[14] These theories cannot be circumscribed within the narrow bounds of purely administrative theory but because consistencies exist between them and the scientific management school of thought they lend reinforcement to the classical position. In particular the notion of an ideal type rational–legal bureaucratic form resonates harmoniously with the technocratic scientific orientation.

The classical position[15] also originated what proved to be an ultimately vain search for *principles* of administration. Despite the failure[16] to provide any incontestable principles the faith in an intrinsic rationality, an underlying logic that could be exposed and reconstructed scientifically, has persisted. The classical view assumes that criteria of productivity and efficiency applied to a combination of techniques, goals, and workers can provide a logical ordering of structure and function that would define and constitute a scientific administration.

The fact that of these conditions only techniques have proven full amenable to rationalization may not have been entirely clear at the onset of Taylor's movement but, increasingly, the complexities and difficulties associated with the human element led to a shift of direction in theoretical emphasis.

The Humanistic Reaction: From the early 1930s onwards attention and study was focused with often great intensity upon the human variable in organizational life and this yielded a rich literature[17] and a rubric known as the human relations or human resources movement. It is well to note, however, that this sizeable intellectual effort was directed primarily at the administ*ered* rather than the administ*ering* and was motivated at first not by any rejection of the classical concern with productivity but by the possibility of achieving the same ends through different means.

The philosophical base for the reaction can be traced to the work of Mary Parker Follett in the 1920s and 1930s.[18] Her concerns with resolving conflict and releasing untapped resources of human potential were well received by the industrial and governmental elite of the times and her ideas were empirically reinforced by the remarkable Hawthorne studies which spanned the era of the Great Depression. It is now somewhat uncertain[19] just what exactly was revealed in the way of scientific truth by these extended socio-psychological investigations but without doubt the studies led to a critical re-appraisal of the elusive and subtle relationship between organization members and administration, between leaders and led. Another consequence is perhaps a certain preoccupation of contemporary administrative thought with the theme of work motivation.[20] Administration of the "human system" now preponderates over the management of the "technical system".

Also emergent from the humanist reaction has been the theme of *self-actualization* whereby organizations include within their constellation of purposes the opportunity for self-realization or self-fulfillment on the part of their members. The extreme case for this was made by the psychologist Abraham Maslow in *Eupsychian Management.*[21] Other researchers such as Herzberg and Mintzberg have extended this notion into the upper levels of hierarchy although that extension was tacit and implicit in the earlier work of Barnard and can be traced as far back as Plato's *Republic.*[22]

Taken to the extreme this logic can lead to a view in which firms and organizations exist not simply to make a profit or render a service but rather to provide opportunities for psychological self-satisfaction and growth. The making of a profit or the acceptable rendering of service then becomes a necessary but not a sufficient condition for the existence of the firm or public sector organization.

At a less extreme level it can be said that this school of thought coalesces about demands for improvement in work conditions and work organization. Its acronym QWL, the quality of work-life, and its proponents would have work become more of an end in itself and less, as implied by classical reasoning, a means to ulterior values determined extra-organizationally.

It should also be remarked that early study of human work motivation, or shall we say the human condition in organizations, led to some simplistic and exaggerated modelling as expressed, for example, in the well-known Theory X and Theory Y.[23] The former showed the worker to be essentially recalcitrant and resistant to administration while the latter imbued the worker with an abundance of altruistic impulses and creative potential. McGregor did however stress that these models-of-man or quasi-philosophical orientations depended on underlying belief systems and world-views.[24] Man is indeed the measure of administration but the measure of man is premissed upon philosophical bases that can range from the divine to the demonic, the sublime to the ridiculous.

Neo-classicism: Two great classics were added to the body of administrative thought in the decade between 1939 and 1949. These are H. A. Simon's *Administrative Behaviour* and Chester Barnard's *The Functions of the Executive*. Both are logical and scholarly assessments of the general nature of administration that have withstood the test of time.

Simon is a declared logical positivist and self-labels his philosophical presumptions. His general reduction or simplification of administration is that it is fundamentally a decision making process. (Administration is decision making.) Decisions are made within bounded limits of rationality and under reality constraints that conduce not to optimizing but to *satisficing* productivity. Within this framework the administrator tends to appear, in our terms, as a manager or factotum. As an organizational artifact he is supposedly value-neutral and a moral cipher;[25] his values are for practical purposes assumed to be those of the organization and they are irrelevant in the same way that an actor's are to his role performance, or the driver of a bus to the buses destination. That this position is not merely theoretical or academic is exemplified by the supposed a-political stance of senior public servants and the widespread fiction that chief executive officers function entirely at the behest of their employer boards.

Barnard, who preceded Simon and was in many ways his mentor, was not an academic but was a successful administrator. Writing out of his administrative experience he, in contrast to his protégé, is pre-eminently concerned with the *moral* component of executive behaviour. This moral aspect is integrally linked to his conception of responsibility and leadership. His work has in fact a Platonic quality and his ideal administrator displays moral attributes that would find favour with the Guardians of the Republic. Such a preoccupation with morality and with the character of the administrator renders him unique in the field of contemporary theory but is apart from his other major theoretical insights which stress the communications aspect of administration, embrace much of the human relations approach, and presage general systems theory.

The groundwork of Simon and Barnard in classicism and of Mayo and his successors in human relations has been continuously augmented by the social sciences. The insights of sociology, social psychology, psychology, economics, and political science have been enlisted at one time or another, in the attempt to render administration a "science". This interdisciplinary thrust[26] gave rise, for example, to General Systems theory, a quasi-scientific formulation springing from the natural science of biology. Systems thinking and its logical derivatives such as PERT, MARS (Model Analysis and Redesign System), especially when combined with quantitative methods made feasible by the microchip and computerology can be thought of as a return, at a sophisticated level, to the classical starting point of scientific management.

Overall, what seems to have happened towards the close of the 20th century is that administrative theory has engaged at some point, to an extensive degree, all of the social sciences and some, but not all, of the humanities. The notable exception to this intellectual effort has been philosophy. For all that,[27] the attempt to create a science of administration has failed leaving open the question, What is the study of administration? The answer would appear to be that it is another great interdisciplinary nexus like education or medicine into which the streams of social science and the humanities flow in a spasmodic and irregular manner. And why is it that, with minor exceptions, administration has fallen into the embrace of social science to the near exclusion of philosophy? Are the two realms of discourse, administration and philosophy, in some way incompatible?[28] This would hardly seem likely since both are professed generalisms that extend their interests across similar territories. And why has organization theory (to the extent that it can be disseminated as such) tended to flourish at the expense of administrative theory? The answer to this last question may be easier to comprehend since the growth of empirical and quantitative research and methodology has favoured the non-qualitative, non-valuational, and ethically neutral side of the administrative–management field of inquiry. Yet in the end it does seem that the great questions of value, interest, and power have gone begging in the broad development of administrative thought.

Organization Theory

A major presumption of an administrative profession would have to be that its members can be distinguished by their superior knowledge of organizations. Superior, that is to non-administrative organizational members. Administrative philosophy therefore is concerned with the substance of this claim. What logic underlies and what values are implicated by organizational theory?

This body of theory is now so large that it would be a forbidding and ultimately irrelevant task to recapitulate or survey its totality of findings, studies, and speculata. It is sufficient for our purpose to consider briefly those elements of organization theory that subtend a logic of administrative behaviour. Let us begin with attempts at definition. Simon has

> Human organizations are systems of interdependent activity, encompassing at least several primary groups and usually characterized, at the level of consciousness of participants, by a high degree of rational direction of behaviour towards ends that are objects of common acknowledgement and expectation.[29]

It may be noted that this definition excludes the family but possibly includes that nation state. As is typical of Simon its emphasis is on the rational character of organizations. A more elaborate definition is given by Bakke:

> A social organization is a continuing system of differentiated and coordinated human activities utilizing, transforming, and welding together a specific set of human, material, capital, ideational, and natural resources into a unique problem-solving whole engaged in satisfying particular human needs in interaction with other systems of human activities and resources in its environment.[30]

This is more sociological, the emphasis now is on *systems* that are devoted to problem-solving. Argyris says simply that "organizations are grand strategies individuals create to achieve objectives that require the effort of many" and, simpler still, is Proposition 23 below. Let us note also the phenomenological interpretation of Greenfield who, in the end, characterizes organizations as "moral orders".[31]

From the standpoint of philosophy organizations can be understood as systemic entities within determining but interactive environments. By systemic entity is meant a discernible integrity of structure associated with purpose—even though the shape, articulation, and locus of that purpose may be obscure, unconscious, or even deliberately hidden. At least two members are a pre-condition of organization and hence there is by definition a presupposition of a social structure and a hierarchy. Also implied are the coexistence of collective and individual purposes. This coexistence creates the fundamental organizational dynamic or tension. Even at the collective or organizational level, however, goals can be in conflict or simply dysfunctional and this reality or potentiality constitutes a conscious or unconscious dynamic in administration.

Although the definition of human organization is not agreed upon by theorists—Simon is content to consider it "a level of human grouping somewhere above the primary group" and somewhat below the entity he calls an "institution"[32]—there is a consensus about the pre-eminent criterion of purposive behaviour. Organizations are intentional. This brings organization theory at once within the purview of philosophy.

The Principle of Hierarchy: Membership in organizations entails some form of social structure, some form of status differentiation. Even in the limiting case of two members, though roles may shift and reverse, at any given time there will be a leader and a led. Also overwhelmingly true as empirical fact, and universal across time and across cultures, is the form of structure known as line and staff. Power and authority are conceived as flowing along a *line* which extends from some philosophical core point within the organizational field to the action levels at its periphery. The line of command or administrative line generates a system of superordinate–subordinate–coordinate relationships. It is the special prerogative of administration to define, clarify, defend, extend, and elaborate this arrangement. Organizational status and reward systems tend to isomorphic symmetry with the hierarchical line and in the conventional wisdom this is considered to be both functional and beneficent.[33]

Collateral to the line are organizational members whose functions are ancillary, advisory, and supportive. In decision theory staff can advise but not command. Thus a cardinal can advise a pope but not subvene to instruct a bishop. Likewise policy analysts are supposed to influence but not direct politicians and their civil servants. This is the general idea but the concept of staff lacks the lucidity of the concept of line. Empirical observation would suggest that staff personnel either fluctuate in their role definition by moving into and out of the line or else they exercise a tacit line authority that is *de facto* if not *de jure*.[34] This blurring of hierarchical logic is particularly endemic in collegial organizations.[35] If the logic were accepted that organizations were purposive collectivities with a "line" from philosophy (purpose) to action (organizational work) then it could be allowed that all members were somehow in this line. The problem then would be how to clarify and define the "somehow" and relate it equitably to the organizational reward system.

Staff and line structure creates the conceptual archetype of the pyramid. This idea is deeply entrenched although various iconoclastic attempts at alternative structural arrangements have been made from time to time as shown in Figure 2.3. Simple inspection reveals, however, that a line (shown by illustrative dotted lines in the diagram) persists in each case. Note also that the apex of this line is distanced or divorced from the "action levels" and that managerial or supervisory intermediaries act as buffers, with the possible exception of the collegial model. The point here is not to argue the relative merits of these organizational arrangements but to point to the depth structure of hierarchy and the pyramidal archetype. Indeed the principle is ancient and is recorded in Chinese history in the writings of Chu Hsi who endorses the Confucian doctrine of "names and parts" (i.e. executive *roles*) as the central principle of governance and social order.[36]

The conservative character of this structuralism does not imply that organizations have a static essence. On the contrary they are essentially compositions in goal-directed flux, essays in goal-achievement strategy. The other face of structure is function, the dynamic aspect of the arrangement of roles or "parts" which form the constituents of structure. And any organizational structure must in the last analysis be functional with respect to purpose.

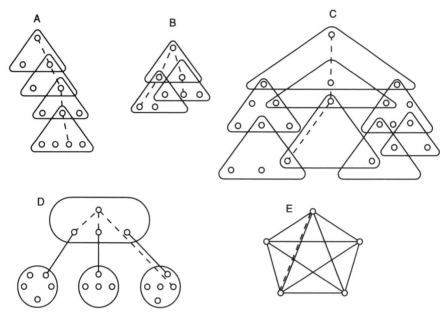

Figure 2.3 Variants on the Line–Staff Theme (dotted lines indicate hierarchy). A, B, C: Linking-pin structure; D: Project team; E: Collegial model.

ORGANIZATIONS AS SYSTEMS

Organizations can be typologized in many ways. One may proceed, for example, from genus through species to individual. At the level of genus the distinction blurs between organizations and institutions. Clusters of complex organizations tend to merge into sociological entities labelled bureaucracy, military, church, and state. At this level society as a whole, national or international, forms the limiting condition. More manageably, at the species level of analysis, classification is more sharply a level of function. Thus, for example, army or navy as species of the genus military, and kindergarten or university as species of the genus education. Finally, each organization can be classified as individual with its own unique phenomenological identity, dependent upon on site conditions specific to itself, and thereby sharpening and delimiting the parameters of administrative actions. There then remains the final classification into formal and informal organization. Each formal organization subsumes within itself at least one informal organization, and possibly more than one. Barnard himself [37] was the first to utter the administrative maxim, "Know the informal organization" and, as a general rule of administrative thumb it can be allowed that the leader or executive needs to know as much as is reasonably possible, at all times, about the network of informal social, collegial, and familial relationships that inevitably cohabit the formal hierarchy and structure. This network is important not only for communications purposes, communications manipulation, and executive intelligence. It materially affects organizational climate, ethos, culture, morale, and leadership. Together the combination of informal and formal organization constitutes a domestic policy rooted in a reward system that interrelates interest, value, and power.

Because organizations are systems that display many features analogous to those of living systems or organisms they lend themselves to the play of imaginative projection. Organization theorists therefore must constantly be on guard against the biological fallacy. The philosopher of social Darwinism, Spencer, illustrates the seduction:

> ... cells of an organism correspond to individuals in a society, tissues to simpler voluntary groups, organs to the more complex organizations. Economic, juridicial, and political activities parallel the physiological, morphological, and unitary aspects of an organism. Merchandise in transition is tantamount to unassimilated food. Conquering races are male, the conquered female; their struggle matches the struggle of spermatozoa around the ovum.[38]

A statement of this extravagance would not be acceptable a few generations later but the general metaphor remains alive and tempting. The idea of organizations as systems of needs existing competitively within environments that force adaptive changes remains persuasive. The contemporary version of this persistent analogue is, however, less organic and biological and more mechanistic, abstract, and mathematical. Figure 2.4 gives the essential elements. These consist of an energic input, a throughput, and an output that is to a degree self-directing by way of targeting and feedback mechanisms. This gives a behavioural illusion of "purposiveness" or even a mechanical analogue of "consciousness". A key concept is the "black box" which provides both logical and aesthetic economy in that it is not necessary for the outside observer to know what occurs within

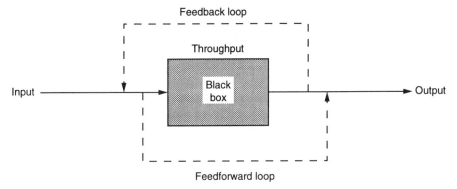

Figure 2.4   A Cybernetic System.

the box in order to manipulate the system or predict its behaviours. It is enough to discern inputs, outputs, and to infer relationships. The system is open because it exchanges energy and information with the environment and it is consequently governed by the laws of thermodynamics. The more complex and ordered the system the more it displays negative entropy or negentropy and the greater the amount of information it is said to contain.[39] Other characteristics of systems are homeostasis, differentiation, and equifinality all of which have corresponding biological analogues.

Every system can be conceptualized as a subsystem of some supersystem and conversely. Carried to the extreme this gives us a Chinese-box vision of the universe, one terminus of which is the closed energy system of the macrocosm (subject to entropy and the Second Law of Thermodynamics) and the other being a limit set by quantum mechanics in the subatomic realm of particle physics and the infinitely small. In other words, between macrocosmic and microcosmic levels of infinity exists a field of flux within which negentropic systems of order are continuously being created, preserved, and destroyed. Some of these systems are individual human entities and others are supersystems of human collectivity. But let us return to the fallacy of biological isomorphism.

The root of this fallacy is exposed by the phenomenon of consciousness. An organization can have neither "consciousness" nor "will". It is quite simply not *alive*. Life, consciousness, sensation, affect, and will can only be properties of *individual* members of organizations. This point is crucial for administrative philosophy. In a complex organization individuals are not whole persons but role incumbents and as such are often treated as replaceable and substitutable parts. The qualities of consciousness, morality, and sensation or emotion are, properly speaking, attributes of *whole* persons not partial ones. Furthermore, as Katz and Kahn observe, "The human organization lacks structure in [an] anatomical sense; its land and buildings are trappings; its members come and go. Yet it has structure; it is not a formless aggregate of interacting individuals engaged in the creation of some random combination of events."[40] Greenfield has perhaps put it best,

> ... In systems theory, the prevailing image of an organization is that of an organism. Organizations exist; they are observable entities which have a life of their own. Organizations are like people although sometimes the image is more that of the recalcitrant child, rather than the mature adult. In any case, the theory endows organizations with many human properties. They have goals towards which they direct their activities; they respond and adapt to their environments. Nor can organizations escape the fate of organisms ill-adapted to their environments. Indeed, the life of organizations depends upon their ability to adapt to an increasingly complex and turbulent environment. Following the Darwinian logic inherent in their image of the organization, systems theorists see small, quick-witted, democratic organizations replacing the ponderous, bureaucratic forms now expiring around us. The fact that bureaucratic organizations appear as large, robust, and formidable as ever does not

appear to shake belief in organizations as living entities subject to stringent laws permitting only the fittest to survive ...[41]

A division exists then in organization theory between those of a social science persuasion who perceive organizations as lawful structures or open systems with biological features that are ultimately amenable to causal determinism and scientific explanation; and those of a more humanistic phenomenological orientation who see organizations as systems structured by human intention, moral orders dependent ultimately on human variables not subject to scientific reduction. In this way the dichotomy between scientific management and humanistic administration is replicated. The dimensions of the debate are most fully set out by Greenfield.[42] The dialectic of argument is in general terms between schools of thought (systems views) which incline toward treating organizations as real entities possessing a sort of "life of their own" and contending schools (phenomenological views) which regard organizations as social inventions, artifacts of a *cultural* nature, created by their membership constituency, past and present.

Each extreme tends to error. An organization is not, in the last analysis, an organism but in the first analysis it is still more than the sum of its parts. It has relative immortality in that it transcends the entries and exits of its members; it has quasi-personality in that its symbolic life institutionalizes values and carries them across shifts in membership. Yet this organizational form is lifeless. What spirit or "life" that invests it is, I shall argue below, a special aegis of leadership, of administration, of, in the French expression, *esprit de corps*. That an organization does not "die" when its administration is replaced means not only that the incoming administration have been able to command the logical system of energy, information, and decision making but also, and more importantly, the valuational and interest complex that is the true beating heart and *raison dêtre* of the organization.

THE NOMOTHETIC AND THE IDIOGRAPHIC

Organizations are not only systems but *cultural* entities for the individuals who compose them. Moreover, each organization member is a social being who inhabits and participates in a larger culture and a variety of subcultures of which the organization is only one, albeit an important or even dominant one. Two diagrams will help us to bring these important and complex relationships into focus.

Figure 2.5 is of some standing in administrative theory.[43] It shows succinctly, from the sociological standpoint, how any organization or social system can be analysed along a formal or nomothetic dimension and an informal or psychological dimension. Formally, organizations can be analysed as a system of

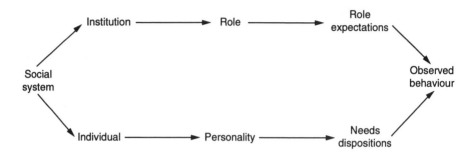

Figure 2.5　The Basic Organizational Dichotomy.

roles or job descriptions which in turn are defined by sets of behavioural role expectations. Informally, the role incumbents, individuals who constitute the flesh and blood actuality of organizations, are defined by personalities which in turn are defined by "needs dispositions", that is, some complex of values, interest, and power. The critical dimension for the administrator is the nomothetic and his peculiar task is to unify this organizational formal collective dimension with those idiographic individual elements that are always tending to diverge from it. In theory this is done through the synthesizing factor of organizational purpose or goals. The task then is to contrive these goals in such a way that what Barnard calls the "economy of incentives" is conducive to optimization of organizational efficiency and effectiveness. In other words the administrator prevents the disintegration of organization by continuously referring the individual to the collective interest.

In contrast, the non-administrative organization member is chiefly concerned with the idiographic dimension. Self-interest, individual satisfaction, not collective, is what counts: the nomothetic represents a constraint or discipline even while it provides the rational–legal foundation for any personal contract with the organization. The nomothetic is a necessary evil rather than a positive good whenever role chafes against personality.

Under this interpretation the task of the executive appears to be one of reconciliation: reconciliation of organizational goals with individual interests and, because no organization exists within a vacuum, reconciliation to the larger encompassing society. The administrative art is that of achieving organizational maintenance and growth—the nomothetic imperative—in the face of contending internal and external pressures, conflicts, and change. Two things can be noted. First that reconciliation itself can be weak or strong, good or bad, short-term or long-term, flexible or firm, creative or uninspired, divisive or harmonious, synergetic or degenerative, entropic or negentropic. In short, not simple. Second-ly, neither in theory nor practice, is it usual for the unifying factor of the goal mechanism to be clearly comprehended or understood.[44] And, as the next figure shows, the eternal presence of an overriding cultural dimension compounds the complexity and confounds the confusion. This point is illustrated by the exceptional circumstance of wartime when nation states become unified about values of survival, victory, and hatred of the enemy. For a time the economy of incentives is radically simplified. With peace and the absence of an external enemy and all its associative value symbolism, the normal condition is restored and the nomothetic override or impress is radically weakened.

In Figure 2.6 we see an extension and modification of Figure 2.5. The concept of roles (or parts in the Confucian tradition) has been expanded to stress the element of dramaturgy or *acting* that is a natural condition and requirement of organizational life. We play our parts and act our roles according to nomothetic scripts and we do so because we seek to attain individual ends within a broad scenario of purposes or economy of incentives dictated by the organizations goals. To paraphrase the economist Friedrich Hayek,[45] each self-interested member goes to work in the morning and does not what he wants but what the organization wants. He contributes not to the extent he prefers but as the organization requires, and he does so not at the price he would like to charge but at a price fixed in the market place. Let us observe also that the administrator labours in like manner. The part now played is called *leader* and the *role* performance given is continuously being monitored and evaluated by a variety

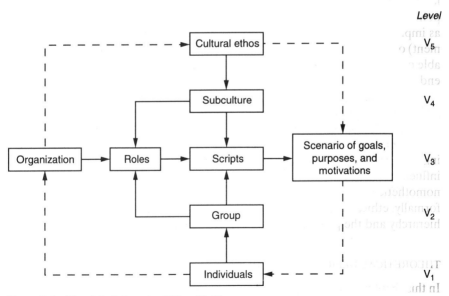

Figure 2.6 The Administrative Value Field.

of audiences, even when the script must be improvised and the scenarios are totally obscure.

The individual encounters the nomothetic dimension not directly but through workday experience with groups, both formal and informal, that in complex organizations act as buffers and modulate the formal administrative dimension. Face-to-face contact with the members of the executive troupe is the exception rather than the rule. In other words the organizational perspective is not that of administration. V_3 which can be taken to represent the nomothetic value orientation is distanced from the individual level V_1 by the mediating experience and subculture of the work group, V_2.

Similarly, from the external standpoint, the overall culture with its prevailing ethos V_5 does not impinge directly upon the organization but is modulated through an intervening subculture V_4. Organizations exist in time and space and each subcultural setting imposes some of its own local mores and norms (V_4) no matter what the *Zeitgeist* (V_5) might be. Geography and history combine as spatio-temporal determinants of consciousness in the workplace. Even such a routinized operation as McDonalds hamburger franchise differs as between Moscow, Tokyo, and Oshkosh, Ohio. This means that the ethos or culture, the large-scale contemporary pattern of value orientation is a matter for continuous executive awareness and concern. Examples are all about. The counter-culture of the 1960s introduced and left a residue of permissive, egalitarian, and anti-authoritarian notions in the workplace. Ecological, ethnic, and gender–political value factors intrude into contemporary administration. Organizations may no longer boldly assert their profit interest but are obliged to couch this motive in politically correct language: they require profits *in order to* render services such as improvements in the quality of life (motor vehicles and television entertainment) or, say, self-assurance (via cosmetic fantasy or the fashion industry). Profitable operation is no longer an end but a means to some semantically acceptable end.

The field of administrative philosophy is thus comprised of five levels of value-orientation and value-action. These levels (V_1–V_5) overlap, intertwine, and interact in complex dynamic and contingent relationships. Any synthetic view of administrative reality must therefore take into account the modulating, buffering, and filtering effects of subcultures (V_4 and V_2) as major determining influences which have to be considered ultimately for their bearing upon V_3 the nomothetic dimension, the dimension of value for which the administrator is formally, ethically, and morally responsible. This above all is the justification of hierarchy and the prequisites of power and status that attach thereto.[46]

THEORETICAL DEFICIENCY

In this chapter we have considered briefly the general dialectics of administrative thought. We have attempted to clarify language by exploring the distinction between administration and management and we have dealt with some of the elements that would constitute any putative theory of organization or administration. These include the components of process, the principle of hierarchy, and organizations as systems. In all of this it can be seen that the two sets of theory, organizational and administrative, overlap and diffuse to the point, perhaps, where the distinction between them, even though it roughly parallels that of management and administration, is neither useful nor ornamental. As to administrative theory *per se* Simon had argued in the preface to his work that it consisted only of maxims or mutually contradictory proverbs. It can be questioned whether today any advance has been made upon this statement, despite Simon's efforts, and despite a wealth of subsequent literature.[47] Organization theory, however, has progressed after the manner of pedestrian social science with empirical studies *ad infinitum* and *ad nauseam*. In the end it can only be concluded that there is neither administrative nor organizational theory *qua* theory; no overall comprehensive articulated set of laws that will permit of predictive certitude. Instead there are only an array of piecemeal subsets dealing with aspects of the whole such as motivation, group dynamics, decision making, and leader effectiveness. Together, these comprise a promissory note for some future unified body of knowledge that would generate hypotheses that could be submitted to rigorous verification but at this point neither the theorists of administration nor of organization can lay claim to scientific status. And this is so because of values. The field is a domain of values, of interest agendas, and of power conflict and struggle, all realities about which science *qua* science is studiously silent.

We have concluded with a multi-level analysis of the dimensions of organizational experience that profiles the value pervasion of the organizational–administrative field. Values, interests, and power manifest at each of the levels shown. If truth-seeking is the objective then this complexity must be somehow rendered comprehensible.

PROPOSITIONS

14. A philosophy of administration must be concerned with the analysis and investigation of administrative concepts, the language of administration.
15. Administration is the general form of human behaviour that seeks ends through organizational means.
16. Anyone can do administration. Not anyone can do management.
17. The administrative specialty is generalism.
18. Since everyone has an inalienable birthright to philosophy anyone can lead.
19. Administration is leadership. Leadership is administration.
20. Anyone can administer, therefore anyone can lead.
21. The philosopher of administration must know two things: where the values are and where the power lies.
22. Administrative philosophy must concern itself with the *Realpolitik* of power and with its psychomechanics.
23. Human organizations are collectivities whose necessary and sufficient conditions are purposes, men and techniques.
24. We are all either administered or administering.
25. Philosophy is a view of man. This alone makes it dangerous.
26. Until social science becomes philosophy it can tell us nothing about how organizations should form their goals, or why they should be pursued.
27. Organizations are purposive and problem-solving. If there be no purpose or problem the organization will create one.
28. The organizational purpose (problem) may be inchoate. It cannot remain static. It is constantly being modulated by events.
29. Multiplicity of ends and vagueness of general purpose will increase with organizational size and complexity.
30. The universe is purposive but inscrutable. Organizational purposes are scrutable. Individual purposes are both.
31. Organizations are the fields of administrative action. Administrators create, preserve, and destroy organizations.
32. Organization theory can only pose the problem for administrative philosophy.
33. The administrative philosopher is a physician of organizational culture. And sometimes a pathologist.

Chapter 3
Decisions and Policy Making

Policy making is decision making writ large. Conversely, decision is the fundamental element of policy. The relationship is also rather like that between micro- and macroeconomics, or between farming and agriculture. Decision making is what people actually do while policy is a pattern superimposed upon a world that has been altered because of decisions. Because the decision process is therefore more behavioural, observable, down-to-earth let us begin our analysis with this universal behaviour and experience that everyone is constantly engaged in and with which everyone is familiar.

That decision making is not necessarily pleasurable—does everyone (or anyone?) really enjoy this apparent assertion of will?—may account for some general animus on the part of the administered, (those for whom decisions are made) towards the administrators, (those who make the decisions affecting other). But administrative decision making can be distinguished from personal or individual decision behaviour.

First, administrative decisions are made for and about others. These decisions are linked to the degrees of freedom surrendered by those others who join the organization on behalf of which the decisions are made. The extreme case is illustrated by the elected politician who decides for *us* once we have surrendered all power of control in the act of election. Secondly, these decisions are *moral,* if by moral one means the exercise of collective responsibility. That is, acting with the intent of furthering the larger interest. Thirdly, administrative decisions are often second-order decisions-about-decisions in that they are power-distribution; they decide who gets to decide what about whom. A typical example would be the establishment of a search committee for an executive appointment or, in another direction, the establishment of a commission of inquiry to produce recommendations.

It is clear then that all true administrative decisions are components of policy making; they are the parts of which policy making is the whole. Such activity is, however, to be discriminated from managerial or routine or technical decision making which is about means as opposed to ends. We can indeed conceive of organizations as patterns of decision flow in which the critical or philosophical decisions having to do with organizational life and purposes are made by administrators in which the subordinate technological means-decisions having to do with organizational process are made by other organization members but are *designed* by administrators.

Because of this persvasiveness of decisional behaviour in organizational life a broad consensus, emanating from Simon,[1] has developed which views decision making as the quintessence of the administrative art. There is the temptation here to be seduced into yet another grand reduction: administration is no more or no less than the making of organizational decisions. But such an oversimplification is untenable. Litchfield,[2] an early analyst, conceived of decision making as the initiatory phase of the administrative cycle which then proceeded through programming, communicating, controlling, and reappraising back to decision making again.[3] He was careful to stress that decisions could be "rational, deliberative, discretionary, purposive" or "irrational, habitual, obligatory, random" or "any combination thereof".[4] On the assumption that the former is the desirable administrative mode logical analysis then provided the sequence: (1) Definition of issue, (2) Analysis of existing situation, (3) Calculation and delineation of alternatives, (4) Deliberation, and (5) Choice. This logic, variously expressed, persists within orthodox organization theory yet one can at once discern difficulties. Just *how* does one "deliberate"?[5] What exactly is calculation and delineation? And what differentiates "choice" from "decision". Is not to *choose* already to "decide"? If there is an accepted calculus then does not that *ipso facto* decide? Can a computer *decide*? Or be programmed to decide? These questions call for philosophical scrutiny but one preliminary assertion may at once be made. True decisions are open and extralogical. Calculations can only be logical. Therefore, machines can never decide.

THE DECISION PARADIGM

Decision making is the most ordinary, familiar, and human of activities. It is also the most philosophical because it raises at once the imponderable issue of free will. We shall examine this question later but for now it can be agreed that there is a universal experiential sense, at the subjective level, of some possibility of choice; some degree—illusory or not—of freedom. We feel as *if* we can choose. And we attribute this liberty to be almost beyond debate. It follows that administrative decisions are special and that the making and taking of them is crucial to the administrative art. But do administrators possess any special expertise in this function that distinguishes them from other organization members? Is there a specialized body of knowledge, in which they are skilled, that can prescribe authoritatively in this domain?

Logically, decision making is a process whereby one arrives at a choice. It is the often quite agonizing business of making up one's mind, a task which Hamlet found quite intolerable. For the process to commence there must come about a state of affairs where the decision maker faces alternative routes in the flow of events. This decision condition extends across an interval of time of varying length and varying intensity. Intensity here refers to both the sense of compulsion to choose and the sense of significance about the consequences of choosing. Within the decision condition a selection must be made between alternatives and one road followed to the exclusion of others. A decision condition entails two and *only* two alternatives. This is so because it is logically impossible to choose between more than two things. What occurs when more than two alternatives are present in the choice situation is that binary options are successively and iteratively considered (a process that need not be consciously conducted) until, in the *final* analysis, the number of alternatives is reduced to two. Thus it might appear on first face that one has options *a*, *b*, and *c* but by the time of decision either *a* or *b* or *c* will have been rejected so as to arrive at the choice between *ab*, *ac*, or *bc*. And so with options in excess of three. Decision making becomes "chattery" or "dithering" only when rejected choices are inadvertently or unwontedly reintroduced into the process. Indeed, one might construe executive decision making as the fine art of sterilization and isolation of rejected options.

No one can claim this complex psychological process is fully understood, nor even that it is entirely conscious. Subliminal and unconscious intrusions confound the paradigm and, as J. F. Kennedy once remarked, "The essence of ultimate decision remains impenetrable to the observer... often indeed, to the decider himself... There will always be the dark and tangled stretches of the decision making process—mysterious even to those intimately involved."[6] Still, we need resort neither to political mysticism nor psychoanalytic obscurantism. If the business of decision were totally inscrutable, administrators might as well play dice with their universe and govern their organizations by means of tables of random numbers.[7] In the practical world of organizational life, administrative decisions and choices have to be made continuously and at every organizational level. Logically each decision can be analysed as an ultimate either-or, this-or-that, to be or not to be. The binary discrimination is entirely congruent with Aristotelian logic and modern science. A thing either is or it is not. Decisions are switches in the ramifying networks of possibility and even a decision not to decide is a decision, the binary alternative of which is the decision to decide. The philosophy of administration must contend with this dualism.

In the ordinary course of administration there is a presumption of rationality (or at least rational intent) and, on this presumption, however ill-founded, the pattern set out below is discerned as the skeletal logic of the standard decision process:

1. Delineation of the ultimate binary alternative. ("In the end it comes down to this or this.")
2. Assessment of the consequences of each alternative. This step can be subdivided as to fact and as to value.

   With regard to fact, the decider is constrained by (a) the sources, quality, and extent of information and knowledge relevant to the case and (b) interpretation of (a), such interpretation being a function of multiple psychological factors, conscious and unconscious predispositions, perceptual sets, as well as qualitative attributes such as insight, competence, and experience.

With regard to value this subject forms the preoccupation and central concern of this book. It goes without saying that it is a function of the psychology and philosophy of the deciding agent.

Notwithstanding the above the rational decider will attempt to determine (quantify) the probabilities of selected outcomes (hereafter referred to as p values) and, in principle at least, to assign to the alternative outcomes respective values (hereafter referred to as v values).

3. Calculation of expected values.

With ps and vs assigned to outcomes the last phase of the decision process becomes a matter of mere calculation since the quantified p and v values can be multiplied to yield the "expected value" of any outcome. The rational choice is then simply that with the highest expected value.

An Illustration

A simplified illustration will make the paradigm clear. Let us take the elemental administrative decision: To appoint or not to appoint a new member to the ranks of the organization. Let us assume that all conventional search procedures have been followed. Four logical outcomes relevant to the decision can then be specified: The candidate either O_1: is engaged and proves to be adequate. or

O_2: is engaged and proves to be inadequate.

or

O_3: is not engaged (but would have proven adequate if engaged).

or

O_4" is not engaged (but would not have proven adequate if engaged).

Suppose now an indifference as between O_1 and O_4 since the whole process of selection is supposed to hire successful personnel and avoid hiring failures. O_1 and O_4 are therefore valuationally neutral as contrasted with O_2 (a hiring failure) and O_3 (also a hiring failure). Both O_2 and O_3 carry negative connotations since they could lead to organizational damage or detriment, especially if similar organizations were competing for similar personnel. Let us therefore ascribe estimates of v from the possible range -1 to $+1$; say, -0.6 to O_2 (a major mistake) and -0.2 to O_3 (a lesser error). Similarly, v values are assigned to O_1 and O_4, say, 0.6 and 0.2 respectively.

Next, for simplicity, let us assume that the statistically best estimate (p) of the candidates' adequacy is 0.8, i.e. there is an 80% probability of the process being successful. The decision matrix then is given as follows:

Outcome	p	v	$p \times v$
O_1	0.8	0.6	0.48
O_2	0.2	−0.6	−0.12
O_3	0.2	−0.2	−0.40
O_4	0.8	0.2	0.16
Expected value	$(O_1 + O_2) = 0.36$		
	$(O_3 + O_4) = 0.24$		

The two expected values sum the respective possibilities for hiring $(O_1 + O_2)$ and not hiring $(O_3 + O_4)$. Given these attributions for p and v the rational decision would be "appoint" (with a 12% margin of confidence).

Quite obviously a different set of values could have been assigned to the variables in this calculus. The object here is merely to display the paradigm and its intrinsic reliance upon the essential factors of analysis (delineation of alternatives) and imputation (the ascription if p and v values). Granted that the paradigm is immensely simplified—organizational context, socio-cultural, personal, and political elements constraining and affecting decision have, for example, been ignored—still it can be seen that the ultimate reduction, immediately prior to choice, is logically and psychologically in the realms of probability and value. And it is further implied that, at least in principle, both of these elements can be quantified. That is to say that essentially qualitative phenomena such as value are amenable to numerical representation, either ordinal or cardinal. And hence to calculus. Thus the decision maker inhabits a world of uncertainty and value in which he struggles to analyse and impute.

To recapitulate: Components of probability and value permeate and determine the decision process. Throughout, p and v values are being guessed, figured, estimated, computed, intuited, "felt", and otherwise entered into the calculus. By and large, in administration at least, rationality is held to as a criterion. This is reinforced by the presumption that in zero sum games the most rational player is most likely to win. Yet the difficulties and impediments to all these analytic and imputational endeavours should be immediately obvious to the administrative mind.

Any non-machined human decision involves p and v elements. Both p and v may be unstable and uncertain. In the case of machine-made or programmed decisions the machine or computer, or in some instances the human manager, can only *calculate* p and v values. And certainly a machine cannot assign a p or v except by derivation from an already predetermined higher level p or v program. Determination of program or *policy*, like the true assignment of v values, is a prerogative reserved for human action and intention, it is a function of *consciousness*.

Simon is of the view that an individual can never possess enough knowledge of p or v ever to arrive at a truly rational decision. He is of course correct. Only a "closed system of variables" would permit approximation to a rational, objective, factual ideal.[8] But even such an ideal, where decisions could be degraded to calculations, would presuppose a "program" of preferences or values which would derive from outside the system and would involve a logically different level of analysis. For readers with a mathematical bent the resonance with Gödel's proof that systems require extra-systemic validation is interesting.[9]

NON-RATIONAL DECISION MAKING

In general, decisions can be classified as open or closed. Closed decisions are those that approximate more closely to the objective ideals of rationality and calculus. For example queuing theory and linear programming provide instances in which the optimal solutions to decision problems can be obtained as with, say, airport and highway traffic control, parking allocation, crop rotation, inventory problems, and bombing or artillery patterns. Such decisions are predominantly factual and managerial, values are "given", goals are precise, alternatives are clearly identifiable, and outcomes are predictable. Moreover, it is possible to optimize or maximize (not just "satisfice"); the utilities or values are given in the decision context and, typically, it is possible to employ sophisticated mathematical and computational techniques. Such decisions acquire the honorific *rational* because they seek the *best* solution. As Simon puts it, "Roughly speaking, rationality is concerned with the selection of preferred behaviour alternatives in terms of some system of values whereby the consequences of behaviour can be evaluated."[10] But this definition is rough because of course it implies at least another *level* of rationality, that which determines the "some system of values", or else it implicitly sets a boundary to rationality itself beyond which lie the irrational, the transrational, the non-rational, or the subrational.

Open decision making includes the following elements which comprise a priori limits to rationality. The following list is not exhaustive: subjective and personal factors related to the decision maker or decision making group, historical factors in the form of organizational sunk costs and binding previous commitments, policy constraints and organizational decision rules, information communication and perception factors which may distort objective reality, unacknowledged affective and self-image problematics, unidentified consequences and unimagined alternatives and, in general, elements of will, volition, or intention that fall outside the rational–cognitive rubric. These latter will be studied in detail in Part IV.

Quite apart from any vagaries of the existential situation within which a decision has to be taken the process invokes two classes of act which are conceptually distinct: the cognitive determination of p values and the *trans-cognitive* determination of v values. The latter refers simply to the value factor and its correlative, interest. It is the essential element in decision making and we shall argue that, though a-rational it is not imponderable. Nor is it intractable. Nevertheless, this irreducible element of values places the entire process beyond the dimension of logic. Wittgenstein[11] has denied the admissibility of value propositions in logical discourse while other philosophers following Kaplan[12] would greatly extend the definition of logic. Philosophers of administration such as Evers and Lakomski,[13] on the other hand, would seek to blur the value-fact distinction altogether. In the present work we are concerned to keep the distinction between logical propositions which can be assessed as true or false and value propositions for which the terms true and false are inappropriate.

In addition to the complexifying factors mentioned above there are important *power* or political questions. *Who*, for example, really decides? The responsibility for an organizational decision is as often as not collective. Sometimes advisory parties to the formal decision maker or decision making group exercise suasion. Or they act as information gate-keepers and control vital data. Standing committees, self-selected and formally selected individuals, representatives of power-seeking factions within and without the formal "rational" decision making processes of the organization—all these and more[14] compound the superstructure of decisional complexity and increase the difficulty of resolution and determination of the v-factors in the paradigm.

Furthermore, decisions never occur in a vacuum. Nor can they be isolated or excised from the living tissue of organizational biology. Each decision is enmeshed in an enormously complex web of contingency, interrelation, feedback, and means-ends concatenations. This web embraces not merely the actual but the possible. Each taken decision becomes both a constraint and a liberating potential for future decisions. Paradoxically perhaps, the most rational decisions tend to be these which are the most constrained, for the fewer the degrees of freedom the greater the amenability to logical calculation and the greater the ease of determination of the p and v factors. but it should also be noted that, in line with our general thesis, the more contingent and determined decisions become the more they fall into the category of the managerial and technical. The truly great administrative decisions are those which tear apart and create anew whole patterns of contingency. Only when the vicious circle of causation can be broken does administrative or philosophical action become possible.

Simon abandoned the ideal of linear or comprehensive rationality[15] in favour of a reality-based paradigm in which the decision maker satisfies rather than optimizes. This practice is rational in that the level of aspiration in adjusting to complexity is pragmatically modified. There are, however, other responses to decision making which can be considered irrational, aberrant, and philosophically suspect. These are particularly likely to occur with respect the v factors.

Because value propositions can never be labelled true or false in the same way as propositions of logic or verifiable empirical propositions, they can be thought of as metafactual or metascientific, beyond the reach of quantitative methods or ordinary logic. To deny this is to commit the naturalistic fallacy,[16] the argument for which asserts that no amount of facts or "is's" can "prove" a value statement or an "ought". This places limits on decision making fact-gathering or information-seeking to the extent that while factual bases may be desirable in arriving at value premises they cannot in themselves prove those premises. In practical administrative life this contributes to two decision strategies that are in effect polar opposites: participation and evaluation. Both of these are apparently rational approaches to the values problem but both are susceptible to irrational degeneration.

Participation is the technique of consulting and co-opting interested or knowledgeable parties so as to enlarge the deliberative scope of the decision making process. It seeks consensus but if this is not forthcoming the v-factor may be determined by some form of vote or weighted ballot. Carried to extremes the method becomes the aberration of determining values and making decisions not on the basis of rationality but of political suasion. A classical instance is the political referendum. Referendums settle issues of *power* rather than value. They are means of terminating otherwise irresolvable value conflicts while leaving the precipitating philosophical value issues intact. That participation can "settle" a value question is one thing, that it can "prove" anything is quite another. And that it can be subverted by force or manipulation quite another yet again.

The opposite strategy to participation is that of assigning values problems to values experts. This may be done *ad hoc* through consultation or formally through the creation of an evaluator role.[17] In either case a distinction is presupposed between deciders or decision takers (administrators and policy makers) and advisors (consultants and policy analysts). The role of the latter is to analyse and evaluate without engaging in executive action.[18] Irrationality, however, enters directly through this front door when the recommendations of the experts "covertly introduce into administrative decisions values of which even the experts are unaware. Further, because non-experts hesitate to contradict experts, experts may inject into administrative decisions value preferences of which they definitely are conscious. And because experts often learn their standardized solutions with little or no understanding of the basic reasons for them, they are often very inflexible and resistant to new ideas."[19] There is in any event a strong odour of illogic in the very concept of an objective analyst with immaculate perception. The mere formulation of alternatives would depend upon the evaluator's "evaluation" and hence in principle would be pre-empting or usurping the administrator's responsibility and freedom of choice.

Given the difficulties inherent in the value aspect of decision it is not surprising that another aberration or dysfunction is the tendency to overconcentrate on the factual and quantitative or managerial aspects of problem-solving. Computerology and the microchip infrastructure has greatly assisted this form of self-deception.[20]

Yet another and more insidious mode or irrationality can occur through the practice of "open" decision making where "open" is used in the sense of accessible to public or organization membership: "Open decisions openly arrived at". Such procedures are commonly constrained by a necessary measure of formality and this can incline towards quasi-judicial solutions where value issues are resolved in terms of precedent or literal interpretation of policy rather than by any imaginative, principled, or creative resolution. Worse, the open forum may become merely a display for manipulative ends, the scene that is the obverse of the obscene, the actual decision having been made prior to the dramaturgy, privately and covertly, thus nullifying the rationale for the procedure in the first place.[21]

Lastly, illustrating but by no means exhausting the possibilities for aberration, administrators may resort to a pseudo-neutral or "bureaucratic" posture—the factotum or "not ours to question why" attitude—whereby the philosophically difficult, valuational, or qualitative aspects of the decision paradigm are treated as external constraints, givens, or simply overlooked or denied altogether as being outside the process.[22] This is of course a pathology, a retreat to managerialism that can extend the roles of evaluators, analysts, consultants, and illicit parties of interest and lead to dysfunctional organizational effects.

From all of this it follows that administrators, who have the charge of making organizational decisions, should at the very least desire to lay claim to some expertise on the topic of values. Value knowledge would constitute for them their special competence and special warranty of office.

POLICY MAKING

Policy making is to decision making as strategy is to tactics. It may be considered as the making of decisions which bear heavily on the organizational life both as regards mission or purpose and as regards the general *modus operandi.* An eminent theorist and experienced practitioner, Sir Geoffrey Vickers, described it as "the setting of governing relations or norms, rather than in the more usual terms as the setting of goals, objectives or ends".[23] Other standard authorities have referred to it as a "body of principle to guide action 'and' a design to shape the future by exerting influence upon trends that flow from the past into the present."[24] Yet others see policy making as the fundamental instrument of governance: "... an authoritative determination, by a governing authority, or a society's intents and priorities and an authoritative allocation of resources to these intents and priorities."[25] In other words a fusion of values, interests, and power.

Policy and philosophy coalesce. An organization is never inert; it is a potent living thing. At any instant it represents in a complex fashion the sum total of its history and, simultaneously, its potential for shaping the future, its own and that of the entire fabric of circumstance within which it has its being. The quality of that being and its potential for the future is the manifestation of its philosophy, the synthesis of logic and value as crystallized in the accumulation and formulation of policy. And this highly philosophical business is a continuous and ongoing affair. "The ever-changing present generates ever new purposes in the continuing organization."[26] Katz and Kahn distinguish policy decisions as those which are large in terms of organizational space and time and refer to policy making as "the decision aspect of the level of leadership which involves the attention, origination, or elimination of organizational structure".[27]

Who then makes policy? Who performs this quintessential administrative act? Is it to be confined, *pace* Downey, to a "governing authority"?

This question takes on a special form because of a powerful political canon which often assumes mythic proportions in Anglo-Saxon democratic cultures. This asserts that the policy function belongs to amateurs or to lay or part-time members of the organization. "The expert should be on tap and not on top." The province of experts (administrators, managers, permanent civil servants, technologist, professional generally) is to do what they are told. They are the experts in means while the laymen are experts in ends, the ones who do the telling. Thus, legislatures of elected citizenry determine policy for nations while boards of trustees and directors do likewise for schools, hospitals, and firms. This blurring of the administrative–managerial distinction obliges us to make a more rigorous discrimination.

First, it cannot be denied that representative or political groups make policy. But it would be naive and fallacious to assume that *only* they make policy and that ranking administrators within organizations do *not* make policy. If this were so then the latter would be in our terms mere managers but, to the extent that directly or indirectly, formally or informally, by persuasion, influence, manip-ulation, control of information, or by whatever means they do in fact determine policy decisions they are authentically executives and administrators.

Administrators are then of three kinds. First, there are those who come to their office by way of some form of political process; by appointment, election, or patronage. These are politician-administrators. Their association with the organization may be temporary and transient, and they may have had no formal or informal administrative preparation: they may even insist that they are not, or do they want to be, administrators. Secondly, there are administrators with or without tenure who have had some kind of career pattern of preparation and who are permanently affiliated members of their organization. They occupy formally designated executive roles. We may call these professional administrators. Thirdly, there is an important hybrid category which is of increasing institutional importance in contemporary society, the collegial administrator. These are career professional members of their organizations but are elected or appointed from within the organization to occupy an administrative role for a specified term.[28] They include most educational administrators as well as doctors, nurses, engineers, technicians, technologists, police and military. Administration is not their ostensible or maternal profession and they may have had no preparation in the field. Their professional allegiance is not administration and may on occasion be antagonistic to it.[29] Let us note that it is only the category of professional administrator which allows any presumption of any preparation or training in the fields of administrative competence. And even here we cannot presuppose instruction in the philosophical skills of analysis and value clarification.[30] Yet all three groups are engaged in administration and the making of policy. All are practising administrators. If rationality were to be a value in organizational life, and if rationality entailed some degree of professionalism then we would have to conclude that present modes of policy and decision making are irrational. But this concern can be deferred to a later discussion of professionalism.

POLICY AS PLANNING

Policy can refer internally or externally. Internally it establishes an organization's *modus vivendi*, its form of life. Examples are the allocation of budgeting discretion, the establishment of flex time, the allocation of secretaries and office space, the status indicators of who has to sign in and who doesn't. In general these sorts of small p policies set up the game rules and the kinds of moves which may be made within the organizational game. The skilled administrator is the adroit game player and through his skill both fixes and changes the game. External or big P policy on the other hand has to do with planning. A course has to be set for the organization in a context of competing and conflicting environmental factors. This calls for a special kind of organizational perspective, for a diplomatic as well as a philosophical overview.

Decisions at this latter level are decisions writ large because the component alternatives, probabilities, and values take on a larger or heightened collective significance. The search for alternatives may expand into deliberate policy analysis or the development of autonomous or quasi-autonomous planning or research and development functions. There may be an elaborate and formal apparatus of investigation, intelligence gathering, analysis, study, and reporting. (All of which may of course be swept aside and ignored in reactive responses to emergencies or "heat of the moment" action). The decisional p-factors will also become more significant because of the greater states of organizational investment. This may place a premium on a certain peculiar administrative attribute that can only be likened to a propensity for gambling or "figuring the odds". This and its concomitant risk-taking faculty would be counterbalanced by organization pressures towards caution, conservatism, and maintenance of the steady state or status quo. Not every administrator possesses the Napoleonic or Hitlerian genius for intuitive risk-taking. It is also clear that the v-factors will have heightened significance; in the extreme, sufficient bad policy will lead to organizational extinction.

Policies or plans can be considered as having two dimensions: scope of intended change and understanding of the intended change.[31] Together these dimensions lead to a basic contrast between large change and small change strategies of planning, each of which involve distinctive philosophical attitudes about future uncertainty and the way in which it should be handled. In general large changes are funded by some sort of overarching theory or ideology or grand intent such as "winning the war" or implementing a utopian ideal. Such ideology may be philosophical, religious, or political. The policy maker who would fashion the organization's future in this grand manner must move beyond the bounds of ordinary rationality and system equilibrium into regions characterized by faith, belief, value, and will—all difficult if not imponderable terms for any putative administrative science.

Diametrically opposed to grand planning is the strategy of incrementalism. This, as opposed to other alternatives such as mixed scanning,[32] or rational synoptic approaches,[33] is the method most deserving of our attention for it is the one which seems to be most widespread and most grounded in the reality of practical affairs. In this type of policy making small decisions are made at the margin and the analytic method employed is based pragmatically on judgements arising mainly from administrative and organizational experience. Goals, means, and ends, values and facts, are not rigorously distinguished but are treated as experientially interactive. The consequences of policy serve as a feedback mechanism in what is essentially a tentative, evolutional, "feel one's way" approach. Policy makers seek to avoid radical action or any large value conflict. Lindblom, in a classic article,[34] called this the branch method contrasting it with the root method of rationally synoptic large-scale change. He also described it as "The Science of Muddling Through." The method has been said to be the basic technique for US budget-making[35] and also the way in which society makes most of its decisions. Any philosophy of administration must take it seriously and, while it may be criticized as inertial, status quo oriented, and unsuited to large scale and rapid change in a system's environment it may also be defended as being the most adaptive and rational method of *coping* with the very same change. Our purpose for the moment, however, is not to enter into this debate or to consider technical details of planning and policy but to alert the reader to the extremes of policy-making and to point out that *any* planning strategy implies, and possibly entails, philosophical commitments and value orientations which may be overt but which also may be unconscious, subliminal, or deliberately concealed. All of these possibilities being contingent upon the live actors in the real policy context.

POLICY ANALYSIS

Policy *analysis* has been stringently defined as "an applied discipline which uses multiple methods of inquiry and argument to produce and transform policy-relevant information that may be utilized in policy settings to resolve public problems."[36] Less stringently the same authority says that policy analysis "in its widest sense, involves the production of knowledge of and in policy processes".[37] There is, however, about these definitions—unassailable as they stand—a subtle quality of detachment or objectivity which could render them deceptive because the key terms of knowledge and inquiry are by no means value-neutral. Indeed Jennings[38] and Wildawsky[39] among others would ground policy analysis in values, interests, and power, going so far as to conceptualize the analyst's role as one of advocacy or "counselling". What would appear to be evident is that the processes of making and analysing policy are so entangled and intertwined, that, while the conceptual distinction is valuable and the practical attempt to achieve a division of labour is to be encouraged rather than disparaged, the underlying reality is primarily valuational or intentional. This can be understood clearly from Figure 3.1.[40]

The line from individual and societal motivational bases and desires to both internal and external policy is clear and it is made or broken only by the intrusion of power. It should also be noted that the extent to which planning and analysis enter into the policy process is a function of the policy maker's inclination

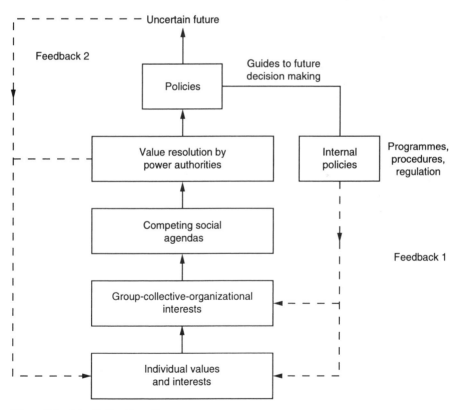

Figure 3.1 The Policy Paradigm.

towards reactive or proactive policy orientations which in turn may be a function of a host of individual and social–philosophical value orientations that together may constitute a complex of variables intractable to analysis. In other words the project of rational analysis may again be frustrated. That analytical complex is further confounded (although, superficially, it may on occasion appear to be *simplified*) by the conflicting demands of representative and participatory democracy. The former assumes that elected or appointed policy makers would consider the whole body of interest relevant to their actions rather than or at least as well as, the interest of parts as manifested through special interest or grievance groups or by lobbies and individuals. The latter, participatory democracy, encourages the influences of parts upon the whole and, of course, enhances political tension between minorities and majority, creating a dialectic in which modern media influences and social–political contexts can be said to favour the vocal minority over the silent or apathetic majority.

Lest these last remarks seem too abstract, an illustration can be provided from academe. Alan Dershewitz, a professor at the Harvard School of Law, referring to an incident on his own campus, wrote "The overreaction [to a student parody] is a reflection of the power of women and blacks to define the content of what is politically correct and incorrect in college and law school campuses ... Women and blacks are entirely free to attack white men ... in the most offensive of terms. Radical feminists can accuse all men of being rapists, and radical African-Americans can accuse all whites of being racists, without fear of discipline or rebuke. But even an unintentionally offensive parody of women or blacks provides the occasion for demanding the resignation of deans, the disciplining of students and an atmosphere reminiscent of McCarthyism."[41] Without engaging at all in this particular debate it can be seen that the power interest nexus is a formative policy element which is culturally conditioned by the representative–participatory dialectic. The implications of this will be examined in later chapters of this book.

LEVELS OF POLICY AND DECISION

Whether at a green baize table or behind a *bureau plat*, whether on the staircase or in a smoke-filled back room the function of policy making is invariably removed from the reality of action. Moreover, the formal deliberative setting is often designed to have an ambiance of detachment, to be a forum for ideas, to be objective, rational, removed from the mechanics of implementation. Between any policy or plan and its translation into factual reality there extends a longer or shorter chain of managerial detail. This hierarchical chain and this physical distancing entail psychological consequences that cannot be ignored in the philosophy of administration. They can, to say the least, be dangerous.

Defective reality or information grasp is not simply inherent in structure, being directly related to levels and hierarchy, but may be deliberately brought about through distortion of the administrative–managerial spectrum. Thus, creative policy alternatives may not come up for consideration on the administrative plane because they are aborted *ab initio*, or held to be "impractical", or else the organization is already committed (managerially) in a contrary direction, or the managerial difficulties are held to be insuperable, or "the eggs are already scrambled". There is a kind of Juggernaut phenomenon wherein the inertial forces of the organization prevent its being halted or changed in direction. This may be bad enough, the administrative dog wagged by the managerial tail but, philosophically, it is in the reverse situation, when there is no impediment to the flow of policy from centre to periphery that the severest changes can occur.

The problem of levels and distancing is another aspect of the problem of the separation of ends and means. Insofar as they can be separated at all we have the logical difference between policy and execution; between value-interests informing policy and the power actualization of those value-interests in the world. That gaps or hiatuses occur in this transition means a choice between the cool of the council chamber and chaotic reality. If the decision maker, committed to logical rationality, is also affectively neutral and detached from any humane-situation comprehension then the result can be pathological. At the policy making desk or table or armchair an *Endlösung* or "final solution of the Jewish question" might seem feasible or even rational. *Lex dura sed lex*. So might a "hands off" policy in the Balkans or support for the Khmer Rouge. Such policy decisions might not have been taken had the actual resultant human agonies been truly entered into the decisional calculus; or then again they might. Ethical questions to which social science could provide empirical answers. Answers for which the philosophy of administration must press.

Against this it may be argued that the administrator must perforce be ruthless. He cannot indulge the luxury of imagination or feelings any more than the surgeon can contemplate with sentiment the person or the body to which (not to *whom*) he is applying the knife. It would be an impediment to rational objectivity and to proper professional detachment. But the analogy is false. The surgeon, like the scientist, is a manager concerned with means, the ends of which have been determined elsewhere. And for that matter, the ends are rational and justifiable and may well have taken into their calculus all or any of the agonizing consequences. The surgeon's detachment is a technically justified attitude, but the policy maker's detachment is of a different logical order: open, not closed, to love and hate. At the policy level of decision making philosophy and psychology interact and coalesce. A humane bridging of the ends–means gap would rightly call for qualities of compassion, empathy, and imagination which are rarely dealt with seriously in the administrative literature,[42] qualities antagonistic both to a *Zeitgeist* of scientific objectivity and to an ideology of political correctness. Cultivation of such qualities is hardly a recognized part of administrative prep-aration. On the contrary we often find dispassion and objectivity being counselled, in line with misinterpreted Weberian prescription,[43] accompanied by an ethos of admiration for the "hard-nosed", tough-minded administrator capable of making "tough decisions" who does not "tolerate fools gladly". Yet none of this is to deny that hard and painful decisions must from time to time be taken. It is only to sensitize us to the inherent structural problem of levels. As Katz and Kahn express it: "The decision-making of organizations may be highly rational within the frame of reference of the objectives of the particular organization, but these objectives may be so irrational in larger terms that the net result is systemic and human destruction ... Organizations are more efficient than individuals, whether concerned with good or evil, sense or nonsense."[44]

While an organization can logically be considered a neutral instrument of power the realities of hierarchy, structural levels, and socio-psychological distancing create a propensity that runs beyond amorality towards immorality. The working administrator who allows his moral sense to atrophy or who retreats to managerialism by one device or another is abdicating his philosophical responsibility. And this holds whether he is political, professional, or collegial; whether his competence in policy making is attributed or achieved, a product of formalized training or the happenstance of experience.

This potential for philosophical difficulty, for crises of *praxis*, is exacerbated in what has been called the postmodern or postindustrial society.[45] Simply, this means we inhabit an era in which the complexities of large organization, science, and technology have led to an "instrumentalization of science".[46] That is, its bureaucratization, rationalization, and disconnection from the influence of the humanities and the associated traditional restraints and inhibitions. This, in turn, has led to contending perspectives on policy analysis.

The contending viewpoints can be classified as either detached or engaged. The first argues that professional analysis should be aloof from administrative decision taking and impartial with respect to decision making;[47] the second that, since value objectivity is impossible, analysts should take activist roles in counselling administrators, thereby becoming policy makers themselves.[48] Both perspectives continue to demand philosophical analysis and scrutiny but both have their origin in social history, namely, the growth of government and the expansion of bureaucratic agencies in both the public and private sectors. It is contentious, but not unreasonable, to argue that the intellectual development of the social sciences has not necessarily matched the rate of change in complex organizations.[49]

POLICY AND CHAOS

Modern mathematical theory makes an interesting distinction between mere randomness and the random determinism of non-equilibrium dynamical systems.[50] The latter include highly complex and unpredictable systems such as the weather, the stock-market, the economy and, conceivably, human complex organizations or policy making systems in general. It has been asserted, for example, that "Any simple-minded statement about how the economy is causally linked to variations in one or more parameters, for example interest and exchange rates, is guaranteed baloney in the long term. The only statements which can be made for chaotic systems are probabilistic ones, based on the inherent uncertainties in the initial conditions."[51] We do not need to enter into the mathematical detail of fractals and non-linear differential equations to appreciate the general notions that (1) incommensurable slight microvariations in the evolution of a system over time, and (2) strange attractors or repellers conduce over time to the emergence of unforeseen or unpredictable states of equilibrium. In administrative life the first condition is represented in the poem about the want of a nail in a horse's shoe leading to the loss of a battle and a change in the course of history. The second condition might be represented by the maxim that crisis equals opportunity, a state of affairs in which innovative organization and intuitive leadership can move a threatened organization to new levels of stability and profitably; e.g. moving a railroad out of passenger traffic and into road freight and airline transport.[52] This is not to suggest that the new, and to some extent oversubscribed, mathematics[53] is directly applicable to administrative philosophy but rather that scientific knowledge of thermodynamical systems might provide conceptual analogues for the theory of decision making at the policy level. Certainly, the concepts of entropy and negentropy (negative entropy) are essential to organizational theorists, and hence to administrative philosophers. Certainly, too, the irreversible factor of time is a too neglected factor in contemporary systems theory. The co-presence of laws that are universal and events that are unique passes for the most part without theoretical recognition or concern. Organizations have a history and exist within a larger history or culture. Such history and culture cannot be construed as chaotic in the ordinary sense of the word; they may, however, be amenable to comprehension under newer and yet to be developed understandings about determinism and causality in natural processes.

INTEREST AND POLICY

For now the term "interest" can be understood as referring to a complex of values organized about an individual or a group. Three kinds of interest can distinguished: (1) *self*-interest, the interest of the individual; (2) *organization* interest, the interest of the collectivity as structured in an organization and; (3) *extra-organizational* interest or larger interest extending beyond the bounds and confines of either individual or group. Each of these types will bear upon policy making but only the first can be rigorously presumed. While the forms of interest are not mutually exclusive the logical possibilities for basic modes of policy formulation yield well-determined patterns that parallel the above categories. They are (1) the *opportunistic*, (2) the *rationalistic*, and (3) the *doctrinaire* modes.

Opportunistic strategies would tend to form policy on the basis of the self-interest of the decider or deciders. An administrator pursuing this strategy consistently would of course find many occasions in which perceived self-interest coincided with or was subsumed by the larger forms of interest. One would also assume that where conflict existed the administrator would couch public and organizational utterances in appropriate rhetoric, disguising and concealing the self-motivations. Opportunism of this kind may also be organizationally benefi-cial to the extent that the administrator identifies personally with organizational success, with keeping the golden goose in good condition. That this need not be entirely the case, however, and the ruthless opportunism can be organization-ally dysfunctional ought not to be overlooked. Ambitious and mobile inter-organizational careerists can trail a wake of organizational distress behind them.

Rationalistic policy orientation has as its dominant thrust the organization interest. Often this conceals or overlays the presumptions that what is good for the organization is good for the individual and good for the larger society. "What's good for General Motors is good for the country." It also connotes an orientation that is positivistic, technocratic, objective, cost-benefit analytical, instrumental and focused on means rather than ends. These connotations imply the risk of at least two kinds of error. First, the risk of committing the ubiquitous naturalistic fallacy (see Chapter 6). This supposes wrongly that ends (and therefore policy) can be logically derived from the study of facts. Secondly, there is the risk of identification with scientific norms of factual objectivity and rationality or econometric norms of cost accounting and quantitative analysis to the exclusion of humane considerations and values. Tribe has criticized the policy science approach by claiming that "the policy sciences tend to partition and warp reality in certain patterned ways, generating a fairly understandable, and sometimes quite unfortunate, system of blind spots and distortions."[54] In the search for a logic of administration the logical–rational approach to policy can itself prove contra-functional and ultimately illogical.

Finally, let us consider extra-organizational interest. Such interest may range from a carefully articulated faith, philosophy, or ideology (Catholicism, Marxist –Leninism, Liberal utilitarianism) to an inchoate, malformed, or embryonic "value orientation" (radicalism, narcissism, opportunism). It may also embrace special or single interest affiliations external to the organization (feminism, aboriginal welfare, the environment). In general, patterned persuasion, if clear enough to the holder of it, can become a determinant of policy, whether or not it aspires to the status of a philosophy or ideology. At the state level of organization these motivating aspirations tend to find form as a political creed or set of political propositions. At the individual level they may not be articulated but are functional as psychological tendencies that are causal factors in interest determination.

It is apparent from this that policy making, whatever the complex of interests underlying it, is always a philosophical activity. More or less articulated bodies of doctrine and belief lead to action. They compound decisions. The sheer complexity of this process frustrates analysis and takes this area of administrative competence—contrary to popular belief and much professional preparation practice—beyond the reach of logic *simpliciter*. Administrators come to their policy making function with interests. And while policy making enlarges the philosophical scope of decision it may simultaneously tend to attenuate or atrophy reality grasp and humane considerations. The body of knowledge on decisions and policy making indicates severe constraints upon rationality. All of which conduce to the eminent desirability of a special set of administrative competencies which can be simply described as the philosophical skills of logical and value analysis combined with a sophisticated comprehension of the human condition. While the first of these my be satisfied the last can never be: the search to understand ourself and our fellows is endless.

It is this which provides some tenuous support for the senatorial principle, the idea that life experiences enhance, or at least ought to enhance, wisdom or the humane grasp of reality. A notion that leads us ineluctably to a consideration of leadership.

PROPOSITIONS

34. Decision is the distinctive administrative act.
35. Policy is strategic decision making.
36. True decisions are open and extralogical. Only calculations can be logical. Therefore, machines can never decide.
37. Rational decision is a mode of problem-solving.
38. In the final analysis all decisions are binary. That is, they reflect an either-or.
39. The basic decision process is analytic and imputational. Analysis explores alternatives, imputation assigns values and probabilities.
40. The quantification of ranked preferences, that is the translation of ordinals into cardinals, would enable and sanction a decisional calulus, if it were possible. But then the resultant decision would need justifying and this would imply a meta-calculus. And so *ad infinitum*.
41. Rationality is always constrained but rarely extinguished. It is a necessary but not sufficient condition for decision making. A norm.
42. Rationality is subordinate to intention. Intention sets the limits within which rationality can be expressed.
43. No true decision process can be designed so as to exclude entirely the personality of the decider.
44. Decisions are both possibility-determined and possibility-determining. They create futures. This is philosophy-in-action.
45. Administrative science would reduce uncertainty while administrative philosophy would clarify values. But each must trespass upon the other's territory.
46. The art of analysis depends upon skills of perception, the ability to discern the contextual factors of a situation. The imputation of probability and values depends upon skills of conception, the ability to discern strategic factors. Both arts invoke imagination but the latter invokes will.
47. Policy goes beyond logic. The only limits are set by the imagination and the will.
48. Policy is a claim on the future. It contains an irreducible element of gambling. Hence it is metalogical.
49. Metamorphic changes in the organizational life are envisioned and realized by way of ideology—before the fact.
50. Incrementalism is the mean between calculation and ideology.
51. Every administrative decision entails unforeseen consequences.

Chapter 4
Power and Leadership

Administration is a practice as ancient as man. So too is leadership, for organizations have always been (and will always be) power structures that discriminate hierarchically between leaders and followers. The ambivalence with which we regard both leadership and power has combined with ambiguity to yield a luxuriant semantic jungle that vastly obscures relevant philosophical clarity. From Plato's *Republic* through Renaissance Machiavelli to contemporary Chinese "Thick Face–Black Heart" administrative literature[1] has always acknowledged the realities of power, but with some embarrassment.

Administration seeks goal achievement—the accomplishment of collective ends. These ends derive from policy making and the technology of management provides their means of realization. True, collective ends always conceal individual ends, from the careerism of the leader to the self-interest of the least significant of followers. Nevertheless, there is tacit understanding that, however phrased, all ends necessitate power and, hence, validate it. Energy force must be expended to achieve the desired changes in condition. There is no worse state for the administrator–leader than impotence.

Power is the ability to gain ends. Physically the gaining is done through energy expenditure and psychologically through force of will. Power can be defined as the ability of A to move B contrary to B's interests but this excludes the reality that power is often exercised with consent or with the perception that the subject's interests are being advanced. This further adumbrates and emphasizes the necessity for some degree of philosophical clarity about the concept of interest.

Foucault on the other hand, has compared the use of power to chess play in which pieces eliminate or inhibit each other, respectively referring to power *over* or power *onto*. Together with other postmodern philosophers he exhibited a pessimistic obsession with the problem of social and organizational power.[2] In general the school of critical theory representative of this philosophy has assumed the burden of making evident and "transparent" the conflicts of power in social action and organization.[3]

Pragmatically, administrative power can be defined as the ability to achieve ends through others. These ends are *ostensibly* organizational or collective ends. *Tout court* administrative power is the ability of the administrator to have his will and get his way. Yet this at once opens wide the psychological doors to *ad infinitum* considerations of conation, affect, values, desire, beliefs, and ego definition.

The power of Man over Men[4] is fundamental to administration. This power has an aspect which is dark, basal, and primeval. Its roots extend deep into the unconscious and its physical correlates may reach to the limbic system of our evolutionary ancestry. Adler notably classified it as an instinct for dominance and ranked it *pace* Freud with sex as an ultimate motivation in the psyche. Lord Acton believed its exercise to be intrinsically corrupting in the moral sense: "Power tends to corrupt, and absolute power corrupts absolutely. Great men are almost always bad men."[5] "Power-seeking" and "power-hungry" are negative epithets. Because of this the administrator will often seek to avoid the terminology and instead euphemize his behaviour as "dynamic", "energetic", or "ambitious"— all putative qualities of "leadership".

The negative connotations of power may however arise simply from the logic that its exercise implies a suspension, diminution, or subversion of the power of the person upon whom it is being exercised. One man's power is another man's impotence; the will of the latter is reduced by the former. Since we have all, from earliest infancy, experienced this impotence (and the first administrator is the mother) we understand at the deepest level what is meant by frustration of autonomy. In consequence we approach the subject of political or administrative power with a sense of unease. Perhaps this partially explains why Simon and Barnard, though expatiating on the topic of authority, are silent on the more basic and primitive notion of power.[6]

Power is a basic and central concern for the administrative philosopher. It is a *sine qua non;* a prerequisite. Very often it is an end in itself. It is the lifeblood of administration. Systems theorists Ackoff and Emory[7] have declared it the *summum bonum,* the ultimate value. One can say that history itself is the record of power conflicts. Such conflicts occur not only in the world, in the administrative realm, but in the mind, in the intellectual realm of ideas. Dionysus vies with Apollo[8] as the idiographic with the nomothetic in endless dialectic. We can therefore postulate a natural tendency for administrators to seek to increase their quantum of power. The individual administrator ought then to question himself about the *interest* associated with his desire for power. Is it personal, egoistic, self-directed and concentrated? Or is it nomothetic, extroverted, directed towards the commonweal? Or is it mixed? And if mixed, how mixed? Such questions may be difficult but they are never vain in administrative philosophy. The two central concepts in administration are hierarchy and power. These concepts vex. They torture the postmodern philosophers, especially the French,[9] and even before them Wilde had declared "All authority is quite degrading. It degrades those who exercise it, and degrades those over whom it is exercised."[10] But what is meant here by degradation? If mere organizational membership—taking the Queen's shilling—is *ipso facto* demeaning or degrading then it is correct. But is it? We must hold off on the answer only noting here that some empirical research, notably that of Argyris,[11] indicates forcefully that personality and organization (idiographic and nomothetic) are forever incompatible.

From the standpoint of sociology power can be defined as the ability to "influence the behaviour of others in accordance with one's will"[12] even if this means dominating, forcing, or manipulating the will of others. The need for power is rooted in the Realpolitik of organizational life. Without it the administrator is literally impotent. With it accomplishment becomes possible; the more power an administrator has, the greater the ends that can be shaped, the greater the range of administrative possibility and hence, the greater the career advantage. Power is the first term in the administrative lexicon but its nakedness must be covered, ethos and mores and popular culture combine to fabricate an elaborate veiling of its appearance and reality. Its use is concealed within elaborate language games; the iron hand is gloved; it must be *re*-dressed and *re*-presented.

Much of this veiling is done through ritual and symbol, most notably through rhetoric and language. Men of power are not necessarily harsh in outward demeanour. Their truer sentiments may be expressed covertly in locker-room language, as was remarkably revealed by the Nixon tapes, but their public personae will be soft-spoken and emollient. It follows that the administrative philosopher and practitioner must be keen observers ever alert to the nuances of interaction and gesture. Consider that language itself is power-based and power*ful*. No utterance is without power implications. Even the mathematically neutral assertion that $1 + 1 = 2$ is semiotically intentional. It can mean (*know that*) $1 + 1 = 2$, an imperative. Or (*know that I know that*) $1 + 1 = 2$, an assertion of presence or status.

There is, however, a division of labour or emphasis between philosopher and practitioner in that the former is concerned with the analysis of administrative terms while the latter is more concerned with language as a working tool of persuasion of attack and defence. Both dialectic and rhetoric, analysis and synthesis, the symbolic and the diabolic,[13] are crucial to the administrative enterprise. The more so as force and domination in the physical, economic, political, or simply *brutal* sense are obliged to yield to *manipulation* and subtler forms of coercion in the exercise of power.

FROM POWER TO AUTHORITY

Authority is legitimized power, rightful power. Its status derives from the organizational language game.[14] It also derives from interest, from the complex of values funding the organization and its purpose. That purpose determines the distribution of authority amongst its members. The clearest instance is war. If the nation-state decides its interests compel war that it becomes administratively legitimate to conscript citizens and wreak violence; the administrators of the organization have not simply the power but also the *authority* to occasion bloodshed, sacrifice, and death. This example is also instructive because it reveals the importance of *perception* to any analysis of interest.

Perception at the level of the organization is a function of ethos and mores; that is socio-political culture (cf. Figure 2.6). The citizens of Athens and Sparta will see things differently. So will Greeks and Turks. Or the membership of an Ivy League University and a State College. If Barnard's thesis that power resides at the base of the organizational hierarchy rather than at the apex is correct,[15] then culture-conditioned perceptions are the formal determinant in the translation of power into authority. The public will or organizational will transmutes the lead of power into the gold of authority. That will is of course susceptible of manipulation through control of the media of communication. Skilled administrators and leaders know how to use the media as well as how to bypass them. But the potential of this manipulation is limited. Cynicism towards the media of totalitarian societies outweighs even that of pluralist democracies and credibility is essential for legitimation. On the other hand, in wartime conditions, public perceptions, consciousness, and will are easily transformed into the agentic state described by Milgram[16] in which interest is identified with authority and administration. *L'état, c'est nous!*

Authority is then legitimized power but, in the ordinary realities of complex organizational and social structures, the clear perception of either organizational purpose or the source of authority is not a simple matter. Both are usually taken on faith. There is a Barnardian zone of indifference[17] upon which the skilled administrator builds. Even the unskilled and inept are, upon taking office, endowed with an automatic ex officio capital of organizational authority and official credibility; a metaphorical bank balance than can be built upon or rapidly exhausted.

Authority manifests through communication. It is "the character of a communication (order) in a formal organization by virtue of which it is accepted by a contributor to or 'member' of the organization as governing the action he contributes; that is, as governing or determining what he does or is not to do so far as the organization is concerned."[18] Here Barnard presumes a degree of free will on the part of the recipient of a command and therefore roots authority ultimately in the followership.

Intrinsic to this classical Simon–Barnard understanding of authority is the idea of a zone of indifference or acceptance. Within this region of complicity subordinates align themselves unreflectively with their superordinate's will. The zone demarcates the frontiers of administrative power. This also goes to the heart of the administrative ethical problem: When am I as a subordinate to obey orders and when *not*? Again, in the classical view, if a subordinate can comprehend and perform an order then his compliance depends on (1) his belief that the order is not inconsistent with the purposes of the organization and (2) his belief that it is compatible with his personal interest as a whole.[19] Later we may consider the implications of this analysis for such cases as My Lai, Watergate, and Eichmann in Jerusalem.[20] For now let us notice the epistemological shift: From a logical or organizational analysis and a proto-psychology or organizational behaviour to the *a*-logic or *trans*-logical realms of belief and value. From behaviourism to ethics.

Orthodoxy thus grounds legitimation in the perception of an identification of administration with the organizational purpose. But what is the purpose, say, of the United States? Or the family? It may be that the more general and diffuse the organizational purpose the easier it becomes for the administrator to manipulate legitimacy and authority. It may be, too, that the more purpose is hidden—deep in the secret labyrinths of the Kafkaesque Castle—the more administration can assume the mantle of priestly authority, sacrosanct and beyond question. Complexity of organization, society, culture, and technology may combine to obscure and mystify purpose as they do occasionally in affairs of state or public education. Who dares to challenge administrative authority when policies are declared to be in the "national interest" or for "educational excellence, improvement, and change"?

We should now consider the concept of influence. although all power is influential and all influence is a manifestation of power the terms differ by way of formality. The formal structures of organization ostensibly define the distribution of authority but coexisting with this design and interpenetrating it are dynamically shifting patterns of influence or informal authority: These patterns are idiographic, they depend on the varieties of organization game that are being played and upon the players. Individuals may have personal characteristics that determine special relationships with power and authority figures, they may be favourites, or burrs under the administrative saddle, or they may have just that skill or knowledge requisite at a critical moment. Interpersonal accounts are established and maintained on the psychological plane with a meticulousness and scrupulosity of remarkable precision. Influence-carriers may even be outside the organization altogether. So wives, lovers, and relatives intrude into political process. In short, the formal *logical* structure of authority and responsibility is continuously modulated by complex, extraneous, and incommensurable forces.

The phenomenon of influence is unquestionably important. It can assume pathological proportions. It is a form of power that evades responsibility because it is not formally accountable to the organization and its purpose. It is subcutaneous and invisible upon organization charts. It is always present, never entirely negligible, and fundamentally irreducible. For philosophy of administration it means that the study of power is circumscribed by the study of human nature.

CHALLENGES TO AUTHORITY

Modern organizations are increasingly dependent on evermore complex technologies and sophisticated skills for the accomplishment of their goals. The instance where the formal leadership is competent to perform all of the subordinate instrumental means is increasingly rare outside of small professional or trade practices and, even here, specialization is increasingly typical of the organizational membership. Specialists (engineers, accountants, faculty, to name a few) are organization members with extra-organizational affiliations, loyalties, and status attributes. As individuals they have made long-term career commitments to their specialties. These invest them in return with a special kind of power, the authority of *expertise*, which contrasts and may conflict with the authority of *position* or hierarchy as represented by the administration–management line. This expert power and authority is orthogonal to the administrative line of command. It is potentially autonomous. Moreover, it is competitive with line authority because expertise may often be functionally identified with the organizational mission in a more direct way than can the hierarchic authority of administration. Thus schools provide teaching–learning situations in which the functional authority figure is the teacher. Similarly hospitals provide healing situations in which the crucial authority figures are doctors and nurses, and economic organizations generally are dependent on researchers, designers, technicians, and engineers.[21] In all these instances professional non-administrators are ostensibly and formally subordinates and subservient to the administrators who, in conventional authority theory, are the organizational members identified with the organizational purpose and who are hence endowed with hierarchical rights, status, and privileges as well as, conventionally, command over the organizational reward system.

The growth of expertise authority can lead to intra-organizational conflict in a number of ways. The experts may claim to have a closer association with and a clearer vision of the organizational purpose. They may challenge the legitimacy of line authority because of an increasingly perceptible disparity between rights and competencies. They may resent taking orders from a "superior" who is incapable of performing their vital organizational function, who is incompetent in their own terms. Conversely the administration may react and exacerbate the tension; threatened in its credibility it may seek to enlarge and enforce hierarchical privileges, to practise *chutzpah* or engage in a variety of well-analysed and documented bureaupathologies, most notably the phenomenon of dramaturgy.[22]

It does not follow from this that a power struggle between the representatives of administrative and technical expertise is inevitable. In general the role structure of a complex organization with its mutual interdependencies is well accepted but the seeds of conflict are nevertheless present and are compounded by increasing specialization and technology. Military organization has provided the pyramidal paradigm of hierarchy in the past and it is significant that modern military structure is much less paradigmatic than hitherto. Air crew, for example, tend to hold commissioned rank and there are an ever-increasing number of non-commissioned officer (NCO) specialists. In the future the generalized private soldier may disappear in warfare as has the unskilled labourer in industry.[23]

Power challenges of this sort are a logical function of the relation between ends and means. In the last analysis authority legitimizes itself by its commitment to purpose. If the organizational ends are clearly dependent for their achievement upon the cooperative articulation of expertise-dependent means, and if this expertise is inaccessible or unsuitable to those responsible for the articulation, that is, the administration, then the organization will tend to have dualistic structure of authority. The threat of withdrawal of services (the power to strike) is clearly enhanced through the technological specialist effect. Indeed, the Barnardian dictum that ultimate power lies at the base of the hierarchy requires modification: in modern complex bureaucracies power is not only diffused but concentrated in such a manner that power-dualism or power-pluralism is the norm. The practical consequence is that simplistic hierarchical authoritarian attitudes must be foregone in favour of philosophical, diplomatic, and political skills. Administrators must become "specialists in generalism" if they are to legitimize their hierarchical rank by reconciling the conflicting authorities of line and staff, hierarchy and expertise, under the aegis of organizational unity and purpose.

Technical or professional competence does not imply or entail administrative competence any more than does the converse. But what may be overlooked in this opposition is the possibility of an administrative profession *per se*, replete in its own expertise and legitimized by its own investment in professional training. The emergence of this putative profession, not yet an actuality but an imminent possibility, would tend to resolve a number of challenges to authority.

Another contemporary challenge to authority lies in a prevalence of anti-authoritarian sentiment. Since, historically, totalitarian systems (most notably those of fascism and communism) have been discredited, and since a liberal orthodoxy with postmodern egalitarian and anti-hierarchical sentiments has for long assumed hegemonic control of most media systems,[24] the classical view of authority has been under both subtle covert and blatant overt attack. The description and explanation of such climates of opinion is a matter for social historians. Many factors are contributory: general affluence and the spread of mass public education, technological advances in media and communication, decline in the perceived quality of life, loss of religious and spiritual values, alienation and loss of meaning, perhaps an ever-sharpening perception that most of the gods (politicians, administrators, executives) are indeed composed of very ordinary clay, perhaps a loss of faith in political process generally. Whatever the causes may be, traditional authority is undermined and an anti-authoritarian climate is formed. Administration *style*, at the very least, will have to be responsive. Administrators may become more overtly conciliatory, more persuasive in communication, more accepting of input, perhaps more anxious to maintain a low profile and to acquire skills in damage control; perhaps, perversely, to become reactively tough-minded and hard-nosed ("When the going gets tough, the tough get going," as President Nixon was inclined to say.). Structural changes such as cooptation, quota-type representatives or tokenism, and extended participatory decision making processes may also be evident and become vogue.

Yet in all of this the point for administrative philosophy is that *logically* the legitimacy of authority is unassailable insofar as that authority stems from and is consistent with *purpose*. Now purpose analysis and purpose formulation are philosophical acts. They refer back to the complex of interest composed first of the individual organization members, second of the organization as a collectivity (interpreted nomothetically by the administration), and third of the extra-organizational environment and polity. That these radiating components or strands of interest should conflict is not only possible but likely. But conflict neither implies nor entails the illegitimacy of authority. On the contrary, it suggests the need for authority and its vindication. A general anti-authoritarian ideology as espoused by some postmodern thinkers is logically defensible only where the orthodox practice of administrative philosophy can be shown to have failed.

THE CRITIQUE OF POWER

Power has valence. It would be fallacious to abstract it from the reality-context and consider it as value-neutral, a mere instrumentality. Power can of course be taken this way in simplistic engineering terms: neither good nor bad, neither right nor wrong—its value only dependent on its application. It should now be clear, however, that power (and hence, authority) in the administrative sense, is always *both* good *and* bad, right *and* wrong, beneficial *and* harmful. Nevertheless, it is an established error in the textbook literature to take power–authority either in the affectively neutral technological sense (Simon, Katz and Kahn) or in the positively benevolent attributive sense (Barnard).[25] We are all, it seems either honourable men or technicians. Yet this is a denial of commonsense and simple observation. It is a blatant denial of reality if that body of esoteric and semi-disreputable literature known in German as *Fürstenspiegel* ("a mirror for Princes")—a literature from which the name of Machiavelli emerges in the West, is in any sense true.

This distortion or imbalance of the classicist view of administration is compounded by the postmodernists but here the error is different. Now it is assumed that power (efficaciously neutral but potentially corrupting) is inextricably associated with hierarchical hegemony, domination, and the malevolent subordination of the powerless. Individual fulfillment or "needs satisfaction" is inevitably frustrated by organizations, the instrumental means of collective action which entail hierarchy and domination. Radical postmodern solutions such as the elimination of hierarchy and differentiation merely intensify the dilemma as is revealed in the following passage:

> An insistence on differences combats the monolith, but a hard-to-abandon allegiance to equal rights (universalist, liberal, and bourgeois though they be) makes contemporaries want to ensure that such differences never place anyone in a social position of advantage or disadvantage (i.e. that the differences not make any political, economic, or social difference).[26]

One cannot, in other words, have one's differential cake and eat it in a non-differential manner. The pre-eminent postmodern fallacy is to deny not only the reality but the inexorable necessity of hierarchy and social differentiation. Hierarchy, we have shown, is intrinsic to organizational structures and differentiation flows from instrumental specialities and competencies. Egalitarianism as a philosophy is rooted in romantic myth: examples are the Rousseauian concept of primitive grace and the doctrine enshrined in the American constitution that all men are "created equal". *Per contra* also, to be born at all is to be born an infant in a power–dependency relationship with an hegemonic mother. Some of the more realistic critical theorists have attempted to deal with this problem as follows:

> Structural power becomes delegitimated only where the egalitarian norm is recognized as applicable to each social sphere.[27]

A subset of the critique of power is to be found in feminist arguments that for millennia the female gender has been dominated by a male hegemony or "patriarchy" that manipulates power structures in society and organizations to the end of subordinating the female of the human species.[28] Such arguments are vitiated on anthropological and biological grounds. There has never been an instance of political matriarchy (the logical alternative) in the recorded annals[29] yet, on the other hand, as already suggested above, both genders are born into a condition of familial matriarchy where the mother for some years has near-totalitarian authority and power. Either way the feminist challenge to patriarchal administration remains highly presumptive and open to post-Freudian challenge. Interestingly, from the administrative standpoint, the evidence suggests that we are all conditioned to some variant of absolute power. In Part IV we shall explore the value implications of power more intensively. For now it can simply be allowed that power, authority, and influence are always value-problematic.

POWER, AUTHORITY, AND LEADERSHIP

The origins of administration predate the historical record. It is primal human behaviour. It has inspired great philosophical debates and great classics of literature such as Plato's *Republic* and *Laws* and Machiavelli's *The Prince*. All this effort has been, in one way or another, a commentary upon power. Especially upon the "right" use of power. That is to say, the discourse has been about values and the problem of value. In historical perspective it is only recently—only *suddenly* one might even say—that the value aspect of administration has been subordinated to the logical. Today a serious administrative aspirant would feel obliged first, and even solely, to acquire whatever knowledge the social sciences could present, in the general form of organization theory—a corpus of knowledge that includes such disparate subsets as "personnel management", systems theory, and "group dynamics" and that aspires to scientific rigour and affective neutrality. Yet all this massive modern endeavour seems in the end to yield little more than elaborations upon the logic of purposive systems with feedback mechanisms. In reality, however, in the messy and untidy world of political rough and tumble and executive hurly burly the sharp edges of logic, the nice frontiers of conjunction and disjunction, and the straightforward exercise of calculative rationality continue to elude us in the face of complexity, uncertainty, and the ubiquity of the value factor. The administrative art resists both rational scientization and moral sanitization.

It is now time to make explicit what has been implicit all along. Administration *is* leadership. Leadership *is* administration. Why should this general proposition be contested? Perhaps because of the power of language and its connotative capacity to imbue one of the terms with magic and the other with disdain. Common usage conceives of leadership very imprecisely.[30] The tendency is to treat leadership as if it were an epiphenomenon—a sort of increment or addition to the administrative–management process that might or might not be present. As if one could administer without leadership or lead without administration. The flaw in this commonsense view becomes apparent when one attaches the unsaid evaluative terms: then it becomes contradictory to talk at one and the same time of having good leadership and bad administration, or conversely. In short, good leadership entails good administration and bad administration entails bad leadership and leadership is what administration does, either successfully or otherwise. It follows that the philosophy of administration is also and always the philosophy of leadership. Semantically the only difference is the degree of affective connotation: administration tending to the neutral or the negative, leadership to the positive.

Also following from this logic is what the Nazis called the *Führerprinzip* or leader-principle. Leadership extends from apex to base of the organizational hierarchy. The SS, for example, ensconced this principle in its system of ranks and titles (*Scharführer, Standartenführer, Gruppenführer*, etc.) so that even the lowliest member was semantically sensitized to his leadership responsibility. Leadership pervades the organization. No one can escape leadership acts and responsibilities since no one can evade the administrative–managerial processes. To put it differently, both leadership and administration are the moving of people towards goals through a system of organization. This can be done well, or done badly, or done indifferently, but it cannot not be done at all.

Of course, the administrative–leadership *emphasis* will differ and fluctuate in accordance with the taxonomy of process, the personalities of actors, and the contingencies of circumstance. Prima facie arguments can be made for some roles being more technical and managerial or staff (i.e. less philosophical) while others are more general, managerial, or live. This is another way of saying that the mix of value and fact varies with process, contingency, and role. Nevertheless, no matter how routinized and homeostatic an organizational role may be it is still integral to its organization. In time of crisis or special contingency it may become supersensitive to leadership action and function. The NCO isolated with his men on the battlefield; the secretary having to "cover" for an employer, the petty bureaucrat suddenly in a "whistle-blowing" crisis; the disgruntled worker with an opportunity to sabotage—all may have to make exquisitely difficult value judgements, and all will be making crucial organizational decision, leadership acts.

If then, in the realities of the world, anyone can administer so too it can be said that anyone can lead. And so they do a fortiori, since everyone has an inalienable birthright to philosophy, anyone can lead. The point of dissension is not about leadership itself but about leadership *effectiveness.* In ordinary language it is positive effectiveness that has come to be equated with leadership and which is understood as a kind of gloss that may or may not be superimposed upon organizational practice. But for our more technical purposes the terms "administration" and "leadership" merge and become synonymous.

While this semantic usage can be agreed to for the purposes of this text an important exception or qualification must, however, be registered. Administrator–leaders practise leadership for and on behalf of an organization. But there are also solitaries, extra-organizational independents such as artists, inventors, critics and scholars, teachers and innovators who by virtue of their private genius and creativity come to alter, at one or several removes, the world at large. These too are leaders but their leadership is of a non-organizational, non-administrative kind. Their leader acts may, of course, have (often unwished for) organizational consequences. Marx declared that he was not a Marxist, Buddha exhorted his followers not to found a church, and Christ said, Render unto Caesar the things that are Caesar's. Yet, inevitably their leadership acts ultimately ramified into the ordinary organizational world of administration while they themselves managed to escape direct or formal administrative responsibility. Power and authority merge in the concept of leadership. At this point they also cease to be abstractions in that they become personified and embodied. Power is felt and authority is visible. Leadership takes on flesh. The concept of leadership also has an intrinsic semiotic power. It is a eulogistic slogan blurring many levels or meaning but also serving as a useful rhetorical instrument. Claimants to administrative office will seek to appropriate this word-magic since the word itself can serve as an utterance which *eo ipso* legitimizes power, authority, and rank. Furthermore, the term is often, indeed usually, accepted uncritically and without analysis. It is almost unthinkingly attributed, as a sort of implicit function, to the administrative–managerial subsystem of the organization and its slogan usage often passes unchallenged. It would be considered somewhat improper, if not downright insubordinate, for a subordinate to question his superior's use of the term by the remark, "Yes, but what do you *mean* by leadership...?" And an administrator who laid no claim to being a leader would be regarded even more askance. There is an a priori attribution of leadership (and its attendant magic) to all administrative roles.

Yet there is also a suspicion that leadership is not an automatic concomitant of a formal authority role.[31] Ordinary language is ambiguous and ambivalent. Its usage contradicts the identity of administration and leadership expounded in this text but this confusion derives from a mythology. The myth comes about as follows. The seekers of administrative office tacitly and overtly claim that they possess, to a greater degree than their competitors, the qualities of leadership. The term typically goes unexamined but the analytical components appear to be: (1) it is a very good thing, (2) its qualities and attributes are known and understood, (3) these virtues reside in the administration of the organization generally and (4) they are embodied most particularly and conspicuously in the person of the claimant. Unfortunately, the empirical evidence for at least the first three of these elements does not entirely substantiate the common understanding ... hence we call it a mythology. On the contrary the concept remains intransigently obscure and hence the great political and rhetorical advantage of the term and the temptation to indulge in its frequent assertion. "There go the mob," said the Comte de Mirabeau during the French revolution, "and I must follow them for I am their leader."

In considering the concept of leadership *per se* it is useful to separate the efforts of empirical social science from the general observations of orthodox administrative thought. The former can be represented by Van Fleet and Yukl who in reviewing a hundred years of leadership research are driven to an analogy with modern physics and conclude that, "Research over this past century clearly demonstrates that leadership is not a simple, indivisible construct. It, like the atom, consists of a multitude of components each of which may have multiple characteristics. To some extent the answers we find depend upon the question we ask, but equally important, we are finding answers. Assuming that there is 'truth' in each answer, we, like physicists, need a Grand Unified Theory (GUT); unlike physicists, however, we may not have sufficient methodological rigor to expect a GUT approach soon."[32]

It can be allowed, however, that leadership (i.e. administration) is a complex dynamic function which has at least the following analytic dimensions: the nature of the task, the psychological relationships between leader and led; the power and authority of the leader, the structure and attributes of the followership, the favourableness of the situation from the standpoint of the leader;[33] the character and characteristics of the leader; the organizational structure, command of resources, history, philosophy, and context.

The alternative viewpoint (i.e. conventional non-quantitative and synthetic approaches to leadership theory) is represented in the expositions of Weber, Barnard, Simon, and McGregor Burns.

Weber's analysis of leadership[34] is a classification into the categories of traditional, rational, and charismatic. Traditional leaders come to their role through social conventions (monarchy, primogeniture, nepotism, oligarchical or kinship privilege) and rational leaders are appointed on the basis of expertise (legalistic, technical, professional, and bureaucratic) but it is the charismatic category that is philosophically intriguing. There is a general intuitive recognition of the type of leader who, by way of forceful or magnetic personality or intrinsic "spiritual" endowment, possesses the elusive quality of charisma. This quality is not properly understood; it is mysterious but its possessors seem capable of inducing extraordinary fealty on the part of their followers, and also seem able to exert their will in an extraordinary way upon the led. This is what McGregor Burns has described as transformational leadership.[35] Though the concept is vague the phenomenon itself is only too real. It constitutes a problem for administrative logic that transcends and supervenes ordinary logic. I am inclined to hypothesize that the charismatic or transformational leader has access to a source of power deriving from the unconscious desires of the followership. The leader voices desires that are inchoate, that they cannot properly express, thereby imparting a sense of meaning or purpose. In the search for purpose, meaning, vocation, fulfillment man will reach beyond life itself. And certainly beyond logic. Therein lies not only philosophical perplexity but political hazard.

Barnard and Simon[36] offer contrasting views. The former enters wholeheartedly into the moral arena and offers the model of the leader as moral exemplar drawing his power and authority not simply from the structures and functions of organization but from personality and character. This view, though authoritative by virtue of Barnard's status, is unorthodox and tends to receive short shrift in the administrative literature. More conventional is Simon's declared logical positivist position that reduces the leader–administrator to a mere executive-manager, effecting as efficiently as possible the values derived from the policy-making subset of the organizational system. Power here is simply a straightforward function of role which can presumably, be derogated or augmented by personality and sundry extraneous or exogenous factors.

It is interesting, if paradoxical, that Barnard—the great exponent of the democratic principle that ultimately power resides in the *lower* levels of the organizational hierarchy—should insist upon the *moral* superiority of leadership, its especial capacity for moral excellence and moral "complexity". Now this is not something that can be constructed or even "specified". Formal authority may indeed be designed, legislated, structured but the Barnardian (and Burnsian) quality of leadership is something that has to be *conceded from the followership*. Though it tends to be claimed by administrators as a specific and transferable competence it is organization-bound to the extent that it is dependent upon follower perceptions and upon the phenomenologically conceived and invented social reality within an organization. In other words charisma may not travel. It requires some critical mass of followership reaction. To that extent it cannot just be traded in the market-place of unemployed executives.

Barnard's explanation is that there are two dimensions of leadership, both representing a kind of superiority. The first kind results in technical proficiency and is a superiority "in physique, in skill, in technology, in perception, in knowledge, in memory, in imagination".[37] The second is

> the more general; the more constant; the least subject to specific development; the more absolute; the subjective; that which reflects the attitudes and ideals of society and its general institutions. It is the aspect of individual superiority in determination, persistence, endurance, courage; that which determines the *quality* of action; which often is most inferred from what is *not* done, from abstention; which commands respect, reverence. It is the aspect of leadership we commonly imply in the word "responsibility," the quality which gives dependability and determination to human conduct, and foresight and ideality to purpose.[38]

Note here Barnard's distinctive contribution. The paragon leader possesses a special quality of restraint, detachment, abstinence, or aloofness—it is deciding when *not* to decide, not deciding what should be decided by others, that which is not *done,* that which is *abstained from* which is important. He also describes leadership as "...the power of individuals to inspire cooperative personal decision by creating faith: faith in common understanding, faith in probability of success, faith in the ultimate satisfaction of personal motives, faith in the integrity of objective authority, faith in the superiority of common purpose as a personal aim of those who partake in it."[39]

Such language moves beyond rationality. Faith. Integrity. Inspiration. And, having identified leadership as the strategic factor in achieving cooperation, he then analyses its components as (1) technical competence, (2) moral "complexity" and (3) a "propensity for consistency in conformance to moral factors of the individual".[40] Power and authority now derive not from logic but from value. Power, authority, and leadership coalesce around and are synthesized by values.

PROBLEMS

The problems so far raised are manifold. First, there is the philosophical unpleasantness of logic imprecision. The concepts of power, authority, leadership are jointly and severally fundamental to the field of administration yet each is vague, obscure, oblique, imprecise. To the extent that these problems are merely logical, having to do with the consistency of a language and its propositions, the difficulties can be practically overcome by agreement upon working definitions and syntax. Or, psychologically, they can simply be ignored through tacit agreement to live with ambiguity and vagueness, leaving any worrying or fretting about all this to scholars and men of inaction. (This latter seems to be the solution most favoured in practice.) Nevertheless, there are problems which go beyond mere disorder and untidiness in the body of knowledge and, though these are for the most part valuational, we have already seen that few administrative utterances can be made before implications of value are raised. And some of these problems are non-semantic.

Consider the organizational reward system. This determines such brute realities as income, rank, status, title, prestige, psychological fulfillment, office space, travel prerequisites, limousines and the like. Who carves and serves up this pie? Orthodoxy insists that it is the function and prerogative of the administration. *Droit de seigneur.* Why? Upon what logic? Upon the grounds that it is the administrative subsystem which has the responsibility for formulating and achieving the organizational ends, and because it has the general system overview and perspective. Eminently reasonable. But we have now seen that there is a challenge to this argument on the counts of specialist competence and the authority of expertise. And this is quite aside from the possibility—all too evident in the real world—of corruption: of using power to subvert collective good to private benefit.

The counter to the specialist argument is the claim to the trans-technical qualities of leadership. To be blunt, to the paragon qualities of morality explicit in the doctrines of Plato and Barnard and generally implicit in the doctrine of veto power of line over staff. On this reasoning one is led to expect (or at least wish for) government by aristocracy, that is, rule-by-the-best or, in contemporary language meritocracy. Superior rewards then flow to superior contributors. We are now led to ask, How do administrators credential this superiority? Is it the result of background and training? Is it a concomitant of some form of professionalism? Or is it simply personal, characterological?

Another sore problem devolves around the concept of responsibility. Does the distribution of responsibility throughout the organizational system parallel the system's distribution of power, authority, status, and reward? Who is capable of the greater irresponsibility, clerk or vice-president? Worker or chief executive officer (CEO)?

These questions have in the last analysis to do with power. But so too does the general problem of administrative professionalism: of how one recruits and appoints and monitors and divests leadership. What are the special competencies distinguishing any administrative profession? I would be the first to concede that such competencies are ill-comprehended. They would, of course, include some special knowledge and understanding of organization theory, relevant research in the social sciences, decision making, and policy analysis. Such subject matter calls for some minimum special competence in logic and value analysis.

The curriculum would also suggest, though it may not be able to deliver, psychological attributes such as imagination, will, empathy, energy, ambition, "vision", which, though randomly distributed as part of the general human endowment, may be especially called upon in the exercise of administration. Yet even all this does not entirely embrace the elusive concept of leadership with all that that might entail by way of morality, character, and interpersonal skills.

The problem is profound. The alternatives to professionalism would seem to be dilettantism, amateur incompetence, happenstance, and a host of pathologies including nepotism, careerism, and an infinite variety of corruption. At stake is the quality of organizational life. We all live in and by organizations, directly as members or indirectly as associates or clientele. We are all accultured and formed by the quality of our organizational experience. We are all, therefore, administered or administering.

PROPOSITIONS

52. Language cloaks power and *has* power. Language is the basic administrative tool.
53. Administrative utterances are in the imperative mood. The administrator must be not only logician but also dialectician and rhetoricist.
54. The precinct of administration is ends, of management, means. Power resides dynamically in each.
55. Administration is a putative profession; its expertise is the specialty of generalism. But it does not follow that everyone is an administrative expert. Only that anyone can lead.
56. There is a moral aspect to administration. Administrative decisions are made for and about *others*.
57. Authority is legitimized power.
58. If one has power one must from time to time wield it. Skilful display augments power, unskilful diminishes. Power is a function of its perception.
59. Logically, authority is self-justifying and self-evident. Anti-authoritarianism is therefore nihilistic or else it is a demand for more authority.
60. Legitimacy of authority rests on the connection with organizational purpose. And yet, authority transcends logic.
61. Illicit authority thrives on obscurity of purpose.
62. The term leadership is an incantation for the bewitchment of the led.
63. Leadership is an event, not an attribute of personality. It is a description given to a dynamic complex of action.
64. Because leadership is a complex intrinsic and unique property of a situation it cannot rationally be detached, isolated, and traded in the market place. Yet this is the expected norm.
65. Leadership is the conjunction of technical competence and moral complexity.
66. Value commitment presages charisma.
67. Charisma plays upon our lust for purpose. The charismatic leader will give hope and meaning to our lives. He will free us from the dreadful burden of responsibility.
68. There is no aspect of administration more dangerous than that which forges the link between power, charisma, and followership.

Chapter 5
Modes of Leadership

The concept of leadership emits more heat than light. Although a central term, perhaps *the* central term, in the administrative language game it is often so muddied by rhetoric and political usage that its sense is lost in obfuscation and manipulation to the point of incomprehensibility or nonsense. Its usage as an academic term has led to a thriving industry as a disciplinary subset comparable to, though greatly exceeding in profitability and scope, that of evaluation.[1] Schools and enterprise abound. From the sublimely motivated like the Matsushita School of Government and Management in Japan[2] to a plethora of commercial videotapes and seminars designed to net their authors rich profits.[3] Despite this expense of energy, however, the semantic mysteries of leadership remain. Leadership can perhaps be better described as an incantation for the bewitchment of the led but efforts have been made to get beyond word-magic. Since in this text we equate administration with leadership and define the former as philosophy-in-action it follows that, since everyone has an inalienable right to philosophize *anyone* can lead. And this entails a value question: What is good and what is bad leadership? But first let us look to psychology and consider the general empirical effort that has been made under this head.

LEADERSHIP THEORY

This subject has been extensively researched. One can indeed talk of a psychologizing of leadership to the point where it now constitutes a subset of academic psychology. This sub-discipline has been divorced from its philosophical connection. What began in antiquity as a profoundly philosophical concern—How to find the Guardians?—has become an empirical area of quantitative research revelling in correlations, factor analyses, and tests and measurements; an industry wherein notions of values, ethics, and morality have been leached away, ignored, bracketed out, or depreciated as irrelevant.

The sequence of exploratory research has proceeded, in its general line of logic, from maxims or rules of thumb through trait theory, to factor analytic trait theory (yielding, unsurprisingly, the two paradigmatic dimensions of task orientation and person orientation), to situational qualifications of this two-dimensional discovery, to interactive considerations (of all the emergent variables considered relevant), to path–goal analysis, to the complexities of contingency theory.[4] Throughout all this body of work it is difficult to discern any explication of values, ethics, morals, intention, meaning, purpose or the psychologically embarrassing factors of consciousness and will. Nevertheless, psychology is grist for the mill of philosophy even if the converse cannot be claimed and we have to ask what the great psychological research effort has accomplished.

To respond to this question I should like to examine one of the most sophisticated, advanced, and substantiated theories of leadership extant, namely, the Fiedler contingency model.[5] This work is prototypical in its underlying logic and an examination of it can serve as a general critique of psychological and empirical studies to date.

The logical infrastructure is simple enough: the leadership concept is conceived globally as consisting of a set of variables which constitute a universe of observation. In Fiedler's studies this set would probably be less than (subsumed under) the set of variables corresponding to administration (certain routine managerial activities being excluded, for example). Nevertheless it would be potentially infinite (v_∞). For practical purposes a finite subset of variables (v_α) is drawn and these are operationalized for measurement and study. Illustrative variables in the model are termed position, power, task structure, leader –member relations and, latterly, intelligence, stress, experience, and task complexity. Two variables deserve special note because of their logical status. These are the input variable (v_i) leader personality and the output variable (v_o) leader effectiveness. v_i is measured in the Fiedler theory by a short paper-and-pencil test, called the Least Preferred Coworker (LPC) scale. The measurement of v_o varies with organizational context but is ostensibly "objective" and, certainly, quantitative. Input v_i as mediated by context variables is then explored for relationships with v_o. The result of this continuing research is a highly sophisticated statistical model which on average, it is claimed, can account for some 25% of the variance among the operationalized correlates of the leadership concept.[6]

Such research is not to be deprecated. It represents the meritorious technical effort of quotidian social science. It should be endorsed, emulated, replicated. But one should also be able to place it within a philosophical perspective and have some understanding of its philosophical critique. That critique can be summarized thus:

First, the central variable v_i engenders a certain philosophical queasiness. Is the essential and relevant truth about personality, even if our focus of interest is confined to something called leadership behaviour, to be derived in five minutes from a unidimensional scale, the LPC? Perhaps it is. Yet we also subscribe to the multidimensionality of personality and a growing literature in the psychobiography of leaders presents us with overwhelming data of qualitative *complexity*, however much simplicity is ardently and scientifically to be desired.

Secondly, it is the rare case where we can say with any philosophical assurance what v_o is. Organizational life is a continuous seamless web and v_o measures have to be taken at a point in time. They are subject to the same strictures as apply to balance sheets when these are used as measures of economic effectiveness. A rowing coach may have his leadership effect evaluated in terms of wins and losses but even in this apparently simple case the measure may be crude since some may row for motives extraneous to the leadership behaviours of the coach. In more complex cases, that is, in *most* cases, the judgement of effectiveness may have to be made by way of expert testimony, such as juries, but this testimony is itself inevitably dependent on the *philosophy* of the evaluators and hence qualitative matter than quantitative, subjective rather than objective.

Campbell[7] has shown that to ask global questions about organizational effectiveness is virtually useless. Fiedler certainly endeavours to avoid this pitfall but the price exacted for operational precision in research methodology may well be an excessive loss of meaning. If so, psychological theory of leadership is again in philosophical trouble.

Thirdly, this sort of research has tended studiously to avoid the value–ethical domain: The positivistic tendency to reduce value to affect and then to subsume the latter in behavioural observations has led to considerable literature of methodological critique.[8] The brute fact that the leader and the follower are always, a priori, value-actors has become obscured and even forgotten. Consider likewise the phenomenon and phenomenology of *commitment*[9] which cannot be bracketed out of any realistic understanding of leadership.

The final critique has to do with comprehensibility. Notwithstanding the misgivings already detailed I am prepared to acknowledge that the general productive effort of this type of research, and its particular embodiment in Professor Fiedler's work, amounts to the best empirical theory that we have to date. Yet it yields, even so, this paradox: the closer such theory approaches the *truth* the more incomprehensible it becomes. Present theory is already unwieldy and confusing, perplexing even to its exponents. An analogue may exist in the field of particle physics and sub-atomic phenomena. Van Fleet and Yukl[10] concluded that research over this past century clearly demonstrated that leadership is not a simple, indivisible construct. In astronomy the Ptolemaic theory gave way to the Copernican in a revolutionary paradigm shift when the former grew artificially overcomplex. Perhaps ultimately the empirical study of leadership may achieve a corresponding simplification but there is no real sign of this as yet. What contemporary theory does have is pedagogical merit in that it may sensitize its students to the existence and interconnection of the multitude of critical variables in the field of executive action.[11]

So far the grasp for comprehension exceeds its reach. It is almost as if leader-science were a subset of nescience, forever expanding the frontiers of ignorance. The philosophy of leadership must certainly take leadership theory into account and must do so indefatigably. But philosophy demands more than has ever yet been forthcoming. It demands both some *comprehensible* grasp of the logic and technology of organizational behaviour and a concomitant grasp of the logic of value as the basis for praxis and administrative philosophy. Not just, How *does* the leader get through the day? How *does* he cope? but How *ought* he to cope? What does it *mean* to be a leader, a man of action, in our times, and what can it mean? What *ought* it to mean? These questions leave leadership theory behind but not forgotten.

TYPES AND ARCHETYPES

The questions raised in the preceding section do break the bounds of ordinary theory by plunging us into the value domain of discourse. This does not, however, mean that the questions are intractable. Only difficult. And not amenable to the quantitative manipulations of conventional empiricism. They imply that real understanding of the modes of leadership must be grounded in qualitative aspects of the human condition and a depth understanding of human nature. This intellectual territory is vast and much of it is *terra incognita* but a first mapping may be achieved by using the techniques perfected by Max Weber in sociology.[12] That is, by seeking ideal types as a first patterning of the administrative modes. Taxonomy is the beginning of science. At present we have no science of administration or leadership but we do have an overload of information and a surfeit of data. How can we make sense of this plethora?

To type is a very basic human instinct. It is a first attempt at imposing order upon a welter of experience so as to derive meaning and form. We cope with an excess of information by arranging its disorder into hypotheses and propositions which can provide us with psychologically comfortable schemes of meaning. The worth of this meaning depends upon the underlying logic of the typological schema and the ultimate use of that schema in practice or praxis. Typing permeates language. Indeed those languages are the greatest which comprise with the maximum precision the greatest multiplicity of names and forms, precepts and concepts. Each *language game*[13] generates its own typing scheme. Science, for example, has a commanding prestige in our culture for its language games of, *inter alia*, biochemistry and particle physics, each of which exhibit exquisite precision and universal scope. Likewise, the ids and animas of depth psychology, the Platonic forms and dialectics of metaphysics, the quasi-mathematical formulae of macroeconomics, though they lack scientific precision and nicety, still persuade, are potent, and have practical effect.

In the study of administration the typing instinct has not been inactive. It has ranged from the trivial to the profound, from Reddin's work in the 1970s[14] to experimentation with the Enneagram in the 1990s.[15] But perhaps the most influential scheme has been Max Weber's formulation of charismatic, traditional, and rational–legalistic administration with their corresponding modes of leadership. Allison[16] explains Weber's approach as follows:

He recognized two forms of generalized schema: the typing which sought to represent the average or approximate nature of phenomena and that which represents "the theoretically conceived *pure type*". Pure types are of course ideal types. These conceptually constructed and theoretically based models can clearly have no empirical form but remain as accentuated abstractions. Weber maintained that "theoretical analysis in the field of sociology is possible only in terms of such types." Hence he is constantly dealing with conceptual parameters, with limiting cases, rather than with empirically derived "average" types such as those yielded through statistical research.

In short, Weber's ideal types are a conceptual tool corresponding in some ways to the mathematical notion of the limiting case.[17] They facilitate at one and the same time inquiry, research, philosophy, and policy.

In addition to the Weberian ideal type and the statistical average type there is also the Platonic Form and the Jungian archetype. The Platonic Form can be construed as a special case of the ideal type, indeed the ultimate and absolute case. It is not abstracted from empirical and sensory reality. On the contrary, empirical reality is subtended from it; what we experience as reality is subtended from it; what we experience as reality being but a dim approximation to that superstratum of transcendental origin in which and only in which Reality can be said to obtain. The Jungian archetype, on the other hand, subsists in the psychological substratum. The suggestion is that there are conceptually distinct forms or types which persist across cultures and throughout history in the universal unconscious mind of the species and that these forms or archetypes are psychologically potent. They manifest in dreams art, religion, culture, and history. Obviously Plato and Jung converge, the one from the philosophical the other from the psychological domain of discourse.

Lastly, there is the much-maligned stereotype. It is the most weakly grounded of types and often tends to a cartoon sort of distortion or oversimplification. Nevertheless, it is a fundamental reality of human cognition and a necessary kind of classificatory behaviour that enables us to cope with complexity. Where the number of variables which impinge on the conceptual field is excessive, as is the norm for interpersonal relations, the device may be unavoidable. Certainly the administrator must both use and contend with stereotypes. At worst they seduce us, as in the phenomenon of political correctness, into the avoidance of thought. At best they provide functional cognitive shorthand and simplifying coping mechanisms with proto-scientific potential.

The archetypes which we shall now consider are a composite of all the above categories of type. In a simple sense they are vignettes, shorthand descriptions of leader ideal types. Their justification would lie only partly in statistical verification. Yet, to the extent that they underlie unconscious affective, cognitive, and conative psychology and have motivating force in individual experience they are archetypical in the Jungian sense. Their logical basis rests ultimately in the analysis of value[18] and their practical worth lies in their hermeneutic relevance to the study of administration. We can then distinguish four basic leadership types or modes, each of which implicitly suggests different criteria of fol-lowership.

CAREERISM

The first archetype in which all administrators participate is that of the Careerist. Any clear-eyed comprehension of human nature in its organizational forms of life must acknowledge the impulse to advancement as a primary motivation, even if it be considered as an inevitable ramification of self-preservation, the "first law of nature". The concept of ambition itself, respectable and often revered in executive circles, may be simply a euphemism for what in earlier times was described variously as vanity or vainglory and in latter days as egotism or self-esteem. The careerist aspires to the status and privileges of rank and the organizational reward system is a template for ambition[19]—a design reinforced by the general social adulation of success.

In ordinary manners and mores, and in ordinary organizational ethos the archetype is overlaid by a complex system of repression, sublimation, inhibitions, and conditioning which preserves an equilibrium of affect, a socio-psychological ordering of behavior, within the organization without which life would be mean, nasty, brutish, and short indeed. Much of organizational symbolism (awards, ceremonies, badges of rank) and many organizational practices (promotion by seniority, examinations) are in fact attempts to channel and harmonize this archetypal energy. To defuse its disruptive or destructive potential. According to Freud civilization is a neurosis. The philosopher's concern with the archetype of careerism has to be that this organizational neurosis does not pass into psychosis.

In the development of ego or personality social conditioning occurs through education and experience. This applies to both leaders and followers. Elemental gratifications are frustrated and culture dictates the game rules, constraints, and modes by which social prizes may be won. The problem of the competitive struggle for prizes: wealth, pleasure, leisure, power, status, fame, sex, success—lends itself to apparent solution through adoption of the correct winning strategies and tactics. Such a technology of success is provided, for example, by the *arthashastra*.[20] The careerist archetype has a natural affinity for such doctrines. It can lead to pathological manifestations when the safeguarding and enhancement of the leader's career subverts other organizational concerns.

Careerism can also be construed as opportunism. Given a context where the major prizes are limited to the few, given evidence of self-seeking and malaise in organizational life, given perceptions that the ungodly prosper while the righteous founder—given these criteria alone it is at least understandable that some leaders may choose consciously (and even conscientiously) to walk the path of opportunism. Or, on the other hand, they may manifest the careerist archetype unconsciously, instinctively, reactively. By one path or another the careerist type is formed.

Other labels have been attached to this form of life: egotist, hedonist, narcissist; but the common factor throughout is a self-concern and self-interest on the part of the administrator that is relatively pure, free from constraint, and contemptuous of convention. Which is not to say that morals, laws, and proprieties go unrecognized. On the contrary, they are sharply perceived but are understood as game rules. And since the objective of the game is winning and the concept of rules implies no ethic of self-restraint it follows that the rules are there to be bent, broken, and evaded if the end result can be unpenalized success. The old-fashioned liberal rule that one was free to pursue one's self-interest so long as doing so did not interfere with another's like pursuit is reinterpreted as a licence to constantly press one's interests to the limits and beyond—if one can get away with it. This is an aspect of careerist ruthlessness. Scruples are for the tender-minded and the inhibited. Thrasymachus in Plato's *Republic* speaks for the careerist when he argues that might makes right and that the evidence is before one's eyes that the unjust reap the rewards of society. His successor Machiavelli reinforces the argument. The value of power is heightened to the point of veneration because power not only determines the possibilities of enjoyment but even the definition or what ought and ought not to be. Power defines the game within which the prizes are to be distributed. *Macht macht Recht*. Power becomes a *summum bonum*.

So the careerist is power-hungry and ambitious. But this ambition is not yet megalomania; it may be displayed or concealed depending on context and the perceived advantages or disadvantages, it has not been amplified to the point of ideological obsession with success, not yet the central focus and meaning of the leader's existence. The careerist is still capable of backing off, accepting defeat when frustrated, changing strategies, tacking with the wind. But private concerns remain such as role security, role advancement, power, authority, deference, status, and perquisites of office. Achievement as a leader is important because the recognition which attaches to achievement, however fleeting, is the leader's reassurance of status, public acknowledgement of worth and, next to promotion and yet greater power, the ideal ego-gratification. Defence of one's *amour propre* is fundamental and if necessary, all the weaponry of the *arthasastra* will be deployed in the maintenance of organizational territory, role, and power base. Given the arts of modern dramaturgy this basic defensiveness can be carefully concealed behind outward facades of *bonhomie*, banality, and even buffoonery. Yet perceived affronts to the ego will be remembered, malice nurtured, and should safe occasions provide the opportunity then the careerist may indulge the luxury of revenge.

The careerist administrator feels impelled to climb any accessible hierarchical ladder the organization provides and, moreover, to move laterally to other organizations if that will permit greater hierarchical progress. In this progression if others—colleagues, superiors and subordinates—get hurt or are left in the lurch so much the worse for them. The careerist attitude to others is essentially that of user. Of what use can this person be to me? Or, on the other hand, what threat might they represent? Ruthlessness therefore becomes increasingly necessary, along with an avoidance of any affective entanglements that might prove detrimental or decelerative. Such ruthless detachment is not entirely to be disdained; philosophers, theorists, and practitioners of administration from Vedic times to the present day, from Hammurabi to Albert Speer and Henry Kissinger, have given persuasive arguments for its necessity.

The archetype gains added potency within a competitive culture. Modern technocultures provide fertile soil for its cultivation. When the realities of large complex organizations and impersonal bureaucracies reinforce a social philosophy which is materialistic, hedonistic, and deterministic, multiple reinforcements obtain for the careerist style of administration. The explicit and implicit reward systems of the culture make ever more ironclad the identification of success with ascent of the hierarchy and of meaning with success. As Mary Midgley says, "Obsessed with success, with examinations, tests, and record-breaking, with competitive sports, trade, and manufacture, we have drifted into behaving as if life were not worth living except at the top of the dominance hierarchy, as if that place alone marked excellence."[21] And, as hedonic satisfaction becomes more and more attached to upward mobility so affective drives initially attached to self-indulgence in the ordinary or non-administrative sense become transformed into work patterns with perceived pay-off. Thus the frequent careerist commitment to hard work, long hours, and the classical work ethic. And this in turn is reinforcing for it assuages any lingering moral qualms and may even endow the careerist with a sense of pseudo-moral righteousness and superiority. Workaholism and careerism share a natural affinity.

The essence of the careerist character is, however, a kind of rugged amorality. Not beyond good and evil in the Nietzschean sense and not psychopathic either; recognizing and accepting the conventions of society that translate into moral codes but working around them without compunction whenever advantage is to be gained.

The careerist is a loner. The empirical workings of the archetype are open to view in the Watergate affair. Here one can observe how instantly and spontaneously public interest is transformed into private career interest and how, in the event of failure or defeat, colleagues and subordinates are ruthlessly abandoned or betrayed. "When the going gets tough, the tough get going."

But the careerist need not reek of brimstone. In appearance the archetype usually displays a pleasant personality, mastery of the arts of *bonhomie*, diplomacy, and flattery. Dramaturgy and the manipulation of others are, after all, essential to careerist success. Moreover, the type exists in all of us to the extent that personal ambition and need for achievement go unconstrained by other, higher level, archetypes. The careerist clearly can be of collective service. Identification with the organization can lead to large personal sacrifices for the organizational good and careerism in itself is no bar to administrative and managerial skills. Organizations can come to revere their careerist leaders even when the façade is stripped away for ruthlessness can be as necessary to the body politic as surgery to the body physical. The record of organizational history show that the prince and the dictator, the tyrant and the man-on-horseback have always been acclaimed for their commonweal success. Richard Nixon was accorded a State funeral and the eulogies of the media.

The careerist is easily perceived as a good leader, beloved of the followership. This image is endorsed and reinforced by visible work habits, energy level, protestations of commitment, busyness, and political skills. Admiration flows from a perception of winning in the organizational market-place. The world worships winners while weakness and vacillation tend to be seen as contemptible. The press to success is thus binding on the careerist-leader; failure is anathema. Political support is also contingent on promised gains and rewards. So time becomes the enemy for with the passage of time some of these promissory notes mature. If they cannot then be cashed it may now be better to move onward, upward, or perform some lateral arabesque that removes one from the ambit of responsibility. Hence, mobility, both within and without the organization is a feature of the archetype.

The risks of exposure of duplicity, of trickery, of cunning, of fast dealing tend to increase with the passage of time. So too does the pressure generated by problems shelved and decisions delayed. Likewise the accumulated resentment from favours denied and egos bruised. For all these reasons time works against the careerist and, therefore, mobility coupled with short-term commitments tends to be a mark of the type. Nevertheless, any ill-feeling caused by the later discovery of having been manipulated or used is but a side-effect of the fact that, in the largest sense, all of the followership is instrumental to organizational goals. Everyone is a usee. But the careerist goes too far; the user thrives while the usee seethes. Morale fluctuates immensely with usage. Meanwhile the careerist has moved on to a new field of predation.

It is amongst the careerist's immediate entourage, the executive suite of intimates and lieutenants, that these pathologies will be most discernible. Psychological and social distancing may protect the leader image at other levels but the inner circle will be privy to the machinations of power. Familiarity need not necessarily breed contempt but it certainly provides more opportunities for perceptive observation. So, paradoxically, the careerist must be most on guard amongst those with whom relaxation should be most possible. Climbers must watch those who climb around them and so the executive suite is often the main site and source of executive stress. And certainly of sub-executive stress.

It is important to reiterate that any critique of this archetype cannot be grounded in mere moralism. *Realpolitik* writes off such sentiments as vain. The leader who would reject careerism must have an alternative or countervailing commitment. Such commitment must in turn be sustained by certain minimal unverifiable *beliefs*. These might include, for example, a Kantian belief in a moral order in the universe or a Confucian belief in a socio-moral order of codes, mores, and laws.[22] Any such belief is inhibiting; it constrains individual freedom of action. In this respect the pragmatist is more constrained than the careerist, under more orders of laws and with fewer degrees of freedom.

Yet the careerist archetype can never be entirely sublimated or exorcized. It lodges within every breast and sinks deep into the recesses of the administrative mind. It is the simplest truth of social wisdom that from time to time self-interest will be in the ascendancy, however and whatever the inhibitions of philosophy, law, religion, morality, or group psychology. We are all of us careerists at some level of our consciousness. Ambition for oneself is natural but if it fixates on the ego it becomes pathological: ambition must reach beyond the ego—to be truly admirable it must become virtuous by transcending ego-interests and thereby seeking inhibition, refinement, sublimation, the greater commitment to the greater good.

Each administrator stands at the conjuncture of an already determined past and an indeterminate future. Indeterminate because no matter how many lines of policy and planning have been projected upon it it remains in the last analysis imponderable. The past is always a lost cause, the future always invincible with hope. It is at this conjuncture that the question of free will forcibly intrudes upon administrative philosophy. A strictly positivist position will logically deny the notions of moral order and free will but the position of this book is that there is limited (perhaps severely limited) free will, some degrees of freedom, and the moral stature of the administrator does depend upon a limited exercise of will. As to the number of degrees of freedom and the latitude of choice within any decision context there can be endless contention.

Careerism is the lowest of the archetypes. But it is fundamental, rooted in our affective nature. All leadership incorporates, subsumes, this archetype and all leaders have egos. There is no escape from this lower-case self. The counsel of wisdom is not to dismay over this but to accept it, to understand to the full the anti-collective forces within us and to seek to refine or civilize them, harnessing the primitive energies of this archetype to higher-level purposes, values, and goals.

In general the forces of order, social conditioning, and prudential reason are strong enough to constrain the careerist archetype and to discipline it, but when these forces for whatever reason weaken then the potential for conversion to charismatic idealism is present and what is good for one many suddenly become what is right for all.

A final caution: the archetype is easier to conceive than perceive. Careerists avoid advertising themselves as such. Modern organizations provide adequate protective cover for their predatory inclinations. It is a perpetual onus of praxis to penetrate all such camouflage, to perceive, to be aware, to discriminate, to act out of awareness—not to be gullible.

PRAGMATISM

Pragma is the Greek for business. A pragmatist is one who gets things done, makes things work—a businessman. And if pragmatism is management by another name then politics is administration by another name. The pragmatic administrator is political, is a politician, but a politician with a business-like sense, a subscriber to the maxim that politics is the art of the possible. The value logic of this archetype lies in the substantive reality of group preferences. The interests of the pragmatist–administrator extend beyond self and beyond the natural ego-extensions of self (family, kin, clan) to a point where they embrace the collectivity of the organization for which the leader is responsible. These interests endorse the Gestalt principle that the whole is greater than the sum of the parts. The political quality of this type is not, therefore, pejorative but rather refers to authentic concern with group preferences and a concomitant concern, less Simon pure perhaps, with group power.

Embedded in the archetype is a metavalue:[23] the democratic principles and democratic ideology of majority rule, in short, collective interest. Legitimacy is grounded not in the individual but in the group. The pragmatic leader seeks then to be the spokesman of the group and the articulator of group interests. The group is a source of energy and moral force. The ordinary narcissism of the careerist archetype is now modulated or sublimated through identification with group values and group interest. This also leads to a certain preoccupation with group harmony (*cf.* the Barnardian concept of "efficiency"[24]) and to continuous maintenance of and search for *consensus*. The pragmatist seeks to mitigate conflict by compromise, by the trading of values and the reconciliation of interests. His forte lies in group dynamics and the arcanum of persuasion.

The pragmatist feeds upon group approach. Group support is meat and drink: the means towards all ends. However lively careerist motivations may be they can be subsumed and sublimated under the legitimizing cachet of the organization itself. Self-interest pure and simple as in the previous archetype now becomes self-interest impure and complex, that is, self-interest enlarged, refined and even, upon occasion, altruistic.

There is overlap between the careerism and pragmatism archetypes. Both call upon the full range of political skills. Both call for a manipulation of group perceptions. Dramaturgy is common to both. Roles must be played out; the executive troupe must put on a good show. Different images—the father, the uncle, the comrade, the fighter, the smoothie—will be presented according to the political reading of the situation. Common to both also will be ingratiation with the constituency of power: those organization members who have power to make decisions or influence outcomes, a constituency that can be sizeable under conditions of participatory democracy. But whereas the careerist seeks what will work for himself as the prime focus of interest the pragmatist *also* seeks what will work for the group.

Inevitably the pragmatist must practise from time to time the techniques of Machiavelli. But the steely hand is well and truly gloved. He does personal favours for the followership; he explains his actions; he backs up members of the group; he does not ostensibly act without consulting members of the group; he does ostensibly treat all members of the group as his equals; he is friendly and approachable; he does not demand more than followers can be, and he does not reject suggestions for change;[25] he is politically correct and alive to the shifting cultural issues of the day. In some ways the type echoes that described by Pope:

> *Some praise at morning what they blame at night; But always think the last opinion right.*
> *And, spite of pride, in erring reason's spite, One truth is clear. Whatever is, is right.*[26]

Nonetheless one can claim that pragmatism is both moral and rational. Moral because the circle of interest goes beyond that of self and extended self, invoking some self-sacrifice by virtue of the value-calculus of group interaction. Rational because of the claim that actualized group preferences enhance the potential for individual welfare. (A claim it can be noted, that runs contrary to the value logic of classical economics as expressed by Adam Smith.[27]) In essence this is primitive or tribal democratic theory: the group knows best, both what it wants *and* what it *ought* to want. The function of the leader is to discover the group values, formulate and represent them, then translate them into reality through the devices of organization and administrative process.

But group chemistry is mysterious, popular support is notoriously fickle, and the signs can easily be misread. It follows that the pragmatist is necessarily committed to a heavy schedule of personal interactions with constituents. He cannot neglect the informal organization nor can he afford to be aloof. He must be busily engaged in a continuous series of personal contacts, his calendar full, his time fragmented, his possibilities for in-depth study of organizational problems limited. At times he must skim the surface like a water-spider. But always remaining jocular, congenial, willing to listen and play to the full the dramaturgy of sympathetic sentiment. His worship at the altar of consensus means eating, drinking, and talking with a lot of people; rarely can he indulge the luxuries of solitude or deep reflection. The world of his organization presses too much upon him. He must be about his political business, persuading, soothing, eliciting and consolidating support.

The archetype implies short-term orientation. It is the immediate problem that is pressing; it is the short-run that counts. Pragmatically the long run can be left to take care of itself. Psychological compartmentalization helps; it is, after all, business-like and systematic. Meanwhile there are egos to be stroked and an overall atmosphere of cooperative efficiency and morale to be maintained. The genius of the type is that this can be done authentically, without cynicism.

Pragmatism necessitates the arts of suasion. So the pragmatist watches carefully his reciprocity index, trades judiciously in favours, gathers intelligence diligently through all the information circuitry of the organization. He is at the centre of a communications network and values this position of command. He values discretion and confidentiality but also knows the value of discreet indiscretion.

Pragmatism derives from a higher value logic than careerism but it remains morally ambivalent. It can be at worst, a base pandering to the herd. "There go the mob," said the Comte de Mirabeau during the French Revolution, "and I must follow them for I am their leader."

> Both Goebbels and Hitler understood how to unleash mass instincts at their meetings, how to play on the passion that underlay the veneer of ordinary respectable life. Practised demagogues, they succeeded in fusing the assembled workers, petits bourgeois, and students into a homogeneous mob whose opinions they could mould as they pleased. ... But as I see it today, these politicians in particular were *in fact moulded by the mob itself,* guided by its yearnings and its daydreams. Of course Goebbels and Hitler knew how to penetrate through to the instincts of their audience; but in the deeper sense they derived their whole existence *from* this audience. Certainly the masses roared to the beat set by Hitler's and Goebbel's baton; yet they were not the true conductors. *The mob determined the theme.*[28] (My italics.)

The line between seeking and manipulating consensus is often difficult to draw. Nor is the process of group aggregation of values any proof or guarantee of rectitude. Groups are often notoriously wrong and notoriously oppressive. By the slightest process of degeneration the ideal type soon yields such familiar forms as the organization man, the confidence man, the trickster, the gamesman skilled in dramaturgical artifice, the peerocratic spokesman for group-think and slavish practitioner of the politically correct. From group suasion to group tyranny is but a step.

Nevertheless, despite its weaknesses and its notable defect of short-term orientation the pragmatic form of leadership is, by and large, most congenial to followers. That this is so may be explained by man's social nature, by the general democratic intent of this leadership style, and by its praxis affinity for idiographic consideration, that is, for its capacity for treating the individual as such in defiance of bureaucratic or nomothetic impartiality. The parallel with Weber's patrimonial or familial type of authority and organization is noteworthy. Thompson[29] too, has argued persuasively on this theme and has described the devices and attempts made to reconcile the form of rational–legal bureaucracy with the demands of the idiographic dimension. He called this the problem of administrative compassion and it is a problem which remains largely unsolved, despite the patchwork of pragmatic panaceas ranging from ombudsmen to guidance counsellors.

For everyone the first experience of organization is the family. The leaders of this organization, father and mother or their surrogates, tend naturally to incorporate the pragmatist archetype, often at its best. As the family extends with maturity to include ever larger organizational obstructions the corresponding value logic of *communitas* and democracy is unconsciously assimilated by the individual. The norm that majority preferences should therefore be given priority in the personal value-calculus is easily, though at times painfully, accepted as a righteous discipline. Thus the pragmatic leader tends automatically to be rewarded with votes, endorsements, and power. Follower approval is reinforced by ethos, subculture, and the human relations movement in administration. The fact that followers are susceptible to manipulation through corruptions of the archetype does not detract from the general appeal of this leadership form of life. Every structured committee, council, or collective policy-making body, however lowly or mighty , is a living homage to the archetype of pragmatism.

The exponent of this archetype must have some sensible, though possibly unexamined, faith in the wisdom of the masses. This need not have been subjected to intellectual scrutiny, it may simply be there as a component of personality. Perhaps, subliminally, the leader believes in the self-correcting cybernetic qualities of large human systems. In any event the pragmatist archetype can be construed as the first form of administrative morality, an authentically moral though elementary, form of administrative life.

The quality of this morality will thus be a function of the authenticity of the leader's identification with the preferences and values of the group. Note that this commitment is to the *authentic* collective will and not necessarily to the nomothetic or formal goals of the organization. *In extremis* this might mean that the leader would assist the followers to mutiny. The point, however, is that to some sensible degree the pragmatist–leader seeks to embody the will, the values, of the followership and is willing to be led where these lead. Hence the import of the Barnardian commandment to know the informal organization.

But the potential for pathology inherent in this archetype must not be overlooked. Plato distrusted the masses while his pupil Aristotle thought that they possessed, unconsciously, the instinctive knowledge of the best course of action, in the long run. But oversocialization leads to the ethics of the herd, the swarm and the insect hive.[30] The pragmatism archetype suffers from such obvious corruptions as tyranny of the majority and the excesses of group conformity. (A paradoxical contemporary pathology in democracy is a parallel tyranny of the *minority* as expressed through various single-issue and grievance groups.) To counter these tendencies the moral pragmatist must cherish variant value orientations and be prepared to embrace what is politically incorrect. Modern theories of bioethics and sociology notwithstanding[31] there is no reason to suppose that the group is invariably right. Groups are often notoriously wrong. Progress is often made against the will of and in spite of the group. So the administrator whose value persuasion would reach beyond this archetype must to some extent take the side of Plato against Aristotle. Democracy has its mobocratic face and within this archetype the axiological slope inclines towards the lowest level and is slippery. The line between manipulating consensus and allowing its authentic emergence is easily traversed. Tempting also is the entropic tendency to take the line of least resistance, to be superficial in the analysis of preference, to avoid hard decisions, to succumb to the group. Authentic democratic leadership is often stressful, difficult, onerous. True pragmatists practise the art of the possible and make the world work. They personify the best elements of an archetype without which there would be no organization. But the archetype is not a limit. One can go beyond it.

HIGHER ARCHETYPES

We have now dealt in a descriptive, qualitative fashion with the two lower archetypes: careerist and pragmatist. These form the basis of administrative morality and leadership modality. There are also two higher archetypes: realist (Technician) and idealist (Poet) which shall be explicated later. All the archetypes derive from the axiological theory to be presented in Part III. For now it will be sufficient to observe that a rough correspondence exists between the Weberian leadership categories of rational–legalistic with realism and charismatic with idealism. The correspondence is closer, however, between the bureaucratic and realist modes and much less so in the difficult instance of the charismatic designation. To understand the latter and its idealistic foundations we need first to come to grips with the theory of value. A philosophy of administration must rest upon defensible axiological foundations. Without these it is wind.

* * *

In this chapter we have examined the tortured issue of leadership in the light of two quite different methods: the empirical–quantitative and the typological–qualitative. The burden of argument has been that while the former is analytical but inadequate the latter sacrifices predictive rigour and scientific cachet on the altar of understanding. Administration remains an art and a humanism, not a proto-science. What has been established is the all-pervasiveness of value in administrative praxis. As a last confirmation consider the classical reduction of the administrative problem expressed by Barnard as the theme of *communication*.[32]

Professor Wilson defines communication as "action on the part of one organism (or cell) that alters the probability pattern of behavior in another organism (or cell) in a fashion adaptive to either one or both of the participants"[33] "conforms well both to our intuitive understanding of communication and to the procedure by which the process is mathematically analysed."[34] But he also submits that "In human beings communication can occur without an outward change of behavior on the part of the recipient. Trivial or otherwise useless information can be received, mentally noted, and never used."[35] One cites this socio-biological neo-behaviourist approach to stress the complexity of *human* communication and its dependence upon understanding or *meaning* each of which in turn depends upon concepts of affect, preference, belief, attitude, and value. In other words mind, consciousness, will, and intention can be deleted from communication between microchips and microorganisms but not from communication between humans. The latter comes down to *interpretation* upon which Nietzsche made his apodeictic utterance: There are no facts only interpretations. We must next examine some of the foundations for interpretation, the discovery of meaning and the process of understanding.

PROPOSITIONS

69. Is there a moral order in the universe? The administrator must ask this question. And answer it.
70. If there be a moral order in the universe then adherence to it would strengthen, departure from it weaken.
71. Virtue enlightens; vice endarkens.
72. The Machiavellian metavalue is success.
73. There is such a thing as the judicious rage, the calculated loss of control.
74. The arts of the courtier govern the dealings with superiors.
75. Where there is opposition seek to divide it. Then redivide the divisions.
76. Beware of friendliness in the realms of power. There is no need to beware of friendship; it does not exist.
77. Authority rests on perception. That is, upon the values of the perceiver. *Esse est percipe.*
78. Administrative authority is a convenient and necessary fiction.
79. Technical competence and role authority are necessary but insufficient conditions for leadership.
80. The best leadership is often followership.
81. Leaders embody (personify) collective values. The sanctity of these values may entail their concealment, and the leader's inaccessibility. Or the values may call for display, and the leader's visibility.
82. The essence of leadership is to know when to raise and when to avoid moral issues.
83. Organizational complexity persuades us of the need for a paragon as leader. We then persuade ourselves that this paragon deserves a robe as well as an office.
84. If our leaders are idols then let us do administrative philosophy with a hammer.

III
VALUES, INTERESTS, AND POWER

If the unexamined life is not worth living the unexamined value is not worth holding.

Chapter 6
Value Theory

Management, itself a subset of administration, is pre-eminently disposed towards facts. Its superset, administration, is pre-eminently concerned with values. Therefore such philosophical questions as, What is value? Is there a fact-value dichotomy? Can one derive a value from a fact? What is a *fact*? are questions of direct interest to the administrator or leader.[1]

SOME PRELIMINARY DISTINCTIONS

Consider to begin with the distinction between values and facts. Without being overly concerned with definition and semantic niceties at this point let us just take values to be *concepts of the desirable* and facts to be, as Wittgenstein would have it, *all that is the case.*[2] Now the first thing to note is that for any given state of affairs the facts can *never* be in conflict while the values (assuming that there are more than one set relevant to the given state of affairs) are *always* in conflict. This difference is fundamental. It comes about because facts purport to be *true* renditions of the objective world of nature and science (and let us also note that natural science would extend its dominion over the internal world of brain/mind events and states[3]). Such facts are by definition true; a false fact is an oxymoron. The legacy of Aristotelian logic and its contribution to the foundations of Western science have been to universalize this concept of fact. A thing (or an event, or a state of mind) is, at any given instant, either *a* or *not a*; it either is or it isn't, that is how the world is made up. Or as Tweedledee put it "... if it was so, it might be; and if it were so, it would be; but as it isn't, it ain't. That's logic."[4] It is worth remarking that this same logic, which is at the root of Western science and materialism, has received considerable experiential reinforcement through the electronic revolution. A computer, after all, is merely a complex of on–off, either–or, is or isn't, binary switches.

But the world of value is altogether different. Whatever internal facticity it may have for the phenomenological subject—the inner observer—the world of public fact, of externality and objectivity, possesses only that value which is imputed to it or superimposed upon it by a subjective private consciousness. By a mind. The world as it is experienced through the mind of an observer appears to be coloured with value, but the world in its factive essence is as void of value as blank videotape before its elements are coagulated into a picture. There is neither beauty nor ugliness, right nor wrong, good nor bad *out there.* To paraphrase Plato, a thing is not valued because it is good, it is good because it is valued. Man values by superimposing an axiological order upon the world at the same time as, according to Kant, he superimposes an epistemological or factual order through the categories of mind such as space, time, and causation. The epistemology tells us what *is*, the axiology tells us whether that *is* is good or bad. Animals other than man do likewise but another crucial distinction now arises. Man appears to be the only animal capable of making *right* or *wrong* types of valuation. He is, as Nietzsche called him, "the beast with red cheeks". The only life-form capable of guilt and shame. We shall return to this distinction later.

Because of the radical difference between fact and value, and because facts are open to public verification whereas values are subject only to private (phenomenological) verification, it is possible for two observers to attribute divergent values to the same piece of objectivity or fact. An object of beauty or desire for the one may be an object of loathing or derision for the other; a supervisor's ambition or goal commitment may be a subordinate's anathema or apathy. And such differences need *not* be available to inspection, they may not be accessible items of consciousness in either party. Moreover, as no one can occupy the same life-space as another—as the world comes up differently each moment for each person—it follows that in some very fundamental sense values are always potentially or actually in conflict.

The administrator need not be driven to despair by this, nor need he accede to Sartre's claim that "Hell is other people." Yet the leader should note that the bulk of collective behaviour, political or social or organizational, is devoted to and dependent upon the establishment of some sort of *modus vivendi* or working resolution of value conflict, either by fiat, or consensus, or manipulation. An organization is, strictly speaking, an arrangement for conflict management through the device of superordinate or overriding goals. When the Pope denies women access to the priesthood and the Archbishop of Canterbury accuses him of failing to "read the mind of Christ"[5] both are appealing a value conflict to the court of organization theory. And in this court there are no facts, only interpretations.

It would, of course, be very convenient if there were such incontestable entities as facts[6] and especially so if one could derive values *from the facts*. This would make administrative life much easier for one would then need simply to discover and be concerned with the *facts* of the case. This, in essence, is the juridical or bureaucratic approach to value conflict: discover the appropriate rules (the legal system is a complex of established rules) and then apply them. The *facts* speak for themselves. Unfortunately we are now brinking upon the naturalistic fallacy, to be discussed later, which says that one cannot get a value from a fact. It is enough, however, to observe that all of the decision rules in law and policy making are themselves ultimately relative to personal choices, traditions, custom, culture, mores, and history and their correlation with any given set of facts is arbitrary rather than absolute. The fact of sheep stealing may cause a man to be hanged in one era and commended for asserting his rights in another. Administrative thought and action has to take into account philosophical distinctions between value and fact; absolute and relative; *is* and *ought*.

One more valuational distinction is useful before attempting analysis of the value problem: the distinction between the study of value in general, what is *good* and *bad* (axiology) and the study of specifically human value problems, what is *right* and *wrong* (morals and ethics). Axiology can be considered to be more "factual" than ethics to the extent that it is more descriptive than prescriptive, and in administrative philosophy a rough correspondence can be made which links the axiological with management and the ethical with administration. This parallel should not, however, be overdrawn since both types of value issues pervade both types of leadership.

Fundamental questions in administrative philosophy are: Ought a leader to be moral or ethical? Or ought leadership at the highest levels to be above ordinary value constraints? At lesser levels ought administrators in general to be committed or neutral? Passionate or professional? Technocratic or partial? Through history these questions have remained contentious and unresolved. Upon the evidence, from the death camps and the gulags to the bombing of Hiroshima, the massacres of Cambodia, and the conflicts of the Balkans, leaders have acted through power to pursue their perceived interests. The sequence is power-interests-values, the last being reinterpreted according to the perspective of the leader–actor.

As an alternative to this relativism Plato had advocated a special breed of leader, the Guardians, who were exponents of the Good and who would administer with virtue and wisdom the perfect state, the *Republic*. Such leaders would be *intrinsically* superior to their subordinates because they had had some experience of the Form of the Good, that which was absolute and *Ideal*, the Infinite, the Transcendental, God. They achieved this authenticating contact with the source of all value by extensive and intensive discipline. The Guardians were of mature years, single, and celibate. Living austerely they had overcome the ordinary corrupting desires of the common man for success, power, wealth, and sensual pleasure. Their burdens of administrative responsibility were assumed, not because they wanted the rewards and perquisites of office but precisely because they did not. They were philosophers. With them the Republic could be born. Without them it could not.

This elitist thought of administrative aristocracy or meritocracy was not confined to Plato nor did it die with him. In some form it appears in many cultures: the Hindu Brahmin/Kshyatria castes, the Chinese mandarinate, the Japanese Samurai. It may seem today to be outrageously romantic or "idealistic" but we are dealing here with an archetype and the appeal of this concept of value-informed leadership has never completely faded. Its lineaments can be discovered in the Society of Jesus, in the Communist party as the vanguard of the proletariat, and in elite leadership schools throughout the world down to the present day. The common factor in all these modern versions of administrative Platonism is that of concern with an ethic, a moral engagement or commitment that both commands sacrifice from its adherents and endows them with a sense of superiority. It is fair to say that there is a religious or mythical quality to this tradition. Underlying it is some vision of the Good whether that be the perfect harmony of the Republic, the utopian Workers' State, Christ's Kingdom on Earth, or the New Order of the Nazi romantics. The mythology provides the value dynamic for the movement and is essentially transrational in character. In other words administration infused with these sorts of values goes *beyond* reason.

At the opposite end of the value spectrum is the tradition of the leader as man (or woman) of power. Such a leader is governed by an ethic of success, of winning. He is totally ruthless in the pursuit of this and in the acquisition, maintenance, and expansion of his power. All efficacious means justify his ends and he is strong, bold, amoral—beyond good and evil in the conventional sense. He is typified by Machiavelli's *Prince* but this school of administrative philosophy can be traced back into the earliest mists of time as, for example, in the Sanskrit *arthasastra*.[7] Its provenance is ancient and perhaps because it is rooted in some psychological truth about the human condition, perhaps because of its reality base as opposed to Platonic ideality, a sizeable literature new exists in the genre known variously as *Realpolitik* or *Fürstenspiegel*—a "mirror for princes". The lure of "success"—undefined but semantically and tautologically *good* —is powerful in itself. Of what value could any administrative philosophy be that aspired to "failure"? Practical formulae for the achievement of success have always had a certain appeal. In general, in the more Byzantine and Machiavellian modes of administrative life, conventional ethics and morals are simply set aside, jettisoned, overruled, slandered, or bent to the will of the leader though careful pains will be taken to disguise all this from the followership which presumably subscribes, at least overtly, to the ordinary canons of morality. Treachery, trickery, guile, and corruption all have their instrumental place in this scheme of things. In ancient China this sometimes secret doctrine or path was known as "School of Thick Face, Black Heart" and is still honored as such today.[8] Study of these techniques and the desire to become an adept in them could not of course be overt or public. Secrecy is a necessary condition and it is noteworthy that secrecy *per se* remains a necessary condition of administrative life. Conventional institutions of learning, however, would be obliged to proscribe such teachings. They would certainly not be politically correct. Nevertheless, the desire for power and success, for wealth and fame at any price, is probably as widespread in human nature today as it was at any other period of history and will be so tomorrow and into the foreseeable future. Consequently, the appeal of this ethos means that such doctrines persist in practice and praxis however much they may be publicly deplored by academic departments of administration, government, leadership, political science and philosophy. Yet even at the intellectual level a counter-Platonic stream of thought persists and has a significant practical appeal. Graduate students have always intrigued me by the sudden liveliness of their interest upon first encountering *The Prince*. And the modern philosopher Nietzsche, though little read and still less understood by administrators in general, has provided for some a transmoral and transitional justification for an ethic of ruthlessness, for the leader who goes beyond the values of the herd to create his own world of value. Shakespeare's Richard III, Othello's lieutenant, Iago, and Dostoyevski's Grand Inquisitor are literary images of the type. And again we can say that this type of leadership too goes *beyond* reason. But in a direction antithetical to that of Plato.

Other value alternatives exist in the philosophy of administration. The leader, for example, need be neither morally corrupt nor morally sublime but simply may take value directions from convention or tradition. Or the leader may seek the bureaucratic option of avoiding philosophical and value issues altogether by becoming a technician, a factotum, a manager. By retreating to managerialism the administrator may seek a sort of disengagement or detachment from the value implications of the role and thus become an impartial conduit for the flow of moral or immoral action. One might call this the Pontius Pilate mode. But in the end even this proves vain if only because personality can never by entirely expunged from role. That epitome of Max Weber's ideal type bureaucracy, the career civil servant void of all political will and totally at the behest of political masters, safely tenured and concerned only with rational analysis and the delivery of dispassionate advice—even this example proves upon scrutiny to be both fiction and myth.

It comes down to this: an administrator, any administrator, is constantly faced with value choices. To govern is to choose. One can accept or not accept the value dictates imposed by the particular organizational culture in which one works. One can aspire to or disdain any of a number of systems of "ethics" from workaholism to neo-Confucianism. One can allow, or not allow, one's leadership to be swayed by values deriving from hedonism, ambition, careerism, or by the prejudices and affinities one has for colleagues and peers. And one can do all of this in the open or in secret or somewhere in-between. But each day and each hour provides the occasion for value judgements with each choice having a determining effect upon the value options for the future.

Since value action is ultimately inescapable upon what grounds can, or should, one choose? What values are the *right* values? How are the values of the case before us to be ordered? How to achieve that degree of certainty, of inner ratification, which can imbue us with a sense of philosophical satisfaction and psychological security?

It must be conceded at the outset that all the classical and traditional theories of administrative ethics fail to finally resolve these questions. The answers which ethics deliver are in the last analysis dogmatic. The business of ethics is a sort of preaching. Perhaps this explains why codes of ethics are, in practice, about as convincing and efficacious as are preachments and moral exhortations in general, whether delivered from the pulpit, the parade ground, the political rostrum, or the chief executive's chair. Let us therefore take a different approach. Let us consider the problem of *value itself.*

Value has primacy in administration. This has already been shown. Our task in administrative philosophy is to elucidate the concept of value and value language. Ideally this should be done in such a way that value terms can be articulated into models yielding testable hypotheses but in any event the terminology should enhance understanding. Affect, motives, attitudes, beliefs, norms, values, ethics, morals, will, commitment, preference, responsibility, duty, integrity, honour— all such terms that enter into the language game of administration demand clarification.

DEFINITION AND UNDERSTANDING

Values are synonymous with meaning but both are invisible. The objective visible referents of action and experience are distinct from whatever meaning or value we might ascribe to them. As evidence of this synonymy try the simple experiment of substituting "value" for "meaning" whenever the latter word occurs in this quotation:

> Reflect for a moment on the *world of meaning* in which you live—in which all people really live. What is meaning for you? You want food, say, or you wish to get some appointment or to see someone. All this is meaning—different meanings in the world of meaning. Now is this meaning tangible or visible? I do not see how you can say that meaning can be touched with the organs of sense or seen by the eye or heard or smelt or tasted. For example, money has meaning to everyone. But is the meaning of money touchable or seeable? It is surely not an object of any of the senses. As an object of the senses it can take any form—paper, silver, gold, scrip, or just credit—but the meaning *remains* the same quite apart from the visible form. It is necessary to point this out as people often take an object and its meaning as identical ...[9]

To this one can add that it is only too common an administrative error, with profound implications for leadership, to seek value and meaning in some sort of objective way, either by reference to the world of fact (which in truth is meaningless) or, at one remove, in some so-called consensus of opinion.

Values (meanings) for the purpose of philosophy of administration can be succinctly defined as concepts of the desirable with motivating force. This is not as tautological as it may appear on first reading since there may be many values or desirables in our phenomenology which either lack motivating force or sustain motivation only weakly. A smoker may, for example, hold non-smoking to be a desirable condition but persist in his habit nonetheless. Or one may subscribe to a political platform without responding to the appeal to vote.

Administrative philosophy can also subscribe, without contradiction, to the more precise and elaborate definition of value first formulated by the anthropologist Kluckhohn:

> A value is a conception, explicit or implicit, distinctive of an individual or characteristic of a group, of the desirable which influences the selection from available modes, means, and ends of action.[10]

Values so defined may be characterized in various ways as, say, political, moral, religious, aesthetic, economic. They can also be considered as phenomenological entities, (that is, components of subjective experience) intermediate between motives and attitudes (see Figure 6.1). Values may arise from conscious or *unconscious* motivational dynamics and they may be determining factors of attitudinal orientations and general predispositions to act. Some degree of value conflict is the normal human condition. Even more so is it the administrative condition. Our aim is to explore the possibilities of an administrative philosophy which will provide techniques, justification, and understanding for the right resolution of conflicts of value and interest.

VALUE TERMINOLOGY

If we have by now disentangled value from fact then this is certainly a step forward in understanding but we must now cope with other orders of linguistic confusion. For example, consider the concept "needs". Maslow, a great psychological value theorist, rarely wrote of values as such but instead preferred to talk about needs.[11] How are needs to be distinguished from, say, wants or desires in general?

The idea behind need is that of a discrepancy or undesirable imbalance in a state of affairs. Needs imply tension and disequilibrium and a consequent dynamic for rectifying or satisfying action. We shall take needs and their cognate terms "desires" or "wants" as being indicators of some state of individual or group deficiency or shortfall, with a consequent potential or propensity for remedial action. As such they are not values but rather *sources* of value. A condition of hunger will make us value food, as a condition of threat will make us value security.

Needs, wants, and desires are intimately related to the concept of motive. The idea behind motivated behaviour is usually that there is for the motivated actor some kind of end-in-view. The trouble with this interpretation is that the end may not be "in view". It may be semi-conscious or even unconscious, or it may be quite other than what it is held to be. The impulse to action may be subliminal; psychological language contains such concepts as "drives" and "drive states" about which there is much contention and inconclusive experimentation. For our purposes, let us accept motives as either conscious reasons (pulls) or unconscious drives (pushes), or some combination of both, which are, again, a *source* of value.

I may be fully aware, partially aware, or totally unaware of my motives for action, but the fact that I myself or other observers can pass value judgements upon these motives is sufficient to show that value is something other than motives, desires, wants, or needs. We may also note a sometimes convention to distinguish between wants and needs on the basis that the former are less legitimate than the latter (I want a Rolls-Royce but need a car). Here again we see the play of a higher order *valuation.*

To return to motives then, we may say that they have a sort of push–pull correlation with consciousness and the faculty of reason. To be completely unmotivated is not to exist as a sentient being. To be fully aware of all our motives would be to be supersentient. And to approve of them all would be superhuman. Whether or not motives can be reduced on psycho-evolutionary grounds to the classic triad of impulses: fight, flight, or freeze; or even further to the Freudian life and death instincts (Eros and Thanatos) they subsist in our psychology and biology as *sources* of value. Motives existing in the depths of the psyche as dark forces of the id as well as those fully exposed in the light of day as validated and justified reasons are in either case correlated with another important value term, *attitude.*

I wish to define attitudes as surface phenomena, predispositions to act or respond to stimuli in relatively stable or persistent ways. As motives provide a source of value so value is a source of attitudes (Figure 6.1). Attitudes are manifestations of values at the interface of skin and world. The world demands our attention in a great variety of ways. How we attend is a function of our attitudes. These attitudes are measurable, observable facts in the world whereas values may be invisible and motives unknown even to the actor. If we take the simplest biological organism we may, by observation, infer, reduce, and classify the number of attitudes to the already mentioned triad of aggression, regression, or stasis. But for the complex human organism, the number of attitudes may be legion because this level of organic complexity is, above all else, linguistic. Humans engage continuously in language games (one of which is called administration) and express their attitudes in language categories, some of which are called opinions. Thus, polls of one sort or another assess collective attitudes and individuals are categorized as open-minded or close-minded, tough-minded or tender-minded, conservative, radical, authoritarian, permissive, and so on *ad psychologium nauseamque infinitum.*

Figure 6.1 summarizes the scheme of value terminology to this point. Let us note the arithmetic of this line of reasoning. First there is the unitary self or ego (we avoid, in the interests of simplicity, the fractured self and multiple personalities of psychoanalytic literature). Next, a very few basic motives: perhaps the "instinct" for self-preservation or the Freudian dualism of Eros and Thanatos. Then, at a closer to surface level, but still interior and closely related to the integration of the personality or self, an emergent system of values. These value complexes or value orientations depend both upon innate motivational structure and also upon education and life experience, upon their holder's

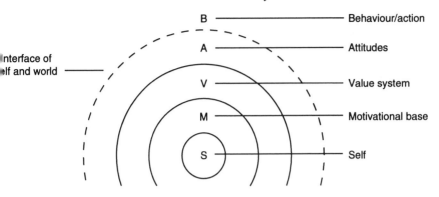

Figure 6.1 Psychological Aspects of Value Action.

circumstances, biology, genealogy, and culture. They may be unconscious and in logical contradiction as, for example, when kindness and honesty are overtly expressed but the ruthless and dishonest acquisition of wealth and status are secretly or subliminally admired. The values are more in number than the motives but less in number than the attitudes. Both, however, are organized more or less cohesively into systems, the degree of cohesiveness being reflected in the integration or strength of the personality. Emergent at the interface of psyche and world are the *attitudes*, expressions of preference and predispositions to act in response to the countless issues of living and life style. They are commensurable in that they can be observed, classified, and organized so as to make conceptual sense and thus lend some element of predictability, albeit probabilistic predictability, to human action. In number they logically exceed the underlying values from which they are psychologically derived. Finally, there is the realm of behaviour and action which is in truth incommensurable because of the infinity of possibilities. This is the domain which is the field of administration, always tense with potentiality and opportunity, always open to the unforeseen, always defying extrapolation and futurology—simultaneously the birthplace of the new and the embodiment of the old.

Behaviours occur as observable facts connected by inference through chains of cause and effect to underlying black-box phenomena of attitudes, value orientations, values, motives, and ego. The schema of Figure 6.1 is not intended to be dogmatic or precise. It does not specify, for example, the locus or function of *will* about which much more shall be said later, nor does it explain how the several components are articulated. But it is pragmatically useful as a descriptive and expository device for the arguments to follow. It postulates a continuum at one end of which are private (but culturally conditioned) value phenomena and at the other end purposive behaviours; strivings taking place in an observable public collective realm from which motives can be spelled out linguistically as goals or collective purposes and from which values can be inferred and expressed verbally as ideas, *summa boni*, social norms, and cultural standards. Such values at the social level may evolve into organized systems of law, codes of ethics, philosophies and ideologies. Between these extremes lie the gamut of attitudes, opinions, preferences. The continuum is dynamic through the action of modulating feedback and feedforward. From its ground in individual consciousness to its revelation in the public play of sensory data the universe is intentional and teleological. Value terminology is our linguistic attempt to express the manifestations of this intentionality.

THE VALUE PARADIGM

Values are subjective because they are concepts. They have to do with the phenomenology of desire. None of these things is simple. Though desire has been much studied, introvertedly by philosophers and artists, extrovertedly by psychologists and social scientists (usually under the head of motivation) we are far from clarity and far from understanding still. Theories ramify and contest with each other. Errors of logical typing and category mistakes abound. Desire manifests itself at different ontological levels and exhibits different relationships to consciousness. It can range from totally unconscious deep psychic drives and complexes to superlatively conscious and highly sublimated intentions of the will. Furthermore, even the concept of *concept* is contentious:[12] it may be vacuous as in *virtus dormitiva* (the power of opium to put people to sleep) or *phlogiston* (the hypothesized explanation of burning before oxidization was understood), or it may be dense with information as with narcosis and oxidization at a later stage of their concept development. Our task with the concept of value as defined so far is to invest it with practical and empirical meaning, to cash it out despite its embeddedness amongst such intractable philosophical difficulties as the mind –brain problem, the existence or non-existence of the "self", and the nature of consciousness and will.[13]

Indeed, given the conceptual difficulties, one might be tempted by Wittgenstein's aphorism, "Whereof one cannot speak, thereof one must remain silent",[14] an utterance often referred to the discrimination of value from fact. But no such resort to silence, however wise for the contemplative, can advance the discourse that is necessary for the field of action. Since Aristotle we have had the notion of *praxis* or *practical* philosophy whereby men, precisely through their actions and administrative efforts, seek to discover and establish the good life. The wonder is that with all the infinite ramifications of complexity and mystery hidden just below the opaque surface of language we can still understand and comprehend with practical simplicity the far from simple notion that "values are concepts of the desirable".

I now wish to present an analytical model of the value concept which can help chart our way across the seas of value confusion. This model is given in Figure 6.2.

The first distinction made in the model is between the RIGHT and the GOOD. This distinction is fundamental and refers to the ontological distinction between

Value type	Grounds of value	Psychological faculty	Philosophical orientations	Value level
I	Principles	Conation willing	religion existentialism intuition	I
IIA	Consequence (A)	Cognition reason thinking	utilitarianism pragmatism humanism democratic liberalism	II
IIB	Consensus (B)			
III	Preference	Affect emotion feeling	postmodernism behaviourism positivism hedonism	III

Right ← → Good

Figure 6.2 The Value Paradigm.

the "desirable" and the "desired".[15] The former is known technically as the deontological (right) while the latter is the axiological (good). The desired refers to what is pleasurable, enjoyable, likable; the desirable to what is proper, "moral", duty bound, or simply what *ought* to be. Good is known directly as a matter of natural preference. We do not need to be told what is good, we already know it. We drink when we are thirsty and prefer beer. Or tea. The knowledge of what is good comes spontaneously from impulse, instinct, or direct introspection. It is a kind of value experience that we share with other animals. It may be innate, biochemical, genetic or it may be learned, programmed, conditioned. The forces of Madison Avenue and of all forms of propaganda work continually upon the malleable aspects. The axiological side of value, being part of our biological endowment, is essentially self-indulgent or hedonistic and can be summed up in the elemental psychology of seeking pleasure and avoiding pain. In the human animal it provides the foundation for a playboy philosophy and a behaviouristic psychology. Translated into a philosophy of liberalism this implies that each can seek to maximize his hedonic satisfaction up to the point where doing so impinges upon the like liberty of another. But this ignores or overlooks the automatic potential for value conflict by way of the general competition for satisfaction from zero sum limited resources. Moreover no one can indulge *all* their desires. On the other hand this value logic apparently relieves non-human animals from "value problems" to the extent that they are "wired" or programmed by evolutionary biological mechanisms. The tigress who sacrifices her life for her cubs is not being altruistic or "moral" but simply doing what she has to do because Nature has contrived this solution to be so desired by tigers. She does *what* she must.

It is the other dimension of value—the desirable or deontological—that really vexes. It is logically quite distinct. Although it would be denied by some philosophers humans are generally understood to have, or at least often claim to have, a distinctive moral sense differentiating them from the rest of the animal kingdom. This faculty, or sense of collective responsibility, or conscience, or superego causes us no end of difficulty and distress. At the personal level it gives rise to internal psychological conflict, tension, and stress whenever the desirable and the desired contend—as when we feel on the one side the pull of affect and on the other the demands of the situation and what ought to be done. The ordinary discipline of daily life continually frustrates our idiographic desires in favour of other more nomothetic demands. It is this superimposition of the nomothetically desirable upon the idiographically desired that gets us out of bed in the morning and makes the trains run on time. It makes duty both a possibility and a reality.

But how is right to be justified over good? Upon what grounds do we override our pressing emotive claims and impulses, our animal selfishness? How can one validate, justify, determine, rank order given concepts of the desirable in given contexts?

The column headed "Grounds of value" in Figure 6.2 classifies the several phenomenological grounds for value judgement and is, so far as I have been able to determine, exhaustive. We can establish or ground our values in one of these four ways and upon these four bases only. If we allow that the value Types IIA (consequential) and IIB (consensual) can be considered as subtypes of a single Type II (rational) category then we have three logically distinctive types of value. Let us consider them in turn.

Type III values are self-justifying since they are grounded in individual affect and constitute the individual's preference structure. Why is *x* good? Because I like it. Why do I like it? I like it because I like it. I cannot go beyond that. Type III values are primitives, facts of nature, justifiable only because the world is what it is and not some other thing. The imponderability of Type III preference is recorded in every language: *de gustibus non est disputandum, chacun à son goût, Es ist bei mir so Sitte*, "There's no accounting for tastes."

Moving upwards in the hierarchy of the paradigm there are three other ways in which a value can be adjudged to be *right*. First, if it concurs with the will of a majority in a given collectivity or context it is grounded in consensus and can be classified as Type IIB. Alternatively, if upon reasonable analysis of the consequences entailed by the pending value judgement, some future resultant state of affairs is held,on balance, to be desirable then it becomes a Type IIA value. Note that Type II values enlist the reason, the cognitive faculty, whether it be to count heads (IIB) or to assess contingencies (IIA); the grounds are both rational and social for they depend upon collectivities and collective justification.

The Type II rationality-of-value occurs, for example, when abortion is declared to be right or wrong because of an expressed social consensus about the issue resulting in a statute or law—the process of this law-making being presumably rational in that it assesses and weighs public opinion and argument through parliamentary and legal channels. Individual preferences (Type III) are here aggregated, averaged, or summed. This is IIB. Type IIA, on the other hand, is a "higher level" of rationality and would obtain if the issue of abortion were to be decided on a cost–benefit analysis: demographic factors and socio-economic costs, for example, being weighed against estimated benefits. In other words a future state of affairs resulting from the value judgement to approve or disapprove of abortion is extrapolated by logical analysis and this state is determined, for policy purposes, to be positive or negative on balance. The analysis of consequences presupposes a social context and a given scheme of social norms, expectations, and standards. If the reasoning is used purely to "figure the odds" for the expedient purpose of maximizing an individual's hedonic satisfaction then this would not be Type IIA but rather Type III value behaviour.

It should be noted that Type IIA values beg (or postpone) the question of grounding since the projected state of desirability must be adjudged in the final analysis either on the grounds of principle (Type I) or consensus (Type IIB), that is, on collective preferential grounds that ultimately (the logical positivist position) can be traced back to individual affect, emotion, or "feeling".

At the apex of the hierarchy of Figure 6.2 are the Type I values. This represents the ultimate level of value. At Level I values are transrational; they go beyond reason. They imply instead an act of faith or intent or will—a *conviction* manifested in the acceptance of a *principle*. Though such principles may often be defended by rational discourse they are essentially metaphysical in origin or location. Often they derive, or it is claimed they derive, from such rationally intractable phenomenological entities as conscience or intuition. Abortion is wrong at this level because Holy Mother Church declares it so. Adultery is wrong because it was so chiselled into the tablets of stone brought down from Mount Sinai. Death for the nationalist terrorist is right and good because he subscribes to the ethic of *dulce et decorum est pro patria mori,* or because Allah has prepared a perfume garden in paradise for martyrs, or because he or she hates the enemy so much that the negative affect is transmuted from Level III to Level I.

Notice that one may or may not have Type I values operative in any given individual or context but that, nevertheless, the resort to a claim of principle is often reserved for the highest and final court of appeal in the attempt to justify or ground a value. Thus in administration there may be organizational loyalty based on affective attachment (III), because of group suasion (IIB), or because of net economic benefits (IIA)—but all of these pale before patriotic commitment to a nation–state organization which can in certain circumstances make the ultimate claim upon the member's life. Such claim could only be grounded on some form of "My country right or wrong" allegiance, that is, transrationally or transcendentally.

Very often Type I principles take the form of ethical codes, injunctions, or commandments such as the Kantian categorical imperative or the Mosaic "Thou shalt not kill" but whether they derive from a postulated moral insight, an essential religious revelation, an aesthetic sense of individual drama, or a sublime or demonic intensification of emotion, their common feature is that they are unverifiable by the techniques of science and cannot be justified by merely *logical* argument. The farthest that rational argument can lead is to an ethic of enlightened self-interest. But this is essentially IIA in grounding, a sort of game theory solution to the problem of maximizing hedonic (Type III) satisfactions. Type I values have, moreover, a quality of absoluteness which distinguishes them from the more selective Type III values. Principles are more meaningful then preferences by several orders of magnitude. Principles and their attendant convictions are also transrational in that, while they *need* not conflict with concerns of rationality they may very well do so and can lead to actions of self-sacrifice (e.g. Kamikaze pilots) which from the Level II standpoint would be considered perverse, irrational, and absurd. The chief characteristic of Type I values is that they are based on the willing rather than the reasoning faculty. Adoption of them implies some kind of act of faith, belief, commitment. That is to say, conviction.

PSYCHOLOGICAL ASPECTS

The column of Figure 6.2 headed Psychological Faculty shows the psychological correspondences for each of the three types and levels of value. Working upwards: Type III values are rooted in the emotional structure; they are affective, idiosyncratic, idiographic, and direct. They are basically a-social and hedonistic. Type II values engage the reasoning faculty; they are pre-eminently rational, cognitive, collective, and social. To the extent that they conflict with and override tendencies to individual indulgence they are disciplinary and nomothetic. They tend in the limit towards an ethic of "enlightened" self-interest or some form of humanistic liberalism, this being as far as logic and the cognitive faculty can go in the determination of an ethical system of cohesive moral imperatives. Type I values invoke the will. They are conative in the strongest sense. An act of faith or commitment is necessary in their activation. Such an act can only be done individually and so Type I values are highly idiographic no matter how much they may be nomothetically endorsed nor how they may be supercharged by ideology.

Some examples. A ballet company pursues aesthetic ideals, a football team is dedicated to winning, a military unit has on its insignia a skull and crossbones with the motto "Or Glory".[16] In each case Type I values are set up which must be individually adopted by the sweating dancer, the battered player, and the bleeding soldier. Dancer, player, and soldier must each, at some point, have made some act of personal commitment to the respective value. If they have not they might still accept the degraded Type I value at the level of consensus (IIB) as the norm or level of expectation peculiar to their respective organizations. Needless to say, there would be change in the quality of commitment in the latter case and administrators would generally prefer to induce the higher level type of engagement in their subordinates. The individual may also *reason* that the only course of action prudent and expedient under the respective circumstances is to dance, play, or fight and the value level shifts to IIA but more than the member's reason must have been involved where Type I values are operative and this *more* is not a simple matter of emotive preference. It invokes a quality of self-sacrifice or self-transcendence, a willingness in the extreme to give one's all for the value at stake. Because of this deontological or duty aspect of value any discussion of the value concept leads easily into questions about the phenomena of loyalty, commitment, guilt, conscience, and responsibility. Such topics are difficult at both the philosophical and psychological levels of analysis but they attend inevitably the distinction between Right and Good and they constitute fundamental components of administrative reality.

PHILOSOPHICAL ASPECTS

Figure 6.2 also encapsulates the main philosophical correspondences under the heading "Philosophical orientations".

Type III values are those which lend themselves to the reductions of logical positivism and behaviorism. In the extreme case it can be argued that *all* values are, in the final analysis, merely expressions of emotive preference.[17] To deduce "Murder is wrong" or "One should not kill" is only to say "Murder, ugh!" or "I do not *like* killing."[18] All levels of value above III can, upon analysis, be discounted as extrapolations of *preference*. Acts of altruism are either manifestations of that actor's preferences or that actor's preferential calculus in a given social context. One may counter that this position simultaneously commits the naturalistic fallacy (*q. v.*) and itself exhibits an emotive preference by elevating logic and science above ethics and values but the strength of the arguments underlying emotivism is not to be underestimated and, in administrative philosophy, the position has been formally adopted by Herbert A. Simon.[19] Moreover at the ethos (V_5) or socio-cultural level the so called playboy philosophy and hedonistic philosophies of self-indulgence generally are consistent with the positivist position. So too are any "me-generation", "self-first", "I'm all right, Jack", or narcissistic value orientations popularly ascribed to the latter decades of this century.[20]

Type II values on the other hand correspond to the broad philosophical categories of humanism, pragmatism, utilitarianism, and democratic liberalism. At this level the move is made from the idiographic to the nomothetic. Contextual values are established and buttressed by the social status quo, the ethos, mores, laws, customs, and traditions of the value context. The fact that these philosophical orientations generally venerate reason and compromise and that they often subscribe to prudence and expediency make them particularly attractive to administrators. One might say, indeed, that level II is *the* modal administrative value orientation.

Type I values, in contrast, have metaphysical or transrational grounds. They are often codified into religious systems, whether sacred as in conventional orthodoxies or secular in political ideologies such as Maoism or Marxist–Leninism. They can also be deliberately irrational or even anti-rational as where the SS recruit swears a blood oath in the forest or where the existentialist convinced that the universe is alien and absurd yet seeks "authenticity" by becoming "engaged" to a self-constructed code of values. Again, to the emotivist or logical positivist such values are literally *non*-sense or at best, high-powered expressions of personal affect. We need not enter the arguments between philosophical schools at this point—our object is only to comprehend the paradigm displayed in Figure 6.2. We may however note that since positivists reject Level I as an autonomous category the adherent of purely rational values (IIA) must walk a razor's edge between the chasms of postmodern fractionated interest (IIB), itself derived from individualistic nihilism (III), on the one side and metaphysical zealotry and fanaticism (I) on the other.

POSTULATES

The paradigm of Figure 6.2 may also be recast as shown in Figure 6.3. From this it becomes obvious that the administrative value paradigm carries with it certain far-reaching implications. These extend both to the problem of the resolution of value conflicts and to the formulation of value theory and philosophical axiology. For example, there is the implication that the value problem is an intrinsic, universal feature of the human condition which is defined by the tension existing between a lower dimension of idiographic indulgence and an upper dimension of self-frustration or denial. Everyone, with the possible exceptions of saints, supermen, and psychopaths experiences this dialectical tension. For the saint it disappears because he *wishes* to do what *ought* to be done—affect and will are unified. For the Nietzschean Superman, as for the common or garden psychopath, ambivalence and tension again vanish for whatever *they* wish is for them *right*. They pass beyond the social categories of Good and Evil. But ordinary people lead lives of inner conflict, they are exposed to the warring clash of moral codes without and to the internal stress between the value dimensions within. This conflict is not simply a matter of the desirable versus the desired. It is as likely to be conflict between two or more desirables or between two or more desireds. We must choose between rights and goods as well as between right and good. Taken together with that continuous 'interplay of interest which is intrinsic to organizational behaviour this value complexity substantiates Barnard's claim[21] that *complex* morality and the *creative* resolution of moral conflict is the chief characteristic of leadership.

The model also suggests three postulates:

Postulate 1: Type I values are superior, more authentic, better justified, and of more defensible grounding than Type II. Likewise Type II are superior to Type III, and the nomothetic or moral dimension to the idiographic or selfish dimension. This may be called the *postulate of hierarchy*.

Postulate 2: Values tend to lower their level of grounding over time. There is a natural tendency (analogous to the Second Law of Thermodynamics) for values to lose their authenticity or force. The force of moral insight attenuates. This may be called the *postulate of degeneration*.

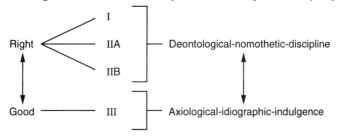

Figure 6.3   The Basic Value Dichotomy.

Postulate 3: There will be a natural tendency to resolve value conflicts at the lowest level of hierarchy possible in a given situation. This is equivalent to seeking the line of least resistance. We seek to avoid higher-level moral issues. This applies particularly in administration and may be called the *postulate of avoidance*.

I will illustrate these postulates by examples from ethics, aesthetics, and administration.

In ethics the notion of adultery as a wrong (and conversely of marital fidelity as a positive good) may originally have been instituted by a creative moral thinker or moral leader on bases of moral insight, intuition, and conviction. In the course of time and with growing public tolerance this institution might degenerate, its original moral force having dissipated, but the value can still be justified on prudential, expedient, pragmatic grounds such as enlightened self-interest or collective well-being; it being argued at the cognitive level, for example, that a society in which adultery is disapproved may be on the whole more stable, functional, and beneficent than one in which it is not. Again, with further passage of time, the force of this cognitive moral reasoning may weaken and degenerate until fidelity or non-adultery becomes a mere norm or social expectation of a waning majority. Finally, all moral force may be spent and the value becomes merely a matter of individual preference. One does one's own thing, subject only to the reality constraints provided by the moral vestiges of marital law and societal norms.

From aesthetics let us take the example of, say, Turner's paintings. These may have been initiated by the artist himself through deep (Level I) insight into nature. He then strove to create representations of these visual, profound conceptions. At first these paintings were neither understood nor appreciated by critics lacking the artist's insights but, with the passage of time they came to be defended at the cognitive or intellectual level (II) by, in this instance, the critic Ruskin. (It is said that the next best thing to genius is being able to appreciate it.) Eventually, larger numbers of aesthetes were persuaded at this level of value (IIA) and then, with the further passage of time Turner became an established aesthetic norm or social convention (art appreciation at Level IIB). Finally, this fashion would also pass and it would come to be argued that Turner's works have value over other works only in accord with individual preference (III) and, ultimately, in the postmodern extreme beauty becomes entirely relative. Nihilistically, everything is now beautiful in its own way (including ugliness). The original Type I vision is no longer transmitted even dimly through the intellect (IIA) or the lenses of social convention (IIB) but, if at all, darkly through idle and fleeting preference (III).

From administration we can take the example of what has been called "the principle of least principle".[22] Blacks marching against housing discrimination or perceived racism (Level I morality—ethical issues) can be arrested or diverted on the grounds of traffic obstruction (a relatively trivial level II norm). Likewise a cheating student can be dismissed on the grounds of non-payment of fees thus avoiding any "moral issue". Or a commitment to open administration (I) suddenly becomes closed by way of perceived expedient reasons for secrecy (IIA) which then are later window-dressed through manipulative group consensus dynamics and dramaturgy (IIB) and ultimately abandoned to the individual whim of administrator and manager (III). More generally, we can state that it is an aim of bureaucracy to rationalize and routinize procedures for the resolution of value issues at the level of least organizational cost. The rationale of this administrative–managerial preference for the avoidance of moral issues or the side-stepping of contests of principle is that lower-level value conflicts may be amenable to compromise and persuasion whereas higher-level conflicts may be irreconcilable—not just moral but mortal.

FALLACIES

The temptations to fallacious thinking in administration are legion. To be generous this is doubtless attributable to the infinity of dynamic variables with which the practitioner must cope and which the organization theorist must somehow attempt to comprehend but the ground becomes more slippery yet when one enters the domain of value logic. Among the many traps to be avoided in this difficult intellectual territory we can single out and label four of the most conspicuous.

1. The Naturalistic Fallacy

The Cambridge philosopher G. E. Moore, author of the Edwardian classic *Principia Ethica,* is to be credited with showing that notions of the good are irreducible primitive terms and *sui generis.* In the end good can only be defined in its own terms. It is unanalysable and, therefore, values are of a different ontological category from facts. No facts, nor indeed any amount of facts or factual information, can *prove* a value. Or, in Popper's famous phrase, You can't get an *ought* from an *is.*[23]

Administrators, like lawyers, are particularly given to consulting the facts of the case. They would very much like to get an ought from an is. But the world of fact cannot of itself yield any value other than that which is projected or super-imposed upon it. The world of facts is *given,* the world of values *made.* A thing is but a thing, an event but an event. Yet because values are inseparable from facts in experience and so constitute a sort of psycho-social set of facts in themselves the problem is subtle and complicated. The temptation is ever present to deduce the values from the facts and so commit the naturalistic fallacy. Nor can administrators, being men of action, avail themselves very much of Wittgenstein's suggestion of silence. They are forced to speak from time to time as well as to utter value judgements, if not in speech then in action—but they must beware the temptation to derive their subjectivities ("oughts") from their objectivities ("is's"). Values are certainly inextricably intertwined with facts but this does not mean that there is any intrinsic or causal relation between the two categories.[24]

2. The Homogenetic Fallacy

Even when values are carefully discriminated from facts there remains the potential error of treating values as if they were all of a kind, homogeneous. As the value paradigm reveals to the contrary values are themselves amenable to hierarchic analysis. They are heterogeneous by rank. When this hierarchical distinction is confused or forgotten the homogenetic fallacy occurs. Values are not all of a kind. Two men may both subscribe to the value of honesty but the one's candor may be the other's lies. One may have a sentiment for his native country but another may be prepared to die for it. Level I is ontologically distinct from Level III and both from Level II.

3. The Excisionistic Fallacy

This fallacy, as much favored by positivists as by administrators, is the error of appearing to solve or resolve value problems by excising the source of the problem and thus removing the apparent need for its consideration. For example, if the source of a value conflict can be traced to a particular organization member then that member can be transferred, removed, promoted, side-pocketed, or expelled from the organization altogether. A delusory appearance of having resolved the value issue is thus created. Nothing is said to the *truth* of the rights or wrongs of a case by the mere exercise of power. The occluded offender may have been right, may have been wrong. Removal speaks to neither possibility, it simply exhibits the distribution of power among the value actors. The root value question is not addressed, it is avoided. Burying Lenin neither invalidates nor validates his ideology.

4. The Militaristic Fallacy.

This fallacy, itself a version of excisionistic thinking, is named after its most obvious devotees. It occurs when ends or terminal values are radically divorced from means or instrumental values, often to the point where the former are lost sight of through preoccupation with the latter. It conflates the ethical error of the ends justifying the means and the vulgar concept, not peculiar to sports, that "winning is everything". The fault is by no means confined to the military, however, and can as easily be ascribed to technological, bureaucratic, political, commercial, scientific, and systems thinking generally insofar as all these orientations share a propensity to factor, fractionate, and atomize problems into means–ends chains. In doing so the proximate devours the ultimate. Within administrative philosophy the position is exemplified by Simon and the logical positivists[25] and wherever administrative value questions are presumed not to exist by virtue of all critical values having been predetermined extraneously by putative policy makers. The countervailing position is that value problems pervade all organizations throughout all levels of the authority hierarchy. Excessive rationality and its attendant value myopia or anaesthesia becomes a pathology, a sort of fascism of the intellect wherein value sensibilities are attenuated or eliminated by an inappropriate military dressage. The Holocaust of the 1940s is only the cruellest example of this fallacy at work.

* * *

These four fallacies do not exhaust the possibility of error. They have been selected from a potential universe of errors in value logic because of their peculiar salience in administration and their special relevance to organizational life. It would be fair to assert that each is committed with greater or lesser degrees of severity many times each day in the average executive's life. Most often, if not invariably, the error is unconscious. To achieve a constant level of awareness of these temptations would represent an incalculable advance in administrative philosophy. In the advance towards that degree of sophistication the first step is recognition and the second, understanding.

METAVALUES

A metavalue is a concept of the desirable so vested and entrenched that it seems to be beyond dispute or contention. It may thus pass unnoticed as an unspoken or unexamined assumption into the value calculus of individual or collective life. Examples of metavalues would be health or life itself. In a democratic society democracy is a metavalue. Amongst academics education and rationality are common metavalues. It is not so much that metavalues are absolute or quasi-absolute that makes them problematic as that they go, for the most part unquestioned, implicitly unproblematic, *beyond* value and so they intrude unconsciously and continuously to affect value behaviour. Amongst them we may distinguish some of the principal organizational metavalues. These include maintenance, growth, efficiency and effectiveness.

Maintenance

If the first law of nature be self-preservation then the first law of organizations is likewise to survive, to maintain themselves. This is most palpable in new and emergent organizations but when an association, organization, firm or institution has become established and apparently secure then the level of consciousness of this value recedes. It does not disappear, however. Organizations do not question their need to be because the desirability of their existence is an a priori given. The metavalue manifests in the principle of organizational and group loyalty. New members are rapidly indoctrinated to a perception of themselves as "us" and a correlative perception of non-members as "them". Threats to the collective interest or security may cause the level of consciousness of this metavalue to rise. It can also be assumed that the maintenance of the organization is pre-eminent in the motivational complex even though irrational responses may lead to dysfunctional effects. Thus a trade union, for example, may put itself and its employers out of business by killing the goose that lays the eggs but this merely shows the distinction between factual "rationality" and valuational transrationality or subrationality.

Katz and Kahn put it this way:

> Since any organization must survive in order to carry out its basic functions, survival becomes a salient goal for organizational decision makers. [Dynamic forces generated by maintenance structures] have as their implicit, and sometimes explicit, goal the survival of present organizational forms. For many administrators and officials, concern with the preservation of the bureaucracy assumes primary significance. Indeed, the term bureaucracy is often used, not in the Weberian sense, but in the sense of an officialdom absorbed only in the preservation of its structure and in the ease of its own operation.[26]

For the administrator it goes without saying (is beyond value question) that the first duty is to maintain the organization. Without an organization there is nothing to administer. None of which denies the occasional necessity to eliminate dysfunctional subsystems—acts of maintenance surgery that merely reinforce the maintenance metavalue from the leadership standpoint.

This metavalue is a fundamental part of the administrator's value orientation. It is ineluctably nomothetic. To escape it one would have to ask the unaskable question, Should my organization exist?

Growth

The second metavalue is a logical corollary of the first. Organizations seek to expand both by the dynamics of competition and by way of insurance against future downsizing. Resources are always limited, change and flux are unpredictable, and growth augments the possibility of environmental control. The metavalue applies within organizations as well as without and the study of bureaupathology is replete with instances of dysfunction traceable to this metavaluational impulse.

Barnard observed that "The maintenance of incentives [...] calls for growth, enlargement, extension. It is, I think, the basic and, in a sense, the legitimate reason for bureaucratic aggrandizement in corporate, governmental, labor, university, and church organizations everywhere observed. To grow seems to offer opportunity for the realization of all kinds of active incentives—as may be observed by the repeated emphasis in all organizations upon size as an index of the existence of desirable incentives, or the alternative rationalization of other incentives when size is small or growth often so upsets the economy of incentives, through its reactions upon the effectiveness and efficiency of organization, that it is no longer possible to make them adequate."[27]

Note that the status of this second metavalue is less secure than the first. It is acknowledged in Barnard's quotation that bigness of itself does not always provide the necessary and sufficient conditions for goodness, or even for maintenance. It is understood that excessive growth can be dysfunctional. Facile biological and evolutionary analogies are sometimes made to cancer and to dinosaurs but the metalogic of survival continues to support placing as many bulwarks as possible between prey and predator, target and threat. Many subordinates mean more protective cover, sacrificial cover if need be. And organizational expansion, even in non-threatening supportive environments, serves to preclude the birth or growth of potential competitors. Growth implies power (itself an administrative metavalue). To gain power is both an administrative and an organizational reflex. It is metavaluational. Perhaps *mega*valuational.

Effectiveness

Effectiveness is the accomplishment of desired ends. An organization is effective if it can achieve its purposes, what in personal terms is called success (though here with overtones of fame, prestige, and power) is in organizational terms called effectiveness. As a metavalue it is tautologous for it simply means the desirability of accomplishing desired ends and, because of this tautological quality, it goes unexamined: Who seeks ineffectiveness?

The only way in which the metavalue can be challenged or raised in consciousness is by an examination of latent functions. These are the unforeseen, unintended, or unpredictable consequences of any means–end chain of action initiated by the pursuit of goals. They are to be contrasted with the manifest or declared functions associated with the same goals. Paradoxically (or hypo-critically) latent functions may subvert the manifest as when, say, a conference has as its manifest function the reading and discussion of presented papers but this function is valuationally outweighed by the latent functions of social intercourse, interaction, intelligence exchange, and "networking". Here the metavalue of effectiveness remains operative but just what is meant by goal achievement is ambiguous and ambivalent. The metavalue is tautologically incontestable but awareness of it can give rise to important administrative questions about the sought and unsought consequences of the ends of action.

Efficiency

The concept of efficiency has caused some confusion in the classical literature because of its idiosyncratic interpretation by Barnard who related it to the satisfaction of individual motives. Organizations were for him efficient to the extent that they succeeded in eliciting individual cooperation. The efficiency of a cooperative system would be its capacity to maintain itself by the individual satisfactions it affords.

More conventionally the idea of efficiency is essentially the ratio of output to input. In an imperfect universe this is always less than unity. Engineering technology seeks to maximize such efficiency. Accounting measures of efficiency such as profit and loss statements are essential to commerce, trade, and industry. More generally the primary economic fact of life is the scarcity of resources. The consciousness of this reality underlies all administrative decision making and establishes a criterion of choice wherein one seeks the largest result or pay-off for any given application of resources. I shall take the term efficiency in this ordinary sense and consider it a metavalue because, on the face of it, no administrator would consciously choose, *ceteris paribus,* the less efficient of two alternatives. But let us scrutinize this basic administrative assumption.

Efficiency entails that (a) given alternative means with the same cost attaching to each means one will seek the maximum return, that is, maximization of ends; or (b) given alternative goals with the same end value one will choose ends so as to minimize the cost of means. In both (a) and (b) there are two possible sources of fallacy: the one having to do with the meaning and specification of costs and the other with the meaning and specification of goals or ends. In each case there are major conceptual and philosophical obstacles which include the incommensurability of quantity and quality, the imponderability of value and intentional factors in decision making, and the problem of ascertaining all cost and benefit functions. Efficiency as a metavalue is applied forward, to the future; but as a value it is measured backwards, in regard of the past. We fly first and pay later. Perhaps this explains why so much inefficiency is to be observed in all organizations despite the universal subscription to the metavalue. Again the metavaluation is incontestable. Administrators cannot choose to value inefficiency but can probe, if they wish, the devious and sometimes intractable implications of the efficiency metavalue itself.

Others

The four metavalues described above do not exhaust the list of candidates for such status. Rationality, especially in bureaucratic–technocratic–legalistic societies is another prime contender. It is, however, subsumed within the efficiency and effectiveness metavalues. Power has already been analysed at the personal level as an administrative metavalue. Conceivably human security is a near metavalue at least in non-military organizations. Others may occur to the reader. Nevertheless the four *organizational* metavalues: maintenance, growth, efficiency and effectiveness can be safely declared as fundamental to the value bases of organization and, because they are so universal and fundamental, because they so easily pass unquestioned and unexamined, they constitute the essential value *character* of organizational life. They are thus determining factors in any administrative philosophy.

THE PARADIGM AND MOTIVATION

If there is one concept which can compete with value in generating intellectual distress and philosophical confusion it is probably that of motivation. In the organizational literature much theorizing and endless empiricizing has been devoted to this topic.[28] It constitutes the theme and focus of much of the journal literature and dwarfs by comparison the study of values. Indeed it tends to overshadow to the point of invisibility the topic of ethics and morals for administrative aspirants, theorists, and practitioners.

This is probably because behavioural science is more at ease with a concept like motivation that has a strong connotation of driving or being driven (and hence a suggestion of determinism) than with a concept like value which, sooner or later, implies a freedom of actors to choose, and hence introduces a factor of uncertainty and indeterminism antagonistic to any project of predictive science. But we must be wary of the lust for simplification, the tendency to reduction in explanation, and the homogenetic fallacy. Human nature is mixed. It is obviously susceptible to much motivational determinism; it can often be overdetermined; but still it retains the possibility of being free.

The value paradigm subsumes and transcends motivational analysis. It permits us to dispense with the motivation terminology. This is so because motivation can be treated as a *source* of values. A fund from which concepts of the desirable can be drawn, or a spring from which they can be thought to well up. Thus Type III values may derive from the unconscious dynamics of depth psychology. Or from simple hedonics—the innate tendency to seek pleasure and avoid pain. Type II values can flow from the "motivation" to rational analysis or collective judgement much of which, if not all, may indeed be social conditioning. And Type I values can be said to emerge from a uniquely human motivation towards transrational commitment.

Again, to take the Freudian obsession, there is no question about the omnipresence of the primal sexual urge. But this motivational drive can translate out at all levels of the desire paradigm: as hedonic gratification (Level III), as all manner of stylized mating behaviours from sock hops to debutante's balls (Level IIB), as legalized prostitution (Level IIA), and as the practice of clerical celibacy (Level I). It should be clear from this illustration alone that the concept of motivational impulse *per se* is not refined enough for value analysis, it is too coarse-grained and, at the most general level, this critique can be launched against all the grand reductionists in motivational theory. Marx and Freud committed the homogenetic fallacy. So too, perhaps, did Weber. In the last analysis all is neither sex, nor wealth, nor property, nor reason though the drives associated with each unquestionably provide us with primary and major sources of our complex value orientations and patterns of the desirable. In the rest of this book motives can be taken as subsumed, implicitly, or explicitly, within the concept of values.

A further complexity arises, however, from the conventional notion, widespread in the literature, that it is the administrator's responsibility to "motivate" his subordinates. The leader's task is often seen as that of maintaining a kind of hedonic balance of trade within his organization or, as Barnard put it, maintaining an economy of incentives such that organization members would choose to remain in rather than leave the cooperative system.[29]

There is truth to this picture of organizational life in much the same way as there is truth to the principles of economic science, but the realities frustrate simplistic explanation: Given a real freedom to move between and within organizational envelopes (wherein we have our administered being) there would certainly be an inter- and intra-organizational market of motivational forces tending always toward some hypothetical state of equilibrium at which the motivational price tag for any given class of organizational member, including administrators, could be determined. But the push–pull of affective striving in the organizational market place is a constrained and partial truth. The market is not free. Inelasticities abound. And as the philosopher Barrett has shown, "the sense of meaning is the primary fact in motivation.[30] Moreover, even the motivational literature acknowledges the operative presence of so-called "higher" motivations as exemplified in the work of Herzberg and Maslow.[31]

Maslow's needs theory postulates a hierarchically ordered set of human motivational needs ranging from the lowest level of physiological and security needs through "higher" needs for social acceptance and status on to a "highest" level need for "self-actualization"—a quasi-mystical state of affairs in which "peak experiences" occur and all the potentialities of the individual are maximized. Similarly, though without Maslow's apex of self-actualization, Herzberg distinguishes between lower "hygiene" needs (e.g. supervision, pay, and working conditions) and higher "motivating" needs (promotion, achievement, responsibility, challenge, and the like). The parallel between such motivational schemes and the value-paradigm is indicated in Figure 6.4.

In general the argument of motivational theorists rests upon the assumption, explicitly *hierarchical*, that lower level needs must be satisfied before "higher" level needs can emerge. There is much common sense to this. One cannot be a philosopher while one has a toothache. Needs must when the devil drives, and so on. In the light of the value paradigm, however, the interpretation is more subtle. Here the assumption is rather of tension: continuously between the socially generated Type II values and the individually seated Type III values; occasionally between Type I and lower levels.

With the exception of saints and psychopaths all men experience the first type of phenomenological tension: between what is moral or right or socially approved and what it is that they would rather do. As a rational and social animal man

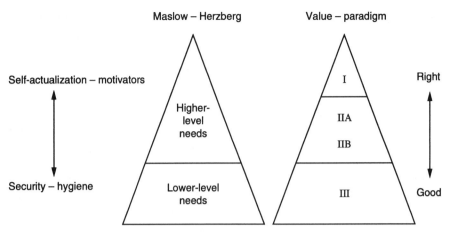

Figure 6.4 The Value Paradigm and Motivational Theory.

constantly experiences the dialectical internal interplay between the affective and cognitive sides of his nature.

The second kind of tension is motivationally more difficult. Type I values are transrational, suprarational, metarational. In theory they need not occur within an individual's value system—on can pass from birth to death without their intrusion—but when and if they do enter an individual's value experience they inform that experience and its associated value system with a power of override. That is, they have a dominant quality of hegemony by which they tend to subordinate, realign, and synthesize lower type values and their contending motivations within the individual form of life. Saul on the road to Damascus experienced what can be called a Type I conversion. The transfiguration on the Mount is an image of such value transcendence and indeed all authentic religious or secular conversions imply an infusion of Type I values and some sort of "transvaluation of values".[32] Albert Speer's initial meetings with Hitler and his ensuing commitment to the Nazi cause is a more ordinary administrative example.[33] Type I values entail deep-seated commitment and powerfully determined motivation. They can, as in terrorist examples, entail the ultimate sacrifice of life itself. When they are present in a field of action the value-calculus is radicalized, polarized, one might say *fanaticized*. Motivation becomes, as it were, supercharged and reason becomes subservient to intuition.

From what has been said it follows that the terminologies of motivation and value are to some extent interchangeable and reinforcing. To avoid confusion, however, the discourse of this text will for the most part be confined to the language of value rather than that of motivation, it being understood that motives are sources or originating factors in our value systems. They can be taken as elements which are subsumed within the general language game of values.

The Paradigm and Weber

Figure 6.5 shows the chief correspondences between the Weberian concept of *rational* value (*Zweck* and *Wert*) and the paradigmatic categories.[34] The parallels are consistent, the most notable exception being the total omission of the Type I level. It is reasonable to speculate that its inclusion would assist in the explication of Weber's difficult rubric of charisma or charismatic leadership and we explore this possibility elsewhere but suffice it to say here that, *mutatis mutandis*, the Weberian interpretation is supportive of the value-paradigm as given.

The conceptual apparatus now provided by this theoretical treatment of values allows us to proceed to a mere concrete and less abstract discussion of the realities of the administrative world.

Value mode	Source	Reflectivity	Logic	Value type
Zweckrational (formal)	Technological considerations	Subjective or objective	Rational	IIA
Wertrational (substantive)	Values, beliefs, attitudes	Subjective	Rational	IIA
Traditional	Traditions, mores	Subjective or reactive	Rational or Irrational	IIB
Affectual	Emotions	Subjective or reactive	Rational or Irrational	III

Figure 6.5   Weberian Analysis (Note the absence of (*Übermenschlich*) Type I values).

PROPOSITIONS

85. The world of fact is given, the world of values made.
86. We discover facts; we impose values.
87. Values are special kinds of facts, but never true or false.
88. The facts and the scenario of events, yield no values at all. But we can project values unto this. That is our will.
89. There is nothing valuable or beautiful or good *out there,* only *in here.*
90. What is good is different from what is right.
91. Desire taints all things; there is no immaculate perception. Desire colours our life. And yet value is other than its field of manifestation. This is a great mystery.
92. Valuation precedes rationality. It pre-empts it. One can only be rational within the limits set by value.
93. Our value system is an expression of our psychological integrity. The more values we sustain the more our need for system.
94. Values stem from the self, from others, and from that which is neither self nor others.
95. Rank is the essence of value; hierarchy is the essence of universal order.
96. Values run down. They are born, live, and die. Like us they are nurtured within the bosom of societies and, like us, finally rejected.
97. Motives are sources of value. They may be in the dark or in the light. In the first case they push us and we call them drives. In the second they pull us and we call them reasons.
98. To approve none of our motives is to be an animal, to approve them all is to be a god. To go beyond approval is to be superman.
99. Pure valuation implies looking at the world and looking at one's looking. Hence valuation is invariably impure.
100. Consciousness and ethics are correlative.

Chapter 7
Organizational Values

The previous chapter has been devoted to establishing the elements of a value theory, universally general but specifically applicable to administrative action and organization life. Of necessity this had to be done in the first instance at a fairly abstract level. It now becomes necessary to examine the value-problem in a more earthy manner and this will be done throughout the remainder of this part of the book. Philosophy as an intellectual activity is often associated with a sort of armchair divorce from the more sordid and pressing realities of everyday life, from the "real world" of which men of affairs are so fond of speaking. But philosophy in this sense is not philosophy of administration; of the latter it can more truly be said that philosophy begins in the dirt and ends in the stars. Or at least the Way of Action might aim at transcendental ends, at ideals generally applauded in the human condition (and sometimes at darker stars not so applauded), whether or not it ever attains to these ends or rises much beyond the mud into which by moral gravity it ever tends to sink. This chapter examines some of the mud that clings so tenaciously to the administrative endeavour. It "begins in the dirt."

Henry James said this, and few have ever said it better. "Life is, in fact, a battle ... Evil is insolent and strong, beauty enchanting but rare, goodness very apt to be weak; folly very apt to be defiant; wickedness to carry the day, imbeciles to be in great places, people of sense in small, and mankind generally, unhappy."[1] Can anyone with the slightest real knowledge of organizational life and politics, of administrative power, interests, and values deny the ring of truth in this? It is not, of course, the *whole* truth but it is a fundamental part of experiential reality, a part we might rather ignore, elide, or forget. Yet anyone visiting the literature of administrative science or organization theory might well naively assume that such unpleasantness does not exist. It is almost as if the executive encounter with ennui, frustration, anger, resentment, envy, hostility, defeat, and occasionally pure evil and malevolence were a chimera. Or else the experience were sufficient unto itself without having also to write about it and incorporate it into an aseptic and technical "value-free" literature.

But the affective experience of life in organizations is in accord with the value-paradigm. At the lowest level this is hedonic, one seeks pleasure and avoids pain. Translated into self-interest this means that leaders and followers seek to maximize their own welfare within the set of game rules or constraints provided by the organization to which they owe putative allegiance and within which they pursue their own interests. If one accepts this assumption—that they are in it for what they can get out of it—then one of the value implications is what might sardonically be called an ethics of the trough. Life, played out through the forms of organizational careers, is a struggle, by hand and mind, of each against all for a better place at the trough, a better share of the rewards–system pie, a ruthless but covert pursuit of self-interest within the organization game, a steady and relentless effort to maximize perquisites, power, and status—ending only with death or demise, i.e. ultimate expulsion from the organization by dismissal or retirement (or else by transfer, voluntary or forced, to another organizational context where the Jamesian battle continues). One could infer from Clausewitze's definition of war as a continuation of policy by other means that the ordinary condition of institutional peace is in fact warfare on a normal scale, but generally unacknowledged as such.

Of course this is oversimplified—one aspect only of the value paradigm has been drawn upon, motives are mixed, and so are morals and ethics; it is all very messy and this gives cause for tender-minded optimism. But, before writing off the negative view as overdrawn, or accusing James of middle-aged anhedonia, or charging the writer with overweening cynicism it might be well to consider the formidable strength of the negative position. Leave aside the arguments from depth psychology, political science, and the historical record. Ignore the Christian dogma that man is born in sin. Instead consider a proposition endorsed by Asiatic millions: the Buddha's First Noble Truth: Life is suffering. To the naive counter that life also contains pleasures and delights outweighing any price of pain the Buddhist would respond that all these apparent pleasures are themselves tainted sources of suffering for they are transient, fleeting, consummated only in the knowledge that they are passing, leaving behind as traces the seeds of painful craving for repetition. It is not without relevance that the Lord Buddha himself commenced his career as an administrative cadet nor that he steadfastly refused to found an organization at the end of his philosophical experiment. Indeed he enjoined his followers against doing so. Notwithstanding, his followers, being lesser men, forthwith proceeded after his death (as did those of Jesus Christ) to found eminently long-lived and successful forms of organization. The point is not to enter into any theological debate, it is only this, that if a degree of unhappiness is the normal human condition then this norm surely deserves administrative recognition. Such recognition is scarcely granted in the literature although Argyris has argued persuasively that human personalities and human organizations are fundamentally incompatible.[2] On the other hand most authorities appear to assume a general benevolence in organizational life.[3] The question thus appears to be moot but, even so, the *moral* problem of the integration of human values, character, and personality into the realities of organizational values and organizational interest remains and deserves scrutiny.

ORGANIZATIONAL IMPRESS

It will be shown in Chapter 9 that organizations can be construed as moral primitives by which is meant that they are without consciousness and will, these latter being terms that can only be attributed to individuals. Only an individual can experience value. Only an individual can *experience*. Only an individual can think and feel. What passes then as group decisions and collective judgements or collective actions are at best quasi-willful and pseudo-conscious. It follows that organizations *qua* organizations cannot be morally responsible. Nevertheless organizations do act in the world and they are collectively more powerful than individuals. Moreover, organizations are collective means for the overcoming and transformation of nature towards a state of civilization and lawful order. Civilization may be a neurosis as Freud claimed or it may even be cities as the Greeks claimed but certainly it is organizations. Whence then corruption? For one thing because of the transmutation of power. Organizations are hierarchical power structures and power in itself can be corrupting. As the philosopher Simone Weil explains:

> Power, by definition is only a means; or to put it better, to possess a power is simply to possess means of action which exceed the very limited force that a single individual has at his disposal. But power-seeking, owing to its essential incapacity to seize hold of its object, rules out all consideration of an end, and finally comes, through an inevitable reversal, to take the place of all ends. It is this reversal of the relationship between means and end, it is this fundamental folly that accounts for all that is senseless and bloody right throughout history. Human history is simply the history of the servitude which makes men—oppressors and oppressed alike—the plaything of the instruments of domination they themselves have manufactured, and thus reduces living humanity to being the chattel of inanimate chattels.[4]

One need only read "leaders and followers" for "oppressors and oppressed" and "organizations" for "instruments of domination" or "inanimate chattels" to have the case, strongly put, for the corrupting capability of organizational entities. And there are other supports for this sort of conclusion. Consider.

The individual experience of organization membership means, even in the very best of worlds, a loss of autonomy. The *soi-disant* voluntary joining of any organization commits the new member to a contract. In exchange for a presumptive net benefit the joiner agrees to forgo certain privileges and liberties such as control over time and form of life. Within the new zone of indifference (Barnard) or zone of acceptance (Simon) the member now obeys without question and ceases to be an effectively free moral agent. The organization impresses *its* values upon the new recruit. To argue that moral autonomy can be restored through critical reflection and review on the part of the member is to miss the whole point of organizational hegemony which is simply to remove the very need for such inefficient, ineffective, dysfunctional and authority-threatening review in the first place. The soldier who takes the King's shilling and buys into a zone of military indifference sells a part of his soul. Or, to put it another way, once in the member is subject to a sort of organizational moral override. Circumstances combine to overdetermine the member's zone of acceptance by way of organizational culture and by both crude and subtle varieties of impress. Constraints multiply. Autonomy diminishes. It will be the rare case (rarer still with ascent of the hierarchy) that the individual is not at some point pushed to or across the zonal boundaries in some sort of moral violation, compromise, or adjustment of Type I or II values. When that occurs one of the easier modes of psychological adjustment is to reduce or eliminate residual value dissonance by conscious or unconscious extension of the area of one's zone of indifference or acceptance. So organizational impress grows until, in the extreme case, it is not mine to question why any more. My organization, like my country, right or wrong!

Both clientele and membership of organizations also experience from time to time the frustrations of perceived lack of consideration for their egos, that is, the impersonality and alienation of bureaucracy in its pejorative common language sense. Certainly this felt impartiality is far from corrupt or evil when, from an objective standpoint, the collective is right and the individual, at best, less right. But it does give rise to such problematics as administrative dispassion and the general void of organizational sympathy. Organizations are not conscious. They cannot feel. Though potent they are faceless. This in turn gives rise to a reaction at the individual level which Thompson nicely labelled *bureausis*.[5] This kind of neurotic response to organizational reality can lead to a variety of dysfunctions including sabotage, vandalism, and aggression. Again the reality is of organizational impress being experienced and interpreted as *oppressive*, even when nomothetically legitimate.

In the executive suite the full force of the amoral aspect of organizational impress is occasionally experienced in the form of Type I conflict. The leader or administrator finds his Type I values threatened or contravened. A choice is imminent between fighting the organization or leaving it and a stand must be taken. "Here I stand," as Luther remarked after nailing his theses to the church door. Such a reality (one might call it the Mutiny Point) is to be dreaded and avoided by organizations and their leaders for the consequences can be tragic and traumatic. Organizations may break and leaders may lose or gain their souls. Yet this Level I outcome of organizational impress is of necessity rare in comparison to the common, everyday realities of moral disintegration at the lower levels of the paradigm. The day-to-day pressures of group decision making, the arm-twisting, head-nodding, and eye-winking that would surely contribute to moral queasiness were they not so easily excused by the bromides of the pragmatic "real world": Don't rock the boat. Don't make waves. If you can't beat 'em, join 'em. Look out for number one, get through the day.

The accomplishment of organizational goals is inevitably accompanied by unforeseen side-effects of process which may be either benevolent or malevolent as well as side-effects of product which likewise may be good or bad. Purposive actions are like drugs; there are always side-effects, and these are compounded as the field of action extends and as organizational complexity increases. The inevitable trade-off for general efficacy in goal accomplishment is some loss of human quality in the work-place. At its worst this loss can be psychologically destructive (stress, burn-out, violence) but more probably it is simply psychologically (and morally) abrasive. This abrasion and wearing down of soul is in proportion to the degree that organizations approach their limit as morally primitive, goal-seeking golems.[6]

ORGANIZATIONAL INTEREST

Scott and Hart have shown how modern complex organizations are increasingly dominant in our lives and have analysed the concept of the organizational imperative.[7] This can be specified by way of two propositions and three ethical values. The first proposition is "Whatever is good for the individual can only come from the modern organization", that is, individual welfare depends upon collective effort and, hence, the second proposition, "All behaviour must enhance the health of such organizations." This implies, among other things, the loyalty of organization members to organization leadership.

The three ethical rules derived or deduced from the propositions are:

1. The rule of rationality. (Administrators must seek to maximize efficiency and effectiveness.)
2. The rule of stewardship. (Administrators owe primary loyalty to the organization and its structure.)
3. The rule of pragmatism. (Administrators must be expedient and must focus on short-term reality to the exclusion of long-term idealism—it's the short run that counts.)

Scott and Hart argue that these philosophical components are now entrenched in American administrative culture. (They can be traced both to the American mode of philosophy known as pragmatism and to the great influence of John Dewey in the interbellum era.[8]) The characteristics of this administrative culture are a deep-seated "anti-intellectual" or "anti-romantic" commitment to rationality, managerial efficiency, organizational culture, in-group cohesion, and pragmatic factoring of problems down to the engineering or technical level. In short, a massive shift away from leadership towards the managerial end of the spectrum. Individualistic values are discounted in favour of beliefs in human malleability, obedience, individual dispensability and disposability, specialization, planning, and paternalism. The organizational interest becomes materialistic, positivistic, conformist, scientific–technological, legal–rational–bureaucratic, and consumerist. The emergence and development of high-tech microchip infrastructure can only serve to underwrite and exacerbate such a value orientation at level V_3.

The general thesis of organizational interest or imperative is largely support-ed by some empirical research that would not now be tolerated under contemporary ethical norms: the famous series of experiments conceived and conducted by Professor Milgram.[9] In these experiments naive subjects admini-stered electric shocks to a supposed victim upon the command of various authorities ("leaders") acting under a variety of organizational conditions. The research showed quite conclusively that the willingness to obey authority figures was much greater than had been supposed. The zones of indifference and acceptance were substantially large, administrators had a most significant power base by sheer virtue of role, and the overriding of ordinary moral scruples could easily be accomplished in an organizational context. Conflating differences across experiments, approximately two-thirds of all subjects committed—in the organizational interest—acts of violence upon their fellows that would normally be considered intolerable. Pessimists about human nature will therefore be tempted to deplore the fact that two-thirds appeared to be without conscience while optimists will rejoice that one-third did resist the organizational impress.

Professor Milgram himself concluded that the experiments were evidence of an *agentic state*. This is a psychological set or condition into which subordinates rapidly fall when placed within the context of formal organization. It is a condition of propensity to obey and willingness to be commanded. The organizational interest is assumed as a metavalue. All that seems to be required is that the trappings and attitudes of authority be appropriately presented. These would include all the outward and visible signs of formal organization, symbols and badges of rank or status, a hierarchy of command, power, and authority—even the mere capacity to assume an authoritative posture and speak with an authoritative voice. The leader need only act as if in command. Man falls easily into the agentic state because, it can be supposed, the history of the species has time and again reinforced the greater survival capacity of the collective over that of the individual. Bioethical advantage resides in submission to authority and organizational interest requires such submission. This interest is also the larger interest of civilization. *Ordnung regiert die Welt.* Our entire culture rests upon a presumption of legitimacy in our institutions. These institutions and their component organizations from superstates down to tribes and families are the constituents of our social reality and, hence, all formally identified functionaries from meter maids to kings induce a spontaneous reflex of subservience. Ordinary language too reveals itself in the ancient and modern honorifics attached to organizational roles; My Lord, His Honour, Your Excellency, the chief executive officer (CEO), the second-in-command (2IC), President, Boss. This primal subservience tendency is of great significance for those concerned with the actual design of power–authority systems, that is, administrators. Agentic state is a factor in any such design. In the event of emergency or threat to organizational survival the factor can assume overdetermining if not overwhelming proportions. This can be most clearly observed under wartime conditions when the larger interest of the state frequently suspends or overrides individual liberties and rights, conscripting citizens into service and commandeering property, wealth, and even life itself.

It is easy then to accept authority, easy to present a façade of authority, easier to obey than disobey, easy to seduce into commitment and easier to be seduced, easier to slip by stages from passivity and condonation into the line of least resistance, to the compromise of reason and principle to, in the end, active participation in organizational wrongdoing, malevolence, and evil. And easiest of all is to overlook the existence of this slippery slope for not to see it at all is a standard ego defence mechanism. All the more therefore that administrators ought not to ignore it. It is but one of many pathologies of organizational interest to which they should become sensitive (see Chapter 10). Those positive qualities of human nature that, at the V_1 or V_5 levels we wish to preponderate over the negative may be modulated through organizational interest (V_3). Because organizations are themselves foci and repositories of power, property, and status men and women compete for these goods both through organizational means and through their interpretation of organizational interest. What may be overlooked in such pursuits is the autonomous or unconscious capacity of the organizational interest to subvert or pervert individual ends.

ORGANIZATIONAL DISVALUE

Human organizations are entities whose necessary and sufficient conditions are purposes, people, and processes. Not one of these conditions is value neutral. More, these collectivities, to survive, have to be efficacious[10] which is but another way of saying that they are underwritten by a will to power, however complex and mysterious this will might be and wherever it might reside. This "will", itself the motive force of a value, can generate disvalue. It is unnecessary to invoke Nietzsche's doctrine of the will to power[11] or to refer back to Weil's remarks on power earlier;[12] it is enough to assert that the larger will of the corporate body can conflict with the smaller component wills of its individual members. When this happens it is felt by those members as oppression.

Organizational oppression is an aspect of organizational life more ubiquitous and omnipresent than the technical literature would indicate. It is not the *only* aspect but it is an aspect of especial interest to administrative philosophers and all the more so for the persistence of the myth or false ideology or mode of political correctness expressed in the assumption that "we are all honourable men". On the contrary the encyclopedia of leadership incompetence, malfunction, and outright malevolence runs the range from managerial lapse to administrative inhumanity. Example of the former: A snow plough is ordered to clear the runway, the sense being to *get off* the runway; the snow plough operator interprets it as get the *snow* off the runway; a plane crash results; lives are lost—true case. Example of the latter: the "final solution" of the Jewish question at the Wannsee Conference—true case.

Administration is constrained always by the factors of time and confidentiality. It is widely accepted that both managers and administrators are busy men of affairs with heavy workloads and often overfull schedules and calendars.[13] Whether or not such a burden, pace, and rhythm really and truly ought to be can be questioned. Even in the last century a philosopher famously referred to our living "in the midst of an age of 'work,' that is to say, of hurry, of indecent and perspiring haste, which wants to 'get everything done' at once. ..."[14] But the reality of time lines, time constraints, and executive pressure, enhanced no doubt by the communications technology of the late twentieth century, conduces to effective superficiality and its corollary, secrecy. Proper and adequate time and energy are not devoted to problems, proposals, projects, personnel. Instead there is the dramaturgy and illusion of concern. Bad policies, plans, decisions, and actions frequently result—bad not merely in the organizational sense of inefficient and ineffective but bad in the ordinary moral sense. Neither the organizational nor the larger interests are served. Leadership is deluded into believing that it has an adequate grasp of the subtleties and complexities of the problem situation. Examples from the realm of foreign policy politics abound and in the military a brilliant and sustained illustration of the pathology is given in Solzhenitsyn's *August 1914* where a staff officer reveals the unwitting inadequacies of his superiors and of the entire administration.

Since superficiality cannot be openly acknowledged, elaborate organizational devices are created to hide the disvalue behind the value of *competence*. Screens of secretarial and support staff, praetorian guards of lieutenants and assistants, façades of pomp and circumstance, proper channels and due process, enable the chief executive officer to project the image of gravity necessary to assure any naive enquirer that all is known that is to be known and all is being done that is to be done. But to maintain this appearance it is necessary to have a system of organizational confidentiality and administrative secrecy. The emperor must not reveal his nakedness. Administration has its inevitable freemasonry. Communications have to be passed in the faith that discretion will be exercised. Sometimes this is done overtly, "Eyes only", "Strictly between you and me", "Not for the record", but often it occurs casually, spontaneously, and tacitly—in the corridor, in telephone talk, in a moment snatched on the staircase or at the beginning or ending of a meeting, in informal contacts at conference or convention. Thus networks operate and thus the goodwill and trust necessary to organizational functioning is built. The explicit values are collegiality, loyalty, reciprocity. The implicit disvalues are deceit, treachery, suspicion, and conspiracy. Moreover, there is the danger that communication which passes in this way tends to be superficial and fact-deficient even if only because of the constraints of time and executive scheduling. And the danger in *this* is that the information passes on into decision making as a determining value factor. In such ways careers can be determined and fates decided in a furtive or casual or mindless manner. Hannah Arendt has written about the banality of evil and the phrase applies with force to many of the informal exchanges, especially about personalities, which are so common and so functional a part of organizational life that they are simply taken for granted. Often, too, there is a sort of robust macho quality (applicable across genders) to these exchanges which cements the understanding that they occur between hard-nosed movers and shapers of the world, a tough-minded elite without pretensions to intellectualism or culture— these being effete mysteries leading only to administrative impotence and futility. Those who can do, those who can't, think.

It also can be assumed that executives are typically ambitious. This attribute is not only condoned, it is deemed necessary and is even admired provided that its manifestation is palatably disguised. Naked hunger for power and advancement must be suitably clothed in socially approved rhetoric. Clever ambition requires social skills and the ability to read or sense values from V_1 to V_6 and Type I to Type III. It also requires a modicum of aggression. Modern organizational and social norms require the concealment of the latter in formal discourse. A persona or figure of calm or "cool" is considered admirable no matter what the churnings underneath. Yet the luxury of indulging personal animosities is also one of the concomitants of power and the exercise of aggression can take many forms, from golf to golden handshake. As Herman Melville remarked, "Who has but once dined his friends, has tasted whatever it is to be Caesar." Administrative reality commits its actors to much dining, and much besides food to digest.

One is obliged to note, however, that while administrative careerism can be interpreted in the negative (Machiavelli makes the classic case) conventional organizational thought tends by and large to adopt a passive neutrality or else a positive view. The contemporary classic by Professor Self on public administration[15] takes this position and discounts careerism as an organizational disvalue or dysfunction. Weil, on the contrary, as always perceives the evil in hierarchy and argues that "... the powerful obtain through persuasion what they are totally unable to obtain by force, either by placing the oppressed in a situation such that they have or think they have an immediate interest in doing what is asked of them, or by inspiring them with a fanaticism calculated to make them accept any and every sacrifice ...".[16]

In Weil's terms oppressed is synonymous with subordination. But need this entail *dis*value? Since an organization is merely an instrumentality towards some hypothetical larger good (the organization's goals) does it not follow that its *internal* instrumentality, that is, leadership and followership; subordinates and superordinates, are not each and all invested with a measure of this good? Yes, at a V_3 level of reasoning. Alas! more often no at the V_1 level. Psychologically— as opposed to logically—the human organization member resists his self-effacement in a hive, Japanese salarymen and assembly line workers not excepted. Alienation, loss of meaning, frustration, resentment, stealing, soldiering, sabotage, even death from overwork (a peculiarly Japanese phenomenon) can result. Clinically, these few examples of a much larger catalogue of organizational disvalues can be treated as the occasional and undesirable "side-effects" of misalignment of organizational and individual interests, malfunctions in the Barnardian economy of incentives—a malaise to be remedied by appropriate therapy—but philosophically the problem is more intractable. Administratively the question embraces all the aspects, known and mysterious, of motivation and all the arts, intuited and acquired, of reconciling the nomothetic and idiographic dimensions. But whether we approach the problem from a philosophical, a psychological, an administrative, or even a managerial perspective it is self-evident that any analysis, any resolution, must be grounded in a *realistic* understanding of organizational life.

ORGANIZATIONAL REALITY

To ask about the nature of reality is equivalent to asking the question posed by a Roman administrator, Pontius Pilate, What is truth? But, metaphysical and arcane though they may seem to be, such questions are very much alive in what is sometimes supposed to be that most eminently practical of fields, administration. A protracted and at times heated debate persists in organization theory about the ontological foundations of the discipline. The extremes of argument extend from positivistic naturalism to phenomenological idealism[17] with a middle ground represented by American pragmatism.[18] A scrutiny of the contents of *Administrative Science Quarterly* over the last quarter-century would also reveal a discernible shift from quantitative empiricism to qualitative studies, the latter ranging from the linguistic to the psychoanalytic. In essence, the debate contrasts the objectivist to the subjectivist or perspectivist standpoints. The factual-orientation of the former appeals to the scientific proclivity and asserts that organizational reality exhibits qualities of order, structure, determinism, consistency, and predictability within which laws can be discovered and the control of human groups achieved. The values orientation of the latter appeals to the affective proclivity and challenges the aforementioned qualities as a set of super-impositions (the social construction of reality) behind which there is an imponderable and unique individual existential reality that ultimately elides deterministic manipulation. The former subscribes to the possibilities of social engineering; the latter to the potency of individual meaning in collective existence.

It must be admitted that this argument about reality returns us to the problematics of will. But once admit free will into the scheme of things, to however slight and proscribed a degree, and the camel's head is within the tent. Soon one must seek in human affairs—and what is administration if not human affairs—a moral as well as a scientific order. It follows that the control of men by Man can never be fully achieved and that the ultimate goals of collective endeavour are precarious, always liable to subversion from the group to the individual, especially the individual in the mode of *leader.* *Self*-control, wisdom rather than knowledge, philosophy rather than science may then be implicit in the grand aim of administration. But in the extremes one side of the reality debate leads to general systems theory and neo-scientific management while the other leads towards unclear methodologies and vague humanistic outcomes; the one dispenses with the value problem in administration as Simon, Katz and Kahn, and the systems theorists generally have done, the other remains profoundly bothered by problems of will, choice, and morality.[19]

One can infer from this that the simplest truth about reality—organizational or otherwise—is that it is not simple. Greenfield cites Ortega y Gasset, "Reality happens to be, like a landscape, possessed of an infinite number of perspectives, all equally veracious and authentic. The sole false perspective is that which claims to be the only one there is."[20] He then goes on to sow the seed of synthesis by asserting [that]

> What is real depends upon the assumptions we make about reality and the way we *want* to look at it. One truth of one way of looking at the world does not *necessarily* deny another *seemingly* opposing truth, for the truths of values and ideas do not exist in an external, independent condition. Such truths are subjective realities that depend upon human belief and action; they have force only as we strive to create them, to *realize* them by *imposing* them upon the world around us. There is a world out there that we do not control and there are certainly other people too whom we do not control, though often we strive to do so. The alternative view holds that the individual is the ultimate building block—the atom—of organization. This view holds too that environment is simply the reflected image of other organizations. Organization and environment are two sides of the same coin and both are created out of human ideas and effort.[21] (My italics.)

Because of this logical and psychological complexity contemporary thought in organizational theory is not only given to polemic but is also suffused with category mistakes[22] and the confusion of logical types. The value paradigm offers a way out of this morass in that it implies a triplex rather than a dualistic analysis. Reality may be considered as a conflation of three logically distinct categories. We may assign numbers to these categories so as to correlate them with the value types. Reality III would then represent the empirical domain of science, the deterministic world of matter and substance, cause and effect, the world of hard edges, tangibilities, and the stuff and furniture of the senses, mechanics, technology, and engineering. Here propositions can be predictive and falsifiable, taking the form of laws such as $I = E/R$ or $E = mc^2$ or Falling bodies accelerate at 32 feet per second squared. It is a reality we all have to live in and, generally, the more natural science can tell us about it the better. Our sense of control over nature depends upon the body of knowledge as construed by science at any given historical time. It represents our reality parameters, our temporarily immutable *givens*.

The second reality, reality II, would be the appropriate province of social science. Here propositions are less rigorously shaped, more probabilistic, cast in such forms as "Organizations which have a high degree of goal specificity will have a greater degree of effectiveness than organizations which have a low degree of goal specificity." Or "$B = f(P, E)$": "Behaviour is a function of personality and environment", or "If I fail to pay my workers they will eventually cease to render organizational services." In this reality there are no rigidities, only discernible tendencies and correlations. It is described by statistical inductions and it admits of degrees of freedom; its realm is therefore only partly determined a priori (though a posteriori all events can in principle be explained deterministically). This reality is therefore opaque and the propositions of its language can be called hypothetical or tentative—suggestive rather than dogmatic. Nevertheless, as with the Reality III in which it is embedded and by which it is constrained, the more propositions, verified or unfalsified, that social science can deliver the better for our sense of administrative and organizational control.

Finally we must acknowledge a Reality I, the perspectivist subjective phenomenological realm of individual *experience*. This internal realm of meaning admits of imagination, interpretation and, in an existential sense at least, the phenomenon of will. Its convergence with the external Reality III and the mixed external–internal Reality II will produce quite different *mises en scène* for the psychotic or for the normal adult, for a child, indeed for any two persons. In this realm each man *is* an island and there is no truth save by individual interpretation. Propositions at this level therefore, while constrained by the "lower" or "harder" realities and falsifiable by them, are not scientific but rather philosophical. Their epistemological status is dependent upon the value orientations, life experiences and "life-worlds" of their audience. The propositions of this reality are, as it were, the raw material for philosophy. We need not so much more propositions as more ordering and validating of the propositions that already abound. And we need to get clear about the language games of the three realities taken jointly and severally so that, *pace* Wittgenstein, our intelligence is not bewitched by our language.

The way in which this logical ordering accords with the general taxonomy of process is shown in Figure 7.1.

Administration is the art of translating ideas into a change of the material grounds of reality (things) through the organization of people. The realities it deals with are three-fold: internal, internal–external, and external. In the first of these is the genesis of leadership, in the second the evolution of interest, and in the last *that-which-resists*. The moral aspect of this complex is implicit within its first two terms. Greenfield expresses it as follows:

> Organizations require two things to make them real: an idea for action (or more likely ideas for action) in someone's head and process that commits others to the realization of those ideas. The development of ideas for action we call inspiration, genius,

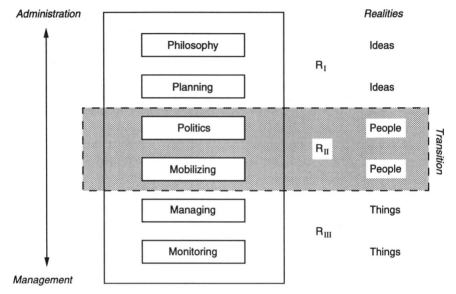

Figure 7.1 Levels of Reality on the Administrative–Managerial Continuum.

policymaking or the work of the devil, depending on our assessment of the ideas themselves. Those who mobilize people around ideas and who commit them to those ideas we call leaders. The job of leaders, of course, is to go about committing people to others' ideas by whatever means they can—by reason, calculation, persuasion, force, or charismatic inspiration. What matters is the commitment and the relationship that orients the action of some people to others' ideas. When some people are related in action so as to bring to fruition the ideas of others, we have a moral order. We have organization and we have power.[23]

We also have values, interests, and meaning set against a material reality that is itself forever in flux. Organizational reality is then what we make it. An *interpretation.*

ORGANIZATIONAL DIALECTICS

This examination of organizational values suggests that the V_3 level of analysis derives its content and structure from the organization's purposes or goals together with such metavalues as effectiveness, efficiency, survival, growth, and rational calculus. The content is reducible to language and can always be expressed, however imprecisely. For example: business organizations (firms) exist to make, over the long term, a profit—public sector organizations (bureaucracies) exist to render some sort of social service; schools and colleges exist to certify or credential their clientele; the military exists to pursue national policies by violent means, and so on. All of these examples exhibit an inverse correlation of goal specificity with size and complexity. That is, the larger and more complex the organization or institution the broader, vaguer, more inclusive and opaque the goals, purposes, and values appear. Nevertheless they represent the (V_3) nomothetic dimension with which the leader, the administrator, has to be identified. In other words this is the overt dimension of administrative interest. The leadership may not in fact agree with the organizational goals and policies but is constrained and inhibited by the V_5–V_1 value structure while at the same time being liberated by the scope of *interpretation* permitted by the language in which the goals and purposes are couched. Language games about value thus become instruments for the transvaluation of values. When the War Ministry becomes a Ministry of Defence there is a reality as well as a value shift.

The administrative interest (V_3) is of course subject to the cultural and subcultural impress from without $(V_{5,4})$ and the individual and group value influences from within $(V_{1,2})$. These contending forces constitute a permanent source and residue of value conflict for the administrator. Axiology is inescapable. Compounding the difficulties, and obviating any naive subscription to a doctrine of achieving value consensus, is the reality of power. Moreover the administrator personally embodies some set of V_1 values that inevitably affect both the executive interpretation of the V_{1-5} spectrum and the realized, manifested value culture, climate, and "weather" of the organization itself.

The countervailing dialectical force of the administrator's own values is dependent upon their congruency with those of the organization. Applying the value paradigm we can see that the administrator may relate to the organizational value system with the following distinctive forms of interaction.

1. Preferential liking or disliking (congruency or incongruency) modulated by personal career interests [Type III].
2. An affiliation (willed or perceived as rationally advantageous) with the organizational norms and subscription to the organizational subculture [Type II$_B$].
3. A rational (or rationalized) commitment to the organizational purposes as a result of deliberate reflection, reinforced or modulated by self-interest [Type II$_A$].
4. A personal conviction of the worth of the organizational values that transcends ordinary self-interest and instantiates a passionate psychological identification with the organization as a meaning-endowed and meaning-endowing entity [Type I].

Empirical referents for these levels of commitment can be hypothesized: for example, observable charismatic leadership effects in the instance of Type I, but actual analysis in given cases is essentially and ultimately dependent upon introspection and self-audit by the leaders or administrators themselves. Furthermore it is clear that, save in the rarest of circumstances, the intrinsic dialectical tension between V_3 and V_1, together with the range of paradigmatic options, gives rise to disvalues. The aetiology of such disvalues and the dysfunctions associated with them will be explored in greater detail in Part IV but some of their complications have been adumbrated above. This discussion has also already brought us face to face with what may be called the central problem of administrative philosophy. This will form the topic of the next chapter.

PROPOSITIONS

101. The problem of the organization is the superimposition of the nomothetic upon the idiographic while the problem of administrative philosophy is the justification of the former in terms of the latter.
102. Administrators lack the value autonomy of subordinates. They are constrained by the nomothetic dimension.
103. The administrator cannot be a mere agent of the collectivity, this would be a descent into management.
104. Isomorphism of organizational hierarchies with the organizational reward system is a logical, but impractical, ideal. Value conflict is endemic.
105. We shape our lives through organizations.
106. Purposiveness translates the future into the present, and conversely, by way of values.
107. Organizational purpose is external, impersonal, objective but for the member it is internal, personal, subjective. Organizational purpose modulates individual purpose. And, to a lesser extent, conversely.
108. Organizations have a double meaning—inward to their members, outward to the world. The administrator seeks to reconcile these perspectives and to do so rationally is not enough.
109. Men are powerfully moved by group pressures. Great is the power of the group. But greater still is the power of the man moved by his true will.
110 The organization can be a source of joy. To some of its members it can give their meaning and purpose in life.
111. We speak of organizational morale, and also of culture, climate, weather—such concepts are functions of administration. That is, the quality of organizational life depends on administration.
112. Organizations are abstractions, unconscious, and without will—they are not real but as systems we endow them with pseudo-consciousness and quasi-will.
113. When the work of an organization contends against deep-seated values in the larger culture it must be transvalued. Hence the glorification of the military, the dictator, the executive. Hence too the professionalism of the surgeon, the undertaker, and the police.
114. Military organizations, like religious, are dependent upon transrational values. Loyalty is their metavalue.
115. There are individual and organizational metavalues; the latter have the force of the collectivity and hence a pretension to righteousness.
116. It is not enough for an organization to be effective, it must be efficiently effective.
117. Organizations generate a value culture. This culture reinterprets (transvalues) the values of society.

Chapter 8
The Common Interest

In its most succinct philosophical form the central problem of administration could be described as the problem of the one versus the many. Viewed from the top down it is the problem of singular leadership and plural followership; viewed conversely it is the plurality of individuals versus the singular collective. Jargonistically this is the contest of the idiographic and the nomothetic. Hardin[1] has analogized it to the medieval problem of the commons, referring to the practice of common grazing or pasture. In such conditions it is quite rational for each peasant to maximize his own use of the commons even if that should result ultimately in the destruction of the land and total loss for each individual. Or, updating the illustration, it is seemingly prudential in underdeveloped countries for each set of parents to maximize the number of their offspring, even if the resulting overpopulation leads to a decline in the quality of life for all. And, in developed countries, the phenomenon of trade unions killing the geese that lay the golden eggs is too familiar to bear elaboration. Larger scale instances can be drawn *ad nauseam* from the field of international policy where the pursuit of national interest by sovereign states again and again invokes the amorality and immorality of power. This basic opposition at the political level has recently given rise to a philosophy of communitarianism, especially as advocated by Etzioni,[2] the central idea being that a third force between state and individual is desirable, namely an evolution of community or localized polity and associated values and morality. It should be noted, however, that this suggestion is largely hypothetical, does not yet constitute a political movement, and does not speak to the possibility of organizations as third force.

All of these examples are instances or expressions of the fundamental conflict between the one and the many, a conflict with psychoanalytic roots in that we are born as idiographic egos[3] struggling to maintain ourselves in a nomothetic cultural context. From the beginning it is a case of rules versus gratification. The parent represents our primordial experience of the administrator. Valuationally, what is good for the one may not be good for the many, and conversely. The line between right and good is drawn early.

There is also another, less obvious and less acknowledged aspect to this problem of conflicting interest and that is the contest between chaos as represented by nature (unbridled emotion) and order as represented by human society (reason). Again the roots go psychologically deep and are established in archetypal myths. These are represented by the opposition between the great gods Apollo and Dionysus. The imposition of Apollonian order in the affairs of men in the constant endeavour to reduce uncertainty and allow predictability finds its apotheosis in technology and the totalitarian State. All organizations are, by definition, Apollonian—nomothetic systems designed to achieve ends of benefit the costs of which are individual submission and the repression of Dionysian instincts. The outcome of this dialectic is what we loosely call culture, civilization, society but the prize, so hardly won, is precariously held. Again and again the attempt to eliminate uncertainty fails, the repressed forces of Dionysian indulgence erupt and in extremes there is violence, barbarity, sabotage, war, and at the organizational level: bureaupathology, resentment, disruption, dysfunction, inefficiency, and ineffectiveness. In some sense the idiographic is always Dionysian; and administration is its natural enemy. The structures of hierarchy and power are devices to regulate this dialectical tension while leadership itself has at times been defined in terms of the reduction of uncertainty.[4] But is there yet another formulation of this value conflict? Another way of explicating these inherent divisions and oppositions, intrinsic as they are to all organizational life? The answers to these questions call for another look at the phenomenon of value-impress.

VALUE IMPRESS

Figure 8.1 recapitulates the essential ideas of Figure 2.6 (p. 45) and indexes the broad levels of value referred to in the previous chapter. Within each of these levels, V_5 to V_1, the value paradigm is itself applicable in the following manner. V_5 cultures may be heavily ideological (medieval Christianity, Stalinist

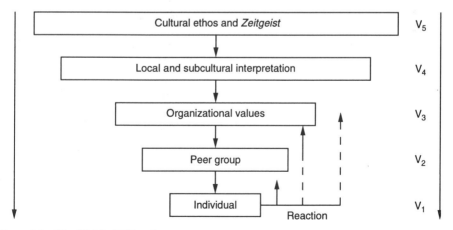

Figure 8.1   The Field of Value Impress.

communism, World War wartime ethos in the democracies). This can be classified as Type I while Types II and III could be illustrated by the post-war Japanese economy and US consumerism respectively. Whatever the ethos, however, it is not directly accessible to the administration of an organization and affects the value climate of that organization (V_3) by an interpretive mediation through the local and regional milieu in which the organization functions. Paradigmatically, V_4 influences and special circumstances can modify and modulate the overall downward impress of the culture upon the organization and its individual members. Type I exhortations to greater productivity in wartime munitions factories could be obviated, for example, by ethnic rivalries and tensions or even by past history of labour–management feuding.[5] The same logic applies, *mutatis mutandis*, throughout the downward travel of value-impress to the point of interaction with the individual. Two points can now be made. First, a paradox. While the individual alone has the only real *experience* of value and in the end the individual alone, by force of will or force of preference, has the sole *capacity* to take value action yet this individual is the constant recipient of value-determining forces beyond his control or even beyond his ken. Secondly, it is to be observed that the leader or administrator or executive is also an individual, albeit one with a split value-personality, to the extent, that is, that he assumes and personifies the collective interest. It follows from this that (a) V_1 and V_3 are central problem levels of analysis and (b) the value-paradigm enters primarily into the overall analysis of value at the V_1 and V_3 levels.

A fortiori, since every formal organization (V_3), subsumes an informal organization (V_2), a composite of subsets, and since no human role incumbent ever perfectly fits the formal role expectations but always embodies individuality and idiosyncrasy, a large part of the art of leadership consists in the observation, judgement, and intuition of character. A great leader is, to use Hitler's term, a *Menschenkenner*—one who grasps, instinctively, intuitively, or otherwise—the motives of men. The leader deconstructs their desires, penetrating beyond the veil of rhetoric with which their ego defence mechanisms self-justify their roles and rationalize their behaviour. Crudely put, to lead is to know what makes people tick and use this knowledge for the common ends. And this implies a heightened sensitivity to the phenomenon of value-impress.

Achieving the common interest means that the administrator's central and unending task is reconciliation. Reconciliation of the idiosyncratic organization member to the organizational interest is the internal task. Reconciliation of the organization to its environment (clientele, public, society, subculture and culture) is the external task. Since both internal and external dimensions are always in flux the administrative process can be defined as the complex art of achieving organizational maintenance and growth in a field of conflicting and changing forces. This again reminds us that what is obvious is not simple. The forces of value-impress in either direction, of value action and reaction, are not necessarily visible. One thinks of Wittgenstein's image of a man in the street viewed from behind a closed window. He appears to be walking upright but in truth he may be in a highly unstable equilibrium, barely balancing against the gale of wind he is leaning into: Generally it is what is *not* seen that matters.

Much of administration is concerned with the unseen, a fact which the general literature tends to slight. Secrecy, confidentiality, role-playing, masks, personae, theatricality, dramaturgy—all are aspects of concealment in organizational life.[6] That there is a theatrical quality to organizational behaviour does not deny that there is also the possibility of authentic engagement of the personality with the formal role but this commergence of interest is an unlikely solution to the problem of reconciliation below the Type I level of value. What is critical is the degree of fit between personality and role. To the degree that there is misfit we can never truly or entirely be ourselves in formal organizations. Our V_1 essence is subservient to the V_3 ends. And this inescapable condition frustrates the Kantian ethical imperative: Never treat another human being as a means. The very nature of organization requires that we treat each other as means—the military commander who sends men to their deaths does that; so do all leaders with followers. At the very least the Kantian ethic would have to be reinterpreted and thus would lose its absolute quality. Yet impress also places another sort of moral obligation upon leadership: to achieve V_3 ends and subordinate the leader's own V_1 ends to the general will of the collective enterprise. Any personal divergence of common and private interest must be masked in performance. The role of leader is public and hence continuously monitored by many audiences, even when the script is improvised and the plot obscure. The administrator is always on-stage whether monitoring outwardly the culture and subculture of the environment so as to make adaptive organizational responses or monitoring inwardly the informal organization and its members so as to elicit optimal performance and commitment.

In the course of action, that is, in the course of *history* all systems interact and change. The river of Heraclitus ensures that the individual experience of value can never repeat itself but the larger V_5 culture itself changes and transvalues all values in time. Whether this transvaluation is patterned or what shape the patterning may take—linear, cyclical, spiral, helical—are metaphysical questions of only tangential interest to administrative philosophy. What is certain is that value impress is inexorable and inescapable. Organizations are always culturally determined.

The contest between personal and common interest in political theory takes the form of divergence of values between the individual and the state, or between anarchy and order, or (at a more sophisticated level of understanding) between nature and human nature. Bloom sees this dialectic deriving from the different philosophies of Locke and Rouseau. "The two outstanding intellectual types of our day represent these two teachings. The crisp, positive, efficient, no-nonsense economist is the Lockeian; the deep brooding, somber psychoanalyst is the Rousseauian."[7] Or, administratively, social science tells us how to manage our systems and industrial psychology tells us how to bandage the wounds. Of course the claim of the latter would be larger than this, namely, to avert or avoid the wounds in the first place. But, from the philosophical viewpoint, this distinction is an over-sanguine interpretation of the underlying dialectic.

Historically, as observed previously, the conflict of interest in administrative thought has evolved into the contending value orientations of scientific management and the human relations movement. While a vast technical literature has evolved about these positions, the models of man and basic presumptions about human nature which underpins them, can still be succinctly expressed in McGregor's Theory X and Theory Y.[8] The postulates of Theory X are:

1. The average human being has an inherent dislike for work and will avoid it if he can.
2. Because of this most people must be coerced, controlled, directed, and threatened with punishment so that they will work toward the organization's goals.
3. The average human being prefers to be directed, prefers security, and avoids responsibility.

The postulates of Theory Y are:

1. Physical work and mental work are as natural as play, if they are satisfying.
2. Man will exercise self-direction and self-control toward an organization's goals if he is committed to them.
3. Commitment is a function of rewards. The best rewards are satisfaction of ego and self-actualization.
4. The average person can learn to accept and seek responsibility. Avoidance of it and emphasis on security are learned and not inherent characteristics.
5. Creativity, ingenuity, and imagination are widespread among people and do not occur only in a select few.

That Theory Y has five propositions to X's three and that the first two of Theory Y are contingent and the last three Rousseauian in presumption is merely reflective of their author's philosophy and of the V_5 impress of the times. Nomothetic conformity (portrayed as Stalinist oppression or modernist drudgery) is contrasted with idiographic potential bursting to be channelled into the fulfillment of common interest. Implicitly Theory Y is preferred as a dialectical synthesis but the dialectic remains. Also implicit in the contrast is the belief that self-interest must either be coerced or seduced towards the common ends. Coercion can be achieved through managerial technology while seduction can be effected through the manipulative techniques of group dynamics, personnel psychology, manipulation of the reward system, and perhaps by the inculcation or intrusion of Type I charismatic values.

The administrative difficulty raised by this central problem—the problem of the commons—can be acutely observed in public sector bureaucracies: Public and political demands for accountability in non-profit service enterprises such as education or health care have generated a large-scale industry of consulting and evaluation. The subversion of the efforts to evaluate is interesting and instructive. Initial "hard-nosed", Theory X, "bang-for-a-buck" attitudes generated Theory Y reaction and opposition. The forces of V_2 group self-interest entrenched in the system (often with tacit V_3 support) have proved in general sufficiently powerful to frustrate any simplistic efforts at X-evaluation and have led to dramaturgical scenarios in which external evaluators are obliged and compelled to enlist the cooperation of the evaluators. This then becomes an instance of "provider capture"[9] whereupon criticism or restraint is diffused and obfuscated into public relations semantics of "participating leadership" or even "leader substitution".[10] That is to say, evaluators are subverted by those whom they seek to evaluate and evaluation proceeds via obfuscation into a form of defence of the established order of interest. In blunter idiom: the fox guards the chicken coop. It is also of interest that this state of affairs forms a counter-example to the general principle of downward value impress. Here V_4 interests are subverted by reactive impress as manifested in V_3 and V_2 maintenance metavalues.

LAYERS OF INTEREST

Resolving the problems set by value-impress and divergent interest is typically interpreted as a problem of motivation. But this terminology is unsatisfactory. Motivation is too general, it can range from brute coercion (the threat of dismissal or the promise of promotion) to the subtlest of psychological suggestions (the warm grip, the hand on the arm, the raised eyebrow). And, at the other extreme, national fervour or religious zeal, sexual enticements, and injured vanity can override the merely rational economic motivations of salary and benefits. Moreover, motivation is *always* less than complete, never pure. It is unstable (often highly volatile) and threatened by contingencies from beyond the organizational domain.

The family, for example, at level V_2 poses the eternal problem of the extended ego (V_1). What mother does not consider her child's welfare before that of others if the issue be forced? What family does not wish its claims to power, property, and status to be preferred above those of others? Charity, as said, begins at home. In this light it is interesting to read Rousseau's solution to the problem of common interest. Simply find a leader who can

... so to speak change human nature, transform each individual, who by himself is a perfect and solitary whole, into a part of a greater whole from which that individual as it were gets his life and his being; weaken man's constitution to strengthen it; substitute a partial and moral existence for the physical and independent existence which we have all received from nature. He must, in a word, take man's own forces away from him in order to give him forces which are foreign to him and which he cannot use without the help of others. The more the natural forces [idiographic] are dead and annihilated, the greater and more lasting are the acquired ones (nomothetic), thus the founding is solider and more perfect, such that if each citizen is nothing, can do nothing, except by all the others, and the force acquired by the whole is equal or superior to the sum of the natural forces of all the individuals, one can say the legislation (administration) is at the highest point of perfection it can attain. (Author's parentheses.)[11]

Naive or not this is a depiction of what would now be called the transformational leader[12] and its theme will recur in the later discussion of charismatic leadership. It represents one arm of the dialectic dealt with earlier and can be associated with such movements as human relations, human resources, democratic and participatory administration while the oppressing arm—the rational as contrasted with the emotive—can be identified with systems theory, Weberian bureaucracy, and scientific management.[13]

The philosophy of the leader does therefore make a difference. If it is truly believed that scientific method and rational empiricism are together necessary and sufficient for an understanding of human motivation—a view reinforced by the scientific–technological spirit of our culture—that is one philosophy. If, on the contrary, one invokes ineluctable constructs such as experience, character, value consciousness, will, emotion, commitment—that is another. The leadership implications of each of these dialectical positions are themselves contrary and contradictory. At best attempts at reconciliation or compromise of the viewpoints can be unstable, tentative, and inconclusive. The underlying conflict is radical and basic.

While administration is indeed a humanism it must be conceded that contemporary value orientations have been subtly and profoundly influenced by the instrumental efficacy of science and technology. Our V_5 culture is scientific–technical–rational–legal–bureaucratic. Space achievements, nuclear science, medicine, and the infrastructure of computerology all tend to intensify and deepen our appreciation of the rational, the logical, the empirical. By extension this means the hegemony of the abstract and general, the nomothetic, over the concrete and particular, the idiographic. Science seeks laws and regularities (*Nomos* in the Greek); it seeks order and predictability; it is, at the deepest level of analysis, antipathetic to individuality, uncertainty, and will. But science works. It pays off. It passes the pragmatic test. It delivers. It endorses the maxim that knowledge is power. Furthermore it rests upon that fundamental distinction between fact and value which, percolating down to the level of mass understanding, has resulted in value orientations of relativism, pluralism, hedonism, behaviourism, and pragmatism. These tacit contemporary public philosophies form the substance of the conventional or orthodox wisdom. The emphasis upon rationalism in modern organizational life, the influences of Weberian ideal-type bureaucratic theory and the development of systems theory all go to endorse the new-scientific management and neo-Taylorian tendency in administrative philosophy.

That this has contributed in a dysfunctional way to achievement of the common good has been shown by Sir Geoffrey Vickers:

> ... An ever more scientific world was never less controllable. A world dedicated to majority rule is increasingly run by militant minorities. "Free" individuals increasingly depend upon each other, are subject to increasing demands to share the commitments, accept the constraints and accord the trust required by the multiplying systems and subsystems to which they belong and on which they wholly depend. And these distribute their favours and, still more their responsibilities, with the equality of a battlefield ...[14]

Our analysis shows that because of intractable V_1 value and because of Type I and Type III elements the ideal predictability of natural science can never be achieved in human affairs. Hence, perhaps, the existential nervousness about nuclear and advanced weapon systems. Despite all fail-safe guarantees, total security remains elusive. In one extreme of administrative philosophy we are led to a totalitarian logic where the values of any individual are rendered irrelevant to the accomplishment of organizational tasks. From an ethical standpoint this social engineering could be construed as fostering that "banality of evil" described by Arendt and others in reference to Adolf Eichmann and the death camps of Europe or by Solzhenitsyn in reference to Stalin and the gulags.[15] On the other hand it could be construed simply as an ends-justifies-means approach to the final resolution of the question of common interest.

The central problem (the individual versus the collective) may also be discussed in political rather than motivational terms. For example in terms of democracy as opposed to monarchy or oligarchy, or liberalism versus authoritarianism, or collegiality contrasted with hierarchy. The socio-psychological work of Kurt Lewin is classical in this approach.[16] He studied group behaviour and organizational climate which he classified as authoritarian, democratic, and *laissez-faire*. His conclusions favoured democratic leadership and were perhaps politically correct in view of the times and his status as a refugee from Nazi Germany. Certainly they imported an ideologized thrust to the movement of democratic administration and foreshadowed a contemporary emphasis in administration upon collegiality, collective decision making, and consensus. Since conflict cannot be eliminated but is considered rather as an essential and healthy part of organizational life the leader has not so much to solve value conflict as to continuously resolve it. The administrator is faced with the ongoing task of seeking to build coalitions and trying to discover and maintain consensus at all levels of the organizational hierarchy.

The interest in Japanese management is an illustrative case. This school of thought and practice is certainly a resultant of the special Japanese V_5 version of value impress and may not be simply transferable to other less hierarchical or homogeneous cultures. A formidable expenditure of time and endless pains are taken by Japanese executives in their political task of consensus building at every level of organization, including that of the nation state. When successful—

and it is not always so, even in Japan—it could be argued that this presents an ideal solution to the central problem of commitment. Group and individual interest are ostensibly reconciled. Yet the reconciliation may be more apparent than real and what has been painstakingly built may nevertheless erode. Consensus is also Level IIB of the paradigm. In concert with the V_2 level of impress it either seduces or coerces the individual into another zone of acceptance. Consensus applies to the part of life within which an individual identifies with an organization and embraces its values. Consensus is also the domain of group-think.[17] Contemporary cultural inhibitors such as political correctness and anti-elitism[18] tend to reinforce the status of democratic administration. Consequently, there is, as it were, a strong consensus against any criticism of consensus and administrators often feel subservient to collective influence and opinion, especially as this manifests at the V_4 level politically and in the media. But a pandering to the power of the group, be it V_2 or V_4, is not the only option available to the cause of leadership. Power is diffused hierarchically and can be analysed at each of the levels of impress. And the paradigm itself applies at each of these levels.

V_3 Power

At this layer we are dealing with administrative power and the point to be made is that this is often underestimated even, or especially, by administrators themselves. Empirical evidence for this contention is provided by the work of Professor Milgram. The Milgram studies[19] were conceived in the 1950s with the intent of proving that the Nazi death camps were an organizational aberration that could not have occurred in a liberal democracy such as the United States. That they proved the contrary is of interest as is the fact that changing ethical norms would now prohibit the replication of these studies themselves.

In these experiments naive subjects were required to administer supposed electric shocks to a supposed victim upon the commands of various authorities. The subjects believed that these shocks could reach such proportions as to cause bodily harm or even death. The results seemed to show conclusively that there was, at the least, a powerful predisposition to obey a superior's commands, even if those commands violated the values of the subordinate and caused distinct and considerable pain and distress. In short, the propensity to obedience was much greater than had been imagined—so great in fact that it could be inferred that atrocities could occur under any system of government. Later historical incidents such as the My Lai massacre in Vietnam would seem to support this inference. That is, administrators simply by virtue of their V_3 office, had a power base capable of overriding ordinary moral scruples and, *a fortiori*, organizational structures could be so designed as to facilitate this exercise of power.

The findings of these studies led the researcher to postulate the concept of *agentic state*. This is a psychological set or condition into which a subordinate rapidly falls when placed in a context of formal organization with the appropriate dramaturgical and symbolic trappings of authority in place. It is a condition of ready obedience and willingness to be commanded. In extreme forms it is present in totalitarian and military contexts but to some extent it is present from the outset in all formal organizations. It is evidenced also by clientele as when we fall easily into the agentic state in the doctor's or lawyer's office or in the presence of uniformed police or customs officers.

It may be, as Milgram himself thought, that submissiveness to authority has bioethical merit. It can override the private in favour of the common interest. This becomes clearly observable in wartime ("There's a war on!") but in even the most ordinary of social conditions a constraint operates which makes it easier to obey than disobey. (This constraint is a V_5 variable and obedience to authority may be more facile in China, Japan, Germany than, say, in the British Isles, USA, Israel.) In short, obedience is the line of least resistance. Because of this the administrator has at his service the capacity to design and manipulate authority systems which can override many if not all of V_1 scruples, preferences, and inclinations. When this is done out of Type I convictions the override may be well-nigh irresistible. In any event the leader may well have more power than realized.

V_1 Power

Apart from self-interest what power does the individual wield in the organizational value complex? Barnard was among the first of administrative philosophers to appreciate that, *in potentia* at least, the ultimate power resided with the followership, the individual components of the structure who can quit, strike, go slow, walk away or sabotage the common good. Hell, as Sartre said, is other people. So long as the flame of individual will is not extinguished there remains a residue of resistance or antagonism between individual and organization and the administrator has to contend with what, from the common standpoint, could be interpreted as not only a deficit of commitment but a sort of moral obtuseness or defect—organizational original sin.

The means to cope with this sin are, as in religion, coercion and persuasion. Argument, flattery, guile, guilt, exhortation, example, charisma, symbol, myth, bribery, force, domination, manipulation, inspiration, energy, resentment, resentment, revenge, malice, sacrifice, love—the whole gamut and range of techniques that is the legacy of the long history of administration, a legacy which each succeeding generation of leaders must either relearn in whole or part, or else practice instinctively. And why? Because the follower has a form of ultimate power and because the common interest is always in jeopardy. Never secure. Always threatened by this lowest layer of interest.

V_2-V_4-V_5 Power

The remaining layers of interest have more subtle effects upon the central problem. These influences are cultural and are often subliminal or unconscious. For example, the mere fact of being a "professional" means that one is subject to a set of norms which are not merely expectations of behaviour but also ways of perceiving and evaluating. These acquired norms are part of the induction and initiation processes of professionalism. In return for a certain power and status the professional subscribes to an *extra*-organizational culture. Here the specific organization and its values are transcended for the larger community of the profession and the waters of the "common" interest may be muddied or clarified in interesting ways.

Organizations also inevitably generate their own cultures, defined by Schein, as patterns of "basic assumptions—invented, discovered, or developed by a given group as it learns to cope with its problems of external adaptation and internal integration—that has worked well enough to be considered valid and, therefore, to be taught to new members as the correct way to perceive, think, and feel in relation to those problems."[20] Such cultures are essentially conservative, dominated by the metavalues—not impervious to change but resistant to it and inelastic. A culture over-rigid breaks, a culture over-flexible never takes on form. The military and the church provide self-evident examples as do those elite schools whose graduates bear the impress of their educational enculturation visibly and permanently into their later lives. But so too do banktellers and sales clerks who must discover and abide by "the way we do things here".

The play of cultural forces from within and without the organization compound the central problem. The leader can in principle create new culture but is more likely to reinforce the old. One set of pressures conduce towards his becoming an "organization man"[21] while another set—the culture of private life derived, say, from an ethos of consumerism—would prescribe individual indulgence or hedonism. An additional complexity is the quasi-moral imperative to monitor both the external value environment (including all those political, social, and media interactions that might affect the organization in any way) and to monitor and investigate simultaneously the internal subcultures.[22] Both sets of activity are directly relevant to the common good and its interpretation.

Practical Implications

The implications of this complex interplay of interest are fourfold. In searching, interpreting, and expressing the common interest four sets of value knowledge and experience are required from the standpoint of *leadership*. For now it can be said that the criteria are (1) V_3 knowledge of the organizational task (aims, ends, goals, objectives, purposes, policies, philosophy); (2) V_4, V_5 knowledge of the situation in its cultural context externally; (3) and (4) are psychological and refer to the malleable internal or subjective side of leadership. The implied methodology for the acquisition of these knowledge sets is observational, intuitive, experimental, practical—one becomes a *Menschenkenner*, for example, by people study, by a special faculty of consciousness acquired in interaction with *people*, and by reflection upon this experience. Herein too lies one argument for promotion by seniority. Against it, however, may be laid the natural biological decline of energies with chronology. The acquired wisdom attributed to political survival has to be traded against the possibility of failing powers of commitment.

TOWARDS THE GENERAL INTEREST

A final restatement of the central problem may be made in terms of selfishness, egoism, and greed. In the final days of the Soviet Union its leader Gorbachev saw the dilemma of Communism in these terms.[23] Individual desire is the matrix of values and the human condition is one of adapting *personal* desire to frustrating reality constraints. This in turn means that *both* the moral *and* the metaphysical dimensions are sources of action that cannot be eliminated from praxis and practical reason despite all the attempts to do so by postmodernists, structuralists, positivists, determinists, behaviourists, and their philosophical bedfellows. The education of desire, the discipline of ego, thus becomes a leitmotif of administrative philosophy if not the central theme.

The spectrum of this commonwealth philosophy is large, it extends from the dirt to the stars. It has aspired to the highest ideals of the species. It has built nations and empires, achieved honour and glory while at the same time encompassing every flaw and defect of the human condition—malevolence, hatred, bloodshed, violence, corruption, envy, vanity, greed, lust, rage. Yet throughout, somehow, it has been vindicated by history insofar as it has sought to place the whole above the part, the greater before the lesser interest, the nomothetic over the idiographic, ends in advance of means. This is its claim upon morality. Great organizations are always in some sense ideological or educational; they seek to change their members, make them conform to their own ideal, subscribe to their culture, and discipline their natural egoism. So the leader becomes a sort of moral tutor, for the better or the worse, *in loco parentis* to adults. True, administrators may fail their charge; they can retreat to managerialism, become factotums or moral ciphers or Machiavellian manipulators or survivors or careerists. Such failures reflect in organizational climate and morale. But when executive responsibility is taken up there is a movement towards the common interest. As Barnard puts it, "Executive responsibility, then, is that capacity of leaders by which, reflecting attitudes, ideals, hopes, derived *largely from without themselves*, they are compelled to bend the wills of men to the accomplishment of purposes beyond their immediate ends, beyond their times" (author's italics).[24] The value direction from *without* is here, in the idealistic view of Barnard, a transcendence of the ego on the part of the leader rather than, as more realistically oriented cynics might have it, an identification of the organization's goals with the leader's career ambitions. (What is good for me is good for General Motors). Moral leadership, that is, is in the general interest. Egoism is transcended, supervened, disciplined. The problem of greed is resolved.

But another philosophical conclusion may be drawn from all this dialectical to-and-fro-ing. The logical appeal of a hierarchy of interest extending in the ideal state from an apex of generality (God, the State, the Commune) to a base of pluralistic individualism (egoistic self-interest) and structured in descending order to create an imperative of moral obligation must now be rejected *simpliciter*. The appeal of this logic has seduced many philosophers: it is the template of Plato's *Republic*, the Great Chain of Being of Christian scholastics, the Taoist Mandate of Heaven of the Confucian Analects, the authoritarian totalitarianism associated with a discredited Fascism. The rejection of this solution to the central problem is based not so much on moral–ethical grounds as was the case with Sir Karl Popper in his defence of democracy[25]— a democracy which itself is perfectly capable of group tyranny and populist dysfunction—as in the ultimate neglect of the individual interest, whatever the moral–ethical rights or wrongs of that interest might be. The problem of egoistic greed, of selfishness, is rightly perceived by Schopenhauer and others but in administrative philosophy it is compounded by the problem of corporate greed, by the principle of "fighting one's own corner", by in-group versus out-group psychology—all of which exacerbate the value problem of the administrator.[26] In the daily encounter with that problem subtle advice can be drawn from the following ancient Sanskrit maxim: "For the sake of the family sacrifice the individual, for the sake of the nation sacrifice the community, for the sake of the world sacrifice the nation, and for the sake of the individual soul sacrifice the whole world!"[27] The sense of this maxim is apt and points to at least a preliminary solution of our problem: Administratively one *in general* ought to subject the lesser to the larger interest, but always with the caveat that the very largest interest is not a man's physical welfare but his soul. And so at last the pragmatics of administration and management come to include the metaphysical. In the last analysis neither values nor metaphysics can be excised from administrative philosophy, theory, or practice.

What must next be considered is a further complication arising from the above analysis. It can be expressed in this way: *can* organizations be moral entities? This forms the topic of the next chapter.

PROPOSITIONS

118. It is a commonplace that the self-interest of one can be a cost to the self-interest of others. But what is meant by *self*? This mystery enshrouds the core of the problem.
119. The administrator must acknowledge the primacy of self-interest. It is the point of origin for administrative philosophy.
120. The commitment to self-interest can be subrational or transrational. It can be sublime, demonic, or merely banal.
121. Both nomothetic and idiographic factors seek expression in the organization's goals but the values of the latter are elastic, of the former inelastic.
122. Administration is a cultural enterprise: it mediates between organization and environment, this is its diplomacy.
123. The basic organizational tension is between the one and the many. Organizations are fundamentally dualistic and dialectical.
124. Organizations have hierarchy of status and a hierarchy of purpose. To unite these in a one-to-one ratio would be the ideal logical form. So far it has only been achieved by insects.
125. Work motivations are dualistic and dialectical.
126. At base men are moved by fear. This assumption is defensible. More so than that they are moved by love.
127. Men seek power as an antidote to fear. But if fear grows correlatively then the cure enlarges the disease.
128. Theory X and Theory Y are not contradictories; *both* are true.
129. Vested organizational interest is a species of neofeudalism.
130. The simplest rule of administrative morality is, "Submit the lesser to the larger interest." But this must be tempered and sophisticated.
131. Individual interest is always tripartite: self (including the extended self), organization (including other organizations), society (including mankind at large).
132. Self-interest is never simple. Metaphysics intrudes.
133. Identification of individual and organizational interest need not be reciprocal; it may be intransitive.
134. Totalitarianism seeks unification of interest while pluralism seeks compromise of interest.
135. The highest and lowest of values are idiographic; between lies the realm of value belonging to the nomothetic mass.
136. Administrators are far from moral impotence; the zones of their acceptance may be wider than they believe.
137. Interest is the active value orientation of an individual or a group. It is value referred to fact.
138. Masking and unmasking interest is the continuous task of leadership.

139. Administrators must worship at the shrine of Apollo; not so their Dionysian followers.
140. The individual is a creature of culture, not the converse.
141. Administration deals with the seen and the unseen in the same proportions as the visible iceberg to its submerged body.
142. Transformational leadership, though it can occur, is Rousseauian romanticism. The ordinary is more modest, and more difficult.
143. Consensus is the mildest form of dictatorship.
144. Political correctness is the politest form of tyranny.
145. Corporate interest is the postmodern form of selfishness; the antagonist of the commons.

Chapter 9
Organizations as Moral Orders

The problem of the One and the Many, however it is phrased: as individual versus collective, as the ego encountering authority, as the particular versus the general, or the subjective versus the objective has been treated in the previous chapter as if the collective nomothetic qualities of an organization were a legitimated abstraction generally representative of larger moral forces overriding the interests of organization members. "What is good for General Motors is good for the country" is a maxim of corporate value that extends downwards as well as upwards, internally as well as externally. This equivocal (ambivalent and multivalent) status of organizations in their own evaluational or ethical right deserves some closer inspection. From the systems standpoint, of course, and from the standpoint of scientific management, organizations are morally neutral. Their ethical status is instrumental in the positivistic sense. They are not *responsible.* They exist, for good or evil, as mere functions of their directive subsystems, that is, the executive policymakers who establish and maintain the organizational goals. If what is good for General Motors happens also to be good for the country then that is a bonus, for the country *and* General Motors. If the Luftwaffe bombs Coventry or the Royal Air Force bombs Dresden no moral qualms need attach to either organization *qua* organization. Organizations, like managers, are ciphers in the moral equation.

The opposing view is epitomized in a proposition of Greenfield's: "Organizations are not objects in nature; an organization is a moral order invented and maintained by human choice and will."[1] The term "moral order" is worthy of note. It suggests that the organization *itself* is a force for good or evil independently of, or at least concomitant with, its *pro tempore* administration.[2] Which in turn leads to a set of questions that form an important part of administrative philosophy. Do organizations possess moral, ethical, valuational qualities in their own right? Is the whole, in some moral sense, greater than the sum of its parts? Do organizations, in terms of the value-paradigm, exhibit socio-psychological features which would permit their classification as Type I, Type II, or Type III? Are they, as Greenfield claims, "moral orders"?

THE PERVASION OF PURPOSE

The entire rationale of organizations must lie in their capacity to serve collective ends. They are in essence goal-seeking entities. However, as the size and complexity of an organization approaches institutional dimensions (the military, the police, the state) the rhetoric of purpose loses specificity. Goals such as "defence" or "the public interest" or even "the prevention (control?) of crime"—though they may have Type I connotations, nuances, or overtones—are, as March and Simon once put it, *non-operational*.[3] To become *operational* purpose must be specified into objectives and subgoals for which some criteria of efficiency and effectiveness apply. Yet this move from the general to the specific is philosophically treacherous and difficult. "Public education", for example, is a purpose which is general and vague in the extreme and, as countless educational administrators have learned, its translation into specifications is deeply complicated by obfuscation, ambivalence, and ambiguity—quite apart from the omnipresence of contending interests and political forces.

Compounding the problem of specification is the unsaid purpose that invests all organizations, namely, the welfare of its component members. This collective selfishness is, however, generally hidden behind a veil of legitimizing rhetoric. Politicians and bureaucrats talk of the "public interest" or "social services" while corporate executives use the language of "satisfying consumers". In all such expressions of purpose the metavalues of maintenance and growth may act to deter or occlude clarity of goal accountability, and hence of organizational responsibility. Unenunciated goals have to do with such items as pay and perquisites of organization members. These, in turn, seek their legitimization in the same rhetoric of organizational purpose (increased productivity) or compensation for extra-organizational pressures (cost-of-living). Any move to downsizing, the euphemism for organizational shrinkage, engenders purposive interest counterclaims in demands for job-security or golden handshakes. These reveal what could be called the intensive or intensional organizational purpose.

The chain of *ostensive* purpose extends from the individual with particular values and goals through the subsystems of organization with their subpurposes to the organizational entity itself and its purpose. The end of the chain merges into the community of context made up of those individuals and groups who interact with the organization and this in turn merges imperceptibly into the social whole and a cultural community defined by some national boundary. Even this last distinction may be superseded as is the case with international corporations and multi-national conglomerates. At each stage in this progression of purpose statements about goals are capable of a double formulation: that which is expressed in the rhetoric appropriate to the next higher level of value (V_1–V_5) and that which is indeed the case but which for political reasons cannot be overtly expressed. In consequence the language of purpose conceals more than it reveals; it is duplicitous. The task then falls to the administrator of reconciling rhetoric and fact, of monitoring and shaping the flow of purpose, of integrating organizational value. Is this a moral exercise? Of course it is.

The logic of a line of purpose from broadly diffused general purposes (make a profit, serve the public, educate) has endowed organizations with a deceptive and often spurious appearance of rationality. This is epitomized in such variations on the administrative theme as MBO: management by objectives, PPBS: planning, programming, budgeting systems and PERT: programme evaluation review technique. The success of all such methods depends on the specification of material objectives or subgoals. If the cause–effect connections necessary to achieve these objectives can be perceived then it is merely a technical managerial problem of planning to connect means with ends—a positivistic quantitative calculus of resources and time lines. Complexity is no bar to this given modern technology, computerology, automation, and robotics. Values disappear from process and the problem of values itself can be made to disappear. The organization SS–Auschwitz or SS–Dachau can be evaluated on managerial rather than administrative criteria.

Several difficulties interfere with this appearance of rationality and logic. First, as already mentioned, there is covert interest on the part of membership combined, it must be noted, with Barnardian power. Such interest may subvert or deflect the attainment of stages in the purposive chain. Then there is the problem of goal category. Is it quantitative or qualitative, objective or subjective? While the rational techniques may work well for clear end items such as building a submarine or placing a man and a vehicle on the moon they may work poorly or dysfunctionally where the end is conceptually diffuse as in "good education", or "the national interest" or even, paradoxically, "maintaining the organization". Moreover, vague end items will connote different values for different people. They may be simultaneously ambiguous and ambivalent. A newly formed film company, for example, may be seen differentially as having as its major purpose (1) making as large a profit as possible, (2) establishing an artistic reputation, (3) providing the service of entertainment (with profit as necessary but not sufficient cause), (4) providing career opportunities for specific members of the organization, (5) providing job security for others, and (6) providing a tax write-off for investors or a parent corporation.

Organizational goals may be, and usually are, pluralistic rather than monolithic. Ends may be competitive. Trade unions may have both political and welfare objectives. Education comprises the competing purposes of literacy attainment, socialization, vocational preparation, and character development yet none of these subgoals can be excised without damage to the overall integrity of purpose. And to make matters worse some of the components may be quantifiable (reading and mathematical skills) while others may be qualitative (literary appreciation, moral development). Given such complexity any rational or managerial bias towards the quantitative may depreciate or discount the qualitative elements of purpose.

Finally the real purposes may be themselves misperceived. A university may in all good faith (let us make the best assumptions) declare its chief priority as teaching.[4] But in fact, and at another level of truth, its chief priority is really research and scholarly production (not necessarily the same thing, of course). Moreover, some of the membership will perceive the organization as a milch cow or rice bowl or use it chiefly as a stepping stone in a career arabesque. In these and other ways organizational rationality may be much more apparent than real and values percolate into even the most sterile interstices of technology.

Nevertheless the formulation and communication of purpose remains the highest of administrative responsibilities. Upon this rests the character or ethical climate of the organization itself. Barnard concedes that this philosophical function does not rest entirely with administration: "The formulation and definition of purpose is then a widely distributed function, only the more general part of which is executive" but he immediately stresses that the "most important inherent difficulty" in administration is the necessity for "indoctrinating" those at lower levels of hierarchy.[5] Because of "insulation" the "function of formulating grand purposes and providing for their redefinition is one which needs sensitive systems of communication, experience in interpretation, imagination, and delegation of responsibility."[6] What is indicated here, in this classical interpretation, is that intellectual and emotional *understanding* of purpose is typically unevenly distributed throughout the power hierarchy of the organization. Indeed, elsewhere Barnard suggests that *intellectual* understanding by itself is dysfunctional, a "paralysing and divisive element".[7]

Not that subgoals do not need to be rationally comprehended but rather that the larger purpose is better associated either with Type III affect or Type I ideological commitment than with explicit sequences of ends and means. The implication is that it is generally insufficient for the administrator to merely rationalize purpose at the Type II level. This latter position is that of Simon where "the content decisions of the higher administrator deal with more ultimate purposes and more general process than the decisions of the lower administrator. We might say that the lower administrator's purposes are the upper administrator's processes."[8]

What is overlooked by these dogmas of orthodoxy are the socio-psychological factors of purposive investment by the non-administrative non-managerial membership in the organization. While the organization may not be mother-and-father to the member it is often, to use the Oriental metaphor, a "rice-bowl". And this is fundamental. But the fact that most people's livelihoods depend on their organizational affiliation does not discount the possibility of conscious commitment to the organizational purpose as a deeper rationalization of their self-interest. Contemporary concerns with job security reinforce this observation. Moreover, while economic security may be provided by organization membership it is an additional reality that a major portion of life *is* organizational life. Private life too is affected by the part commandeered by the organization. The impress, then, of collective purpose is of no mean motivational significance, at *any* level of hierarchy. It is here that organizational function intersects with personal value experience, ethics, and morality. And it is here that the organization itself assumes what may be called a moral character. Is the organization, say, elitist (Type I), productive (IIA), politically correct (IIB), hedonic (III)?

Of course a dialectical tension exists between the individualist view of Barnard and the collectivist view of Simon. Barnardian purpose is an amalgam of individuals trading in the values market place ("the individual is always the basic strategic factor in organization")[9] while Simon (and Katz and Kahn) would make the organization, not the individual, the pre-emptive strategic factor.[10] While it is certainly true that there must *ultimately* be a favourable balance of trade in value for the individual if services are to maximized this truth must be quite radically adjusted for the various inelasticities of the employment and career market place. The would-be contributor to organizational purpose has a limited number of organizational opportunities. Perhaps only one organization is desirous of his services; certainly mobility—laterally and vertically—is limited and a formidable array of disincentives accumulate in the form of vested interest, natural inertia, structured retention devices in the form of seniority increments, pension schemes, and the like. Individuals' capacity to bargain in their own interests and to take risks in the pursuit of their career goals can also vary greatly. Any change involves some inconvenience and the known evil may be preferred to the unknown good. Collective purpose carries with it a further override of affective coloration for the individual. Once one becomes a member and is thereafter on the "inside" one becomes increasingly subject to a continuous, often subliminal, process of identification with the organizational interest. The many intrudes upon the one. The shifts of value and psychic alignment which occur as a result may rarely be sufficient to fuse individual and collective purpose but they are nonetheless significant. The processes of value integration are unremitting and therefore rightly remain a key function of the executive. But the executive is not uncontaminated either. As Churchill remarked of architecture, "We shape our buildings and then they shape us." *Mutatis mutandis* the same holds for organizations.

The empirical question as to which value-interest factor—organization or individual—is the basic "strategic factor" goes unresolved but it is clear that varying degrees of harmony and conflict may result along a putative continuum from that of the organizational zealot to that of the individual saboteur. What is to be noted about nomothetic purpose, however, is its generality, rationality, logic, and delusive simplicity as contrasted with the particularity, complexity, richness, affective intensity, "reality", and sheer protean multiplicity of idiographic values. That the latter are subordinated to the former constitutes a minor miracle and concedes the overriding quality of the organizational interest even if it also means the triumph of the unclear over the clear. But one must avoid the biological fallacy. Organizations are not organisms; they do not live. They are contrived social entities which find their reality and make their historical mark through the power they can exercise in the affairs of nature and society. In general this power will reside with the administrative subsystem, although all organization members may contend from time to time for influence and participation. The administrator's philosophical task is to establish the value bases for control of this power. The organization's goals are neither autonomous (the biological fallacy) nor dictated by the environment (the teleological fallacy) nor derived from the membership (the humanistic fallacy). The basic leadership difficulty with the pervasion of purpose seems to be that of reconciling the rational Type II explanations of human behaviour in organizations with the larger view which would embrace the transitional and subrational elements of value. And this difficulty is compounded by the fact that organizations themselves may be classified as Type I, Type II, or Type III.

The *meaning* of an organization is twofold. One source of this meaning grows out of the collective phenomenology of its members, which is to say that human chemistry determines morale (as well as morals). The other source derives from logic, whether that logic be grounded in economics, politics, sociology, or ideology. This too yields ethics, ethos, morals, and value. The administrator is positioned at the interface between these two realms of value, and must accommodate both.

RECONCILING THE IRRECONCILABLE

Administration is schizoid. Discipline forever wars with indulgence. The value paradigm draws our attention to the distinction between the hedonic values of individual indulgence (which might well include such administrative desirables as power, social approval, reputation, and prestige) and the collective "social" values of morality, convention, duty, and transpersonal commitment.

For the organization to survive, to satisfy its metavalues, sanctions must operate to ensure at least a partial hegemony of discipline over indulgence. Typically, these are of two kinds. First, there are the collective sanctions, reinforced by society, of conventional norms, conventional morality, the "axioms" of political value,[11] the constraints of consensus, law, rules, regulations. The pay cheque, the time clock, the executive diary, the computer, and the balance sheet all illustrate this Type II kind of pressure.

The second sanction to discipline occurs when there is self-commitment, the individual attachment to or investment in an organizational collective value by way of ideology, religion, or philosophical reflection. Despite any potential dangers from this sort of sanction (extremism, myopia, zealotry, fanaticism) organizations will usually seek through their administrations for some measure of this Type I value infusion into their ranks, it being commonly acknowledged that self-discipline is better (more efficient and effective) than imposed discipline. The alternatives are Type II persuasion through appeal to rational self-interest and the coercions described above.

The paradigm example for these disciplinary efforts, all of which seek to reconcile individual and collective, is the military. Here where the collective interest may demand the ultimate sacrifice (literally so) value theory yields a praxis running the gamut of the paradigm from ceremonial ritual and indoctrination in regimental history and tradition (I) through combat training, drill, hazing and initiation rites (IIA, IIB)[12] down to decorations and badges (III)—all of which seek, in Selznick's terms, to infuse with value beyond the rational needs of the occasion, beyond the technical requirements of the task at hand.[13] At its best this value praxis may engender Level I commitments but, in any event, it serves to buttress the Type II sanctions of discipline and maintain the hegemony of the nomothetic dimensions. It may and should be noted that soldiers die for other than nomothetic reasons. At the individual level of analysis they may do so out of love for comrades (Type I), out of fear of comrades or group conformity (Type IIB), out of panic or despair (Type III), even out of stoical rationality, "The occasion demands it" (Type IIA). But these individual acts lend support to rather than detract from the organizational effort of value indoctrination.

At less extreme levels than the military example the same principles apply. Japanese employees assemble each morning to sing the company song. American high schools engage in pep rallies, as do salesmen and entrepreneurs. "Team spirit" is invoked in many places and many ways and the invocation always seeks to define the line between in-group and others, between us and the rest. The psychological need for belonging is manipulated into an identification of individual with group to the explicit benefit of the former but the implicit benefit of the latter.

Katz and Kahn have analysed the motivational patterns of organizational commitment into four logical categories.[14] First, legal compliance where contributions are compelled and a machine theory applies as in conscription or prison labour. This is the realm of naked power and Theory X. Second, inducement through rewards and incentives, the lower Barnardian realm. Modified machine theory and behaviourist psychology is here appropriate. Third, the opportunity to exercise special talents and skills, professional expertise and careerism; and fourth, the opportunity and desire to seek self-actualization through identification with the organization's purposes. This is clearly a Maslovian type of analysis and an ideal assumption would be that administrators and executives would be operating in the self-fulfillment/self-actualization range of motivation. Even more ideally *all* organization members would function at this level. This does not deny that at the leadership level the divergence between organizational goals and the administrator's private purposes may often be deeply schismatic, necessitating much in the arts of concealment and dramaturgy. Nevertheless, for practical purposes the fair assumption is that the modal range of purposive behaviour will be somewhere between the extremes of individual opportunism and collective fanaticism. Which is to say, the split goes unreconciled, the reconciliation fails.

The problem of organizational value conflict resolution will be considered again. It is essentially one of alignment of idiographic and nomothetic values (V_3

and V_1). For the ordinary member this always means inconvenience at the very least, always some accommodation and compromise. For the administrator it means, properly speaking, a careful analysis of V_3 values as expressed both in formal goals and policies and in informal processes. This analysis has to be extended to V_1 for the administrator personally. These values do not have to be entirely reconciled; it is improbable that they ever would be, or could be—but there is a limit of discrepancy beyond which the administrator cannot go without either dissociation or war. Later there will be discussion of value auditing and conflict resolution. For now the point is that success in this kind of organizational analysis calls for some degree of withdrawal and reflection; both of which are behaviours which do not particularly recommend themselves to action-oriented administrators.

ORGANIZATIONAL MORALITY

The philosopher Ladd[15] has forcefully argued that organizations are antagonistic to ethical outcomes: they frustrate, delimit, and even degrade the moral enterprise and they do this from structural considerations now familiar to the reader, namely the metavalue of rationality and the nomothetic principle of depersonalization. Obviously Kant's dicta that humans should *always* be treated as ends and not means, that one should *never* lie, and that one should *always* act in accordance with the categorical moral imperative are violated every minute of every organizational or bureaucratic day.

In complex human systems individuals are not whole persons but role incumbents, partial sets of skills that are of utility to the organizational whole. They are *parts*, replaceable and substitutable parts at that. In the rationally construed organization no one is indispensable. Morality on the other hand, even at a less purist level than that of Kant, invokes the whole of the personality while in the organization this exceeds, overflows (and inevitably interferes with) any role save perhaps that of generalissimo or tyrant. Of course, the personality component will vary considerably with role, professional artists and administrators having more personality latitude than machinists and corporals, but the principle remains. There would be a "personality surplus" even in the most *laisser-faire* of organizational roles.

The direct psychological implication of organizational power, *vis-à-vis* its membership, is that individual sentiments, affects, and interests are discounted. The organizational language game is impersonal, even anti-personal. It reveals the values appropriate for the social and collective decisions made in its name. Organizational goals as ends combined with rational procedures for their attainment as means (glossed and glazed where necessary by rhetoric, political correctness, and the refinements of the human relations movement) make organizational life curiously analogous to chess. Within the game there are no metaphysically "right" or "wrong" moves only moves which are more or less efficacious within the overall set system of rules (V_3) which cannot be challenged from the inside, from "within the game". The ordinary organization member becomes a logical factotum, a good soldier, whether alienated or enthused or merely manipulated is beside the point. Even that *extra*ordinary member, the administrator, is not an author of acts but an *agent*, one who does things in the name of others.

There is a specially insidious way in which this character of the organization as principal with its administrators as agents can become malevolent. It occurs when, by a corruption of philosophical analysis and psychological detachment the administrator comes to the belief or attitude that the organization (collective) is bigger than any individual and possesses a destiny and logic of its own. Then the organization is not only reified but deified. And the agent ceases to be personally or morally responsible for the acts which derive from the authority and *authorship* of the collectivity. Bureaucrats and civil servants, officers of the state, administrators of industry, trade, commerce, education, no less than the Adolf Eichmanns of history, faithfully execute policies of which they may or may not personally approve—and outwardly benevolent organizations can become latent and potent collective forces for evil. From this the hypothesis springs intuitively forth that the larger, more impersonal, more complex, bureaucratic, technocratic and even meritocratic, the more nomothetic and hierarchical the organization—the greater the malevolent potency.

We are not concerned here with the legal aspects of agency but rather with the socio-psychological and philosophical ramifications of collective or social decision. In the case of contracts, for example, the official concluding the agreement is neither personally bound nor personally responsible for the consequences of what becomes an organizational obligation. And there may well be a certain *frisson* of irresponsibility when the will of the group, or the leaders of the group, is allowed to sway and prevail over valid opposition.

Legally an agent acts in the interest of a principal. An administrator is supposed to act in the interest of an organization. So far so good but organizational interests may conflict with other levels of interest (V_5, V_4, V_2, V_1). Thus the agent/administrator comes to find that from time to time his agency is doing things, or causing things to be done, that conflict with personal values at either the Type III or Type I levels. A parallel dilemma might be that of the utterly professional lawyer burdened with the task of seeking to prove a client innocent, who is known by the lawyer to be guilty. The organizational decision is made according to Barnard "non-personally from the point of view of its organizational effect and its relation to the organization purpose".[16] Simon's corresponding positivistic text is "decisions in private management must take as their ethical premises the objectives that have been set for the organization."[17]

So much is taken formally for granted in the literature of organization theory but it would be simply naive to assume that this surface appearance of ethical neutrality cannot serve as cover for, or even an instrument of, Type III malice, spite, and animus or Type I ruthlessness in the pursuit of an individual rather than a collective agenda. That is, the appearance and façade of Type II rationality can be made to serve as an excuse for most, if not all, of the well-documented record of bureaucratic injustice. On the other hand, Victor Thompson, in a cogent defence of bureaucratic collectivism coined the useful term bureauticism, on analogy with neuroticism, to refer to individual resentment at the subjugation of unwarranted individual desires to the collective interest. Bureauticism of itself however, real phenomenon though it be, cannot explain away all anti-bureaucratic, anti-collective, anti-authoritarian sentiments. Organizational dehumanism or organizational inhumanity extends even to organizations which are by definition humane or even Type I (hospitals, the Roman Catholic Church). Administration, it seems by its very nature, can devalue value in the cold light of reason and the cool detachment of agency.

The philosopher Ladd goes so far as to say that social (organizational) decisions cannot be moral.

> Thus, for logical reasons it is improper to expect organizational conduct to conform to the ordinary principles of morality. We cannot and must not expect formal organizations, or their representatives acting in their official capacities, to be honest, courageous, considerate, sympathetic, or to have any kind of moral integrity. Such concepts are not in the vocabulary, so to speak, of the organizational language-game. (We do not find them in the vocabulary of chess either!) Actions that are wrong by ordinary moral standards are not so for organizations; indeed, they may often by required. Secrecy, espionage and deception do not make organizational action wrong; rather they are right, proper and, indeed, rational, if they serve the objectives of the organization. They are no more or no less wrong than, say, bluffing is in poker. From the point of view of organizational decision making they are ethically neutral.[18]

The philosopher Iris Murdoch expresses it somewhat differently, but to the same end:

> ... The charm and power of technology and the authority of a "scientific outlook" conceal the speed with which the idea of the responsible moral spiritual individual is being diminished. The fragmentation of morality menaces this individual, as it menaces the society in which he flourishes.
>
> Political utilitarianism may also lead people with high motives into "specialized" fragmented morality. In extreme situations of this sort, which may seem to some young people the only "moral" situations with which they can engage, the idea of the virtuous individual tends to vanish. A cynic (or structuralist) might say of our age that it is the end of the era of "the virtuous individual".[19]

These philosophical comments by non-administrators are interesting for they highlight the paradox that while morality governs relations with *others* it is itself interpreted as an *individual* matter. In our analysis of value this standing dilemma has been shown as a contest between discipline (II) and indulgence (III/I) and it has been suggested that the administrator ought to identify with the collective interest (II). But this ethical quasi-imperative now needs qualification, for organizations are not necessarily benevolent nor forces for the social good and the public interest. As Ladd asserts, "actions that are wrong by ordinary moral standards are not so for organizations", and as Murdoch maintains, "political utilitarianism [that is, the IIA conventional mode of bureaucratic function] may lead even people with high motives into a 'specialized' fragmented morality." Power corrupts and organizational power corrupts insidiously.

What must not be overlooked, however, in this grimmest vision of organizational life—the view that organizations are morally stultifying and ethically dangerous entities—is the power possessed by the administrator *qua* person. This power can be exercised in creative or destructive or preservative ways from within the organization so as to modify morale, ethos, and collective intentionality. Of course, if the administrator abdicates this potential by adopting the *persona* of the agent he offends as Pontius Pilate then and the legalistic bureaucrat now. Functionaries and factotums *are* moral ciphers. Yet, to fuse individual morality with collective decision is difficult; as Barnard constantly stressed, it demands much in the way of moral complexity. In comprehending this complexity it is necessary to cope with two difficult concepts: self-interest and responsibility. The first is only simple on the surface. The administrator has to engage in continuous self-scrutiny and difficult introspection to discover the truth of private motivations. And perhaps the true self can never be perceived save through a glass darkly. This topic will be considered later.

The second concept, responsibility, is equally vexed and tortuous. If *all* are responsible who *is* responsible? One cannot, as they say in the law, hang a common seal. We can, however, discriminate between legal, formal, and moral responsibility.

Legally both bodies-human and bodies-corporate are held "accountable" for their acts to the system of game rules established under the heading of "law" at local, national, or international levels. These rules usually have their genesis in Type II consensus values or Type I principles as historically interpreted. The difficulty is that corporate acts cannot always be reduced to the acts of individuals. If I own 10 shares in General Motors I am not responsible if that firm violates the anti-trust rules or does things that are not good for the nation. And if I am a director of Baring's Bank and it goes broke overnight I am not responsible beyond the rules of legal limited liability even if the greatest individual economic havoc has been wrought.[20] On the other hand *accountability* (as opposed to responsibility) can be impressed upon the individual actors who are *agents* of a corporate body through such legal retributive devices as fines, imprisonment, and loss of licence or credentials. Law has the sanctions of naked power. The force of legal responsibility is real enough, especially since the corporate agents are usually administrators, but this sort of responsibility is extra-organizational and distinct from moral responsibility.

Formal responsibility can be conceived as intra-organizational legality. It refers to the accountabilities sanctioned by the game rules of an organization. Acts are constrained by a potent system of rewards and punishments, including salaries, bonuses, promotion, demotion, and termination. The monitoring functions of administration and management are a part of this responsibility system. Just as law seeks a ground in societal values so the system of formal responsibility seeks its ground in organizational values and policy. This in-organizational parallel to corporate bodies acting as independent entities is to be found in group acts and decisions stemming from group processes and structures (committees, boards, *ad hoc* groups) established formally and internally within the organization. So, if a committee of peers decides by secret vote or unrecorded consensus that a colleague should be dismissed, or denied promotion, against *whom* can the injured finger be pointed? The popularity of committee action is understandable. It can be a way of responsibly avoiding responsibility. But the responsibility thus avoided would be moral responsibility.

Moral responsibility reduces to the individual only. It is intrinsically phenomenological. Since responsibility of any kind is always responsibility *to* somebody *for* something in the moral sense it is the responsibility of a person to himself for his adherence to his entire range of values and especially to those Type I values to which he has become authentically engaged. It is the ultimate sense of responsibility.

It makes no sense and much confusion therefore to talk of organizational morality without a great deal of conceptual ground-clearing. Organizations are abstractions, unconscious entities that do not feel a thing. They are not sentient; they do not have a will. To say otherwise is to commit the biological fallacy. The nexus between organizations and their human components, however, does create what Greenfield calls a moral order. It is exemplified in Michel's "iron law" of oligarchy which derives from the principle of polyarchy: that rule can only be by the few and never by the many.[21] Michels showed that those who control the life of an organization, typically but not necessarily administrators or officials, can generally smother, head-off, or ignore the views of dissident and usually disunited non-hierarchical members of the organization. These *de facto* leaders can also usually modify the ideology and formal goals of the organization in their own interests. This type of subversion is therefore a major qualification to the general axiom that the administrator's values should be equated with the collective.

Administrative morality, it follows, is self-referent and psychologically complex. It is private in genesis, public in effect. It comes to stand for an organization even though bred of factors such as conscience, will, consciousness, commitment to principles and attachment to preferences. At best the academic disciplines of ethics and moral philosophy are only ancillary to moral action and only relevant to the administrator's understanding of responsibility insofar as they can clarify concepts, set out the arguments, and make the case for Type I and II value. They are aids to moral navigation that can be, and often are, ignored or swept aside in the tempest of conflict and the heat of action.

In this light it is necessary to reiterate the point that has now been made *ad nauseam*. An administrator insofar as he is a leader is not a manager: he designs and creates roles for himself as well as for others; he monitors and reconciles the nomothetic and idiographic aspects of his organization; he determines in part or in whole the organizational values; and he does these things within the constraints and inhibitions of the metavalues. None of this is pure agency. When one considers that the administrative role also embraces such activities as settling value disputes among organization members, determining the organizational language game, and negotiating with parties and levels of interest outside the organization it is clear that moral agency (as opposed to legal or formal agency) is inescapable.

Barnard recognized this and stressed the need for moral, or in our terms valuational, skills. He defined moral as "personal forces or propensities of a general and subtle character in individuals which tend to inhibit, control, or modify inconsistent immediate specific desires, impulses, or interests, and to intensify those which are consistent with such propensities."[22] An interesting definition suggesting the suppression or repression of Type III values by levels higher on the paradigm. When such Barnardian "morals" were "strong and stable" there would exist a "condition of responsibility".[23] He goes on to illustrate: "I know men whose morals as a whole I cannot help believe to be lower ethically than my own. But these men command my attention and sometimes my admiration because they adhere to their codes rigidly in the face of great difficulties; whereas I observe that many others who have a 'higher' morality do not adhere to their codes when it would apparently not be difficult to do so. Men of the first class have a higher sense of responsibility than those having, as I view them, the higher ethical standards. *The point is that responsibility is the property of an individual by which whatever morality exists in him becomes effective in conduct*"[24] (Barnard's italics). Here the point at issue seems to be will, or the lack of it, *akrasia* as the Greeks called the latter. We may subscribe to a value but fail to implement the subscription in action through loss of nerve or failure of the requisite desire or will. In terms of our value theory this would simply indicate a lack of *presence* of the values in contention, even though publicly or orally or even subjectively avowed. The operative Barnardian phrase is "whatever morality exists within him" but this only means whatever the components of his value complex happen to be. This does not alter in any way, however, the thesis that the response to the demands of organizational life will be a function of the moral substance (i.e. values) of the administrative actor. And this leads to a general hypothesis: that the character of the leader in an organization, analysed in value terms, is directly related to charisma and to organizational morality or moral climate. Insofar as organizations are moral orders the values of their leadership makes them so.

ORGANIZATIONS AS METAPHORS

Perhaps the most comprehensive treatment of organizations as metaphors—things standing for something else—has been presented in Gareth Morgan's brilliant *Images of Organization*.[25] This would appear to exhaust the possibilities of conceptualizing organizations. Its perspectives range from classical machine and systems theories, political systems and socio-cultural orders to imaginative interpretations such as organizations-as-brains or holographic arrangements or "psychic prisons". All of these may be considered as valid "takes" on organizational life but it is curious that the terms values, ethics, and morals do not find a place in Morgan's index despite quite thorough and fertile discussions within the text of such value-saturated issues in organization theory as Marxist dialectics and "organization as domination". Perhaps this reflects a certain philosophical diffidence or sophisticated caution but, nevertheless, in his conclusion the author moves from the constraints of description to overt prescription. His declared philosophy is deserving of quotation at length:

> ... I believe that people can change organizations and society, even though the perception and actuality of power relations passed down through history may at times make change difficult. Prescriptively, I would thus like us all to recognize that reality is made, not given; to recognize that our seeing and understanding of the world is always *seeing as*, rather than *seeing as is*; and to take an ethical and moral responsibility for the personal and collective consequences of the way we see and act in everyday life, difficult though this may be.[26]

Morgan goes on to express his own preferred metaphors: the organization as psychic-prison, as culture, as politics, and as brain; each of which presents both the picture of individual entrapment in a deterministic context and the (hopefully according to Morgan) possibility or potentiality of either release from that entrapment or fulfillment within it. "I believe that the domination metaphor helps us to confront the gross exploitation and inequality on which so many of our organizations build. ... Consistent with my overall orientation, I firmly believe that we need to break the hold of bureaucratic thinking and to move toward newer, less exploitative more equal modes of interaction in organizations."[27]

Just what this new organizational egalitarianism might look like or what forms it could take, the metaphors having been surveyed and exhausted, is left to the realm of hope and for some yet to be born administrative arrangement. In short, the philosopher of administration is forced to conclude that the moral potentialities of organizations are primitive, despite the prima facie appeal of subordination of individual to collective interest.

ORGANIZATIONS AS MORAL PRIMITIVES

It will be recalled that *ur*-values of organizations, the metavalues, are universal and apply not to individuals but to collectives. When conceived as organizational laws they form quasi-moral (or *pseudo*-moral) imperatives; commandments for the administrator which could be distilled into the single injunction, "Thou shalt preserve the organization!" The natural corollary is "Seek the organization's interest always!" and thence, by way of easy stages of increasing identification with *us* (the organization) and disidentification with *them* (the rest of society) to "What's good for General Motors is good for the country" (What's good for education, the military, etc., etc., is *good*.) to, finally, "My organization, right or wrong." The conventional wisdom acknowledges all this. It allows that the administrator must maintain the organization, must seek its growth rather than its diminution, must seek the organization's ends and goals and their accomplishment as efficiently and as effectively as possible. All these are *values*. This primitive value structure or base has imperative force for the leader prior to and without regard for personal value orientation. It is in this way that organizations can be called morally "primitive". The collectivity is neither person nor biological entity nor simple sum of its component interests but its constitution as a corporate entity establishes *ipso facto* a value pattern with governing effect on its administrators and this pattern or template, measured against humane individual standards, can be called elemental, primitive, unsophisticated, and even inhumane.

This does not mean that organizations are of necessity corrupting or degrading to the morality of their members. What it means is that they can work a subtle or malevolent influence if their primitive imperatives (the metavalues) are allowed to impose themselves, achieve dominance, and pass unexamined. An efficient organization effectively maintaining itself, expanding its influence, achieving its goals can be a source of self-fulfillment and well-being both to its members and its clientele. But it can also be an engine of corruption, a Juggernaut, a moral anathema—the more so as it clothes itself via its public relations subsystems, in the garments of moral righteousness. (And, nowadays, of political correctness.) The administrative philosopher and the administrative practitioner must therefore, from time to time, ask the following questions:

1. Is the organization justified in its basic (*real*) purpose?
2. Does that justification in turn justify the complex of ancillary purposes and subgoals?
3. Which of growth, consolidation, and reduction is the most *morally* defensible?
4. What are the latent functions and how can *they* be justified?

The point of such metavaluational scrutiny or audit is simply to reduce the primitive unconscious influence of organizational values and to re-enter them into the value calculus of administration at a more conscious and sophisticated level. That is, at a *philosophical* level of awareness.

Metavalues are by definition *good*. The question is always whether they are *right*. To even ask that question implies already a degree of philosophical sophistication, of consciousness and moral complexity that augurs well for the immanence of authentic leadership and the ultimate harmony of individual and collective.

ANSWERS

The questions with which this survey of organizational morality began may now be reconsidered. Do organizations possess moral, ethical, valuational qualities in their own right? Or, is the whole in some moral sense, greater than the sum of its parts? To this the answer must be, not quite felicitously, in the affirmative. Yes the organizational value-complex is, like language itself, an inter-subjectivity. And yes, also like language, it is attached to a substratum of culture. This culture has its own history. The institution outlives its members and human chemistry affects the ethos of the organization as it flows through its structure as blood and lymph through an organism. Socio-chemistry imparts to the organization a residue of value which can be summed up in the terms tradition, mores, ethos, moral climate, morale, *esprit de corps* and so on. This organizational quality of intension is closely linked to its overt (and even more so to its covert) purposes: an organization can be malevolent. Can be morally corrupting. Can be evil. And conversely for the positive value attributions to which organizations typically aspire.

Do organizations, in the terms of the value paradigm, exhibit features which would permit their classification as Type I, Type II, or Type III? Again the answer is affirmative and respective examples that are clear-cut would be The Society of Jesus; a Ministry of Highways; a Golf Club on the one hand and the SS, the Mafia, and a juvenile gang on the other. All organizations may be assigned a place in the paradigmatic typology[28] although most will exhibit mixed rather than pure strains of value orientation so that the classification tends to definition by salience or dominant profile.

Are organizations then, in Greenfield's terms, moral orders? Yes, though the understanding of this characterization is both subtle and complex. Nevertheless, our personal lives are in large part organizational, or functionally dependent upon organizations, and morality enters into every aspect of this interaction. There is no such thing as value-neutral or value-free organization. The impartial bureaucracy is not a myth but rather a subscription to a quasi-morality of rationality and objectivity.

SUMMATION

The aim of Part III of this book has been to treat directly, but at a theoretical level, the linked concepts so fundamental to administrative philosophy of values, interests, and power. It has been argued that among these the key administrative concept is value and to that end a paradigmatic analysis of value was undertaken. This analysis is philosophically robust and within it values manifest themselves in three hierarchical levels as Types I, II, and III. They enter the complex processes of valuation, evaluation, and motivation at five levels of interest: V_1 through V_5. While this analysis can serve to sophisticate the administrative leaders of organizations it also points to complex unresolved philosophical issues. These refer to the valuational status or character of organizations themselves (moral primitives) and to the central conflict in organizational life, namely, the problem of the commons, or collective interest in opposition to self-interest individual and egoistic tendencies. This has in the past also been known as the problem of the social ethic.[29] The nature of organizations as moral orders is also philosophically contentious but nonetheless draws attention to an inexorable administrative commitment to some set of values, whether drawn from the range approved as valid by philosophical opinion, or not. An effective leader must adopt a private position on the central issues of values, interests, and power. Administrative morality depends upon the quality of this position which in turn depends upon the degree of technical knowledge of the concepts involved.

Part IV, the concluding section, will build upon the preceding theoretical foundation and treat of practical difficulties (disjunctions) which beset both the practice of administration and the philosophy informing it.

146. Administration is schizoidal. Discipline wars with indulgence, self-assertion with self-sacrifice.
147. Detachment and commitment, consistence and inconsistency, to be engaged or disengaged: these are the extremes of administrative philosophy. Their function is to direct our attention to the middle ground of ambivalence and ambiguity.
148. True purpose is rarely enunciated. The administrator colludes in this.
149. The organizational analogue to the legal corporation is the decision making group.
150. Committees: a sometime mode of responsible irresponsibility or irresponsible responsibility.
151. Administrative rhetoric must seek to make organizational welfare appear as extra-organizational good.
152. The administrator is bound by the metavalues. He can exceed or transcend them but not deny them.
153. The fiction of agency can be ethically lethal.
154. A corporation is a legal fiction. An organization is a conceptual fiction. Lawyers and administrators are both agents of fantasy.
155. In the private sector the profit motive is a necessary but not sufficient condition for organization. In the public sector the service motive is a necessary but not sufficient condition for organization.
156. Organizations are evaluated upon criteria which are extraneous to organization and administration. These criteria are metavalues.
157. Organizations are morally primitive—especially when defined by their metavalues.
158. As chess is amoral so is rational administration.
159. The metavalue prophylaxis is periodic analysis, that is, value audit.
160 Collectivities cannot be punished; organizations are immune from retribution; they feel no pain.
161. Organizations do not question their need to exist. They need to exist because they do exist.
162. Growth of organizations is growth of interest. Growth of interest implies the growth of power.
163. An organization is a state of inadequacy. It strains to close the gap between what is and what can be. To have a goal is to be dissatisfied by definition.
164. Organizations are not organisms but neither are organizations equivalent to the sum of their parts.
165. Organizations exist for the welfare of their members. This is the simplest and most basic truth.

166. The essence of the organizational quasi-life is symbolic. It is a matter of the manipulation of symbols.
167. Ceremony seeks to motivate at the transrational level. At the rational level it is absurd. At the subrational level it invokes the daemon of the tribe.
168. Organization members surrender a part of their autonomy (of their soul?) simply by their belongingness.
169. Organizations are pseudo-moral and quasi-immortal.
170. Role incumbency need not reduce moral responsibility. For the administrator it could exalt it.
171. Collectivities author but do not own their acts.
172. Responsibility is transitive: from x to y for z. But $x = y$ is possible and z may be a part of x.
173. The system of law is a language game of responsibility. It is not moral. Though it may seek its ground in morality.
174. The factors of moral responsibility are value structure, value complexity, value strength, ego, will, role, situation, and sophistication. Compounded by the organizational language game.
175. The progression of interest is reciprocal, from self to society. But within this progression organization mediates.
176. The chief fruit of administrative philosophy is moral complexity. Sophistication. At the apogee: authenticity.

IV

DISJUNCTIONS

Virtue is secretly in love with vice
for without it neither can exist.

Chapter 10
Pathology

This book began with the thesis that philosophy and administration were intimately related and that in the ideal case they were conjoined. In the light of the intervening chapters, however, it should now be clear that this conjunction is an uneasy one, fitful, and tortuous ... a vexing problem for the individual, for the group, for organizations, for society, for culture, for civilization, and for the quality of human life in general. This final part explores in greater depth the extent to which the disjunctions of this relationship make themselves manifest and the responses by which, in accordance with the value theory expounded in the previous part, the administrator of the late twentieth and early twenty-first centuries might see some honourable self-reconciliation with the dilemmas of his vocation. Of necessity this concluding part will be an investigation into morality, that is, into the catalogue of value sicknesses—the pathologies of organizations and their leaders in our times. The administrative task does not change essentially through history; what changes is only technology, the content of values, and the battleground of ideology.

THE PLATONIC DISJUNCTION

The epigram that virtue is secretly in love with vice, for they depend upon each other for definition, takes on an interesting form in administrative philosophy for it reveals the paradox or dilemma exemplified at the surface level by the differences between rhetoric and reality and, at a deeper level, between the world-views of Plato and Machiavelli. As Saul Bellow once said, "With everyone sold on the good how does all the evil get done?"

One of the difficulties of discussing administration with sympathy and understanding—one of the difficulties in becoming sophisticated about it—is that a gulf exists between the unreal value neutrality or sterility (or worse, political correctness) of the textbooks and the so-called "real world", the knowing world of "hard-nosed" practice, the world of cut and thrust that has converted more than one political scientist to doctrines of cynicism and despair, the world in which radical evil exists.[1] Stereotypes emerge. At the sterilized extreme is Weber's ideal-type bureaucrat, an organizational instrument or agent whose essential humanity has been sacrificed on the altar of pure rationality or the humbler positivistic "bounded rationality" of Simon. At the other extreme is *homo politicus,* the political animal, the careerist barbarian who would again sacrifice essential humanity, this time at the altar of fortune and the Goddess of success.

This dichotomy is central to Plato's *Republic,* the classical statement of administrative philosophy in antiquity.[2] Trying to answer the question of why men should do right rather than follow the apparently more rewarded practice of injustice, Plato had to develop a whole theory of the ideal State and its administrators or Guardians. The Guardians are peculiar in that they are philosophers who have had some insight into the nature of truth which is synonymous with the ideal of the Form of the Good, Plato's analogue for God. Such insight smacks of mystical or quasi-mystical experience, a sort of personality conversion and reformation that paradoxically not only fits the Guardians for leadership and governance (by virtue of moral superiority) but simultaneously dissolves any ambition to engage in administration, much less to enjoy its perquisites of power, prestige, and fortune. Rather they would wish to withdraw from the public rough-and-tumble *pour cultiver leurs jardins* and therefore can only be obliged to administer out of a pure sense of duty, moral obligation, and a vocation of responsibility. This they do out of Type I motivations: a motivation that is altruistic, ethical, ideological.

Russell has outlined a threefold classification of men into aggressives who seek to dominate (the commanders), submissives who seek to be dominated (the obeyers), and those who wish neither but would rather withdraw. This last represents, presumably, the philosophical type which again is considered to be in some way superior to the other two categories.[3] The Platonic type administrators would then have to be obliged out of a higher moral sense to engage in that which they do not like. The paradox is that this work—of leadership, governance, and administration—is the very work which appeals as eminently desirable to the class of persons most unsuited for it, namely, those who wish to exercise power for their own gratification and self-indulgence; the egoists, the careerists, the megalomaniacs, the lusters after rewards of office. This accounts perhaps for the rather despairing note sounded by Plato when he says, "I was forced, in fact, to the belief that the only hope of finding justice for society or for the individual lay in true philosophy, and that mankind will have no respite from trouble until either real philosophers gain political power or politicians become by some miracle true philosophers."[4]

So the pathology is this. To be reasonable we must concede that *both* of Plato's alternatives are unlikely. By and large, administrative roles will be filled from the ranks of the ordinary and the less than superlative. Power will be their basic reality with all its corrupting influence. It is to counteract, to mediate and meliorate that influence that they need the aid and conjunction of philosophy—not so much to make them into Guardians as to inoculate them against the other extreme. Philosophy as prophylactic, perhaps as propaedeutic.

It is also reasonable to assume without trace of cynicism that self-interest is the prime dynamic. But the Guardian's concept of self is out of the ordinary. While the ordinary administrator may rationalize an enlarged self-interest to include kin, clan, or organization this extended self does not disqualify and may even exaggerate that Realpolitik in which the weak and tender-minded go to the wall. In the patois of the American success-wisdom: "Nice guys finish last" or "Show me a good loser and I'll show you a loser."[5] The Guardian's concept of self, on the other hand, would seem to reach beyond this to a vision, however dimly perceived, in which the ego (extended or atomic) is sublimated into some sort of union or harmony with the whole order of things. The Guardian does not deny the lower perspective but transcends it. Self-interest sublates Type III and Type I values. The individual is not lost in this grander order but fulfilled. The Platonic Republic does not impose an Hegelian, Marxian, or totalitarian "ethics of the hive". On the contrary, the latter would be a product of the merger between Type III and Type II value orientations. Guardians, did they exist, would look *beyond* mere order and harmony in the organization and the State, beyond social welfare and egalitarian equilibrium.

To repeat, the Platonic vision is idealistic. Guardianship is an ideal. The masses and their administrators are for the most part neither saints nor psychopaths but are normally distributed between the extremes of the value paradigm. Nevertheless, in the ordinary practice of administrative affairs the comfortable but dangerous assumption can only too easily be made that "We are all honourable men." And while Theory X is often applied with rigour to the non-administrative ranks, it is often overlooked altogether, or given insufficient weight when applied, if at all, to executives. In view of the fact that control of the organizational reward system is a prerogative of administration, and in view of the presumptive bias of honour attaching to leadership roles; in view also of Milgram's evidence and the agentic tendency—it might be only conservative to make the worst assumptions: that those in office or seeking office are motivated (in addition to whatever higher motives) by vanity, greed, and egotism rather than by any self-denying spirit of service in the Guardian tradition. Furthermore, being successful and professionally sophisticated (having won out in the political contest) they are the better able to disguise, conceal, and *re*-present their basal motivations. Above all, perhaps, are they able to do this to themselves. To confirm their sense of righteousness. Such loss of altruism would be not only a psychological defence mechanism but a disjunctive pathology.

BUREAUPATHOLOGIES

The useful term "bureaupathology" has been coined to refer to those things which can go wrong when ostensibly benevolent and rational complex organizations set out to accomplish their purposes in the real world.[6] Technically the term is associated with those dysfunctions which are commonly associated in the public mind with the pejorative sense of bureaucracy: bigness and complexity, overspecialization and circumlocution, inertial inflexibility, obsolescence, impersonal alienation, intra- and extra-organizational imperialism, and the like. There is nothing new here. Dickens expressed a Victorian perception of the problem in his entertaining description of the Office of Circumlocution. Kafka's view was grimmer and deeply sinister. Orwell imparted a postmodern and perhaps even more ominous overtone to which I shall advert in a later chapter. What is to be remarked here is that for over a century the consensus of the arts has been growing about the problems of bureaupathology and the organizational imperative. The consistency and negativity of this consensus is striking. Clearly there is some reality about organizational life which tends to threaten and offend artistic sensibilities. That this reality might be traceable to Type III affectivity may induce or seduce administrators into discounting it, the more so as Type II arguments for the efficiency and effectiveness of classical Weberian bureaucracy are rationally persuasive, but the value conflict is at least noteworthy when the lines are so forcibly drawn between the spokesmen of the humanities and the proponents of political practice.

LOSS OF COMPREHENSION

Bureaupathologies proliferate. The sociological literature alone is replete with case histories. The folk-wisdom is vindicated and affirmed again and again in the academic archives. Consider but a single example, chosen because of its central importance to administrative philosophy. It has to do with the problem of generalism which in itself, it will be recalled, is the a priori specialism of administration. Organizations are hierarchical power structures (it has already been shown that they cannot be otherwise).[7] The conception of power and authority is conventionally pyramidal and is loosely expressed in the theoretical notion of line and staff. The central nervous system, so to speak, of this power hierarchy is the administrative *line* running from apex to base of the organization and carrying command and veto power with it all the way. In Scott and Hart's terms it runs from the significant people of the executive suite via the professional ranks of staff expertise through to the insignificant people of the lower organizational echelons.[8] Traditionally these lowest ranks were made up of workers who (paradoxically like administrators) possessed only general or undifferentiated skills but, in a technological society, where even private soldiers tend to be specialized, this classical pattern no longer holds. On the contrary, the quality and quantity of specialization increases with ascent of the hierarchy, particularly at the staff or professional levels. These strata tend to be occupied by organization members with a special kind of power, the power of *expertise* sanctioned, usually, by some sort of professional cachet. In other words this power is kept exclusive by means of professional or guild credentials. Such power holders can often be the "cosmopolitans" whose feudal allegiance to the organization may be suspect[9] when contrasted with the "local" affiliation to the organization of both the significant and the insignificant people. This gives rise to a very general endemic source of conflict where the expertise required to perform the organization's work rests with *staff* while the power of command and veto rests with the *line*. Executive authority is thus dependent on the acquiescence and subservience of lower levels of hierarchy and this creates the potential for a variety of pathologies not the least of which is dramaturgy or role-playing with concomitant executive stress.[10] Such a divergence, inevitable under modern technology, between the myths and the realities of power is perhaps the most significant and pervasive of the ills deriving from the organizational imperative. It can stifle creativity, distort collective energies, and corrupt authentic leadership. Yet it is only an aspect of the general pathophysiology of organizations.

This is, however, a structural (Type II) technopathology, what might be called the pathology of lost comprehension because the decision makers, the policy makers, and the holders of the veto are themselves *naturally* divorced from the technological interface with reality. The general does not know what it is like in the trenches or the jungle; the principal cannot teach the subjects his instructors are teaching, the Minister has no inkling of how his will is translated into action. And conversely those who man the guns, the microscopes, the blackboards, and the VDUs have no proper sense of how their superordinates decide and act. Thus, to take a historical paradigm, in the long-run analysis the Soviet system of order collapses under the weight of its own corruption and inefficacy and thus, as revealed in Robert McNamara's latter-day confession,[11] the American catastrophe in Vietnam is perpetrated in the cool of the council chamber with the logic of general systems management.

The pathology of lost comprehension is exacerbated in modern complex organizations when the distribution of power is perceived to be out of phase with the distribution of rewards. Since the latter is a structural function of administration (the executives cut the pie) it may in the pathological version follow that rewards accrue disproportionately to the administrative–managerial line. Professional staff and other workers, increasingly conscious of their own power of expertise, may react to this perceived inequity. Executives in turn may counter-react by dramaturgical assertion of authority, "pulling rank" or manipulating subordinates. The insecure administrator may interpose his desk as a symbol of authority or, worse, come out from behind it in an attempt to declare his egalitarian pretensions. The aetiology of such behaviour, when and if pathological, can be traced to an incapacity or inability to grasp or cope with the technical dimensions of the situation.

Variants abound. Committee-ism in all its forms from the *ad hoc* group to the Royal Commission derives essentially from the inability of line to comprehend expertise, technicality, and the realities of political complexity. Delegation of decision making, problem solving, and policy formation to non-administrative groups, "off-line", *can* be efficient and effective but it can also be, and often is, dysfunctional to the point of pathology. Lesser devices such as formalistic delaying routines, executive inaccessibility behind ranks of subordinates and protective secretarial cover, inaccessibility by travel, by conference, by conventions, by being "tied up", or simply by non-response to calls, and correspondence—all these are used to decelerate or retard conflict resolution or in the effort to derail, deflect, and deter criticism and opposition.

Although this particular subset of organizational malady can be expected to grow with technology and with professionalism it is important to note that, of all the value illnesses besetting organizations, this may be the easiest to treat. It occurs primarily because administrators fail to make a profession of their own specialty, namely, generalism. This fault could to a large extent be remedied by training and education. The administrative profession, if it is to become such, must achieve credibility on grounds other than power, hierarchical status, and political or careerist skills. Moreover, the credentials must go beyond the narrow pseudo-expertise of the Master of Business Administration (MBA) or MPA into the wide reaches of the humanities and liberal arts.[12] For generalists to earn this recognition cannot happen, of course, without at least a modicum of authenticity. This in turn would imply an ethical commitment to the nomothetic value aims of the organization under their administration. To the extent that administration is recognized as a legitimate profession commanding generalist knowledge and skills to that extent will this pathology be attenuated.

Yet there are difficulties here. While this argument may hold true for the professional career administrator, that is, in the non-pejorative sense for the bureaucrat, it applies less easily to the amateur, the purely political and, in general, the non-professional. One thinks, for example, of the so-called collegial administrator who at least has the option of hedging career bets when failure in executive labours can be compensated by a suddenly rekindled desire to return to the glories of teaching and scholarship. Nevertheless the principle remains of the overall desirability of generalist credentials (not necessarily formalized) for all seeking serious service in the hierarchical line.

SUPERFICIALITY

Information overload is a characteristic of our times. It was accurately predicted in Marshall McLuhan's concept of the global village and it has special relevance to administrative practice. It is only in part a direct consequence of electronic technology: E-mail, voice mail, cellular phones, faxes, and lap-tops are symptoms rather than causes. While digitalization has multiplied information potential (ignoring any problems of signal-to-noise ratio) it has done nothing to increase the number of hours in the day available for information digestion in the human machine. These remain at an absolute limit of 24 and some of those have to be disallowed for "down-time". Managers notoriously, and administrators hardly less so, tend to manage their time resources through calendars, diaries, and structured appointment routines. In this they are no different from doctors, dentists, and airline crews but they retain more control of their diary content and are able to project an image of ostensibly very busy workers whose time constraints are greater than their fellow organization members. Mintzberg and others have shown, however, that much of their apparent busyness is characterized by superficiality.[13] It is not uncommon for serious reports on controversial organization issues to go unread, or to be merely scanned, despite the labour that may have gone into their production. (Indeed the report or consultant study may often be used not to solve a problem but to defer it or to "buy time".) Problems demanding action may repeatedly be deferred through other executive engagements and priorities until events force a decision point. It is then found, not unnaturally, that only the briefest time is available for any kind of serious value–fact–probability–consequence analysis and none at all for any philosophical reflection.[14] Specialist literature, trade and professional journals, important books, are simply not read. There is no time after all. Reliance for critical intelligence is placed on informal contacts with peers inside and outside the organization, or with cultivated sources in the informal organization network. Gossip in other words. Problems are not dealt with in their full right but on an *ad hoc* or "firefighting" basis. Impending confrontations are deferred or sidestepped. Time itself becomes both friend and enemy but is always in short supply.

All of this creates an appearance of busyness and an air of pseudo-efficiency upon which skilled dramaturgy can impose styles of either coolness under fire or bravura and braggadocio. As a pathology this has to be distinguished from the perfectly hygienic and quite necessary practice of compartmentalization. The practice of structuring agendas, of keeping to the point, of dealing with one thing at a time and one thing only is technically admirable in the main but it can also lead to strategic error through tactical focus, to dysfunctional myopia, and to affective psychopathy when the membranes between compartments become too impervious and opaque. (Apocryphally it was said that Hitler could interrupt a temper tantrum when the bell went for lunch, to resume in mid-scream when lunch was over.)

Reduction of time for reflection through busyness techniques reduces the probability that all points of view will be entered into the decision account and increases the likelihood of minority positions being suppressed, overlooked, or lost on the agenda through pressure of time. More ominously the new-imaginative idea, the breakthrough, will simply not be conceived or if conceived then not received. V-factors in decision making will be affected by time pressure and the given situational bias of the moment: attitudes, however, disguised by miens of gravity or levity, will be pressed towards the shallower rather than the deeper limits of their range. The scope for unauthenticity expands in inverse proportion to the diminishing opportunities for the exercise of true consideration and principle. Meanwhile errant administrators will find in all this neither guilt nor misgiving but rather comfort, for does not their very busyness serve to persuade the world of their worth to the organization? Are their diaries not crammed to capacity? Do they not put in excessive hours? Is their energy not poured forth in the organizational service? Ought not then the organization to acknowledge this by providing them with still more support staff and the assistance that they so evidently need? When this state becomes chronic the work ethic itself subserves and reinforces value-pathology.

THE PARAGON FALLACY

Administration can go wrong in an infinite number of ways. Much of this can be traced to a lack of theory. No substantive or overall theory exists. In this, administration parallels education—another great generalism—and suffers in consequence in its aspirations to a fully professional status. Despite the best efforts of social science, and despite the technological infrastructure available through electronics, managerial proto-science and administrative theory itself have hardly progressed beyond the mutually contradictory sets of proverbs famously castigated by Simon.[15] But this need not be cause for pessimism; it is rather a reaffirmation of human will and complexity. Human organisms are notoriously perverse in refusing to sit still under scrutiny and submit to the quantitative reductions and simplicities demanded by scientific methodology. Their complexity will not be contained. But, nevertheless, it breeds its own version of error.

Because administration is irreducibly unscientific and yet so obviously vital to so many interests, quite apart from the common interest, it is easy to attribute sterling characters and superlative qualities to its role incumbents. Add in the facts that reward systems and the distribution of honours are commanded by administrators, that a long conditioning to authority is universal across cultures, and that the executive competencies are supposed to be wise decision making and leadership. The Milgram studies in particular and bioethics in general support the concept of susceptibility to the agentic state on the part of followers. All things considered it then becomes easy, partly out of sloppy thinking (we have seen how vague are the concepts of leadership and decision making), partly out of a perception of the gravity and complexity of organization, and partly out of herd instinct, to impute paragon proportions to the administrator. Job descriptions for administrative positions bear out this assertion. The sought leader is not only to be wise and virtuous but is to be extensively and intensively experienced and should have this that and the other qualification from academic credentials to the politically correct attributes of gender, age, race, and ethnic or subcultural affiliations. In the end the executive searchers fill the role with a mere mortal, often promoted from within—a mortal draped, however, with an authoritative mantle as a result of the paragon fallacy. The organizational world is very familiar with the phenomenon of the presidential honeymoon; and the fairy tale of the

Emperor's new clothes should be required reading for any administrative aspirant, indeed for all who would understand organizational behaviour.

Because the paragon fallacy works to the advantage of executives, and because it is a construct of sceptical critique, it may feed into a certain spirit of anti-intellectualism in administrative ranks. This tendency may be compounded by a trait of machismo or pseudo-machismo not uncommonly affected by powerful executives. Administration and management are seen as practical affairs: the former a subset of politics, the latter a non-reflective set of skills, and both misperceived as strictly or simply pragmatic. Both call for action and decisiveness to the discount of passivity and reflection. Though it would be improper to generalize the accusation of administrative anti-intellectualism, administrators (with notable exceptions such as Barnard and Vickers) are not renowned for their contributions to scholarship. More usually, when they write at all, they tend to add substance to the paragon fallacy by additions to the self-vindicating autobiographical literature of "great men". The memoir of Robert S. McNamara, an apologia for his conduct of the Vietnam War, is unusual in its acceptance of blame and admissions of error.[16]

A peculiar affirmation of this fallacy derives from another American source: the unique and freakish circumstances of the Watergate affair whereby an American president was forced to reveal the administrative intimacies of his executive suite. However idiosyncratic these data may be they indicate at the highest levels of echelon the hidden subsurface quality of administrative discourse and they do give ample evidence of the machismo and anti-intellectualism associated with the paragon fallacy. Although other examples abound in the arts—the prizewinning German film *The Wahnsee Conference* is a poignant example—the Watergate transcripts are authentically empirical and it is a matter of academic regret that decades after the event serious administrative and sociological research has not yet been conducted on this material. This case study would seem especially worthy of the attention of administrative scholars because the principal actors in the drama were committed to success, the work ethic, and a number of apparently Type I values. Moreover the often-cited pathology of administrative secrecy, itself a derivative of the paragon fallacy and superficiality, is open to academic scrutiny in an intimate and informal exhibition. Other pathologies such as disengagement, compartmentalization, vanity, and aggression are also accessible for study.

Of course it should be noted that an administrator may *be* a paragon, Plato and Barnard would have him so, but the fallacy lies in the belief that the acquisition of office endows the incumbent with paragon proportions.

NEO-FEUDALISM

Loyalty to the organization and commitment to its values are generally considered an efficacious and necessary virtue but it is well to remember St Paul's dictum:

Nothing in excess, and Aristotle's conception of beneficent value as the mid-point of extremes (courage, for example, being a mean between cowardice and foolhardiness). Excessive loyalty can easily become pathological and the reader will recall from the previous chapter that collectivities, the focus of loyalty, are immune to punitive sanctions. One cannot execute the Gestapo or even bankrupt General Motors. Only individuals can be penalized. Some forms of collective, however, deliberately seek to induce Type I commitments. The military provides a clear example.

Since military organizations are agencies of brute force and possess a monopoly of violence within any nation state they require their members to overcome ordinary psychological inhibitions and revulsions about bloodshed and the destruction of human life and property. This is done in large part by psychological countervalence, that is, by value-conditioning about the themes and rhetoric of honour, duty, loyalty, patriotism. Pomp and circumstance including a whole division of music are invoked, together with uniforms, ranks, colours, decorations, parades and ceremonial ritual in a veritable theatre of glamour designed to redress (i.e. re-dress) the brute reality of slaughter. When individuals commit atrocities as agents of a military collectivity it is difficult to apportion blame—though courts martial regularly seek to do so. Whether or not overconditioning can be taken as exculpation does not obviate the general pathology—applicable to organizations other than the military, indeed to all organizations. The question: Where does my primary loyalty lie? is one which were better not asked in the ordinary run of administrative life. It might lead to awkward questions such as, Which comes first, my career or my family? My health or my work? My duty or my pleasure? Who is my liege lord? Better is it that organizational loyalty be taken as an unexamined assumption. But when fealty does come to the sticking point then the question of pathology re-enters. At that time the road forks between the consequences of neo-feudal uncritical subservience reinforced by indoctrination and the consequences, often dire, of resistance to the collective hierarchical will.

It must be added that in a pluralistic society where traditional values are under threat the patterned order of neo-feudal organization may be a source of psychological assurance. For here, as in the microcosm of a ship, each man knows his role and all are guaranteed sustenance and identity in return for fealty. Even in the old medieval feudalism this was so. Not all serfs felt downtrodden. So it is, perhaps, that some administrators may come to retreat into managerialism, to moving material from the in-basket to the out-basket, in strict observance of procedures, careful to be politically correct, keeping a loyal and dutifully low profile.

DECEIT

Niccolo Machiavelli is the eponymous exponent of this art in the West. His thought remains a living force in administrative praxis. His great text *The Prince* is still fully applicable to the realities of organizational and political life and it has often been a source of some wonder to me, in my teaching of administration, that experienced practitioner–students often come visibly alive and receptive when introduced to *Fürstenspiegel* as if, like Molière's character, they are astonished to discover that all along they have been speaking prose. Or as if they had at last come upon an oasis of meaning amid the aridities of management science.

Egotism is common to us all. Certain schools of psychology consider it to be healthy and to the extent that it is correlated with ambition it is generally assumed to be a natural prerequisite to the administrative career. The point at which it crosses the line into pathology is often associated with an over-subscription to success and *a fortiori* to the presumed doctrines of the evil genius Machiavelli. The connotations of the latter have come to be associated with slyness, intrigue, deceit, and scheming manipulation—all attributes and skills denounced at one level of propriety while being admired and practised at other levels of action. The Machiavellian administrator is presumed to have personal goals or ends to which the organization is a means and thus will self-righteously scheme for the betrayal and downfall of superiors and rivals and will use peers and subordinates as necessary means, not as Kantian ends-in-themselves. He (or she) will do all this unhesitatingly, ruthlessly, without remorse or compunction but without its being *seen*. It must not be perceived or be at all obvious in any way—quite the opposite, it must be masked and disguised.[17] Such an administrator will take pains to be especially charming, guileless, likeable, candid, persuasive, congenial ... perhaps even diffident and shy, professing denial of any power ambitions and avowing all the collegial and politically correct values. This kind of dramaturgy can approximate the dimensions of high art but such is the power of the paragon fallacy that even much lesser performances can be eminently successful. Occasionally the Machiavellianist will self-deceive and be convinced that all this effort is for the greater good but the true exponent maintains a clear grasp of Realpolitik and his own sacred interest.

Occasionally, too, the naked lust for power is defended on quasi-utilitarian or social Darwinist grounds as satisfying organizational needs for strong leadership by way of free play in the marketplace of ambition. Lord Thomson, the newspaper magnate is said to have castigated British administrators for their lack of ambitious drive. In his native Canada they would have been motivated by the principle expressed in his words as "I want that bastard's job."[18] Not that Lord Thomson was going to let them get *his* job but he thought it good that subordinates should want it in this way. The belief, *pace* Adam Smith, would seem to be that if each pursues with sufficient ruthlessness his selfish ends then the whole and the collective would benefit in some optimal way. A divine hand in human affairs even if the hand be wearing chain mail under its velvet glove.

The Machiavellian administrator may indeed possess qualities (political skills, value sensitivities even) which are organizationally advantageous but the practice can also breed fear of counter-ruthlessness, indeed it implies it, and hence the possibility of paranoid and dysfunctional defensive expenditures of energy and effort. More subtly and more speculatively it has been suggested since ancient times[19] that the practice of virtue heightens intellectual clarity while indulgence in vice tends to dull the mental faculties. The basic question, I would stress, is not whether egotistical vanities and power-seeking can be expunged; most certainly they are administrative realities ever with us, but whether their excessive Machiavellian manifestations can be detected and deterred. Whether, that is, they can be raised into consciousness and become truly observable.

DOMINANCE

Aggression or aggressivity is an aspect of ambition. It can be fairly assumed that this psychological attribute is distributed amongst administrators in average to above-average proportions,[20] One is unlikely to climb far in the organizational hierarchy without it. Pathology arises because of the Milgram effect and the agentic state. Opportunities proliferate within the administrative role which can magnify or exacerbate the malevolent effects of aggression leading to domination of subordinates and deleterious conditions of compliance. The fault here is simple moral or valuational abuse of authority.

The converse, and symbiotic, condition is overcompliance. To cite Milgram: "Any competent manager of a destructive bureaucratic system can arrange his personnel so that only the most callous and obtuse are directly involved in violence. The greater part of the personnel can consist of men and women who, by virtue of their distance from the actual acts of brutality, will feel little strain in their performance of supportive functions. They will feel doubly absolved from responsibility. First, legitimate authority has given full warrant for their actions. Second, they have not themselves committed brutal physical acts."[21]

This is one putative explanation of "how the evil gets done" and the sinister suggestion is that it is within the conscious scope of administrators to deliberately design such systems of dominance. But a reservation must be entered. The philosopher of administration has two difficulties in studying any organization. First, to discover the true allocation of power (which would necessitate an intimacy with the informal structure); secondly, and even more importantly, to discover the true allocation of value (which would necessitate an even deeper intimacy with the collective personality structure). When organization members are ready, for whatever reason or lack of reason, to overaccept authority they permit and even sanction the actualization of the administrator's values, both idiographic and nomothetic. Thus the stage can be set for tragic pathology as in the administrative histories and psychobiographies of Heinrich Himmler, Robert S. McNamara, and unnumbered Stalinist functionaries. It is not enough to declaim that the price of liberty is eternal vigilance. The price of morality is continuous monitoring of the bases of authority and the realities of power.

ALIENATION

Rationality, legalism, bureaucracy and technocracy constitute framing conditions for our everyday experience of life. They are parameters of the social condition. And they can alienate. The sociologists Cohen and Taylor have thrown an interesting light upon organizational reality in a remarkable study subtitled *The Theory and Practice of Resistance to Everyday Life*.[22] They had set out initially to discover how convicts serving life sentences and long-term prisoners without hope of parole managed to cope with the realities of their enforced institutional life. How did they get through the day? The answer is provocative. In their research they found that people within prison walls coped in much the same way as people outside those walls. Psychologically (and philosophically) speaking, the escape attempts within paralleled the escape attempts without. Or to put it another way, we are all serving a life sentence. The major difference between walled and unwalled servitude is that the paradigm of resistance and escape is more amenable to direct observation in the former, more concentrated situation. We are all confined and oppressed in some way by organizational and institutional life. We all nurture to some degree a romanticism of escape. From the standpoint of the affective ego life-experience itself can be a frustrating confinement with but a limited range of modes and means of quasi-escape. These might include the temporary solaces of alcohol, drugs, and sex; the anodynes of television, cinema, media, conversation and gossip; the "enclaves" provided by hobbies and holidays and travel; the distraction of visitation and participation in socio-drama with family, relatives, and friends; the attitudinal postures of irony and cynicism, the sustenance of philosophy and religion. But—and this is the incontrovertible "but"—however and whenever we "escape" or "resist" we must eventually always return to the phenomenological reality of the walls of our respective cells. Life is an open prison. And so are organizations. One aspect of the administrator's role is custodial wardenship. And once more *Quis custodiet ipsos custodes?*

The voiced or unvoiced, realized or unrealized, conscious or unconscious sense of work-imprisonment and organizational alienation is a function of time and its structuring. A dominant characteristic of organizational time is routine. Routine is the hallmark of what Cohen and Taylor describe as *paramount reality*.[23] In the "inner theatre of the mind" we are constantly confronted with "the nightmare of repetition" and the never-ending problem of the "mental management of routine". Paramount reality is a world of timetables, routines, chores, duties, drudgeries, responsibilities, obligations, fixed times, fixed places, boredom and repetition. We have to learn that our "escape attempts" are only "binges", "arousal jags", "crazy interludes", "flings". They do not lead to any permanent escape, any alternative reality. However consoling they may temporarily be they are but compartmentalized features of everyday life the predominating characteristic of which is alienating and oppressive. We might think that the organization serves us but the paramount reality is that we serve it. We think we design our own life projects and are masters of our fate but the paramount constraints of attending meetings, pushing clocks, dealing with in-baskets, catching planes, commuting and, in general, being on parade negates our illusions. Discontent is the ordinary and normal condition of organizational life, would (or could) this be admitted. The search for escape from the organizational prison leads to a corresponding over-evaluation of the free areas or enclaves of liberty provided under the head of private life. It can also lead to a quasi-ethic of "me-first-ism" or "I'm all right, Jack" in which the concept of the organization as "person" or "collectivity" or "service-worthy ideal" is nullified.

But is this analysis complete? Is it adequate? Is it not possible that work itself can be an escape attempt (especially for the careerist and the workaholic)? Can the ego even rejoice in submission to paramount reality? Yes. Surely. There are those for whom the organization is home. Or at least a haven, an escape area (this time from *private* life), a place of order and security and routine the very impersonality of which is laden with psychological consolation and philosophical meaning. From what, in this analysis, does the organization, the work-life, provide escape? From the full range of human unhappiness: tedium, ennui, guilt, despair, sadness, worry, anxiety, insecurity, inadequacy, grief, meaninglessness, a vexing wife, a boring husband, millstone parents, millstone children. Anodynes to life's problems are to be found both within and without organizations. It is, however, the ones *within* organizations that are of most administrative interest: workaholism, mindless absorption in task, the plunge into politics, intrigue, even the escape into administration itself for this too, with its vistas of prestige, power, and liberty of action may seem an alternative to alienation: a way out!

Alienation and anomie are related terms, originating with Marx and Durkheim respectively.[24] Alienation at first referred to the loss of relation between a worker and the product of his labour under capitalism. By extension it came to refer to a loss of relationship generally, especially where there is an excess of formal over informal organization, of *Gesellschaft* over *Gemeinschaft*. Most generally it refers to the loss of commonality, of collective values, and of human meaning.

Anomie likewise underwent a radical extension of meaning. At first it referred to *loss* of regulation[25] leading to "weariness", "disillusionment", disturbance, agitation, discontent", "anger", and "irritated disgust with life",[26] perhaps even to the point of suicide. It now refers rather to an *excess* of regulation, such as might be imposed by a complex organization or system inducing the negative Type III affect just described. Anomie and alienation may be in the last analysis sicknesses of the individual psyche but they are also names for pathologies which are organizational in aetiology and which therefore enter into administrative philosophy. It is axiomatic that it is within the logic of organizations to have the potentiality of structuring socio-psychological reality so as to create the conditions for anomie and alienation. Any administrative agenda to counter this pathology would of course be a matter of morality and ethics rather than management theory but it would entail a more complicated praxis and a heightened awareness and understanding of the psychological substrata of the administrative field.

ENNUI

This pathology is a subset of the preceding one. The mass of men lead lives of quiet desperation according to Thoreau. So then do administrators. Some of them abhor their work to the point that their shrunken horizon of fulfillment consists in merely getting through each day. It is also true that the context of organizational life necessitates routine, a routine leading some to infantile dependence and others to dullness, boredom, and even a sense of mental and spiritual suffocation and exhaustion. These negative Type III evaluations are to be found not merely on the assembly line or the factory floor but also behind the executive desk. When major challenges have been met, problems resolved, structure established, decisions scrutinized, power grown secure, leaders too, like Alexander, may suffer from a deficit of worlds to conquer. Moreover, a sort of psychological second law of thermodynamics obtains: in time things run down, novelty wears off, familiarity breeds disinterest, one ages on the job, and even the salt of achievement loses its savour. Churchill's reputed last words were that he was bored. And, even without pursuing these aspects of the human condition to their pathological limit a general truth can be conceded that human nature seeks a dynamic balance between stimulation and quietude; between stress and the absence of stress; between work and play. It is in imbalance that pathology resides.

REALPOLITIK

Realpolitik is a German loan word now well understood and attached, often with negative connotations, to Machiavellian praxis. It is, however, intended to be neutral and objective in a valuational sense. If politics is the act of the possible then Realpolitik is this principle unhampered by moral inhibitions. But there is also a clearcut denotation of commitment to success (for individual or organization) when it is applied to praxis. At its root is the notion that moralities are relative and manipulable. There is no absolute morality and certainly no Kantian categorical imperative. Rather there is the Nietzschean notion of two moralities; the morality of the master (leader–administrator) and the conditioned morality of the herd (those born to follow). To function best, in fact, Realpolitik endorses strict codes of morality for *others*. The proponents are, by contrast, amoral. The links to the *arthasastra* (see below) are obvious and in the extreme case the seeker of success would be the *sole* moralist—a one-eyed man in the kingdom of the blind. That the victim have a healthy body is best for predator and parasite alike. The social conditioning and programming provided by public morality and organizational norms renders subordinates predictable and manipulable. The ruthless administrator will therefore enforce Type II codes and will frequently enunciate the highest of Type I sentiments. Moral image and moral credibility are always a matter of prime concern to administrators, whether or not they are pursuing a policy of Realpolitik, for the deployment of power is ultimately dependent on trust.

Bombing Hanoi on Christmas Day by virtue of one's clear-eyed comprehension of the logic of power; eliminating one's opponent by betrayal, bribery or deceit, obtaining funds, advancement, promotion, perquisites by flattery, obsequiousness, manipulation; these things occur. Are they pathological? Or merely distasteful? It depends upon the value analysis employed but to be ignorant about such realities is to be unsophisticated, philosophically and politically virginal, and administratively inept.

One's attitude to power is crucial. It is a nice test of honesty and self-knowledge to ask where on the value-paradigm one's own evaluation of power rests. Is one, for example, rationally committed or *more than* rationally committed to the acquisition of power? Pathology is all too often the correlate of overevaluation.

ARTHASASTRA

Arthasastra as a philosophy of success has already been mentioned several times. It can now be considered in further detail because of its affinity to several of the pathologies already listed. Those pathologies can be traced to defects of motivation, of character, and of organizational structure but their sickness or wrongness or badness is itself a value-judgement derived only from Type II conventions or Type I subscriptions that have some common endorsement such as, say, Judeo-Christian ethics. For the individual who takes as a basic philosophical truth the overwhelming priority of self-interest, the limited supply of prizes, and the consequent clash and struggle for power, the *arthasastra* may be not only logical but ethical: a vision of the world as it really is (Realpolitik) and self-endorsement for having the courage to embrace that vision and the consequences it entails. To act accordingly could then be either Type I heroism at best or Type III megalomania at worst.

The *arthasastra* suggests four principal modes or strategies for dealing with people politically (or administratively).[27] All are power-based. The first applies when one is in an inferior power position to an opponent (and in the jungle savagery of the competition for success *everyone* is an opponent, including those whose passing role is that of friend, ally, political bedfellow, or even family member). It can be called the technique of conciliation or negotiation. Here one seeks appeasement of the superior by whatever means: by ingratiation, personal charm, rhetoric, flattery, diplomacy, all the arts of the courtier. The superior must be soothed, lulled, made to feel secure, unaware of any threat from his subordinate, confident, trusting, and dependent upon him if at all possible. It prevails among administrators when, for example, we courteously keep the lines of communication open, even with those whom we detest. Power demands that the more powerful be treated with respect, conciliated—one can only "negotiate" with someone in command.

But suppose oneself is in the superior position. Then the appropriate modal option is that of *force*. If one has power one should wield it, and be seen to do so. Legend has it that Napoleon would periodically hang a man from the ranks *pour encourager les autres*. Chastisement and punishment should be visible occasionally lest the superior be perceived as weak. Cabinet reshuffles in parliamentary democracies are often a case in point. In modern jargon it is advisable to "lean on" subordinates from time to time, exert pressure, make demands, show who is boss, make sure it is the lieutenants who get the ulcers and not the CEO. The surprise firing, the swift punitive action, can be most salutary. All done judiciously, of course, and with an accurate sense of timing and audience. The steel beneath the velvet can be delicately displayed and so can the dramaturgical rage or tantrum.[28] The seeker of success will master all these techniques and use them without moral inhibition or compunction.

A third technique, donation, is well understood in its common modes of bribery and graft, less so as the universal social exchange principle.[29] Indeed sociology provides philosophy with data to elevate the principle to a metavalue of reciprocity. One advances one's social reciprocity index whenever one takes a colleague to lunch and manages to field the cheque. The underlying tacit force of *quid pro quo* is very pervasive and subtly powerful, whether it be the tip to a waiter or the lavish entertainment planned to suborn the recipients in the donator's interests. In parts of the Orient the practice is often semiformalized (*kumsha, baksheesh*) but its usage transcends cultures and is susceptible of infinite variation. Noteworthy is the delicately phrased "conflict of interest" which can, of course, be engineered to bring an opponent's downfall. "Donation" seeks to bind by gift, interpreting gift in its widest sense.

The fourth major mode is the principle of division, the Roman *divide et impera*. This should be second nature to the true success-seeker who will be skilled in splitting the ranks of any opposition, in spreading ambivalence and doubt, playing upon peers and superiors alike by sowing dissension and rumour, in undermining competitors, rivals, colleagues by the wrong word in the right ear— maintaining throughout the persona of candour and integrity. For the praxis of division ambiguity is good and ambivalence even better. It thrives in an atmosphere of secrecy and confidentiality. It lies close to the heart of darkness.

These four major strategies are to be employed in concert with an array of minor tactics such as "deceit", "overlooking", and "feint". One must be as ready to resort to any trickery, treachery, or fraud as one is ready to assume the guise of moral outrage if those behaviours should be detected in others. One is most friendly to the intended victim against whom one will strike without warning. Occasionally rivals will succeed and then the right attitude is "overlooking". One discounts the opponent's successes by ignoring them; or one feigns disinterest or damns with faint praise. Alternatively one might lavish praise under the mode of donation. The skilled practitioner will generally contrive not to be at those meetings at which his agenda may fail. It is important, too, to master the art of false appearance, to "feint" where necessary. Especially desirable is the image of honesty, conviction, authenticity. It is not too difficult given modern techniques of public relations and group dynamics to make the satanic appear as angelic and the demonic as the epitome of virtue.

Enough has been said to give the flavour of the *arthasastra* but quotations from both East and West drive home the perennial and contemporary quality of this value orientation:

> As clouds change from moment to moment, just so thine enemy of today becomes, even today, thy friend.
>
> Power grows out of the barrel of a gun. *Macht macht Recht.* (Might makes Right)
>
> Might is above right; right proceeds from might; right has its support in might, as living beings in soil. As smoke the wind, so right must follow might. Right in itself is devoid of command, it leans on might as creeper on the tree.
>
> If men think thee soft, they will despise thee. When it is, therefore, time to be cruel, be cruel; and when it is time to be soft, be soft.
>
> God is on the side of the big battalions.
>
> Whoever desires success in this world must be prepared to make deep vows, swear love and friendship, speak humbly, and pretend to shed and wipe away tears.
>
> My enemy's enemy is my friend.
>
> The last word of social wisdom is never trust.

This doctrine is timeless. Though ancient it has its place in contemporary administrative studies. It is not because I subscribe to it that I have dwelt upon it at such length, but because it is a benchmark in the search for higher wisdoms. If administrative aspirants are not exposed to it, given the opportunity to observe it in action, and reflect upon it then they can hardly be in a position to combat it, to contest it philosophically, or even to know that it is there and that they are, from time to time, themselves being manipulated and used. The *arthasastra* sensitizes us to the darker side of the moon, makes us aware of the administrative id, and serves as a point of initiation for higher aspirations. It can only fully succeed where there is a sort of liberal or tender-minded failure of nerve, a refusal to recognize its presence, a surrender to cynicism, or an abdication of value analysis through ideological positivism, pragmatism, relativism, or pluralism. All of these conditions are, however, significant aspects of the postmodern world. Philosophy may aim for the stars but it has to begin in the dirt. And administrative pathology is the disease of which philosophy can be the cure.

CAREERISM

The archetype of the careerist as derived from the values paradigm has already been sketched in Chapter 5. Many if not all of the preceding pathologies are intimately linked to phenomena of ambition and career progress. Other things, however, remain to be said under the dark light of this heading.

First let it be noted that executive aggression (and its concomitant energy) is harnessed to ambition. Both serve the ends of the organization and the administrator, and ideally so, when these ends unite. Value difficulties arise because the ascent of the hierarchy is not, under the general Western system, a simple matter of seniority combined with an unsoiled copybook. Career progress is made by moving on and up; sometimes sideways in a lateral arabesque; not by staying put or stuck, certainly not by moving down. And the climb is competitive in every way because the game is zero sum; there is *not* "more room at the top". That this need not necessarily result in naked competition or internecine warfare in the administrative ranks, is shown in the phenomena of executive succession and cliquism. In the former there is the practice of like appointing like; in the latter of mutual reciprocity (the "old boy" system)—both often deserving of pathological status in their own right since they can clearly operate to the collective disadvantage. In fact, the development of some form of mutually regulated competition and reciprocal cooperation is more likely than one of solitary savagery. In large complex bureaucratic systems it is axiomatic that no one is indispensable, that office-holders are substitutable. Moreover, checks and balances emerge at an informal level to restrain individual pushiness. And this in turn need not be pathological; it may assist the rhythms of organization life and serve to dampen incipient resentments.

Given these countervailing tendencies it is within the compelling logic of careerist ambition that one moves to ascend the hierarchy and the prerequisite to ascent is entry. The aspirant often leaves behind an established record of expertise, this perhaps being the very price of entry to the career ranks, and thus there comes about the well-publicized pathology known as Peters' principle.[30] Good teachers are promoted into administration and cease to teach; good salesmen likewise become sales managers and cease to sell; physicians and surgeons succumb to the glories of hospital administration, airmen fly desks; all in a sort of Gresham's law of administration were it not for the fortunate fact that there is no law or principle which dictates that aggression, ambition, and competence cannot flow together or that adequate or even superior morality cannot be combined with the mix. But careerism does imply that successive organizational roles are left behind and that return to them is commonly viewed (though not necessarily overtly so) as a form of failure or loss of face. There are structured quasi-exceptions to this such as the return of an academic administrator to lecture hall or lab, or the return like Cincinnatus to his farm of the amateur administrator to some former role, but for the professional or careerist administrator these face-saving exits do not normally obtain. There is only one road, and that is up.

Executive advance by extra-organizational movement creates its own subspecialty of irresponsibility. The office leaver can then bequeath unfinished work, stalled decisions, unfulfilled obligations, and a host of moral and ethical discontinuities. To a lesser extent this can apply when the career progress is intra-organizational; the climber can effect the same shucking of responsibility and the unfortunate successor is obliged to pick up the pieces.

In short, when careerism takes on imbalanced proportions it can not only prevent any of the potential benefits of role recycling but can generate an insecurity which can lead to self-perpetuating cliques with an elaborate control of the reward system that is organizationally dysfunctional. Alternatively, when the career system is manifestly open and competitive it can lead to executive stress and defensive–aggressive insecurity. The third (or Japanese) option of assured tenure with seniority advancement leaves open the further hazards of executive impotence, irresponsibility, and anomie. Whatever the structure of the reward system and whatever the historical or cultural content, in postmodern no less than in ancient times, one assumption is surely defensible: that ambition and careerism are facts and realities of administration and organizational life.

DRAMATURGY

Dramaturgy has been referred to often in this text. It is an aspect, an important one, of administrative theatre and refers both to the presentation of self on the administrative stage and to the contrast between *playing* a role as opposed to actually *functioning* in a role.[31] It embraces as subdivisions the arts of rhetoric, image-making, and persuasion—the whole legerdemain of the administrative language game—in contemporary cliché, of "talking the talk rather than walking the walk", of style as opposed to substance. The concept is further recognized in the coarse vernacular in impolite references to animal functions but none of this denies its efficacy in the careers of salesmen, politicians, and more specifically, administrators. The crime of dramaturgy is that it sins against truth. Like all art it presents an image or a "lie" in place of what is "real". This upset Plato greatly causing him among other things to allow that a carpenter who made a table was better than an artist, however acclaimed, who merely painted a representation of a table; and to propose that censorship of the arts would be a necessary institution in the ideal republic. The latter suggestion may have some appeal in these days of populist mass entertainment but the former fails to appreciate the positive aspects of dramaturgy: Churchill's "blood, sweat, and tears ...", Nelson's "England expects ...", Hitler's *"Ein Reich, Ein Volk, ein Führer"* leap to mind. Any assessment of dramaturgy in the executive sense must be ambivalent for administration is a value-saturated and emotional activity, not a robotic or rationally analytic calculus, and the leadership role is, after all, a *role*.

It has to be played out. The pathological threat to this role performance comes when its unauthenticity becomes potent or obvious and, most of all, when the executive self-deludes and comes to believe his own rhetoric, when, so to speak, unauthenticity becomes authentic. When the followership come to discern with greater or lesser clarity of perception the degree to which illusion is separate from reality the curtain begins to descend in the organizational theatre. Dramaturgy is not necessarily pathological, it may be a positive accompaniment of leadership style, its success or failure (like the success or failure of a monetary currency) is a function of an elusive quality called credibility. Maintaining that credibility is an enduring and persistent concomitant of the administrative task. All Cretans may not be liars but some Cretans may be better liars than others.

IDEOPATHOLOGY

This term may be coined on analogy with bureaupathology. It refers to the state of affairs when the ideological commitments of the administrator, say, for example, to gender equity in hiring, or to ecological value issues, or to a secular or religious worldview affect the organization dysfunctionally. A distinction must be drawn between ideopathy (negative behaviours deriving from ideology) and idiopathy (negative behaviours deriving from individual characteristics). Both are value-based and may overlap and reinforce each other but ideopathy, having an external aetiology (we do not normally construct our own *ideologies*), is best reserved for discussion in the next and final chapters while idiopathy, of course, is already implicit in the variety of pathologies discussed above. Their interaction, ranging from the trivial to the dire, is seen for example in the degree of "trendiness" exhibited in administrative style, a phenomenon often revealed in the use of language as, say, in the repetition of buzzwords such as "impact" or pointed use of gender-neutral or "inclusive" terminology. The extent to which this sort of thing is harmless or harmful is a function of context at the V_1–V_5 levels. Pathology need not necessarily be in question.

MALADMINISTRATION

The question posed by Saul Bellow can now be partially answered. In this preliminary catalogue of malaise, one which is surely incomplete and suggestive rather than exhaustive, I concentrated on some of the more obvious ways in which the administrator, by one vice or another, can contribute to organizational value pathology and I have dwelt, in particular, upon the so-called philosophy of success. Why, in an age of supposed scientific enlightenment, of technical rationality, liberal ideas, mass education, and advanced jurisprudence would an administrator consciously, as an act of individual free will, that is, of morality, secretly subscribe to such a philosophy?

For several possible reasons and in several ways. First, the administrator may come to believe from private experience and personal phenomenology that this philosophy best reflects the truth about the world, a truth about inimical reality that the tenderminded would rather not face and one which demands courage and nerve to encounter and grasp. In this sense it is adopted as a reflective and reasoned response: to fight fire with fire, to be evil in an evil world, to beat the world at its own game, and so on. Or it might be supposed that, true or not, a differential advantage can be gained by its adoption. Most people are too socially conditioned at Level II to adopt such a philosophy; the comfortable half-truths of liberalism and the soft sentiments of the human relations, human resources, and personnel counselling views of the world are more to their taste; and so they are likely dupes and proper victims for the ruthless spirit. This would be the wolf in the sheep-pen theory. Again, the administrator may not totally accept the secret doctrine but may acknowledge it as being partially and significantly true and therefore worthy of conditional acceptance. Pragmatically, then, he will embrace the philosophy from time to time as and where he judges it appropriately self-serving. This would be *ad hoc* commitment. Or the administrator may succumb, as many have done, to the lure of the Grand Temptation: that the end justifies the means. Thus the philosophy can be used to achieve power so that, once achieved and secure, the true and righteous administration can follow. This is the rationale of Stalinism, of Pol Pot, of Dostoievsky's Grand Inquisitor. It also smacks of Nietzsche's binary division of morals into Master and Herd moralities, and of his perceptive and disturbing depth analysis of ressentiment.

In such ways, and in other ways, whatever the revulsion or offence to ordinary sensibilities, the doctrines of power and their associated value orientations can come to be accepted. In the end, however, it is a matter of individual choice and it portrays the administrator's intentionality. If free and conscious, then that choice is ethical, however much disapprobation might be heaped upon it from yet other moral perspectives. If unfree (programmed, mechanical) and unconscious it is accidental, irresponsible, and amoral. Either way that is how some of the evil gets done.

Lest there now be stirrings of unease it were as well to remember that any philosophy professing to wisdom is a search for meaning. Meaning for some can be found in what is pathology for others. Meaning can also be found in success of the socially accredited variety. But Marlowe's words are deeply ambivalent,

Is it not passing fair to be a king,
And ride in triumph through Persepolis?

PROPOSITIONS

177. The essence of political skill is the concealment of manipulation.
178. There are lines between ambition and prudent self-preservation; between moral cowardice and moral detachment. Administration crisscrosses these lines.
179. Will or hedonic compulsion can override reason; so can line overrule staff.
180. Administration appeals to the unfitted while it repels the fitted: the Platonic dilemma. But administrative office may be sought to prevent its being held by others presumed worse: *faute de mieux* administration.
181. Dramaturgy is compensation for incompetence by competent *performance*.
182. A career ladder has a ratchet effect. Descent is devalued and deterred.
183. The principle of hierarchy prevents functional recycling.
184. Cliquism is a defence against careerism, a form of self-insurance.
185. The dialectic of organizational value is unending but biased.
186. Organizations are tainted with ineradicable irrationality; status coordinates are not necessarily purposive coordinates.
187. Supervision has an ethical connotation. Its imperative lies in the collective good. And it must look outside the organization as well as in. It also implies distrust.
188. Morality inexorably reduces to the individual. Ultimately only an individual can be responsible.
189. The problem of the moral economics of organization is to ensure that the gains from membership outweigh the losses from role incumbency and instrumentality. There is a razor's edge between welfare and alienation.
190. Lower values seek to replace higher. They are transvalued by extinction of desire (psychology) or the will to the desirable (philosophy).
191. Opportunism is the first organizational value sickness. Executive succession is congealed opportunism.
192. Humane comprehension, or at least its possibility, varies universally with distance from action. Compartmentalization is the second sickness.
193. Means and ends are always intertwined. Their disentanglement is a problem in administrative philosophy. While ends can dictate means they cannot justify them. Each means is an end in itself.
194. It is but a step from the moral to the mortal. Safety lies in amorality.
195. There is a point, the Luther point, at which the administrator must fight his organization, or leave it, or tread the paths of unauthenticity.
196. The nature of administration is such that it rewards the skills of guile. The arts of concealment and dissembling can be advantageous. Or they can be necessary.

197. As disbelief is suspended in the theatre so conscience can be suspended in administration.
198. Ambition and love of power motivate the administrator. The question then is, Can these values be civilized?
199. Careerism conduces to irresponsibility since responsibilities can be shed by *moving*: onward, upward, outward.
200. When career progress is paced by seniority and guarded by tenure the dangers are irresponsibility, impotence, and anomie.
201. The principle of *quid pro quo* is universal and external. All things have their price. But the price is subject to negotiation and one gives in order to receive—more than one gave.
202. One binds by gifts. Donation supplements structure. The administrator is a merchant of reciprocity.
203. Ambiguity and ambivalence may be cultivated, for they favour deceit.
204. The object of dramaturgy is to appear, at the least, honest, committed, credible. Competence can then be assumed.
205. One can choose what the world calls evil and call it, privately, good. To do so rightly would be principled behaviour.
206. It would be reasonable to assume that most administrators are neither psychopaths nor saints. But in the middle ground is there a trend?

Chapter 11
Ideology

The *arthasastra* and the Machiavellian doctrine of success represent systems of ideas which may be subscribed to by administrators. There are many other such systems which could loosely be classified as ideological but the term ideology is vague; it requires clarification. Its original sense of "knowledge of ideas" has broadened into a conflation of beliefs, religions, political worldviews, and loose coagulations of sentiments which serve to order a form of life. Marx and Mannheim in particular used the concept to establish the discipline of sociology of knowledge[1] and were concerned with the interactions between belief systems and political–social structures. In this light not only axiology (our values) but epistemology (our "facts", our science, the way we see and understand the world) are at least partially determined by cultural patterns. Geertz in anthropology saw ideology more neutrally as one symbol system among other symbol systems such as those provided by religions, art, and science. In the specifically administrative sense, however, it refers especially to Type I value investments which serve to guide, direct, and determine the administrator's action, behaviour, style, and response to value conflicts. Although this is its main sense and one which is intimately linked to the phenomena of charisma, it should be observed at the outset that the paradigm applies *across* ideology. Thus, for any given ideology, say, Roman Catholicism, the commitment could be merely preferential (Level III), a matter of upbringing and conformity (Level IIB), an adoption confirmed by reason (Level IIA) or—in the full ideological sense—a deep-seated psychological and philosophical engagement.

THE TRANSVALUATION OF VALUE

Type I values are Type III values writ large. Type Is are fundamental to ideology in its strongest sense. They are values for which people are willing to kill and be killed: affect transmuted by will and transcending reason; affect grounded in unshakeable belief.

To understand value would be to understand affect—something which science, even in this postmodern era, does not yet attain to and can only approximate. While all animals exhibit affect (and the positivists reduce all value to affect!) the human animal is peculiar in possessing a distinctive cognitive capacity to use language and symbols in the discourse about value. When this is combined with a *belief system* (true or false, no matter) then the potentiality exists, in certain instances, for a sort of transvaluation or transmutation of value. That is, a mutation from Level III to Level I. When this occurs specific values and their attendant value clusters may be activated as central value features of the ego structure, integral to the personality of the value-actor. The life-meaning of that actor is then bound up with some set of Type I values.

Illustrations are plentiful. The ordinary Type III or Type IIB values of patriotism, of ethnic or national affiliation, are easily transmuted in time of war (or by way of terrorist resentment) into Type I adhesions entailing sacrifice of life, limb, and the blood of innocent or accidentally engaged persons. Similarly martyrs and saints are created in the name of religion. And likewise lives are laid down upon the battlefields of art, science, letters. What we are talking of here is not ordinary dedication or commitment—that too, by sheer application and persistence can lead to great things—but something which is abnormal, supernormal, transcendent in its origins, whether these be divine or demonic in extraneous value judgement. It is as if, by psychological processes not yet understood, an intensification of affect achieves some critical mass with a resultant locking-in or irreversibility which entrenches the value that then becomes a critical determinant of its holder's form of life. Such Type I values are resistant to modification, conversion, or degeneration because they are so integral to the ego and its defence. Although emotive in origin they have become transvalued, mutated to the level of will and, while they may be subject to rational discourse, that is rational*ized*, they are essentially *trans*rational. Since any value can appear at either level III or I it becomes an important administrative skill to discriminate between them. Figure 11.1 gives a partial listing of the contrasting elements by which such discrimination can be made.

The distinction is vital for administrative practice since value conflict (to be discussed in the next chapter) depends mightily upon the presence or absence of Type I ideological motivations.

Ideologies then are quasi-philosophical systems of thought and belief which structure meaning, establish cardinal values, and determine the life-world or form of life of those who embrace them. Their genesis and etiology lie in Type I values but once an ideology comes into existence it does not necessarily elicit Type I adherence from all of its subscribers. Not all Muslims are zealots nor are all romantics radicals. The field of cultural ideology is a rich and confused tapestry but the specifically administrative variations seem to derive from a single source: rationalism. All other administrative ideologies could be said to various reactions against it.

Type III factor	Corresponding Type I quality
Subrationality (infrarationality)	Transrationality (suprarationality)
Preference	Intuition
Impulse	Choice
Transience	Permanence
Intermittence naturalistic compulsion (habit)	Persistence transcendental freedom
Abandon	Commitment
Affective programming (heteronomy)	Conscience (autonomy)
Instinct	Belief/faith
Weak or normal motivation	Super or hypermotivation

Figure 11.1   Factors Discriminating Between Affective and Conative Value.

THE ROOTS OF ADMINISTRATIVE IDEOLOGY

From the eighteenth century Enlightenment to late twentieth century postmodernism our culture has been characterized by science and epistemology rather than religion and axiology. The values of logic and reason have dominated this emergent worldview and its attendant ideology of rationalism. That is desirable which is logical, empirical, mathematical, technical, explicable in terms of causality, in a word, scientific. Implicit is a bias towards the sensory, and towards the material as opposed to the metaphysical or sublime.[2] One acknowledges of course that scientific advance at the frontiers of quantum level physics and relativity has attenuated earlier and cruder materialistic interpretations of reality but this does not yet appear to have funded any corresponding idealistic ideology at the public level.[3] Moreover, the presiding value of rationality remains triumphantly ensconced in the culturally revered institutions of science and technology. And in administration where rationality is typically metavaluational. Rationality with its connotation of logical cognitive processes, that is, ratiocination, is to be distinguished from "reasonableness" on the one hand and "rational*ism*" on the other. The former implies a satisificing making do in a pragmatic world where the ideals of logic inevitably fall short while the latter implies an overemphasis in the *value* domain upon reason—an excess, as it were, of rational rectitude. This root value of rationality depends upon an underlying epistemological conception of truth. Since truth negates falsity, and since the latter is undesirable (except, be it noted, in the realms of myth and fiction, that is, in *art*), and since administration is primarily (or ostensibly) concerned with a real world of fact then rationality achieves automatic metavalue status and rationalism becomes the concomitant ideology.

Of course administration, being inescapably bound up with means–ends causality and the metavalues of organization, is intrinsically rational in some sense. Taylor's ultimate logic—that there *must* be one best way of performing work—still goes unrefuted. Only a philosopher might stumble over the word *best* but no such conceptual perplexity need deter or decelerate the managerial administrator who has unreflectively underwritten the metavalues of efficiency and effectiveness and takes his ends as given. Large complex modern organizations are a priori rational. They are also *a fortiori* rationalistic.

High technology and computerology reinforce this natural tendency, perhaps in a paradoxical intellectual swerve driving it *out* of the Type II cognitive domain into the affective Type III and Type I reaches where it serves to fund both metavalues and ideology. Examples can be drawn from the conduct of the Vietnam war[4] and from the bureaucratization of public education.[5] General systems theory itself is but the unexceptionable endeavour of seeking to introduce logical rigour into the understanding and control of complex human arrangements. Likewise the influential philosophy of logical positivism is quintessentially rationalistic. The impress of a rational scientific ideology is evident everywhere in organizational life: no administrator will contest for long against a rational argument and, since decision making and policy analysis are conducted within a language game of rational discourse (typically cost–benefit calculus), then the ideological impress becomes overwhelming. Often it would require a high degree of philosophical sensitivity to even perceive this state of affairs as a problem, much less expose the weaknesses and fallacies concealed within it. In Wittgenstein's words "... someone unpractised in philosophy passes by all the spots where difficulties are hidden in the grass, whereas someone who has had practice will pause and sense that there is a difficulty close by even though he cannot see it yet. ... How hard I find it to see what is *right in front of my eyes!*"[6] And so the homogenetic, naturalistic, militaristic, excisionistic and *rationalistic* fallacies become embedded in administrative praxis under the aegis of rational ideology and pass unnoticed into the flow of events.

Bureaucracy provides an ambivalent justification of the rational ideology but an unequivocal example of Wittgenstein's principle. Were our sense of wonder not anaesthetized by familiarity we should be full of awe at the marvels of cooperative endeavour which so miraculously *work*. Planes fly, taxes are collected, trains run, meals are served, the sick are tended, children learn to read and write, presses roll, prisons are filled, hospitals are emptied, and filled again, wars fought and won, planets explored, and the dead buried. How wonderful! How wonderful that it all *works*, that there is *order*! Rational bureaucracy—ignore for this moment its shadow side of irrational bureaupathology—sustains and maintains our collective form of life with its commanding institutions of science and technology.

The nomothetic–rational ideology inherent in administration is nevertheless tempered by the idiographic–humanistic countervailing tendencies and their associated ideologies. Weber discriminated between *Zweckrationalitat* (the rationality of purpose) and *Wertrationalitat* (the rationality of value) while Tönnies, in sociology, drew the distinction between *Gesellschaft* (formal rational structure) and *Gemeinschaft* (Informal human "rationality").[7] The administrator, once again, is faced with philosophical divergence for while the one rational option might appeal to our individuality and to the amateur in our souls the other rational option appeals to the dispassionate professional spirit. This dialectical tension refers of course to the main countervailing or contending source of administrative ideology, namely, humanism. Applying the value paradigm one could say that if rationalism represented level IIA, humanism was the proponent set of ideas and values associated with IIB and III. This leaves us with level I, that is, level III writ large. Where does this fit in? The answer is to be found in what, for want of a better *-ism* category, can be called transcendentalism: the source, I shall argue, of leadership charisma. Nevertheless, despite the offsetting and dialectical influences of humanism and the aberrations of transcendentalism it can be fairly said that the roots of administrative ideology lie in rationalism. In a technocratic legalistic bureaucratic scientific culture it could hardly be otherwise.

While the paradigm maps cultures and ideologies it also implies archetypes—ideal types of leadership modalities. Two of these, careerist and politician derived from the lower non-ideological levels of value hierarchy, have been discussed in Chapter 5. It is now appropriate to apply the same logic to the higher ideological levels of the paradigm. These yield the archetypes of poet (charismatic leader) and technician (bureaucratic administrator) for levels I and II respectively. The labels are chosen in deference to Heidegger who identified the crisis of our age as the conflict between technician and poet.[8] What Heidegger meant by "poet" will soon be apparent.

CHARISMA

Formation, Transformation, Eternal Mind's eternal Recreation. (Faust)

Certain values, Type I values, have for some the magical property of transforming life, imbuing it with meaning, giving to it a sense of conviction and purpose. The ordinary ego of workaday self-concern and common sense is somehow transcended. The terms "charisma", "devotion", "fanaticism", "zealotry", "passion", "love and hatred" enter into this field of value and when an actor becomes committed in a Type I way, the field of action is affected both rationally and emotionally. The influence of a Type I personality, whether directly or at many removes, can be transforming.[9] Those who come into the presence of a charismatic leader experience this reality directly. I have called the associated archetype of these phenomena, *pace* Heidegger, the Poet.

The poet "carries the fire", makes things and flesh grow warm, extends the reach of language (and hence of concept and rationality), steals fire from the gods, even—in the limit—seems to reconcile for that instant God and Man. House puts it more soberly: "Such leaders are people who have a vision of the future, of society or an organization, and usually state that in ideological values ... They motivate people by appealing to universal end values and call on people to go beyond the call of duty, to put their self-interests aside ...".[10]

Poetry in this technical usage, refers to higher or deeper sentiments and intuitions, to some sort of transrational grasp which can only partially, if at all, be expressed in the linear logic of ordinary language. There may be an element here of Wittgenstein's *Das Mystische*.[11] Such language speaks to the Will; it is not mythos opposed to logos but mythos subsuming and transcending logos. It is the rhetoric that moves masses and inspires sacrifice, often verbalizing the inchoate desires of the followership. And it is unlikely to be learned in any conventional academic school of public or business administration.

Type I values, and their poetic manifestations, create awesome difficulties in a variety of milieux—in theory, in philosophy, in the social sciences because of the homogenetic fallacy and the problem discussed above of differentiating between Type III and Type I affect—in the untidy world of administrative reality because these intrusions do violence to pragmatic conventions and the ethos of compromise and bargaining. They are threatening because they invoke the will in its highest registers of motivating force and because they represent ultimate commitments. Because of their singularity we can correlate them with charismatic phenomena and advance the hypothesis that true charisma is a function of Type I commitment.

The attitude of the administrative philosopher towards the charismatic phenomenon is necessarily cautious. The record of history gives us Churchill and Gandhi but also Hitler and Genghis Khan. At the level of leader-inspired events we have the French and American Revolutions but also the Bolshevik revolution and Mao Zedong's Great Leap Forward. On the one hand the course of social evolution is often accelerated by the poet-leaders, on the other hand we bear the historical scars of their leadership. One approaches this archetype, therefore, with a strong sense of inadequacy for here analytical discourse falters. What is before us is philosophy-in-action *extraordinaire*.

The archetype can be approached through the Platonic ideal of Guardianship insofar as that entails something other than a rational technology of administration, a something other which could be described as "religious". It may indeed be that true religion is the highest experience that life has to offer and the ultimate of which we are capable. In the poetry of the Academy Plato expresses it through an acquaintanceship, however fleeting, with the Form of the Good. Zen masters would express it as *satori*. The leader then becomes a *moral* leader, calling followers beyond their petty rationality, their bourgeois comforts, their prudential insecurities. Such a leader has charisma. He knows men do not live by bread alone. He knows and voices for them their deeper, hidden yearnings. He knows too that men are led by baubles. (Is this *he* correct? Is this not primarily a male phenomenon, the mythology of Joan of Arc notwithstanding? Is the corresponding female quality "glamour" likewise undefinable? Was Mrs Thatcher charismatic? Such questions, whatever their answers, are ancillary, and need not detract from the line of argument.)

The poet archetype subsumes lower forms on the hierarchy. The type is often portrayed with adulation and yields cross-cultural and cross-historical instances of mythic stature: Moses, Arjuna in the *Bhagavad Gita,* Marcus Aurelius, Nietzsche's *Übermensch.* All of these have some special Vision of the Good. (Hitler too had his vision of a Thousand Year Reich.) To the extent that the special faculty of the poetic archetype is to impose the leader's *own* will upon the unfolding of events through the art of administration (a will which the leader may see as divinely inspired or transcendentally given) then indeed the aphorism is justified that history is the biography of great men. Of course, history is continuously in process through collective action anyway but the special role of the poet is reserved for mutative leaps in human affairs. The poetic shatters the humdrum.

Science provides us with no rational explication of charisma but its reality is undeniable in administrative experience.[12] Perhaps it is too affective for strictly rational investigation but social science would allow that it is an attribute of personality manifesting in social interaction with motivating force. It must also be in some profound sense valuational and communicative. The poet has to be seen and heard but once established in the leader role the power of myth and image as conveyed through modern media confirm and reinforce the mystique. Often the poet is in fact just that, a master of language. Mao Zedong wrote poems. Churchill achieved literary renown. This type of leader has the gift of playing language games in such a way that ideas, desires, values, affective longings which might wither and die in the light of Type II reason and pragmatic commonsense become instead invested with transrational motivating force, alive with fire and inspiration, evoking Type I commitments.

Poetry, ideology, and religion run together hand in hand. They cannot be entirely eliminated from organizational life though they can of course be perverted and degraded through the power of the planner and the philistine, through the best intentions of the technician and the politician, and the worst intentions of the careerists and the masses. The fact that our higher and deeper yearnings remain and are in some sense ineradicable renders the poet archetype dangerous. This is so when the type appears to us in the form of the Good Leader, the virtuous administrator who impresses us with character and integrity at close quarters but even more so when the imaged leader, never met, nevertheless talks to our hidden depths touching resentments of which we cannot speak; dangerous in the extreme; brinking, like genius, on madness, luring with dreams of honour and glory, self-sacrifice and fulfillment, revenge and the settling of accounts. The poets represent the ultimate in leadership but they command by will, not reason. Theirs is a different ideology and its persuasiveness lies not in mere positive affect modulated by some rational calculus of incentives, but in the triumph of the Will.[13] The poet lives by and is prepared to die for the values to which he is committed. These (Type I) values form his depth-personality infrastructure and engage the whole force of his will "What *am* I but what I *stand for?*" To be sure, in administration the poet may make full use of the technical and political modes of negotiation and compromise, the archetype subsumes the lower forms, but in the end there is no compromise, "Here I stand," said Martin Luther and afterwards, "I could do no other." This may break the organization, as it did the Roman Catholic Church. Or it may make it, as it did the Protestant Reformation. The intense personal commitment of the leader, the leader's embodiment of ideology, can have galvanic affect, infusing the organization with synergetic purpose and bringing about extraordinary accomplishment; or else leading it to self-destruction! The archetype goes beyond the limits of normality; it exhausts normality. It gives birth to a new order.

Hitler

In applying the value paradigm as an analytic tool for deriving the ideal types of careerist, politician, technician, and poet we encounter a difficulty which logically stems from the established conventions of morality and ethics. Can we admit to the ranks of actual leaders representative of the "highest" archetype—an archetype embracing the Platonic Guardian—those supposed charismatic administrators upon whom history has handed down judgements of shame, condemnation, and ignominy? How is megalomania to be reconciled with an archetype that certainly accommodates Christ and Buddha?

In dealing with this problem the special case of Adolf Hitler is instructive because of the scale of his offences, the nature of his charisma, and the degree to which his character and career have been the subject of academic scrutiny and interest over the half century since his suicide. Many theories have been offered and many books written in explanation of his demonic power of which perhaps Lord Dacre's (Hugh Trevor-Roper) *The Last Days of Hitler* and Alan (Lord) Bullock's *Hitler: A Study in Tyranny* are the most famous and authoritative. As Rosenbaum has concluded, in a careful study of the literature, rational explanations fall short while contention and mystification still confound expert opinion.[14] The issue most relevant to administrative philosophy is whether Hitler was in essence either a careerist mountebank, a charlatan dramaturgist of inordinate skill whose vision was driven by sheer lust for power (Bullock) or whether he was an authentic ideologue (Trevor-Roper). In our terms whether he was a true Type I or a remarkable Type III. The issue also runs to the distinction between these two types of affective value (see Figure 11.1). The former position was initially taken by Lord Bullock while the latter has been held continuously by Lord Dacre since his investigations into the leader's death in 1945. Contemporary comments by Lord Dacre are illuminating. Of Hitler he said, "He certainly had an extraordinary power. When he wanted to mesmerize, he did have this effect. It didn't work on—to put it crudely—aristocrats or on people who were sensitive to the vulgarity of his behaviour."[15] Dacre was still convinced, a half-century later, that there was "a frightening mystery" at the heart of Hitler's charisma but more to our point he was also convinced that he was not an actor, not a dramaturgist, nor an archetypal Politician but a true believer, a man of conviction (however one may judge those convictions)—"not a cynic but rather, horrifically sincere. He was convinced of his own rectitude." Bullock, on the other hand, took the position that Hitler was a charlatan, a poseur, a cynical manipulator. But his antagonist draws attention to Hitler's capacity for philosophy (again no matter how one judges such philosophy) and points out that *Mein Kampf* was a self-wrought ideology: "There was a powerful and coherent, if horrible, message which he had thought out, a philosophy, he obviously took himself deadly seriously. He was not, as Bullock calls him, an adventurer. He considered himself a rare phenomenon, such as appears only once in centuries. It was not a joke he was selling."[16]

This is an obvious approximation to the pure Type I archetype although it was contradicted by Bullock who for almost half-a-century insisted upon an interpretation of Hitler as an extremely astute and able politician (IIB) sub-suming a careerist and megalomaniac love of power for its own sake. Lord Bullock has, however, recently modified his position to coincide (almost) with that of Lord Dacre. He invokes the following insight of Nietzsche to justify his interpretation of Hitler as an actor who had come to believe his own role:

> Men believe in the truth of all that is seen to be strongly believed. In all great deceivers, a remarkable process is at work to which they owe their power. In the very act of deception with all its preparations—the dreadful voice, the expression, the gestures—they are overcome by their belief in themselves, and it is this belief which then speaks so persuasively, so miracle-like to the audience. Not only does he communicate that to the audience but the audience returns it to him and strengthens his belief.[17]

This is dramaturgy taken to its extreme. Auto-hypnosis. The actor who merges with his act. The mesmerist who mesmerizes himself: In Bullock's words, "I changed my mind about Hitler, in that I originally took him as solely interested in power. *I now think the ideology is central.* I think it's what armors Hitler against remorse, guilt—anything. Hitler was unmovable on this ideology, this belief he was the man sent by Providence. The belief in himself."[18] (My italics.)

The dialogue between these scholars thus finally yields, from our axiological perspective, the definitive conclusion that Hitler incarnated the Type I archetype of the Poet. This is so whether he was in our judgement evil or not, or whether he was insane or not, or whether he was historically and psychologically determined or not. At this level leadership can be angelic or demonic and moral judgement can, for the purposes of theory, be bracketed out. The significance of this for the resolution of value conflict at this level will be dealt with in the next chapter. For now it can be assumed that Hitler, Genghis, Stalin, Mao Zedong, Pol Pot and all the despots and tyrants of history that can lay claim to charisma have crossed the threshold from III to I. And, like the great *religious* leaders of past and present they impose the force of their poetic will upon *others* through organization and the mysterious power of Type I values and commitments.

None of this is intended to rehabilitate the tyrants of the world. But, from the perspective of administrative philosophy, divorced from any private sense of moral misgiving or squeamishness of scruple, we must accept that history is written by the victors and that the principle of *Macht macht Recht* is not confined to the *arthasastra*. In this instance the forces of liberal democracy triumphed but if Hitler had won, and the informed consensus is that he came very close to doing so on more than one occasion, then vilification and damnation would have been replaced by laudation and justification. If this truth is disturbing to some of us then let us be consoled by the fact that it is itself a proof of the power of Type IIB conditioning and, therefore, an illustration and exemplar of the necessity of that level of value as an instrument of moral value formation and civility.

Further Note

In the end it can be said that the mystery of charisma remains. Indeed without mystery, without inexplicability, the phenomenon might vanish. Given the value paradigm, however, one need not pass over this mystery in silence. The paradigm applies to charisma itself as it does to any value phenomenon. Thus Type III (simple affective) charisma may refer to the qualities of personal charm evinced by the careerist or opportunist in his general praxis. Provided that disbelief is temporarily held in abeyance, as it is with the persuasive salesman, this low level charisma can work its effect. The courtier and the diplomat exude their own professional glamour but it is a glamour and mystique easily dispelled by scrutiny and examination of their authenticity. Nevertheless, while it lasts, it too works its short-term magic.

Type IIB charisma is that of the politician. The charm of the manipulator raised to some degree of identification with consensus and the common good. It is the charisma of the bargainer, the negotiator, and the trader, a side-effect of the dramaturgy contingent on the fulfillment of those roles. Beneath it ripples the undercurrent of power and this, of itself, has an hypnotic quality, especially to the susceptible, to the unsophisticated, to those easily led.

Type IIA charisma, where it exists, endows the technician, whose archetype is next to be explored, with attributes deriving from *rational* ideology. That is, essentially, from science and technology, from the institutions of law and bureaucracy, and from the might and majesty with which these are invested in a postmodern culture. The individual physician, surgeon, judge, airline pilot, minister, chief executive officer may themselves be void of charisma but yet they participate to some degree in the power and magic of those values which surround and maintain the icons of our techno-civilization. And when role incumbents add to this value endowment the force of their own will, commitment, and investment in the values of this archetype then again the phenomenon of charisma becomes empirically and forcefully apparent.

True charisma, however, of the transforming and radical variety discussed above is a Type I property that remains, possibly forever, enigmatic. By definition it is transrational and ideological. Some would call it, simply, religious. Kierkegaard discriminated between the aesthetic individual, the moral universal, and the religious individual. The first and third are private and obscure belonging to the secrecy of the individual soul. Only the second, being rationally explicable, can serve as a public (or what we might call "administrative") model.[19] But paradigmatic analysis implies the manifestation of *all* levels of charisma and the subsummation of lower levels by higher.

While the most congenial form of leadership might be that of the politician following the consensual ideology of the day and while the most beneficial, as I shall later argue, that of the technician, the most committing, demanding, and in its own way fulfilling is that of the poet. Because of the religious quality of this archetype the followers themselves, transformed, intoxicated, may become as dangerous to themselves and others as is their leader. They become invested with a quality of fanaticism or zealotry which can lead within their own ranks to internecine rivalries and, outside these ranks, to violence against the infidel. Paranoia, persecution mania, is a concomitant contingency.

The followership of this archetype also risk the trauma of disenchantment, the crisis of loss of faith, the despair of deconversion. This is compounded by the fact that the prime pathology of the poet is megalomania. When the vision fails, or is frustrated, madness and tragedy ensue. The Holocaust, the gulags, the *Götterdammerung.* When Type I value idols topple, ashes and nihilism sweep in their wake.

Poetic archetypes are the ultimate leadership force for good or evil and the problem which is intractable has been phrased in the ancient question *Quis custodiet ipsos custodes*? To which the unhappy answer must be, no one. No one guards the Guardians. No rational ideology can account for them. The poet answers only to intuition (*in*-tuition), to an inner guide and voice: There is much in common between poets, saints, martyrs, supermen, and psychopaths.

Genius, when it appears in administration, is wondrous to behold but sometimes terrible in its consequences. Administrative philosophy can at best offer the maxim, Beware charisma! The charismatic leader may wish to lead where others cannot or ought not to follow. To beware does not necessarily mean

"Avoid!": there can be greatness and glory here as well as danger—superlative rewards for superlative risks—but it does enjoin consciousness. Be *aware*! Then choose.

THE TECHNICIAN

The remaining archetype restores the theme of rationality that, I have argued, is the characteristic ontological and ideological form for administration and organization in modern and postmodern society.[20] It derives from the second level of the value-paradigm which is modal for administration. Most administrators tend either to the politician (IIB) or technician (IIA) archetype. Both types can be classified as rational, humanistic, and pragmatic but it is possible to discriminate between them. The former (IIB) grounds its value logic in the politics of consensus and the ideology of the day while the latter (IIA) is utilitarian, consistently grounded in the rational analysis of the consequences of value-judgements (policy) in action. The Technician archetype is pre-eminently rational–cognitive and rational–legal. As such it resonates and is deeply congruent with our culture, deeply imbued with the ideology of reason and calculation. I have chosen the term "technician" but it is clear that, used properly and in its correct sense, the terms "bureaucrat" or "technocrat" or even "professional" or "expert" might serve as well and would agree with Heidegger's sense. Ideal-type bureaucracy *pace* Weber and its approximations in the real world constitute a technology of organization that must rank as one of mankind's greatest accomplishments. The values of the archetype are primarily those of intellect and logic—intrinsic values subserved by the extrinsic values of dispassion, impartiality, efficiency, effectiveness, planning. Justice is interpreted as fairness, economic distribution finds its path to righteousness in equality of opportunity and a seeming reconciliation of elitism and egalitarianism. The greatest good of the greatest number is an underlying tenet. Implicit too is a faith that if human problems can be stated then they can, in principle, (ultimately) be resolved. The chief instrument to this end is knowledge, pure and applied. A preference follows for the quantitative and factual over the qualitative and subjective, the nomothetic over the idiographic. The Technician is a social engineer and the morality of the type subsumes that of politician and careerist. It looks to ends that are preferably given rather than responsibly construed; but this does not mean that the technician is necessarily a-valuational or amoral. On the contrary the type is the guardian of its ideology. It would be a mistake to treat the technician–leader as being either a value-neutral or value-neutered agent and factotum of other-directed imperatives.[21] The moral commitment of the archetype can extend beyond organizational interests to the value-clarification of larger and more extensive interests. In the mode of Weberian bureaucrat the technician is the self-effacing and self-sacrificing civil or organizational servant rightly directed by a deontological sense of duty, committed to the public interest and the ever-better determination of that interest. This form I suggest, is not without its own charisma, a charisma deriving from a Kantian transcendentalism; but it is without the romantic and dangerous charisma that imbues the higher ideological type of Poet. The technician archetype subsumes, comprehends, and acknowledges the lower archetypes but transcends them. It is elitist and aristocratic—susceptible to the ideology that administration, governance, leadership are the more desirable the more they manifest rule by the *best*—often phrased "the brightest and the best"—as opposed to rule by consensus or by the merely powerful. The realities of power and politics are thought to be amenable to meritocracy, to the ultimate virtue of expertise and professionalism. The logic runs that the body of knowledge (a summative, intrinsic value) must of necessity be continually compartmentalized and refined through the subdivision of its disciplines. As the unity of science is cooperative and interdependent but increasingly molecular and articulated, so too must be social structure and organizational life. So, too, administration creates its own expertise and becomes a matter for professionals rather than amateurs.

In the public sector the technician sometimes acquires the tag of mandarin. The term may be used pejoratively but, if so, it overlooks the possibility of a form of administrative life with a vocation of service. Depictions of the type are to be found in the novels of Lord Snow and in the biographical literature of great public servants.[22] At its best the type approximates the ethos of Platonic guardianship.[23] The archetype can also take the form of the *eminence grise;* the clever staff officer behind the titular commander, the expert deputy minister who both informs and forms the mind of his minister.

Those administrators who consciously or unconsciously manifest this archetype (Robert McNamara; Albert Speer) can lay claim to the best of intentions, with which of course the road to hell is so proverbially well paved. Theirs is not any defect of motive nor any deliberateness of malice. They wish merely to better achieve organizational aims; even to achieve better aims. At worst they are guilty of philosophical myopia, of a failure to comprehend the complexity of human nature, the richness of its intuitive and affective side, its *trans*rationality, its susceptibility to all ideologies alien to the rational spirit. Ironically, for this archetype of knowledge, this is the defect of ignorance. Nevertheless, this is in a real sense the safest and most honourable of the ideal value types despite its capacity for degeneration into the modes of faceless bureaucrat, apparatchik, and disengaged organization man. Together with the politician this type represents the component of reason in the logic of administrative value. The technician approaches the limits of such logic.

As organizational life becomes increasingly bureaucratic and technological the technician archetype moves into the ascendant. If the dysfunctions of bureapathology are to be avoided followers as well as leaders must somehow come to accept a rationalistic ethos. Here is the crux of the problem of leadership in the twentieth century. Generally, professional and technical norms resonate with the archetype but the values of detached objectivity do not necessarily penetrate to the idiographic level.

In praxis the utilitarian ideology of the technician must be refined to achieve the best reconciliation of organizational interest and the largest possible compass of humane responsibility. The Socratic dictum that the unexamined life is not worth living has to be raised to the organizational level and this entails some kind of value audit. Examples of this reconciliation of *Zweckrationalitat* with *Wertrationalitat*—of a logic of worth as well as of purpose—are to be found in the biographies of Frederick W. Taylor and Bismarck, the former protesting to the US Congress that he was improving the lot of both society and the worker; the latter sitting down to write letters to himself in his several offices as Chancellor and Minister of War.

This archetype, identified as it is with the dominant administrative ideology, is by its very nature prone to praxis errors of compartmentalization, psychological distancing, abstraction, and the scientistic and excisionistic fallacies. I once asked a true exponent of the type, a high-ranking bureaucrat, about the religion of a Prime Minister whom he had long and intimately served. He was indignant. What difference did his religion make? What one did at the sacred level was not to be confused or contaminated by what one did at the secular level which was public and official. Nonetheless, when all the risks of praxis have been accounted, we must honour the technician's role for it represents the highest of the archetypes that it is ordinarily possible for an administrator to aspire to and attain. Rationally consistent it sets a prudential limit to the moral ambitions of administration. Schools of leadership can with confidence set their sights no higher—charisma cannot be taught though it can and should be learned about. It could be fairly argued that the technician –leader is the true standard bearer of rational virtue.

CAVEAT

In this chapter the ideological and value ramifications of the two higher leadership archetypes have been considered, and in Chapter 5 the two lower archetypes were discussed. Together these four analytical "pure types" theoretically exhaust the paradigmatic value possibilities. It is now necessary to repeat that these "forms" are immanent, inchoate, teleological, potential entelechies which are manifested only incompletely and impurely at the empirical level. This impurity of realization is further compounded by the principles of subsummation and conflation. These state that any value-actor is the bearer at any given time of a complex of values which are hierarchically distinct but which coexist contemporaneously, the higher value types subsuming the lower. Moreover, actors need not necessarily be aware of any affective dissonance in their axiological state.[24] Not all values need enter into consciousness. And others may be sublimated or repressed. Ignorance can be bliss. Simple ideologies such as political correctness can be an easy way out. We are forced then to acknowledge the extreme complexity and subtlety of value phenomenology while at the same time having a practical faith in the possibility and utility of its analysis. This leads to the topic of praxis which is the subject of the next chapter.

PROPOSITIONS

207. Administration is a humanism. It is not a science. But its natural ideology favours a scientific humanism.
208. Whoever makes policy is engaged in administrative behaviour. In this way managers become administrators and in this way ideology permeates the organization.
209. If administration is a practical affair then the intellectual is suspect. He is in the way. And if it is a political affair he is more than in the way—he is dangerous.
210. Administration is a perpetual becoming in which the future is more pressing than the present. Hence the search for an ideology.
211. Ideology is both disjunctive and conjunctive. It simultaneously unites and divides.
212. Ideology tends to the metavaluational: undisputed, unexamined.
213. Technologically, there must be one best way of performing work. Humanistically, there is no one best way of performing work.
214. The ideological roots of policy require discontinuous philosophical and continuous moral scrutiny. That is, value auditing.
215. Meritocracy is logically preferable to democracy.
216. A man consists of the faith that is in him. Whatever his faith is, he is. (*Bhagavad Gita*).
217. Our faith, our administrative ideology, is our own transvaluation of value.
218. Organization enshrines reason. Order is metavaluational.
219. But to be reasonable is not necessarily to be rational.
220. The crisis of our age is the conflict between the Technician and the Poet. (*Heidegger*)
221. As you believe, so you think.
222. Charisma is the mark of the Poet.
223. Charisma goes beyond reason, but reason can have its own charisma.
224. The demonic and the divine; both show themselves charismatically. How to discriminate between them?
225. Charisma calls us to commitment, to reach beyond our grasp. It is danger and risk in glamorous array.
226. Do not listen to your reason, it will betray you. Listen to your heart, it always tells the truth. (*Adolf Hitler*)
227. Men believe in the truth of all that is seen to be strongly believed. (*Nietzsche*)
228. At some point the administrator must ask, and answer, this question. Do I believe in *myself*?
229. In psychology, as in administration, higher subsumes lower. The lower cannot have the vision of the higher. This is the law of hierarchy.
230. *In*tuition is the leader's ultimate resource.

231. Mandarin, brahmin, samurai, aristocrat, guardian, technocrat, bureaucrat, meritocrat ... all synonyms for an elite the honour mark of which is the vocation of service.

Chapter 12
Praxis

Do the duty that lies nearest thee which thou knowest to be a duty! The second duty will already have become clearer. (Carlyle)

There is an ideology behind ideology in administration. One might almost call it a meta-ideology. It is inchoate and amorphous but it has a name: pragmatism. Pragmatism is a philosophy of practice, a philosophy of getting through the day. For the ordinary business of administration, whatever higher ideology might pull or push it, is inevitably pragmatic, and this is because the daily menu of administration and management consists in large part of *ad hoc* problem-solving, of dealing spontaneously and directly with those problems that arise out of the flux of events and intrude themselves, demanding attention, into the sphere of administrative action. They may stem from minutiae or be the fruit of long-breeding complex chains of cause and effect. They may be trivial or of magnitude. No matter, they must be dealt with.

Fortunately for human nerve and tissue there is a middle ground between the commitments of ideology and the fluctuating turbulence of affectivity. Between the Type III flux and the Type I dogmas lies the vast region of normality, of the everyday workaday world of organizational life. A banal world, perhaps, but one of relative ease and comfort: routine, habit, regularity, ordinariness, where potential ennui or fatigue is offset by security and modest satisfactions. This middle ground is the realm of common sense and *savoir faire*. Its affective tone may be neutral and void of ideological override, providing a context within which the ego can subsist without excessive wear and tear. Instead of the ultimate values of Level I and the proximate values of Level III there are the *ap*proximate values of Level II. These are themselves subject to the criteria of consensus and consequences, criteria which are pragmatic or utilitarian in their philosophical orientation—the former asking "Will it get the job done?", the latter "Will it pay off?" Within this region of the mean organizations approximate their goals, organization members approximate job satisfaction, and administrators approximate their ideals. It is a field of practice rather than praxis, of action satisficing values rather than values infusing (and enthusing) action. But this is the most ordinary, the most typical, and the to-be-expected pattern of organizational life within which the administrative actor must perform. For that reason alone it is at the heart of administrative philosophy. The cognitive socio-rational instincts of pragmatism result in a world of experience which is not philosophical at first blush but is rather a field of behaviour, a hurly-burly where, in the short term at least, action is favoured over reflection and doing over being. The pragmatic spirit assumes that emotions can be subordinated to rational manipulation and control. It abjures the ideological and treats the intellectual as a suspect domain. It worships the great god Common Sense. It seeks the *via aurea mediocritas*, the Golden Mean and, if it fails to find it, then it muddles through anyway.

But pragmatism is no more value-free than any other mode of administration; its focus upon practice does not divorce it from praxis, it only renders that praxis more deserving of attention so, before approaching the general problem of value conflict some more discussion of this praxis-style is indicated.

TYPE II PRAXIS

The pragmatic attitude consciously or unconsciously subordinates or excludes the extremes of Type I and Type III valuation. This attitude endorses practicability and workability. The test of this form of practical reason is, Will it work? There is an emphasis upon the short run, upon getting through the day, even upon the moment. Problems of value are muted or elided since value direction is always available, either as given in the positivistic sense or through reference to the working consensus. As Scott and Hart put it:

> The organizational world of management is one where complex problems of short-term duration must be dealt with expediently in order to advance the a priori propositions (of the organizational imperative). Pragmatism demands that managers direct their energies and talents to finding solutions for practical, existing problems within an immediate time frame. The language, reward systems, and activities of management demonstrate this concern for the present. Its attention to putting out fires, meeting competition, adjusting to inputs from the public, insuring the smooth day-to-day running of departments, and short-range planning horizons indicate its devotion to securing an orderly, purposeful world composed of interesting, narrow puzzles to be solved. This pragmatic puzzle-world encourages managers not to reflect on larger, less immediate issues of long-range effects or needs.[1]

The authors are here of course referring to the managerial end of the spectrum but the administrative extensions are obvious and, as another author says, "It's less a matter of doing what's right, than of doing what's possible, or even what's expedient. The administrator gives up what he might like to do, hoping that the opportunity will come again at a better time ... he concludes that principles and values can only be partially realized, and almost never in the short run, or that it will never be possible to do more than mediate among the demands of others ...".[2]

Pressures towards this mode of praxis are ubiquitous and relentless. An organization is a forum of contending interests, a market-place of values. Within this context the pause for reflection is often not allowed. Stimulus begets unmediated response. Principles and ideals tend to be treated with formal respect, and shelved. Stage and actor, context and experience, are interactive and under the unforgiving constraint of time. The pragmatic impress acts to distort, to elevate management over administration. In this the most prevalent, typical, and common of organizational styles, the chief characteristic is busyness.[3] The busy-syndrome includes a preference for oral contact, a fragmented schedule of interruptions and tasks which are undemanding in terms of critical analysis, concentration, or philosophical reflection. It has already been discussed as the pathology of retreat to managerialism but, even at best, in its legitimate and most hygienic form the maxims and contradictory proverbs castigated by Simon as pseudo-administrative theory[4] tend to be favoured. Hands-on down-to-earthedness and commonsensicality are the preferred praxes and, in policy making, the strategies of muddling through and disjointed incrementalism[5] triumph over rational comprehensive planning or overarching ideological agendas. Politics is the art of the possible. This pragmatic orientation and practice leads to two types, logically implied by the paradigm, of organizational praxis: consensus and results praxis.

CONSENSUS PRAXIS

We feel first, we think later. Type III values colour all our affective experience. The translation of these individual qualities into a collective or organizational expression is on the face of it most easily accomplished through consensus; that is, the working aggregation or averaging of the several component individual values. In principle such a consensus is possible for any group although it should be noted that averaging in any strictly mathematical sense does not occur.[6] What does happen is that within individual phenomenological boundaries concessions are made and victories achieved without disturbance to the overall zone of indifference. The consensus arrived at depends upon a prevalence of Type III values—where Type I values are present the consensus may be difficult or impossible (see below). Because of this the pragmatist seeks to avoid engagement on matters of principle and searches instead for the politically possible. The political arts of discovering, sensing, interpreting, manipulating, and persuading the values of others are necessary to achieve consensus. So too are those processes of compromise, cooperation, trade-off, negotiation, conciliation, dealing and bargaining which occur whenever parties posses differential power and divergent interests. So long as these diverse interests can be accommodated within the general scenario of purposes of the organization the pragmatic administrator has room for manoeuvre. The praxis functions best, therefore, when there is a lack of clarity about goals, a certain semantic obfuscation, and an absence of ideological commitment. In the pragmatic organizational context no one is ever entirely satisfied but neither is anyone dissatisfied to the point of sabotage or disruption or separation. The soldier marches with his eye on the pack of the man in front of him, paper moves from in-basket to out-basket, customers are served, the work goes on—all proof of tacit working agreements about values. Such agreements between role incumbents are not scrutinized or raised to the level of consciousness in the normal working mode. This is not necessary. Things work. They go on. That is enough.

Shifts in consensus occur in the same subliminal way. The equation of human chemistry can alter subtly or radically as individuals move into or out of organizational roles. The skilled administrator monitors these movements and senses when changes in consensus transpire. At the societal or macrolevel the skilled politician does likewise and finds intuitively the correct language game in which to couch the rhetoric that will synthesize the collective energy.

To identify the true consensus (depth as opposed to surface) is the mark of administrative genius at best and great pragmatic leadership at least. Nor is this task simple; surface harmony can disguise decay in the polity while volatile group behaviour and rebelliousness can distract and distort perception of an underlying unity and moral integrity.[7] Consider Albert Speer's account of the first time he heard Hitler (addressing an *academic* audience):

> Finally, Hitler no longer seemed to be speaking to convince; rather, he seemed to feel that he was expressing what the audience, by now transformed into a single mass, expected of him. It was as if it were the most natural thing in the world to lead students and faculty of the two greatest academies in Germany submissively by the leash. Yet that evening he was not yet absolute ruler, immune from all criticism, but was still exposed to attack from all directions.[8]

In the end, however, what can be asserted of pragmatic praxis is simply this: organizations demand some minimal degree of value consensus in order to be viable; there must be a level II modicum of general agreement about the way things are and the way things work, what the organization exists for and what the roles within it are intended to accomplish, the *status quo* and the *modus operandi*. But in the common or garden organizational context pragmatism prospers and all is usually well enough. *Laisser-faire* and the line of least resistance extend from human nature into organizational reality. Disjunctions diminish.

RESULTS PRAXIS

There are two sides to the pragmatic coin. The one—consensus organization—establishes an ambiance of Type IIB values the mark of which is working compromise or *modus vivendi*. The other—results organization—is concerned with Type IIA values and the achievement of organizational purposes. It sets the *modus operandi* and seeks to justify the maintenance of the organization via accomplishment and growth. The values which build the results ambiance are characterized by rationality and consequential analysis. The test, for either side of the pragmatic coin, is the same: Does it work? Do the subscribed values result in organizational maintenance and growth? Are the metavalues fulfilled? Again it can be noted, and should be stressed, that results organization is the modal, ordinary, common form of organizational life. The *raison d'être* of such organization is quite simply the well-being, usually the economic well-being, of its component members. Implicit here is a healthy sense of *cui bono*? Who gets what, and from whom? How will the pie be divided? Because of this underlying spirit of libertarian self-seeking, and because pragmatics tend naturally to the material and the objective as opposed to the ideal and the subjective, it follows that the philosophical infrastructure of IIA is typically utilitarian. The greatest good for the greatest number becomes the eminent maxim of justification. Sometimes indeed this becomes metavaluational in praxis and the organization assumes self-validating moral proportions. What is good for General Motors (or education, or health, or defence) is good for the country and the commonwealth.

In results organization the metavalues of maintenance, growth, efficiency and effectiveness become imperative. They also provide a protocol for the resolution of value problems. First, defend one's vested interest in the organization (as defined either by the larger organizational envelope or by some subunit within that membrane) against any threat.[9] Second, extend and expand that interest whenever opportunity allows. (This follows naturally since growth is itself a form of defence. The more territory one commands the more one can afford to lose. The more fat, the more cutbacks one can sustain.) Third, act so as to minimize costs while maximizing results. (The principle of rational efficiency.) The first two of these protocols are political, and thus take precedence, while the third is economic.

Results organization represents a world of work which can be divorced from "private" life. Interests, that is, can be compartmentalized. Some theorists have observed that this can obscure the individual's relation to the final organizational outcome or the larger consequences of organizational action. Using the term "fragmentation" Silver and Geller [10] say that this permits the individual to function effectively and contentedly in a limited context without ever being aware of the larger purposes of the organization, and without having to accept any personal responsibility for the organizational results. This must be qualified, however. It depends whether praxis is at level II or level I. The stratojet bombardier over Vietnam is to be distinguished from the Nazi death-camp guard. The first is psychologically distanced in aseptic technological comfort while the latter is in dirty hands-on contact with human misery and suffering: both perhaps doing what they pragmatically must but the latter under a radically different value-impress.

In results praxis IIA language games assume an added importance for they must be concerned with the nuances and innuendo of justification. Often the jargon of accounting and systems theory ("bottom line", "up front", "in place", "track record") enters into administrative speech patterns and thought processes.[11] This idiom may be contrasted with the politically correct usage of consensus praxis but the language games are in continuous plastic flux and in either case colloquial fluency in them tends to establish the players' mutual legitimacy and credibility. Language also acquires a shibboleth function which absolves the players from any commitment to literal interpretation and generally expresses a tacit agreement in favour of satisficing ends. Results praxis is distinctive, however, in one important feature: a commitment or orientation to professionalism.

PROFESSIONALISM

Professionalism is the logical outcome of rationalism applied to patterns of work. The topic is sufficiently large to have engendered a literature of its own but for a philosophical understanding it is enough to acknowledge as necessary, if not sufficient, the following criteria of a profession:

1. An esoteric body of knowledge. An expertise not immediately or readily available to anyone.
2. Command of entry into and expulsion from the ranks of the profession. The right to include and exclude.
3. Pretensions to an ethical commitment. A putative ethical concern.
4. A significant degree of institutional and intra-organizational autonomy. Often sanctioned by the meta-organization of the State or, at least, by an organization independent of the organization or setting within which the profession is to be practised.
5. Some dignity of style or title implying a certain status with the social structure of deference patterns.

These criteria refer to an ideal type and clearly administration is deficient upon several, if not all of them. This is not to deny the general aspiration towards professionalism throughout many levels of the work force. The pragmatic question is, How is professionalism implemented? And the invariable answer is by *credentialling*. The mark of professionalism in practice is the establishment of a credential, or better, a chain of credentials that entitle the holder to lay claim to professional status and the rights and privileges that accompany it. Credentials are formal documents (degrees, diplomas, licences, certificates) issued by state-empowered authorities to establish the status of an aspirant or license a practitioner in some technology or art. They are characteristic of bureaucratic rationalism. To be without credentials in a techno-legalistic culture is to be in some degree of economic jeopardy. But the practice of credentialling is itself competitive. Economic devaluation of currencies through inflation is paralleled by inflation and devaluation of credentials. A bachelor's degree may now serve only, in terms of market value, as a prerequisite part of a credential chain. More and more areas of work formerly open to all (childcare, insurance, real estate sales) aspire to professional status. Paper barricades must be scaled to gain access to the perquisites they defend and in Shaw's famous opinion "all professions are conspiracies against the laity."

Professionally, administration remains anomalous. It may lay contentious claims to the criteria of a profession but it is still one of the few fields of prestigious endeavour in which the amateur and the ambitious can make a career without regimentation by diploma. Nevertheless, in all categories of administrative enterprise the influence of credentialling grows as MBA and MPA degrees, law school and business training, the *hautes écoles* of governance, administration, and politics; the background in economics, or accounting, or philosophy, politics, and economics (PPE), become increasingly established as part of a system of proto-professional controls. Only at the political level is it still widely possible for the pure amateur to gain access to organizational power and at this level (school or hospital board, mayor, or government minister) the office is likely to be well-buffered by echelons of credentialled professionals who provide the requisite expertise. Thus the influence of results praxis acquires salience if not dominance in the general philosophy of administration and thus the branch of sociology of knowledge dealing with professional training is of prime concern for any professional administrative education in values and ethics. Any such education would require, from a praxis standpoint, an understanding of value conflict and resolution and it is to this theme that we now turn.

THE LOGIC OF VALUE CONFLICT

Value-conflict is not necessarily pathological. Rather, it is the logical outcome of the combination of individuals in cooperative systems and of competing systems of interest at group and macrolevels. Its resolution, of course, can lead to pathology and disjunctive rifts in holistic praxis. But if health can be defined naturalistically (*pace* Nietzsche) as the ability to overcome disease[12] then healthy praxis is the capability of resolving value conflict.

In any real situation the first question to be asked must be analytical: Is the conflict *inter*hierarchical or *intra*hierarchical on the value paradigm? That is, Are the values in conflict *between* different levels (interhierarchical) or are they conflicting at the *same* level of the paradigm (interhierarchical)?

Interhierarchical Conflict

The point of importance for praxis is that here the values in conflict are at different levels; they are different logically—different in kind, not just different in degree (Figure 12.1).

A Type I value (such as devout religious or patriotic commitment) may be in conflict with a Type III value (this teacher is a congenial member of my staff but as headmaster I must ask her to resign because of her impending divorce). Or

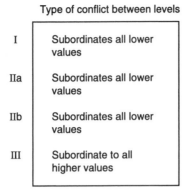

Figure 12.1 Value Conflict Analysis.

Type I may conflict with IIA (Forestry practices must be maintained to keep a local economy viable)—but this would involve environmental deterioration (opposed on ecological principle). Or I versus IIB. (Staff threaten to withdraw social welfare and care services by union action but this violates the administrator's conception of public responsibility.)

These examples illustrate conflict between Type I and other levels of value but level I need not (and ideally should not) typically be engaged. The general problem of the commons, for example, of the common weal versus selfish interest—or simply the dialectic between the idiographic and the nomothetic—can appear as conflict between levels III and IIA or III and IIB. (A simple example: a careerist colleague seeking promotion who would on prior evidence be deleterious to the organizational good.) Again IIA may conflict with IIB. The dilemma provided by the phenomenon (a phenomenon which itself constitutes a praxis) of whistle-blowing or breaking ranks. How far should the known incompetence of colleagues be indulged in the interests of professional solidarity?

Having identified the conflict what is the maxim for its resolution? Prima facie the answer is simple and has already been given. In the Sanskrit ethic the individual was to be sacrificed for the sake of the family, the family for the community, the community for the nation, the nation for the world and, finally, the whole world for the sake of the individual *soul.* The end of this chain of logic converts what was simple at first to what is subtle at last. The metaphysical intrudes ultimately upon the physical even though administrators these days do not normally think in terms of souls. Nevertheless, this ethic does provide us with an escape clause from what might otherwise be an inhuman collectivist logic of the hive. In practical or praxis terms it can be interpreted to mean that the administrator or leader should be willing to apply the general rule except where it would cause harm of a gross or spiritual nature to the individual concerned—what we might legalistically call cruel and unusual harm. Thus, it is conceivable that the loss of a job might prove utterly destructive to a given individual. In such special circumstances the administrator might feel ethically justified in using this high level escape clause to abrogate the general logic of the primacy of the larger interest. (Or the leader might try to finesse, say, the shock of dismissal by organizational generosity—the golden handshake.) What is happening here is that the administrator is in effect *reinterpreting* the larger interest so as to include the threatened employee's psychological security. This then is the first exception to the general rule.

It can be called the Principle of Most Principle. In the example given the deficient employee is kept on, the telescope is clamped to the blind eye, even as the organization becomes less efficient and effective thereby. Excellence may be sacrificed on the altar of humanity at times, and vice versa. The maxim is not mechanical or computational; it is a function of leadership and moral art. It is the particular as opposed to the general. In each real praxis situation each executive is a philosophical monad and, as with all exceptions, $n = 1$.

Psychologically one must add that no amount of value-education or experience or praxis necessarily ensures the administrator a good night's sleep. Thickness of skin, or of the membranes between mental compartments, might help but praxis has nothing to do with administrative comfort and everything to do with what is *right*. It is a sad truth that the perception of emotional stress deters many from the administrative calling but if they are faint-hearted with good reason it is also true that they could be more courageous with better reason. The value conflicts that they fear are in the end susceptible of intellectual understanding and psychological mastery.

There is a second exception to the rule of higher subordinating lower. It can be called the Principle of Least Principle[13] in contrast to its reciprocal exception. The Principle of Least Principle applies when the administrator is capable of negotiating or reducing the level of value conflict among others, always assuming that the leader's own values or those of the organization are not critically engaged. Thus a CEO whose organization is affected by militant political activism or grievance group activity might contrive to keep any such coalitions as informal as possible and to reduce potential controversy to the level of individual opinion (III); always assuming Type I values are not in the equation. If coalitions do organize (IIB) they may be kept out of the formal structure and formal processes of the organization as long as possible and, failing this, they can be incorporated (co-opted?) into the formal structure (e.g. by way of task force, committee of inquiry) but only when politically compelled to do so. At all events the leader will seek to prevent and deter the transition to Type I conflict. The logic here is one of conflict reduction and the psychology is one of "cooling off". The defensible assumption is that less conflict is preferable to more. That is, the lower on the hierarchy the value issues can be contained, or the "less principle", the better. Resort to the Principle of Least Principle is of course not justified if the leader's higher values or those of the organization are at stake. The following illustration is instructive.

A minister approves changes in his ministry which will involve long-term economic costs (e.g. provision of costly but IIB popular welfare services). These the minister perceives as having the merit of temporarily satisfying all vocal stakeholders and ensuring re-election. Here political survival (III) and political calm (IIB) are bought at the price of deferred economic costs (IIA). The reason Least Principle does not apply as a legitimate exception is that the minister's own values are engaged. The minister is not detached. Long-term interests (those of the organization) are also engaged. These interests would necessitate the mid-term losses (value-conflict and dissatisfaction) which were being discounted for the short-term gain. Such an analysis might shift the conflict to an intrahierarchical type where the logic of resolution is radically altered.

Intrahierarchical Conflict

Rarely in practice are we faced with a clear choice between good and evil and, if we were, there would be no conflict for the right choice would be automatically before us. Typically the praxis problem is one of choosing between good and good, or between lesser and greater evils. Value-actors always act to maximize what for *them* is right or good. Furthermore, ultimate choice (conflict resolution) must in the end be between *two* goods. One cannot decide between three or more options. In the last analysis any multiplicity of choice must be reduced (by an internal process of conscious or subconscious rank-ordering) to a final pair of contending values from which one must be selected. This process is not necessarily easy or painless. Consider the difficulty of choosing wallpaper! The process is illustrated by the typical administrative hiring problem of selecting the winner from a strong field of eligible candidates.[14] Iteration may be necessary. Multiple considerations intrude, fade, and re-intrude. Wallpaper or candidate rejected at one stage may be re-entered later if the process appears to be stalling. Over-iteration can of course lead to juddering, waffling, and even paralysis but,

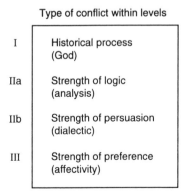

Type of conflict within levels

I	Historical process (God)
IIa	Strength of logic (analysis)
IIb	Strength of persuasion (dialectic)
III	Strength of preference (affectivity)

Figure 12.2 Value Conflict Analysis (2).

ultimately, the conflict must be sharpened and narrowed to the point where only two values remain. These may be, both of them, at any level of the paradigm (Figure 12.2):

Level III: At this level the strongest preference wins out so that the praxis problem resolves into introspective determination of what *is* the strongest preference. What does one *really* want? The choice of restaurant, of entertainment option, of office furniture ought to be decided by maximal preference although it may not be immediately clear what this is. If all values could be reduced to this level (as positivists and relativists would argue) then all value conflicts could be resolved by a sort of valence vector calculus largely inaccessible to consciousness. One need not go so far. It is enough to say that, in the individual case, conflict between Type III values van be resolved by adequate introspection. In interpersonal conflict at this level (Party A wishes x; Party B wishes y) the resolution is again on the basis of strength of preference—whoever has the strongest emotive preference wins out. On the surface this may be mistaken for a "triumph of the will" but in fact it can be a simple determinism as can be confirmed by observations of animal behaviour. The greatest difficulty of resolution (from a theoretical as opposed to practical standpoint) occurs when the contending values are very close in assessed magnitude. The closer they approach equality of valence the less significant the conflict resolution becomes and praxis could resolve it on a random basis—the toss of a coin, or the roll of a dice.

Level IIB: Examples of conflict at this level are opposing public opinions and voting behaviour and group dynamics generally provided that no Type I values are at issue and cost–benefit or utilitarian aspects are not in question. The strategy for conflict resolution then becomes dialectic or, simply, talk. The process of resolution must be allowed to persist (and the dialectical tension must be endured) long enough for the parties to the dispute to express themselves and exercise their several powers of persuasion. It is here that the German concept of *Sitzfleisch*[15] or the ability to "suffer fools gladly" may be a sterling administrative asset. In this way strength of preference again operates but manifests at a group or collective level. This is also referred to as compromise but can be technically described (given a properly free market of contending values) as Type IIB vector resolution.

Level IIA: Type IIA conflicts are resolved by cost–benefit analysis. The rational examination of the context for cause–effect chains determines the ultimate perceived or hypothesized outcomes of a choice between investing the pension fund in Plan A or Plan B; or initiating or delaying a project; or deciding whether to close or keep open a plant. That is to say, force of reason or force of logic should be sufficient for answering the question, Which of two Type IIA values is the best? Granted that our rationality is always bounded and our horizons limited we can, nevertheless, pursue analysis to a point of justification and, hence, this type of conflict is theoretically straightforward.

Level I: Finally there remains the ultimate value-problem—Type I intrahierarchical conflict. Upon this rock men and nations have broken the past, break now, and will continue to do so in the future. How are Type I value disputes resolved? Or even, Can they be resolved? How does one logically determine the superior value as opposed to merely reconciling (or disarming, or segregating, or somehow suspending) the *actors* holding the contending Type Is? Historical and contemporary conflicts between Protestants and Catholics, Hindus and Muslims, fascists and communists, terrorists and the established order, pro-life and pro-choice activists, serve as examples but, in general, any "life-or-death" or no-compromise issue invokes the type of irreconcilable value contention. If the administrator holds such principles and finds them in conflict with opposing principles held with equal vigour by either his subordinates or superordinates then something or someone will have to go. Career or organization may suffer alike.

This level of conflict is the stuff of drama, of art and literature. But in art, unlike life, resolution, is within the creative gift of the author. In life or reality the disappointing analytic answer is that there is no mode of resolution, no maxim, no strategy for determining the "best" value. There is no naturalistic answer to supra-naturalistic phenomena. Conviction locks against conviction leaving only anguish, dilemma, tragedy, and the despair of negative emotion. The pseudo-solution is provided by history itself for history gives the appearance of resolving these conflicts. The war is won or lost. The leading actors die off, are killed, or are otherwise removed from the stage. Yet this is resolution without solution. The actual value problem is left unsolved and humanity is none the wiser in the end. That the Fascists lost the war does not *prove* that fascist values were wrong nor does the collapse of Communism negate its values. Had the Nazis won or the Stalinists triumphed democratic values would not be negated either. History is an arbiter not a judge. After enough historical process, and enough bloodletting, violence, and death the contending religious, political, and ideological factions may come to an accommodation and learn to live, however grudgingly, with each other. The passion that funded the Type I commitments may spend itself over the long term and thereby degenerate the original values to level IIA, or lower still on the paradigm.[16] The initial charisma that attached to the leader dissipates and the organization, minus zeal, devolves into a rational bureaucratic mode. But history's retrospective on Type I values can tell us nothing about their future prospective. As Oscar Wilde said, "A thing is not necessarily true because a man dies for it." Value conflict analysis here comes to a halt. There is no rule. Except it be the administrative maxim to avoid if at all possible, or for as long as possible, the emergence of this category of conflict to the extent that it is within the power of office or of personal capacities to do so.

HISTORICISM

A further comment is warranted for the benefit of those readers who wish for some ultimate ethical dictate. One can, if one so prefers, substitute for the concept history the concept God or the concept evolution. One can then make the further step of assuming a purpose, a teleology, to the unfolding of events thus endowing the procession of history with what Lessing would call a quality of "divine education".[17] Thereby one may arrive at Pope's metaphysical defence of the status quo:

> *All nature is but art, unknown to thee; All chance direction which thou canst not see; All discord, harmony not understood; All partial evil, universal good; And, spite of pride, in erring reason's spite, One truth is clear, Whatever is, is right.*[18]

Such philosophy would, of course, resolve some of the conflict we have asserted to be intractable. Analytically, however, it can be denied on the grounds that any such move *at the Type I level* would simply constitute yet another Type I belief–value system with no greater grounding in higher affect than any other contrary system. The question remains whether these are genuinely supra-historical phenomena which are valid only in a certain place and time.[19]

Figure 12.3 consolidates the discussion for both types of value conflict.

The advantages to using the value-paradigm in praxis are these. First, and most importantly, it is universal in application to all administrative value-problems. Practice with it leads to proficiency and confidence on the part of the reflective

Type of conflict

		Between levels	Within levels
	I	Subordinates all lower[1] values	Historical process[2] (God)
Level of conflict on paradigm	IIa	Subordinates all lower values	Strength of logic (analysis)
	IIb	Subordinates all lower values	Strength of persuasion (dialectic)
	III	Subordinate to all higher values	Strength of preference (affectivity)

Notes: (1) Between-levels resolution has two exceptions: Principle of Least Principle and Principle of Most Principle.

(2) Type I within-level conflict can be interpreted by believers as resolution through divine intervention.

Figure 12.3   Conflict Resolution Logic.

administrator. Secondly, it prevents us from committing the homogenetic fallacy since it constantly reminds us that values are differentiated by degree as well as by kind. Finally, it provides us with a discipline: a relatively neutral conceptual tool which, nonetheless, is capable of expressing and representing the most idealistic systems of ethical thought and belief. The analyst individually determines from context and situation what values are crucial and at which levels of hierarchy. Thereafter the axiology applies. Paradigmatic analyses and praxes import order and knowledge (logic) into a domain where otherwise practice might be impulsive, uninformed, inchoate, dangerous, and potentially damaging to self and others. Of course it is not a mechanical calculus replacing art by science: leadership remains a moral art but it is an art that can be increasingly sophisticated by technique and understanding.

THE VALUE-AUDIT

Value-auditing is the administrator's most sincere response to Socrates' condemnation of the unexamined life; it is also a demanding form of praxis, "a courageous becoming conscious".[20] A value-audit is something done privately and personally; it is a stock-taking of one's own values. A reflective and contemplative effort that seeks to bring into the light of consciousness the range, depth, and breadth of one's preferences, conditioning, and belief. The means of doing this is introspection—self-observation. The concomitant demands are for ruthless honesty, the courage to remember, and not to look away. Value-auditing can be done hypothetically, apart from consideration of any particular case or problem, but more importantly it can be done with a specific praxis focus on a problem being faced in a real situation.

In the praxis case the audit should be as sophisticated as possible within the reality constraints of time pressure and peripheral commitments. It should not be a mere back-of-the-envelope calculus of value pros and cons followed by a rush to closure and action. Closure should rather be withheld until a threshold of inner certainty or conviction is crossed or, if that cannot be accomplished, then at least until there is some sense of inner confidence that the best efforts to reach judgement have been exerted. Certainly the following questions must be asked, even though altered to suit the idiom of the practitioner.

1. What *are* the values in conflict in the given case? Can they be named?
2. What fields of value impress (V_1 through V_5) are most affected, relevant, salient?
3. *Who* are the value-actors? Who gets what from whom and why?
4. How is the conflict distributed interpersonally (between actors) and intrapersonally (within actors)?
5. Is the conflict interhierarchical or intrahierarchical on the value paradigm?
6. Are ends dominating means? Or vice versa?

7. Could the conflict be resolved by removing an actor or actors? Can the excisionistic fallacy be entertained?
8. What are the relevant metavalues?
9. Are there Type I values that (a) should be invoked or (b) should be avoided. Is the Principle of Least Principle applicable?
10. Is the Principle of Most Principle applicable?
11. Would the tension of non-resolution be tolerable? Must the conflict be resolved, now or at all?
12. What consequences are foreseeable from alternative scenarios?
13. What is the internal and external political analysis? Who is for and against? What is the surface and depth consensus on the issue?
14. To what extent does one have public relations, human relations (informal organization), and general communicative control? Can one form (inform, reform) opinion?
15. What is the analysis of affect and *commitment* amongst the parties to the case?
16. What is the collective interest? Short term? Long term? How high can or need the level of interest be invoked?
17. What is *my true will* in the case before me?

These questions need not be taken as exhaustive but it is by careful and painstaking reflection upon such questions that administrators achieve their ultimate leadership cachet and exercise true leadership responsibility. Of course, to cite Goethe, life is short and art is long, so audits may fall short of the ideal. But administrators are not always in the heat of battle and organizations endure, according to Barnard, in proportion to the quality of morality by which they are governed.[21]

Perversely, alas, it is the intrinsic nature of the affective (Type III) side of our being to avoid just this very kind of responsibility. In the contest between Dionysus and Apollo the former tends to win. The press to release of tension, the urge to closure and action—oft times defended as decisiveness—conduces to avoidance of value-auditing, bad praxis, and irresponsibility. In this we are close to the heart of the problem of administrative morality. Know thyself is not an easy maxim. But value-auditing is a rational technique. Even imperfectly performed it sensitizes the pragmatic leader to the importance of principle and the ideological leader to the importance of pragmatics.

The final phase of value-auditing is action. This includes the possibility of inaction since, logically, the latter is merely negative action. Action (and righteous inaction!) necessitates the deployment of power, authority, and influence through the modalities of communication. This alone justifies the Barnardian emphasis on communication but, above all for the leader, action entails the commitment of will. Value-auditing leads ultimately to this crux of engagement. The analysis it requires also cannot but enhance the prospects for the resolution of organizational problems by enlightened praxis.

SELF-CONTROL

The analysis of affect in others, the observation of emotion and its play in organizational life, is an important administrative obligation but the achievement of affective control and the observation of emotion in oneself is quite a different matter. The former is more difficult than the latter. It is easier to judge than be judged. But the absence of affective control in the administrator is inherently dangerous. A sudden impulse, acted upon, can consign the finest analysis or value-audit to oblivion. Analysis in itself is merely academic if not complemented by right action. Praxis is always a function of the leader's affective state. What can be said about this?

The formal leader has a specialist function and role which creates both philosophical and psychological expectations. These assume a perspective that affords a measure of detachment, non-attachment, and affective disinterest which is different in kind and degree from that to be expected in other organizational roles. The leader is expected to be clear-eyed and cool-headed quite apart from any personal complex of interests. Value analysis itself presupposes this but there are obstacles to this desideratum. The administrator is human (*menschlich, allzu menschlich* in Nietzsche's phrase) and all too humanly shares in the ebb and flow of affective impulse. The range of emotive reaction embraces both panic and insensitivity. Primal motivations are continually being triggered or inhibited, occasionally indulged. Such emotive response is free-floating and uncathected. It is crude and primal, directly related to ancestral instincts to fight, freeze, or flee. Hormones play their part. Aggressivity lurks. Ego, id, and the principles of self-preservation are permanent components underlying an affective drive that is *prior* to the conceptualizing of the desirable. This primal drive, akin more to Nietzschean will to power than to Freudian libido, does not necessarily *specify* particular values or objects of intentionality but nonetheless is a powerful behavioural determinant often passing the subliminal threshold and forcing action, even if only by the dynamic of forcing the actor to seek relief from self-generated tension.

To counter the tides of affect surging in the psyche calls for an effort at consciousness.[22] The more consciousness (self-consciousness) the more control (self-control) and the more self-knowledge the more the possibility of detached analysis of interest and accurate value audit. Short of some sort of mystical enlightenment one cannot, of course know oneself fully.[23] To some degree it must always be through a glass darkly but no one can have more intimate access to the nature of one's being than oneself. Given the inaccessibility of such private phenomenology to public inspection and granted that the nature of emotion is at least as much a psychological mystery as leadership itself, it may seem presumptuous to say anything on this subject. But the problem of *negative* affect, affect which can be administratively dysfunctional or dangerous cannot be ignored even if the good can take care of itself. It is in the coping with adverse emotion (rage, anger, frustration, fear, hatred, greed, envy, anxiety, resentment) that the problem of self-control emerges most saliently in praxis and it is here that controls are most to be desired.

THE ART OF ZEN

The Japanese word Zen, now familiar in the West, derives from the Chinese ch'an which can roughly be translated as concentration. The practice of Zen and Zazen (sitting or meditative Zen) has for a long time been incorporated into administrative, managerial, and worker experience in Japan.[24] Murdoch refers to "car factory Zen" and the clichéd titles of "Zen and the Art of This and That" are by now a commonplace.[25] Since it is a discipline of attention and consciousness there is of course a prima facie relevance to administration. The administrator cannot attend properly to more than one thing at a time and, having decided what that one thing is to be, he ought not then, despite the constant importunings and pressures of affect, to allow the intrusion into his field of attention of irrelevant material. Whether or not one undertakes, Japanese style, the practice of meditation to achieve this discipline,[26] it will be agreed that the ability to concentrate and compartmentalize is desirable and it is true that every efficient administrator must be to some extent master of this psychological art-form and praxis of self-control. Simone Weil has said that "true morality lies not in judgment but in attention"[27] especially, one might add, in *inner* attention. Iris Murdoch also points out that attention can be regarded as the higher wisdom.[28] We are responsible for the contents of our consciousness—an amazing and terrible freedom if we truly reflect upon it.

Attention is equivalent to awareness. Awareness as a general attitude is partly a function of our will (or effort), partly a function of our innate form of life (genetic endowment and cultural conditioning), and partly a function of our philosophy (our acquired aggregation of values and beliefs). One can imagine a continuum from concentration with its sharply focused surgical attention-to-task at one end and an open-ended widely focused receptivity of consciousness at the other. This latter would accord with a remark of the Buddha who, when asked whether he was a god or a man replied, "I am neither. I am *awake*." Between these extremes lies the intermediate range of ordinary practice within which our attention ebbs and flows and is typically captured by the mechanical progression of events so that emotive impulses rule and escape from any conscious direction. But what is at the heart of emotive control is the ability (achieved through effort, experience, and discipline) to concentrate and focus attention and then to shift that focus at the behest of will. This is also the ability to build and maintain compartments within the field of consciousness and to sustain them against affective flooding. It is the ability to be present, to *be here now*, and to do one thing right and well. It is also the ability to inhibit negative emotion and however powerful the negative impulse to deny to it the consent of will. For the leader to be overwhelmed by emotion would be dangerous in the extreme but equally it would be organizationally disadvantageous to be impervious, insensitive, and stubbornly phlegmatic. Once again a golden mean is to be sought, a mean this time of live but disciplined emotion. Towards this end the following would seem to be desiderata:

1. A general *mindfulness;* a quality of alertness to the situation one is in; an "awakeness", a sensibility of the will.
2. Continuous monitoring of the ego and the id; their overriding by superego (conscience) when necessary in the interests of administration.
3. Not identifying with the ongoing flux of events, the ups and downs of happenstance. Achieving a degree of philosophical detachment. Outwardly this might resemble the sangfroid of the accomplished gambler but inwardly it might require heroic struggle.
4. A determination, resolve, value-ethic not to place one's own interests above those of the larger collective under one's leadership.
5. A general inhibition against *expressing* negative emotion, unless it be for deliberately calculated political purposes. This is not to say that the administrator will not feel negative affect, only that he will not internally consent to it or externally express it.
6. Commitment.

COMMITMENT

This difficult concept escapes precise definition and provokes the questions, to what?, and by whom? (or even by *what?*). Like the leadership concept itself it is elusive and protean and, under the head of organizational commitment has been the object of empirical investigation only in recent decades. Buchanan drew attention to the component elements of identification, involvement, and loyalty and defined its organizational form as "partisan, affective attachment to the goals and values of the organization, to one's role in relation to goals and values, and to the organization for its own sake apart from instrumental worth."[29] This definition is generally concordant with other empirical research authorities.[30] It is also consistent with the value paradigm and has been researched in that respect at the empirical level by Lang.[31] Sir Geoffrey Vickers, on the other hand, seizes upon the moral aspect of commitment and treats it as a sort of internalized set of self-expectations which can be acquired either by socio-cultural programming or by "an act of conscious artistry on the part of the ego, desiring him to emulate some human possibility which experience has revealed to him and which claims his commitment."[32] The suggestion of deliberate "artistry" is noteworthy. It is to be expected that biographical factors determine one's initial attachments to family, tribe, nation but the actor—especially the educated actor—is presumed to be able to *choose* other commitments: to organization, to task, to person, to idea, to play, to symbol, to myth. All of these are laden with significance for the praxis of leadership.

If now we consider commitment as the degree of attachment of the will to a project (and projects can include human relationships, ideas, sentiments, and symbol systems as well as organizations and specific organizational tasks) then the paradigm applies. A child's commitment to play is affective and transitory (Type III). Work, by contrast, introduces higher levels of value: obligations to and expectations from the group or team (IIB), a rational pay-off (IIA), or service to an ideal, ideology, or religion (I). Our commitments are often thrust upon us by birth, accident, chance, or the manifold persuasive forces of culture. Choice may be much less than we think. Artistry, in the Vickers sense, much rarer than we might care to admit. And engineering of commitment is a praxis possibility.

Any leader's greatest accomplishment is to motivate—to invest the organization with meaning and value above and beyond prudential calculus; to captivate the will of the led. It follows that much of the leader's art has to do with cultivation, manipulation, and education of the will. One wishes almost to say that leadership (administration) is moral education: a shaping and development of self (the leader) and others (the followership). This psychologically precarious term has been described as "deliberative desire", the place in our psychic landscape where reason and appetite meet; where wishes and emotions submit to reason; and reason in turn is activated by desire; hence the central pivot of the human being as a practical agent.[33] There is sufficient mystery in this, both philosophical and psychological, to allow the reader to construct his own philosophy of commitment but one can fairly presuppose the following praxis stages: initiation, commitment, disengagement.

In the first stage the new organization member (or administrator) is exposed to a V_2 group. Initial enthusiasms or misgivings are quickly tempered by these earliest experiences and commitment is either aborted or established at one of the paradigmatic levels. Symbol systems and language games become incorporated in the self-system as a set of socio-psychological expectations. This is followed by a plateau of commitment proper which may be very uneven. Temporal fluctuations in task interest, energy level, health, personal circumstances, perceived behaviour of colleagues, ambivalence or confusion are some of the perturbing factors any of which, carried to excess can lead to the third stage. Thirdly, the member becomes decommitted or disengaged. Infinite are the avenues towards entropy and disenchantment: disaffection with peers, superordinates, subordinates, clients: routine and alienation, understimulation, overstimulation, stress and distress—one way or another the will erodes and the attachment breaks.[34]

If this cyclical character of motivation and commitment is allowed then administrative praxis leads directly to the necessity for both its external study through observation and its internal study through self-examination. Where are the others now? And, more importantly, where am I? The administrative art extends to manufacturing ethos and to the study of its rhythms: inspiration, aspiration, expiration.

THE ART OF INDIFFERENCE

It is hypothesized by way of ideal type that a psychological accomplishment of leadership would be a degree of self-mastery or affective control which could be characterized as *indifference*. Of course what is meant here is not indifference in the ordinary sense of not caring but in the special sense of non-attachment, non-identification so that the outcomes or fruits of an agent's actions are not attributed to either the enhancement or disenhancement of that agent's *ego*. The administrator cares very much about outcomes but not about vanity. His indifference is philosophical; an acquired art form. Success or failure are subordinate to duty in this Kantian model. How could such a model of affective management be achieved in practice?

The following phases occur, recur, and overlap in the affective conduct of leadership: a progression from problem to problem, decision to decision, plan to plan, crisis to crisis. Into the administrator's field of attention flow consecutively, concurrently, recurrently the matters to be dealt with, the problems to be solved, resolved, shelved; one question after another, each with its stresses and affective demands.

It is suggested that the first requirement towards philosophical detachment is a general attitude of mindfulness, of sensitivity, of *perception.* Combined with this should be an imaginative function of *conception,* an awareness or awakeness as to the creative possibilities of the situation. Given these attitudinal factors analysis can then proceed through concentration: the focusing of intellect, affect, and will on the task at hand and the imputation of values to the contingent facts.

The next step in this art is discrimination: between subjective and objective; between role and role-incumbent, between actor and performance or agent and agency. This step is the most difficult to achieve and the easiest to neglect. It is internal and subtle, breaking identification and freeing actor from the impending act. It is the pause, the fateful pause, before commitment. Thereafter comes the flood of action with all its ramifications and ever-widening circles of consequence and interaction. This pausal detachment of ego from its ever-present and ever-pressing demands in favour of a transcendent preview of larger interest and higher value is the praxis ingredient of the art of indifference. This, if anything, allows the leader, his duty discerned and acted upon, to sleep at night. The arrow has left the bow ... what is done is done ... what comes next, comes next.

THE COGNITIVE IMPERATIVES

Administration is not mechanics. It is closer to art than to science. Therefore it is legitimate to adopt pragmatic rules of thumb and the resort to maxims or value axioms[35] ought not to be considered improper or be vetoed on the grounds of being unscientific.

Maxims, including Simon's mutually contradictory proverbs,[36] have emerged over time as a form of administrative folk-wisdom intermediate in the hierarchy of knowledge between speculation or guesswork on the one hand and the empirically verifiable predictive assertions of any putative administrative science on the other. They are propositions whose value lies in experiential efficacy and the continuous pragmatic testing of organizational life. The most important have been already introduced in the chapter on leadership above but it is appropriate to re-enter them once more under the heading of praxis. Cast in cognitive form as injunctions to know something they are nevertheless deeply imbued with moral and ethical force.

1. *Know the task.* What is the mission of the organization? What are the subfactorings of the mission? Where does *this* task fit?
2. *Know the situation.* What are the significant features of the context surrounding the task? Which of these need special attention?
3. *Know the group.* There is no upper limit to the desirability of this form of knowledge save that imposed by the reality constraints of space and time and any sociological constraint that demands a separation of leader from led.
4. *Know oneself.* The mega-maxim and the unending obligation—the apogee and quintessence of administrative philosophy.

These practical maxims are conducive to the best praxis but the last and most difficult of them deserves an additional comment. Administrative morality in its highest sense (that is, *ethics* in the terminology of the paradigm) is a progressive discovery of the administrative will: of the truth that the leader has a will and can manifest it to the world through other people and *their* wills. This is the obverse of the truth that all organizations and all politics involve the exercise of power over others. If the blind are not to lead the blind, nor the sleep-walking to lead sleepers, then the leader must have vision. Moral vision. Ethical vision. This means becoming more conscious and this means obeying the Delphic oracle and the ancient injunction to Know Thyself. But while this axiom of practical reason has been remembered with lip-service throughout the ages it has been honoured more in the breach than in the observance and it is almost forgotten that there was a second commandment at Delphi: *Nothing too much.* Praxis should take note of this also.

To conclude: Praxis is value-driven practice and cannot be entirely reduced to cognitive formulae. The administrator should be especially aware of the three differentiated value-actor roles which leadership shares with every member of the followership: carrier, educator, and judge. Carriers are the bearers of values, their own and those of the organization to which they subscribe; educators are those who persuade others to values as in the politically correct cliché of "role-modelling" but the concept also includes those value-bearers who are open through experience of organizational life to learn as well as teach and thereby modify their own values; judges are those who become critics and deciders, praxis philosophers, visibly refereeing and resolving value disputes and consciously moving values into and out of dispute. All of these roles in complex interplay affect the texture of meaning and the normative structure that comprises an organizational form of life. Observing the cognitive imperatives is a necessary, and to some degree a sufficient, condition of achieving the axiologically superior design of that life.

CONCLUDING PROPOSITIONS

232. Intellectual understanding of organizational purpose is unevenly distributed; it is, finally, the prerogative of administration

233. Administrative praxis is the activity of logic and the activity of value judgements.

234. Management has a natural affinity for the middle realm of value.

235. Participatory decision making improves the possibilities both for consensus and for manipulation. The process is aberrant only when it beclouds intentions. To the extent that it inhibits intuition it is not aberrant, only inefficient and ineffective.

236. The negotiator seeks to conceal values, the arbitrator to reveal them, the administrator to understand them.

237. Administrative workloads can be organized so as to prevent reflection. Busyness is correlated with superficiality and purpose is frustrated.

238. Compartmentalization is necessary but beware of its dangers: insensitivity, unimaginativeness, fragmentation, freneticism.

239. Equity would require rewards commensurate with contribution. In all organizations is the administrator's contribution the greatest? In most?

240. Administrative professionalism would re-legitimize the principle of hierarchy.

241. Administration lacks theory because it is not a discipline but an interdisciplinary nexus; it is a profession in which many amateurs are engaged. It is also the profession of amateurs.

242. We require of our doctors that they study; we do not do so of our leaders.

243. The first law of organization is maintenance; the second is growth. These together constitute the organizational will to power.

244. Responsibility entails an act of will. This takes it at once beyond mechanical accountability.

245. The ultimate ground of decision is consciousness. That is, intention. The raising of value consciousness is an ethical imperative, perhaps the *only* one.

246. Moral conflict, the normal administrative condition, is the unending war between assertion of the ego and self-sacrifice. Pessimists would call this a lost cause; optimists a dialectic.

247. Compassion, empathy, and sympathetic imagination are necessary conditions of administrative morality. But as the oracle declared, Nothing too much.

248. Conscience is that which informs us first of collective responsibility, and then of higher responsibilities still.

249. Between Machiavelli and Plato let us choose the latter. Better, let us not choose but rather assimilate the former to the latter.

250. Commitment should be renewed and refined throughout the administrative career. This is done by philosophy.
251. Consciousness is intrinsically valuable; the means to its own end.
252. The frustration of the ego and its discipline under a collective and hierarchical regime can be the most valuable part of organizational life; it can mature and refine the ego and be a means to growth of consciousness.
253. Commonsense is a necessary but not sufficient condition for praxis. Praxis is the reciprocation of the mind and the will.
254. Self-observation precedes self-control. The former is the condition of the latter.
255. If there is a moral order in the universe then adherence to it would strengthen and departure from it weaken the leader. A hypothesis.
256. No one is indispensable. Everyone is irreplaceable.
257. Work for the work's sake only.

Chapter 13
Polemic

Administration is philosophy-in-action—the proposition that began this text. If this is valid then all else follows, including the principle of praxis to which the last chapter was devoted. It also follows that there can be in administration no *tabula rasa* of the sentiments, however fervently objectivity and neutrality are lauded and professed. Our vision is sullied, our intellects muddied, our hands dirtied by all our action-in-the-world. The universe of action is infinitely complex and beyond any comprehensive grasp of control and predictability. But beyond factual constraints, scientific knowledge, technological power, and coexistent with them, lies also a world of argument, theory, opinion, speculation, and polemic. This can be called the polemical context of administration. That is, levels V_4 and V_5 which form the cultural surround of the organization. In this chapter we consider the sources of that cultural environment. The origins of those beliefs, attitudes, and values with which administrators have to contend.

These strata value (V_4, V_5, and a possible but contentious V_6), whether expressed as ideologies, philosophies, fashions, trends, tendencies, or mores— or simply as the *Zeitgeist*—are all rooted ultimately in intellectual foundations about which blow the shifting sands of polemic, for though a philosophy may last for millennia, may even be "perennial", still it will only feed into the moment of a given epoch. And along with it come all the contending voices raised against it, to yield what is tritely called the conventional wisdom; the orthodoxy of the day and the hour. The *Zeitgeist* feeds upon the efforts of all intellectual workers: artists, scientists, social scientists, critics, analysts to produce this wisdom of the day and its associated morality. In this complex process of axiological evolution cause and effect are intertwined, yet often reversible, but hard to disentangle.

The benefit of studying this process is of course open to question. It may be analogous to studying climate and weather where the cliché has it that everybody talks about the weather but no one does anything to change it. Yet meteorology has its uses, obviously, and the understanding of value climates and weather has its appeal for the active side of the administrative philosophy equation as much as it does for the more contemplative side of philosophy *per se*. The question of benefit may also serve to throw light upon the division between the theoretical and practical aspects of administration. In general, philosophers do not make good kings as Plato and Aristotle (and perhaps Heidegger) discovered. And, in general, administrators have not contributed much, outside their own subset, to philosophy. For one thing administrators do not have the time to study philosophy in depth, and may well not have the inclination to do so anyway. Philosophers for their part are too busy in their armchairs. Legend has it that Socrates in his army service once held up a parade because he had to "stop and think". This is a familiar, but real, disjunction. But because neither specialist can master the other's specialty does not mean divorce but, rather, as this book has laboured to show, the need and the possibility for the establishment of a middle-ground, a logical space for communication and interaction, some prospectus for the sophisticated, educated, and balanced executive. Both poles, active and reflective, share after all a common central interest: the collective good, and if leadership implies vision then vision implies understanding.

Of course a disjunction will always persist (and rightly so upon the principle of division of labour) between practitioners and aspirants to administration on the one hand and theorists (professors, scholars, researchers) on the other. The onus upon the latter to acquaint themselves with the discipline of philosophy is of course much greater than it is for their symbiotic colleagues in the field. And here something has been lost in our times on both sides: the concept of the educated humanist with a command of both the classical and the contemporary polemic of ideas.

Such an administrative education, fascinating and entertaining though it may be, can only be hinted at in these pages. What can be done here is to offer suggestive notes towards some essential outline of the contending worldviews affecting public, private, and organizational life at the beginning of the twenty-first century. To do this means at least to survey, however briefly, the contributions of European thought—for ours is still a European culture, multiculturalist faddisms notwithstanding. It also requires at least a conspectus of the postmodern condition and a delineation of trends and options facing those who choose to do administrative philosophy in our times.

THE GERMANIC INFLUENCE

The life of the mind (as Hannah Arendt titled her major work) is, like administration itself, an arena of contest. Within this turbulent arena doctrines, ideas, formulations, and theories—paradigms and laws even—strive for supremacy, for their short moment in the sun and their long moment in the shade of history. Polemic permeates this strife at least as much as does the force of logic. Sometimes long periods of stable systematization endure (the Scholastic era of Christianity in medieval times, the Darwinian orthodoxy in our own). Sometimes this duration is disrupted by paradigm-shattering events such as the Copernican revolution, Einsteinian relativity, Freudian psychology. The evolution of knowledge and its interpretation by philosophy is integral to the movement of cultures; their genesis, flourishing, and degeneration. Practically this means two things: first, that administrators and leaders are always located within an epoch (V_5) the culture of which has antecedents which are both historical (temporal) and geographical (spatial); second, that this culture forms the substratum or infrastructure of ideas out of which contemporary controversies and issues emerge. To know something of the cause is often to have some power over the effect.

In the West we are, of course, the heirs of Greece and Rome and all their consequents. From classical Mediterranean antiquity to modern Germany, France, and the English-speaking world many lines extend. The heritage is rich, too rich in fact to allow for any simple answer to the question of selective relevance for administrative philosophy. In some sense, of course, it is *all* relevant but practicality demands selectivity and, hence some principle of selection. This could be, for example, the study of great men—the biography of leadership. Or we could apply the criteria of movements, seeking synopses of significant themes and ideas. Or, more pragmatically yet, the delimitation could be to acknowledged authorities such as the Americans Barnard and Simon to whom much homage has already been paid in the text.[1] No criterion, of course, will be universally acceptable. The rationale chosen here is idiosyncratic and to some extent arbitrary: one possible tracing of how we got to here from there, an interpretation heavily dependent upon the reader's suspension of judgement and certainly far from definitive. Nevertheless, it may serve as a mapping of the territory.

It is a curious fact that the literature of administrative theory and philosophy in the Anglo-American world pays less than adequate respect to German foundational sources. This is regrettable for what Annan calls the German Renaissance ("It transformed European culture and, like a star exploding, it continued to hurl radioactive particles into space well into the twentieth century")[2] is at least as influential for the administrative context as its Italian predecessor of the fourteenth to sixteenth centuries. Goethe, Schiller, Fichte, Schopenhauer, Nietzsche, Hölderlin, Kleist, Burckhardt, Hegel, Heine, Kant, and latterly, Einstein, Wittgenstein, Simmel,

Weber, Freud, Husserl, Heidegger ... the pantheon is illustrious no matter how it may be eclipsed by ignominies of political history and the shocks and aftershocks of modern world war. To be sure few of these thinkers were directly concerned with administration[3] but all are part of a rich cultural composition that frames our ways of seeing and thinking about reality, and many were closer to the art of moving men than they perhaps imagined. Their ideas are important and significant for the business of leadership. For example, in all too brief and telegraphic a visitation, consider: Marx and Marxism. Karl Marx (1818–1883) felt that the time had come for philosophers to engage in political action (praxis) rather than detached analysis or speculation. The results of course, in historical retrospective, have been no more salubrious than those of Plato or Aristotle or Machiavelli but the impress on all modernity has been massive. To this time of writing, in a post-Soviet era, citations of Marx in learned journals exceed those of any other social scientist and, for that matter, of Shakespeare.[4] Heavily indebted to Hegel in philosophy his central ideas of dialectical analysis of change,[5] of class struggle, of the economic infrastructure and cultural super-structure, of the primacy of economic motivation and capitalistic determinism are as important conceptual baggage for the administrative philosopher as are his humanistic concerns for the disadvantaged and the victimized members of society, concerns which later were glossed in the "Frankfurt School", the Institute for Social Research exiled from Germany to New York between 1925 and 1949. Adorno, Habermas, Harkheimer, and Marcuse *inter alia* developed a post-war critical theory of Marxism (Marxism with a human face) which was antithetical to positivism, crude materialism, Stalinism, and historical dogmatism. The scholarly output of the Frankfurt School was a highly influential contribution to postmodern philosophizing. But does the administrator as philosopher-in-action need to know about all this? Not necessarily. Suffice that these ideas and their substance are comprehended in the scheme of administrative things. There is no power that can withstand an idea that has reached its time.

Amongst the greatest of ideas are interpretations of history itself or more precisely, historical process. Since history is a succession of events and since administration is the orchestration of events, indeed a historical art form, it is well to consider Marx's predecessor Hegel (1770–1831). His "dialectic" has already been referred to several times and, to recapitulate, it suggests a triadic or spiralling movement whereby an initial impetus (thesis) encounters and engenders resistance (antithesis) which either frustrates the initiative or results in an new state of affairs (synthesis) or *Aufhebung* in which the original opposition, without being negated, is sublimated into a more complex form of order. The dialectical principle would also refer to ordinary processes of argumentation or value conflict as has been suggested in the previous chapter. The applications to administration are plain but again the time-constrained practitioner need not necessarily drink deep at this fountain, a task more appropriate to the academic side of administrative philosophy. In passing it can be noted that the Marxian dialectic was materialistic and understood by Marx to have rectified Hegel's original *idealistic* version—"standing Hegel on his head" or putting him "the right way up". Given the historical verdict such judgement would seem to be *de trop*. The Hegelian *Geist* (world spirit), a sort of meta-physical V_6 force manifesting through evolution might yet be vindicated in subtler interpretation of events.

The most directly administrative German theorist was, of course, Max Weber (1866–1920) and his ideas of leadership, power, and authority need not be recapitulated here. Weber is almost unique in having actually practised (and enjoyed) administration. A sociologist rather than a philosopher his rich legacy has reached the English-speaking world only latterly and it has suffered through inadequacies of translation, interpretation, and scholarly appropriation.[6]

Nevertheless his works are essential to the administrative discipline and his concept of *Verstehen* (understanding), an idea central to anthropology, holds great promise for both research and praxis.

The great philosopher Kant (1724–1804) is noteworthy for his strict deontological position in ethics as reflected in his concept of duty (an administrative concept if ever there was one). His categorical imperative has already been criticized in the text but one may note also his conviction that human worth is not a given (*gegeben*) but a project, an assigned task (*aufgegeben*).[7] This has a clear leadership resonance, an administrative ring.

Also frequently referenced in the text is the near contemporary Ludwig Wittgenstein (1889–1951) who has been influential in the English-speaking world more so than on the Continent. His emphases upon language, linguistic analysis, and the concept of language games are of relevance to both theory and practice of administration. Rhetoric has always had its place in the executive art, sophistication about verbal logic is a more modern acquisition.

For prophetic insights into contemporary culture we must turn to a thinker who died as the twentieth century was born. Friedrich Nietzsche (1846–1900) has been the most quoted and most misunderstood of modern German intellectuals. A radical genius and literary stylist his status in administrative philosophy is as a rich repository of startling insights yet to be explored and developed. Spurious and false identifications of his philosophy with the Nazi movement may be partially responsible for this[8] but Nietzsche was in fact more of a neo-Socrates and a contrarian individualist than any lover of authority and the State. Because of his slighting in the administrative literature a little more may be said by way of compensation.

As much psychologist as philosopher Nietzsche became convinced that a single motive—the will to power—lay at the root of all human behaviour. This places power as a grand motivational reduction on a footing with Freud's libido or Marxist wealth. His analysis is built upon the universality of fear. Power is the defence against and the overcoming of fear (and resentment and inferiority). Such a proposition cannot be amplified here but, if allowed, it would enable us to replace the classical evolutionary triad of psychological and biological responses to a threatening environment—fright, flight, or freeze by a single desirable: the power to overcome. Thus even asceticism, martyrdom, and the sacrifice of life itself can be interpreted as expressions of desire to overcome this world entirely and gain supernatural power in an after-life. Associated with the will to power is the concept of *ressentiment*: slaves (subordinates) resent their masters (governors) but powerless themselves seek ideological–religious outlets for vicarious revenge. Thus St Thomas Aquinas: "The blessed in the kingdom of heaven will see the punishments of the damned, in order that their bliss be that much greater."[9]

These ideas are not without fertile administrative resonance as is Nietzsche's leadership ideal in the *Übermensch* or Overman: not *Super*man but rather one who has overcome *himself*, that is, his chaotic impulses and emotions. The ideal is "the Roman Caesar with Christ's soul."[10] A leader who, like Goethe, "disciplined himself to wholeness" and became "the man of tolerance, not from weakness but from strength."[11] *Per contra* note the remark on Napoleon as a leader who "had been corrupted by the means he *had* to employ, and had *lost* the *nobility* of his character".[12] Or the derogatory reference to administrators (political men) as men of jest, cunning, and revenge.[13] (Do we not know them?) But, to return to the will to power, its correspondence to the first two metavalues (preservation and maintenance) is striking and surely deserving of further investigation within the disciplines of both administrative philosophy and administrative psychology.

Nietzsche's epistemological position is likewise radical and sceptical. His proposition that "There are no facts, only interpretations" is convincingly argued and is technically known as perspectivism. This presaged phenomenological subjectivism and the Greenfield treatment of organization and administration.[14]

In axiology Nietzsche called for a "Revaluation of all Values". This is not a call for new ethics—there *are* no new ethics—but an appeal for recommitment ... "a courageous becoming conscious"[15] and a Socratic "vivisection" of the very *virtues of the time* [V_5] revealing "how much hypocrisy, comfortableness, letting oneself go and letting oneself drop, how many lies were concealed under the most honoured type of their contemporary morality, how much virtue was *outlived*."[16] In effect, that is, a value audit of unrelenting and heroic audacity. Again this is suggestive for another central concept in administration: commitment. On the other hand, although Nietzsche's philosophy of value was not fully worked through his recognition of the paradigm is only implicit. As Kaufmann declares: "... Perhaps one could even construct a three-level theory of values on the basis of the three-fold conception of 'physiological,' 'psychological,' and 'ontological' interests; but such attempt would lead far beyond Nietzsche, who never explicitly distinguished between these three. ... He did not develop any systematic theory of values."[17]

Power, authority, leadership, "greatness", commitment, will, culture, order, governance, the overcoming of the self, values... all the concepts central to philosophy of administration have been concerns of the Germanic *Geist* and the genius of that spirit flowed into and formed our present (V_5) condition. Benn writing at the midpoint of our century said of Nietzsche, for example, "Virtually everything my generation discussed, tried to think through—one might say, suffered; one might also say, spun out—had long been expressed and exhausted by Nietzsche, who had found definitive formulations; the rest was exegesis."[18] Now, another half-century onwards, at the beginning of the third millennium some knowledge of the German philosophic contribution remains essential to an understanding of the human condition and its organizational forms.

POSTMODERNISM

In the latter part of the millennium a popular philosophical congeries emerged known as existentialism. It flourished for several decades after World War II before yielding the field to what are loosely known as structuralist or postmodern critiques.[19]

Existentialism itself was, like its successors, a very mixed bag. It encompassed such diametric opposites as atheistic communism (Sartre) and religious conservatism (Marcel). Conspicuously French it was above all European and represented a post-war confluence of Germanic and Gallic thought. Jaspers and Heidegger joined Marcel, Merleau Ponty, and Sartre in opposition to rationalism and empiricism. The stress was upon the individual as an existent, isolated will cast into a universe which was essentially alien and antagonistic to human interests. Angst, anxiety, alienation and absurdity characterize the experience of this condition and pose the problem of creating value in a world where the moral life depends on individual choice. Authenticity and engagement (commitment to values in defiance of logic) were terms often used to describe the tragic heroes and heroines who peopled existentialist novels, plays, and films. Difficult though generalizations are, given such an amorphous movement, it seems fair to say that it was, in mood at least, anti-rational, anti-organizational, anti-administrative. It was also individualistic although the existentialist V_1 orientation never excluded V_3 political action; it merely challenged it on the grounds of absurdity or inauthenticity. In any event the V_1 emphases of existentialism were to give way in their turn to the next movement in the dialectic of ideas, a movement which shifted the emphasis from V_1 to V_4. From individualism towards subcultural identity.

This movement is variously known as structuralism or postmodernism. It too is heavily Gallic in its sources and development and is even more difficult of definition than its existentialist precursor. The term first emerged in the arts as descriptive of the new experimentalism consequent to the traditions of modernism, that is, the arts as they developed up to, say, the period of the World Wars. Later it acquired a post-Wittgensteinian linguistic cast with the ideas of structuralism and deconstruction. This was coupled with a central interest in the concept and phenomenon of power. From these bases it presented a challenge to conventional humanism and, hence, is of direct administrative relevance. Bradbury describes it as a "still amorphous body of developments and directions marked by eclecticism, pluriculturalism, and often a postindustrial hi-tech frame of reference coupled with a skeptical view of technical progress."[20] In a definitive scholarly analysis McGowan[21] draws attention, however, to the preoccupation of postmodernists with power, politics, and sociology detailing the contributions of French theorists such as Bourdieu,[22] Deleuze,[23] de Man,[24] Derrida,[25] Foucault,[26] and Lyotard[27] as well as German contributors from the Frankfurt school[28] and modern American exponents[29] such as Rorty and Said.[30]

Of the many contributors to the debate Foucault and Derrida can be singled out as being of especial interest to administrative philosophy, the former for his analyses of power and the latter for his analyses of language. But while Foucault is content to explicate the evidences of power-as-domination in its ramifications through social structure, language games and Type IIB conditioning generally Derrida is much more sinister in that his doctrine of deconstruction strikes at the very heart of meaning and consciousness.[31] Postmodernism here reveals its essential nihilism (another Nietzschean prophecy amply fulfilled). Language, for example, is but the *jeu des significants*, the play of signifiers without ontological foundation. What is supposed to be signified in any *grounded* sense is otiose— there is no *Ding an sich*, no reality beyond language of which language is a picture or to which language points or refers. Instead, all *meaning* is entirely enclosed in the self-referential system of language itself; an intersubjective set of symbolic conventions, ever shifting and in flux. The consequences are profound. For there can now be no rigorous concept of truth or tablets of morality set in stone. (Pontius Pilate is vindicated 2000 years later.) Meaning is reduced to the *play* of language which is a sort of transcendental field dominating the individual users of language and beyond their accessibility. Any text can be read any way. Nietzsche is reaffirmed: there are no facts, only interpretations.

Of course, polemic being what it is, this pillar of postmodern thought has its critics. Murdoch, for example, construes a persuasive counter-argument from the standpoint of metaphysics[32] and Annan, from a more administrative perspective remarks that while he and his colleagues remained sceptical "Structuralism 'decentred' the individual in the same way that Darwin had decentred the human species by showing how it had evolved. All the French savants—Barthes, Braudel, de Man, Lacan, Foucault, Derrida—were relegating the individual human being to insignificance. Authors and books, events, and sexuality itself, disappeared beneath waves of abstraction."[33] Neither technical critique nor scepticism should detract, however, from the administrative praxis imperative to know the situation. Indeed three of the four cognitive imperatives are involved since an intellectual appraisal of postmodernism applies also to understanding of the followership and of oneself.

That the V_5 context of administration is, in some sense postmodern, is equivalent to saying—allowance being made for the inevitable distortions occasioned by such a plastic and obscurantist development, a body of ideas which, even if not wrong-headed, is certainly muddle-headed—that V_1 has been de-emphasized in favour of V_4. One encounters here not just a Nietzschean death of God but a fatal illness of tradition and authority—the epiphany of Yeats's intuition that

Things fall apart; the centre cannot hold, Mere anarchy is loosed upon the world, The blood-dimmed tide is loosed, and everywhere The ceremony of innocence is drowned; The best lack all conviction, while the worst Are full of passionate intensity.

A Dionysian triumph over the Apollonian modernism. Meaninglessness, multiplicity, complexity, pluralism, multiculturalism, relativism, alienation, nihilism, hedonism, narcissism, are some of the ephithets applied to the condition and, in the arts, Habermas, and Lyotard talk of avant garde exhaustion while Barth laments "The exhaustion and 'used-upness' of forms."[34]

Other features with which the administrative mind must grapple and which are rooted in this neo-existentialism are radical egalitarianism and utopianism at the political level, political correctness of behaviour and speech, single issue agenda politics, identity culture, victim culture and some considerable loss of nerve or tender-mindedness on the part of all levels of governance and authority. These trends will be discussed in more detail in the next section but attention may now be drawn (in paradoxical contrast to Yeats) to the political shift of both Right and Left towards the Centre, a centre which, at the price of "holding" has lost form, clarity, and commitment. In religion, by contrast, the opposite seems to have occurred. The centre has lost its hold to charismatic and fundamentalist movements towards the extremes. It can be noted that paradigmatic value analysis is competent to explain both the political and the religious phenomena. The former is consistent with Type II reactions to postmodernism, the latter with Type I. Again, the V_5 level which once spelled out the ideologies of large masses has also descended to a V_4 emphasis on vocal minorities and agitating interest groups. Postmodernism exacerbates the problem of the commons and undermines the inhibitions to corporate greed.

TRENDS

Trends and fashions are not philosophy, but they are bred of and by philosophy. Of course, once again, fact must be discriminated from value and certain changes are, at least in essence, factual rather than valuational. Thus, the technological discoveries of nuclear weaponry; the great advances in biology, genetic engineering, and medical science; the evolution in communication and transportation effected by television, microchip computerology, and aviation have all contributed to a globalization of humanity, the "global village" predicted by Marshall McLahan in the 1950s.[35] Beyond this, however, beyond this technical infrastructure the rest is valuational. How one responds to postmodern conditions, to ecological problems associated with population explosion, to an increasingly unified global economy and polity in the wake of convulsive wars and the destruction of the verities of older generations ... all this is valuational. Valuational and evaluational. Postmodernism suggests an interpretation which, while polemical and contentious, at least puts forward hypotheses for verification.

It can be suggested, for example, that the bloody shock of two world wars in which entire generations of youth were sacrificed and horrific acts of inhumanity were undertaken has affected political will in the largest sense. Since 1945, with the exception of totalitarian states the trend of democracies in the developed world has been towards some kind of liberal orientation; social democracy and welfare statism in some form, with rightist and conservative tendencies in the minority or in eclipse until the end of the Cold War, the collapse of the Soviet system, and the shift towards the centre in the latter decades of the century. Characteristic of the long postwar period was a reactionary egalitarianism and, often, a utopianism which sought to provide cradle to grave securities and social welfare, a broad general movement which was often antagonistic towards traditions and older forms of ethos and mores discredited by association with the wars and the "errors of the fathers". New technology and a steady rise in living standards created a climate of optimism and a progressive belief in social betterment. This phase lasted, despite such critiques of conformity as Whyte's *Organization Man* and despite the Cold and Korean wars until the Vietnam conflict and its countercultural reaction in the 1960s. This last social convulsion, itself largely a youth movement, was anti-establishment and overtly radical and anti-authoritarian. Later, after its subsidence in the 1970s, a legacy began to emerge. Multiculturalism, encouraged by emigration demographics and the revolution of expectations endorsed and stimulated by the media of communication, challenged many of the established V_5 values. Allan Bloom in *The Closing of the American Mind* depicts in detail the intellectual effects of the contemporary liberalism and the failure of administrative will upon the American academy.[36] Women's emancipation and liberation movements, feminism,[37] and the growth of higher education provided fertile soil in which such ideas could flourish and further accelerated the decline, if not demise, of traditional social morals. Racism and ethnicity became rallying cries and invocations for political action. Minorities such as homosexuals and aborigines, hitherto considered *sub rosa* or at least politically irrelevant, adopted activist agendas and assumed socio-political prominence. Much of this confusion and turmoil found expression in a new form of almost neo-Victorian stricture called political correctness: a code of speech and behaviour which sought to prohibit offence by word or thought to any social grouping other than the stereotyped white male of European provenance. The Deity too acquired a sexual persona and litanies and scripture were subjected to linguistic revision and censorship. Also associated with post-counterculture postmodernism was, what came to be known towards the end of the century as a victim culture. An emphasis on rights as opposed to duties or responsibilities led in many instances to demands for preferential treatment by perceived or self-perceived disadvantaged groups (women and "visible minorities") and these perceptions were reinforced by de facto or *de jure* quota systems in hiring or the distribution of social and economic privileges.

A consequence of this late-twentieth century Babel—and one could certainly hypothesize that the confusion of voices was a philosophical consequence of the positivist, nihilist, and relativist precursors of postmodernism itself—was a sort of loss of individual (V_1) identity and its replacement by identification with a group (V_4). Thus one asserted one's identity, for example, not so much by being *oneself* as by being, say, a woman, a single mother, a gay black person, a professional, a senior citizen, and so on. Individuality or eccentricity did not fit well with the conformities and group allegiances of neo-feudalism.

Meanwhile, at the national level of organization, the increasing inter-nationalization of economies and the sheer technical complexities of finance and governance rendered many political leaders and their parties impotent in the face of factors beyond their control. The V_1 decline in significance also undermined the sense of democratic citizenship and fostered cynicism and scepticism about the forms and viability of government in general. Massive levels of taxation and spending, budgetary deficits and national debt all contributed to anomie and loss of civic faith, as did, in many advanced countries an unprecedented rise in crime and a disturbing growth of terrorism at domestic and international levels.

It must be noted that many of these trends can be given a more euphemistic evaluation. Thus, Tarnas, in his comprehensive *The Passion of the Western Mind* concludes, for example, that the most radical and beneficial shift in ethos has been the emancipation of women and prognosticates a feminization of culture as a resultant.[38] This shift from yang in the early part of the century towards an undeniable yin in the latter part can, of course, be evaluated in more than one way and, postmodernism being what it is, no criteria for definitive evaluation are forthcoming—one woman's liberation may be another man's deprivation. This ambivalence and, worse, multivalence can be imputed to all of the trends described. This axiological anarchy contributes to the Dionysian V_5 context within which millennial administrative philosophy must be conducted.

This fractured (one might almost say fractalized) mosaic of conflicting and contradicting themes—global and macronational unity versus rabid nationalism and ethnocentricity; centralization and subsidiarity; egalitarianism and elitism; technology and poverty; mass education and illiteracy to name but a few of the polemical dichotomies—does not prohibit the search for larger and more embracing trends in the movement of ideas. Out of the hubbub and tumult the following can be discerned.

A steady overriding trend towards rationalism, despite reactionary tendencies towards, for example, astrology, mysticism, New Age-ism, and fundamentalist dogmatism. Somewhat paradoxically this *Geist* of the rational reinforces nationalism. The rational and the national are complementary. The logic is straightforward. Scientific and technological development entail specialization and large scale resources. Simultaneously growing populations conduce to complexity of organization and articulation. Society becomes increasingly *organizational.* The nation state to some extent compensates for the loss of V_1 individuality in the mass social structures. By myth, symbol, and history it defines each of its members in terms of a legal but also emotive nationality. Despite the growth of international organizations and arrangements (UN, EU, NATO, etc.) the State remains the governing power in the lives of individuals and groups. Social welfare and social security nets further enhance the dominance of the

State. Nations provide the ultimate credentialling and "identification". For most people birth determines an initial identity which will last all their lives. A minority, by emigration or upheaval or excess of wealth, may acquire changes of label but for everyone there is some sort of value initiation into a national culture (V_4). Within its territory a State is sovereign and is the ultimate source of power, authority, property, and law. Its sovereignty places it beyond moral good or evil and the pursuit of its self-interest is constrained only by *Realpolitik* and the philosophy of its leaders. It pervades all social life and intrudes directly and constantly into private lives. (In Chinese there is no word for private.) Its power is absolute. It can through its military expend its citizens' lives in warfare. All property is within its eminent domain. From birth to death the modern State is so much with us that we become inured and insensitive to its formative power over us: even our minds, that which we take to be our most private and intimate possession, are products formed at every turn by the omnipresence of State.

Administration then is not simply a function of the State, an entailment of governance, but its very style and form is a product of an overlooked and often invisible ideology of statism. All states of whatever political colouring and persuasion necessitate large bureaucracies. This constitutes another clearly discernible trend. Growth of bureaucracy is amply documented; what may be overlooked is its reinforcement by the scientific and technological forces of rationalism, the infrastructural demands of globalization, and the explosion of welfare expenditure. Philosophically, the question posed by these trends towards what might be called neo-feudalism (in which the individual identity is first and foremost a national one) is this: If organizations are goal-seeking entities, what are the goals of the State? Or better, What is my nation *for*?

Because of statism a quasi-profession of public or civil service is everywhere an established vested interest. The political and economic funding of this administrative system ensures the propagation of an ideology of bureau-rationalism and legalism. This is a key parameter of the quality of work life. Extensive and intensive regulation. For some this may bring Type III reactions of anomie and alienation, for many a Type II calculus of pragmatic benefits, and for a few a Type I subscription to rational order and an ideal of scientific–technological progress.

A countervailing trend to rationalism is provided by the many forms and varieties of humanism. The dialectic between scientific management and human relations has already been discussed but it is also a persistent feature of postmodernism, occasionally erupting in critiques of V_1 tendencies such as materialistic narcissism.[39] In the 1960s there were antecedents in the counter-cultural anti-authority and anti-establishment radicalism of that period. An interesting administrative by-product of the dialectic is the phenomenon of workaholism, an overcommitment to organizational work behaviour which can, however, find its philosophical support as much in social approval, pragmatic success, or fulfillment ethics as in the narcissistic variety of individualism.

When rationalism preponderates over humanism, or conversely, there will be reaction. The more the preponderance, the more the reaction. Thus the aberrations of narcissism, hedonism, victimization, and egalitarianism can be analysed as reactions against the impress of a rationalistic power culture. Ultimately these reactions fail to replace *Gesellschaft* by *Gemeinschaft* and often their long-term effect would seem to make the last state worse than the first: more alienation, more anomie. Nevertheless even when motivated by *ressentiment*, they march under the broad banner of humanist concern and contribute to the process of ultimately unpredictable syntheses (*Aufhebungen*).

Finally a word can be said about another characteristic of our age: the loss of ideals and the failure of administrative nerve. Idealism as ideology deserves to be distinguished from idealism as philosophy. The latter remains pristine in all its classical glory and an argument could be made that it is in the last analysis the *only* philosophy—all other philosophies being merely commentaries upon it or reactions against it.[40] But ideological idealism is merely an axiological device, a way of treating values; albeit an attitudinally motivating one. When concepts of the desirable are regarded less as end states to be realized and more as ultimates or absolutes that are unattainable but yet are functional as *criteria*, as guides or directors of behaviour then ideals serve as instruments for determining lower-order value judgements. Thus Justice, Truth, Beauty, Goodness: the eternal verities are ever approximated in an imperfect world but never fully attained. Never defined but ever redefined, they serve as guides to action in every field of behaviour including the purely administrative. The assault upon the foundations of belief in such ideals wrought by the postmodern age has shifted them semantically in significant ways. Justice becomes a demand for rights, Truth becomes opinion, Beauty whatever the eye beholds, Goodness political correctness.[41]

As the century draws to a close the cultural cacophony deafens the ears and dulls the sensitivities. Squeaky wheels get grease, power turns politicians into big spenders overnight, celebrities and personalities masquerade as arbiters of excellence; aristocracy is an absurdity and royalty human, all too-human; tradition, religion, both are discounted and discarded; change is considered synonymous with progress ... the jeremiad could be continued in many ways, with different *Leitmotiven*, different, even opposite, emphases. In the end, however framed, it would amount to a sense of malaise, of unease, or dis-ease, a claim that all is not right with contemporary values and culture (V_5). Under such a perspective administrators could perhaps be forgiven for some loss of nerve, for confusion, for failure to develop leadership vision, for favouring compromise over principle, for pandering to the vocal, for taking the expedient road rather than the difficult, for unauthenticity, for self-justification and self-seeking, for fear and trembling. Above all for denying the malaise, for being positive thinkers, optimists, for mouthing that challenge means opportunity while scurrying to maintain the status quo.

But, polemics aside, what options do face the postmodern administrator? *Quo vadunt*?

OPTIONS

While there is no non-speculative rational answer to the question of where V_5 and V_4 are going, that is, where history is going or evolution is going, it is always theoretically possible from an axiological perspective to lay out at any time the options before us in the way of alternative ethics. This is so because of the separation of value from fact, because of the non-natural (noumenal) quality of ethics and, lastly because there are no new ethics under the sun—only the possibility, as Nietzsche would say, of the revaluation of all values: in the terms of this text, personal value-audit and recommitment. Some delineation of the options and some commentary may therefore be apropos, especially in view of the rather negative picture just painted of the V_5 backdrop against which administrative philosophy must be formed and carried out.

First it may be noted that the four archetypes described in the text are ideal-type analytical devices which operate within the administrative psyche as psychological components of the complex ego-ideal. Each of us is at once, and has within us always, the careerist, the politician, the technician, and the poet. The salience of these components varies and shifts within each personal biography and pure types do not empirically occur. This is simply to say that motives are always mixed and that we do not know ourselves. The more we do know ourselves the more the possibility of real will (as opposed to Level III impulse) exists and the more ethics (as opposed to values and morality) becomes possible. *Consciousness and ethics are correlative.* Ethics are implied by archetypical composition; they are not prescribed. Prescriptions can, however, be deduced from the paradigm.

The classical Level III ethic is, logically, the *arthasastra*. Enough has been said already about the doctrine of success and the careerist option in administrative life. One can merely add that contemporary postmodernism would seem to favour the covert adoption of this ethic and, even, on occasion its overt defence. That any element of psychopathology is prerequisite to such commitment is, analytically, merely a second-order value judgement. Contrariwise, the administrator might argue that nothing succeeds like success. Certainly it will always be a paradigmatic ethical option and the text has sought to make this plain.

The paradigm ethic applicable to Level IIB would be that of group-careerism (careerism via group solidarity), or sectional interest. The leader should seek the group interest (V_3 *or* V_2) over that of competing groups. A rationale for such ethics could be derived from a belief in *lasser-faire* economics, that the macrosystem and the market-place together ensure in the end the collective benefit. Competition is righteous and vision is limited therefore, Fight one's own corner. Thus the military pursue great budgets even in peacetime and thus trade unions and corporations acquire a deafness towards protestations of the larger polity.

Level IIA suggests a rationalistic ethic of professionalism. Written codes of professional ethics abound and no matter what the cynic may think of them the fact remains that they are present as options for the free agent to act upon. Such values provide both an opportunity for existentialist engagement and for Nietzschean revaluing. The ethical ideal of professionalism is generally one of service: the placing of specialist expertise at the service of a clientele and the subordination of self-interest to that of the clientele in certain cases of conflict. Pursuing the marketplace rationale of IIB utilitarian logic one might also consider such an ethic to be conducive to the larger good (the good of the polity as opposed to just the clientele). Where the profession is administrative it may lead, as in classic bureaucratic theory, to a *summum bonum* of hierarchical loyalty. In the public service this means ultimately loyalty to the Minister who in turn is supposedly *vox populi*. When disagreement or value conflict occurs between the professional administrator and his amateur superior the differences are argued in private and never in public. At the end of the day the will of the polity is supposed to have prevailed.

These three broad ethical options represent the very general schema of the archetypes up to the charismatic level. Beyond them is an unspecified range of ideology permitting of infinite variation any aspect of which can be subscribed to at Level I. It must also be noted (and conceded) that the lower paradigmatic levels (especially Level III) can themselves be elevated and transmuted to this level as, say, in the case of megalomanic careerism. But among the more conventionally accepted of strong (Type I) ethical orientations let us note the following, each of which can become a component part of a larger and more complex ethic. Greek letters have been used to mitigate the distracting connotations of semantic labelling.

Alpha: The administrator ought to be the self-effacing and dedicated agent and servant of the largest good—perhaps even of the Platonic Good. The general outlines of the ethic have been discussed in the text in relation to Guardianship. It is idealistic in the philosophical sense of the term. The leader is prepared for personal sacrifice and adopts a strong ethic of duty. Illustrations in literature exist in both East (the *Bhagavad Gita*) and West (Marcus Aurelius' *Meditations*).

Beta: Applicable more to the East than the West this ethic nevertheless resonates with modernist Victorian values. It is an ethic of tradition, culture, and established hierarchy and would therefore be antithetical to the postmodern *Zeitgeist*. The administrator seeks to perpetuate through organizational means an ethic of manners and a reverence for historical and social continuity. Extremes are anathema, as are fragmentation, lack of discipline, disorder. Haste is dangerous, rudeness is deplored. It includes the Oriental concept of "face" (Western *amour propre* and *infra dignitatem* are cognate concepts).

The style and the ethic may ramify to include doctrines of Zen and Buddhist or Hindu notions of Karma. Basic attitudinal qualities are detachment and concentration, seemingly antagonistic features that are reconciled in as much as detachment refers to the loss of egoistic self-concern by way of commitment to collective responsibilities and concentration again means loss of egoistic self-concern by way of absorption in the tasks at hand. It should be noted also, as empirically evidenced in Japan, [42] that Zen is a followership as well as a leadership discipline.

Gamma: The gist of this ethic is an administrative concern for other people. In postmodern times it occasionally becomes part of feminist polemic, the argument being that female executives will import nurturing and caring qualities into a presumed patriarchal organizational environment with a presumed meliorative effect. In the text it has been partially discussed under the rubric of human relations and its basic conceptions are rooted in humanism. Sometimes it may take on egalitarian or utopian overtures and sometimes the leader who adopts this ethic subscribes to what has been called the "new public administration" that is, using administrative office and organizational power to advance a political agenda favouring some interest group perceived as disadvantaged, e.g., women or visible minorities.[43] Such an ethic is naturally congenial to certain postmodern contexts such as, say, the academy.

Delta: The administrator commits to intensified professional values. The leader role is seen as deriving its legitimacy from the profession in which it is embedded. Thus, to be a soldier, a policeman, a teacher, a doctor, an academic, a scientist, or a priest is the defining factor and vocation becomes a passion. Vocation provides not only form of life but life-meaning and its values dominate and override other concerns. Such an ethic can bypass postmodern pluralism or turn it to its own ends.

Epsilon: All religions whether sacred or secular provide ethical systems to which administrators can subscribe. Type I values need not be shared with the followership but when this occurs an intensification of organizational coherence and *esprit de corps* is likely. Religions can constrain an administrator's options but they can also infuse direction and inform conduct. Paradoxically, the postmodern context is favourable to epsilon in that "When God is dead, all is permitted." All belief systems are equally sanctioned from the V_5 level while from the V_1 level personal commitment is intensified and defined against a multicultural background.

Zeta: Certain constellations of value such as order–honour–discipline–

hierarchy–duty–power–loyalty comprise a quasi-militaristic ethic which again stresses the subordination of individual to some larger group. Zeta is not congenial to postmodernism and is likely to be denigrated as fascist or totalitarian. Its reactionary dynamic is however a viable option despite, or perhaps because of, the *Zeitgeist.* Excesses of postmodern nihilism or absurdity would foster the appeal of such an ethic and, paradoxically, the growth of statism and unresponsive democratic systems might further heighten that appeal (the rise of militias in the US, for example).

Eta: One thing hastens into being, another hastens out of it. Even while a thing is in the act of coming into existence, some part of it has already ceased to be. "Flux and change are forever renewing the fabric of the universe, just as the ceaseless sweep of time is forever renewing the face of eternity. ..."[44] Or, as Heraclitus put it more succinctly, "One can never step into the same river twice." Deep convictions about the empirical reality of change may lead to an ethic of flexibility, even non-commitment. To go with the flow may become the maxim or, more myopically, One day at a time. While this may fall short of an actual ethic (beliefs about change may range from utopian optimism to deep scepticism and pessimism) the reality may conduce to a pragmatic quasi-ethic which seeks to maximize general or private benefit on a *carpe diem* basis.

Theta: A leadership ethic of personal and private honour (moral integrity) is possible. It may even be deliberately *secret.* Maxims such as the following could characterize such an ethic: "Work without concern for reward." "Do one's duty and let the chips fall where they may." "Work for the work's sake only." Inherent is the idea that man does not live by bread alone and that the bases of duty and vocation (of administrative responsibility) extend into transrational and metaphysical space. Work and responsibility become a means of self-overcoming.

* * *

It is to be reiterated first that the above examples are illustrative and not exhaustive; secondly, that they are susceptible of infinite permutation, combination, and recombination; and thirdly, that each or any can be the focus of commitment or engagement at *any* level of the paradigm. Eclecticism is of the essence. In a postmodern context or, if one prefers, a neo-existentialist condition the leader will, indeed must, construct personal ethical guidelines individually and eclectically. A merit of postmodernism is its prohibition of dogma. Ethical options always lie in abundance before us. The selection is a function of consciousness and will. And it is to be remembered that, in a much cited Barnardism, organizations themselves only endure "in proportion to the breadth of morality by which they are governed".[45] And while the preceding options have been directed towards the ethical it must also be allowed that administration has its aesthetic. To cite Greenfield:

... organizations are social inventions, They are like theatre, all artifice. We go to the theatre to see a play about life. The lights dim and the curtain rises. We know that these are actors we see, playing roles. Yet we go along with the trick and will ourselves to believe; we suspend our disbelief, so that we can be entertained, enlightened, and sometimes deeply moved. We make theatre into life by believing the illusion before us. More importantly, we also make life into theatre by believing that illusion. What we recognize as organization is a constructed reality, a social invention, and an illusion ... .[46]

And to cite an eminent Japanese administrator:

The administrator's task is equally creative. He, too, [like the artist] starts with a blank slate. In setting up a business, he first formulates basic policy, decides where to get capital and how to obtain manpower, what kind of factories to build, what to produce, how to go about production, and how to sell. From nothing he creates something complex, adding one element to the picture at a time. As in art, close attention must be given to the overall effect so that the proper balance can be maintained among the elements. Administration produces something from nothing through the constant exercise of human ingenuity. Moreover, the creation process is never-ending, for its various facets must be maintained and improved continually. If a sufficient balance is achieved in the administration of a complex business the enterprise is vibrant with the spirit of its leader, and the observer is moved to applaud what has been created. I believe that leadership, in essence, is an *artistic* endeavour to which high intrinsic value should be attached.[47] (My italics.)

All these expressions of belief, of conviction even, are impressive and yet when it comes to options: ethical, moral, preferential, or aesthetic it must be said that in its present state of evolution administrative philosophy cannot be prescriptive. At best it can do little more than offer the legendary last words of the Buddha, Work out thine own salvation. But that *little more* is important: it points the way towards a programme of rigorous axiological investigation, one which would include canonical ethnographic studies of leadership in all fields, and which would also embrace the whole of intellectual history for, at the end of the day, administrative philosophy becomes the deep study of human motivation.

Power and motivation are the mysterious core concepts of any putative discipline of administration and, if they are a mystery still, then it can be said that at the heart of every great discipline lie undefined mysteries: in physics, energy; in chemistry, matter; in mathematics, number; in biology, life; in medicine, health and pain; in education, teaching and learning. The vast edifice of knowledge rests upon imponderable concepts—all of which epitomize the human struggle with language: The limits of our language are the limits of our world.[48] And, of course, all philosophy must be conducted in language. What goes beyond language is mysticism.[49] Correspondingly, all administration must be conducted in language; without language there is no administration. What goes beyond language in administration, what cannot be *said*, is Night and Fog.

Finally, a simple sentiment. In this long investigation of the valuational and evaluative administrative art one wishes somehow to have expressed a preference, if only an insinuation, a suggestion, a composition of hints, for the classical ideal of the first great Enlightenment, the Hellenic Platonic concept of the Guardian—an archetype totally unsuited to our times but crying to be reborn. Can it be that this rough beast, its hour comes round at last, shuffles towards another Bethlehem?

Administration is the art of designing and engineering events; administrative philosophy is therefore about the very architecture of reality.

Notes

CHAPTER 1

1. The *Cambridge Dictionary of Philosophy* (1995) lists entries for the following subsets: (Philosophy of ...) Anthropology, Art, Biology, Economics, Education, History, Language, Law, Linguistics, Literature, Logic, Mathematics, Mind, Politics, Psychology, Religion, Science, Social Sciences, and Theology. No mention is made of organization, management, leadership or administration although material of relevance to philosophy of administration occurs in many of the listed subsets.
2. Castiglione, *The Courtier*. Harmondsworth: Penguin, 1981.
3. Political correctness is a socio-cultural phenomenon developed in the 1980s in the USA and spread throughout the English-speaking world. It is generally associated with a conventional orthodoxy that inhibits and constrains the use of language to avoid giving offence to any special interest group and to promote radical or liberal causes. Concern about its pervasiveness ranges from an authentic fear of Orwellian 'thought policing' to a dismissal by *reductio ad absurdum*, e.g. the use of 'differentially challenged' for 'disabled' or a mindless insistence upon 'gender inclusive' language ('No man or woman is an island/Entire unto himself or herself.'). The phenomenon is, however, enforced and reinforced by radical, liberal, and general bureaucratic and public relations practice.
4. Peter Self, *Administrative Theories and Politics*. London: Allen and Unwin, 1972: 50.
5. See Chester I. Barnard, *The Functions of the Executive*. Cambridge, Mass.: Harvard University Press, 1972.
6. Bryan Magee, *Modern British Philosophy*. St. Alban's: Paladin, 1973.
7. F. Fiedler, *A Theory of Leadership Effectiveness*. New York: McGraw-Hill, 1967; Chris Argyris, 'Personality and Organization Theory Revisited.' *Administrative Science Quarterly*, 1973, Oct.
8. The eminent philosopher Ludwig Wittgenstein (d. 1951) embodied a contradiction in that while considering *professional* philosophy an anathema he continued to occupy the Chair in that subject at Cambridge.
9. *Cf.* Karl Popper, *The Open Society and its Enemies*. London: Routledge and Kegan Paul, 1966. Philosophers are generally, of course, not averse to having wisdom *imputed* to them, by attribution or insinuation.
10. The position of orthodox Vedanta and Hinduism generally.
11. Swami Prabhavananda and Christopher Isherwood tr. *Bhagavad-Gita*. New York: Mentor, 1972: 117.
12. On the question of human/animal difference *cf.* E. F. Schuhmacher, *A Guide for the Perplexed*. New York: Harper and Row, 1977.

13. Colin E. Evers and Gabriele Lakomski, *Knowing Educational Administration*. Oxford: Pergamon, 1991.
14. Peter Ribbins, ed., *Greenfield on Administration. Towards a Humane Science*. London: Routledge, 1992.
15. Dwight Waldo, *The Enterprise of Public Administration*. Novato, Calif.: Chandler and Sharp, 1980: 99–117.
16. Herbert A. Simon, *Administrative Behavior*. New York: Free Press, 1965: 62–66; B. F. Skinner, *Beyond Freedom and Dignity*. New York: Knopf, 1971. The concept of metavalue will be discussed below, Ch. 7.
17. This is H. A. Simon's metaphor (*loc. cit.*).
18. Rosamund Thomas, *The British Philosophy of Administration*. London: Longmans, 1978 and Waldo, *op. cit.*
19. Albert Speer, *Inside the Third Reich: Memoirs*. New York: Macmillan, 1970.
20. An interesting cross-cultural historical parallel for this phenomenon occurs in the appeal of Zen philosophy, itself anti-intellectual, for the samurai and governing classes of Japan. Daisetz Suzuki, *Zen and Japanese Culture*. Princeton: Bollingen Foundation, 1959: 59.
21. Alfred C. Kinsey *et al.*, *Sexual Behavior in the Human Male*. W. B. Saunders, 1969; do., *Sexual Behavior in the Human Female*. W. B. Saunders, 1953.
22. Colin Evers and Gabriele Lakomski, *Knowing Educational Administration*. Oxford: Pergamon, 1991: 118.
23. E. Goffman, *The Presentation of Self in Everyday Life*. Harmondsworth: Penguin, 1959; C. Geertz, *The Interpretation of Cultures*. New York: Basic Books, 1973; A. Giddens, *New Rules of Sociological Method*. London: Hutchinson, 1977.
24. T. B. Greenfield in P. Ribbins, ed., *Greenfield on Administration. Towards a Humane Science of Administration*. London: Routledge and Kegan Paul, 1992; H. G. Gadamer in P. Connerton, ed., *Critical Sociology*. Harmondsworth: Penguin, 1976.
25. T. J. Sergiovanni in T. J. Sergiovanni and J. E. Corbally, eds., *Leadership and Organizational Culture*. Urbana, Ill.: University of Illinois Press, 1986: 2.
26. Evers and Lakomski *op. cit.* 134 ... Naturwissenschaften ... ; W. Dilthey, 'The Rise of Hermeneutics.' In P. Connerton, ed., *Critical Sociology*. Harmondsworth: Penguin, 1976.
27. J. Habermas, *Knowledge and Human Interests*. Tr. J. Shapiro. London: Heinemann, 1972; J. Derrida, *L'écriture et la Différence*. Paris: Editions du Seuil, 1967; M. Foucault, *Power and Knowledge*. New York: Pantheon, 1980; J. F. Lyotard, *The Postmodern Condition*. Minneapolis: University of Minnesota Press, 1986.
28. *Cf.* e.g. the entire opus of F. Fiedler, and F. E. Fiedler *et al.*, *Improving Leadership Effectiveness*. New York: Wiley, 1976.
29. David Van Fleet and Gary Yukl, 'A Century of Leadership Research.' *Papers Dedicated to the Development of Modern Management*. US Academy of Management, 1986: 12–23.
30. Van Fleet and Yukl, *ibid.*
31. H. Simon, D. Smithburg, V. Thompson, *Public Administration*. New York: Knopf, 1950: 395.
32. N. Machiavelli, *The Prince*. London: Routledge, 1886.
33. Christopher Hodgkinson, *Towards a Philosophy of Administration*. Oxford: Blackwell, 1978: 19.

34. E. Marini, ed., *Toward a New Public Administration*. New York: Chandler, 20.
35. *The Theory of Social and Economic Organization*. A. Henderson and T. Parsons trs. London: Oxford University Press, 1969; *Staatssoziologie*. Berlin: Duncker u. Humblot, 1956; R. Bendix, *Max Weber: An Intellectual Portrait*. New York: Doubleday, 1962.
36. Sir Geoffrey Vickers, *Freedom in a Rocking Boat*. Harmondsworth: Penguin, 1972; Peter Drucker, *The Future of Industrial Man*. New York: John Day, 1962; Alvin Gouldner, *The Future of Intellectuals and the Rise of the New Class*. New York: Oxford University Press, 1982.
37. Rosamund Thomas, *op. cit.*; Waldo, 1980: 16.
38. Matsushita Corporation, *Introduction to the Matsushita School of Government and Management*. Kanagawa, Japan, 1980: 18–19.
39. William G. Scott and David K. Hart, *Organizational America*. Boston: Houghton Mifflin, 1979: 225.
40. M. Dimock, *A Philosophy of Administration*. New York: Harper, 1958: xi.
41. *Ibid.*, 5.
42. Chester I. Barnard, *The Functions of the Executive*. Cambridge, Mass.: Harvard University Press, 1972: 296.
43. Alexander Pope, *An Essay on Man*. II: 1.

CHAPTER 2

1. Sir Geoffrey Vickers, *Public Administration*, 1979: 57.
2. Andrew Dunsire, *Administration the Word and the Science*. London: Martin Robertson, 1953 gives fifteen separate meanings of the word 'administration.' Also C. James Gardner, 'Organization and Methods Development in the Government of Canada.' *Public Administration* (U.K.), 1976, Autumn: 283–309 on the confusion wrought by misunderstanding of terminology in the Canadian Civil Service.
3. Derek Allison, *Canadian Administrator*, 1983, 23, 1.
4. Chester Barnard, *op. cit.*
5. G. H. Litchfield, 'Notes on a General Theory of Administration.' *Administrative Science Quarterly*, 1956, January, Vol. I: 1.
6. Michael D. Cohen and James G. March, *Leadership and Ambiguity*, 2nd edn. Boston: Harvard Business School Press, 1986.
7. S. S. Ker, 'Substitutes for Leadership: Some Implications for Organizational Design.' *Organization and Administrative Sciences*, 1977, 8: 135–146.
8. D. L. Stufflebeam *et al.*, *Educational Evaluation and Decision Making*. Itasca, Ill.: Peacock, 1971.
9. Dwight Waldo, *The Enterprise of Public Administration, op. cit.*, 61–62; Peter Self, *Administrative Theories and Politics*. London: Allen Unwin, 289–299. Machiavelli, Nietzsche, and the Sanskrit *arthasastra* are outstanding. *Cf.* James Burnham, *The Machiavellians, Defenders of Freedom*. New York: Day, 1963; Herbert H. Gowen, *A History of Indian Literature*. New York: Appleton, 1931; also Heinrich Zimmer, *Philosophies of India*. New York: Bollingen Foundation, 1956 on *Matsyanyaya* or the 'law of the fish.'
10. Simon, *op. cit.*, 45–77.
11. See e.g. Harold R. Pollard, *Developments in Management Thought*. London: Heineman, 1974 as a representative example of historical summaries.

12. Frederick W. Taylor, *The Principles of Scientific Management*. New York: Harper, 1915 and *Scientific Management*. London: Harper, 1966.

13. Henri Fayol, *Administration, industrielle et générale*. Paris, 1916. Tr. J. Coubrough, London: Putman, 1929.

14. Much of Weber's work remains untranslated but the standard English text is *Economy and Society: An Outline of Interpretive Sociology*. Guenther Roth and Claus Wittich, eds. Berkeley, Calif.: University of California Press, 1968. For a general bibliography see Reinhardt Bendix, *Max Weber: An Intellectual Portrait*. New York: Doubleday, 1962. Bendix's work has, however, come under some criticism in the field.

15. The standard exposition is found in Luther Gulick and L. Urwick, eds., *Papers on the Science of Administration*. New York: Columbia University Press, 1937 and J. D. Mooney, *The Principles of Organization*. New York: Harper, 1937.

16. Herbert A. Simon, *Administrative Behavior*. New York: Free Press, 1965.

17. The seminal work for this movement was provided by the famous Hawthorne Studies described in F. J. Roethlisberger and W. J. Dickson, *Management and the Worker*. Cambridge, Mass.: Harvard University Press, 1939. See also Elton Mayo, *The Human Problems of an Industrial Civilization*. London: Routledge and Kegan Paul, 1969.

18. Mary Parker Follett's major work was *Creative Experience*. London: Longmans, 1924. For an assessment of its contribution see Harold R. Pollard, *Developments in Management Thought*. London: Heinemann, 1976.

19. *Cf.* esp. Alex Carey, 'The Hawthorne Studies: A Radical Criticism.' *American Sociological Review*, Vol. 32: 403–416.

20. A perusal of article titles over the decades of the 1970s and 1980s in *Administrative Science Quarterly* will suffice to confirm this assertion; the existence of a journal literature devoted specifically to work motivation notwithstanding.

21. Abraham Maslow, *Eupsychian Management*. Irwin, Ill.: Homewood, 1965; see also his *Toward a Psychology of Being*, 2nd edn. New York: Van Nostrand, 1968 for a clear exposition of the self-actualization concept.

22. Fred Herzberg, *Work and the Nature of Man*. Cleveland: World Publications, 1966; H. Mintzberg, *The Nature of Managerial Work*. New York: Harper and Row, 1973.

23. D. McGregor, *The Human Side of Enterprise*. New York: McGraw-Hill, 1960. For a critique of Theory X and Y see Christopher Hodgkinson, *Educational Leadership*. Albany: State University of New York Press, 1991: 71–72.

24. D. McGregor and W. G. Bennis, eds., *The Professional Manager*. New York: McGraw-Hill, 1967: 77.

25. Simon, *op. cit.*, 252.

26. Ludwig von Bertalanffy, 'The Theory of Open Systems in Physics and Biology,' *Science* 1950, III: 23–28; *General Systems Theory*. New York: 1968.

27. Dunsire, *ibid.*

28. Clearly the interface was effected in earlier times; Plato, Machiavelli, and later writers in political theory.

29. Simon, *op. cit.*, 157.

30. E. Wright Bakke in L. von Bertalanffy and A. Rapoport, eds., *General Systems Yearbook*. Society for General Systems Research, 1960: 37.

31. Thomas Greenfield and Peter Ribbins, eds., *Greenfield on Educational Administration: Towards a Humane Science*. London: Routledge, 1993: 217.

32. Simon, *ibid.*

33. Barnard, *op. cit.*, 46. This leads to anomalies and pathologies such as exorbitant salaries for CEOs and reward disparities between professional-technical staff and their line superordinates, e.g. in hospital administration and some educational administration. If carried to extremes one logical interpretation would have the salary of a nation's president or chief executive officer set as a percentage of the gross domestic product.

34. Victor A. Thompson, *Modern Organization*. New York: Knopf, 1961. Professor Ribbins in his Inaugural Lecture at the University of Birmingham (May, 1995) clarified this point concisely citing A. Sinclair, 'The Seduction of the self-managed Team ...' *Leading and Managing*, 1995, 1, 1: 44–63. Peter Ribbins, 'Leadership Matters in Education: Regarding Secondary Headship.' University of Birmingham, 9 May 1995.

35. Cohen and March, *ibid.*

36. Chu Hsi, *Tzu-chih T'ung-chien* (An Imperial Guidebook for a Successful Government.) cited in Daisetz Suzuki, *Zen and Japanese Culture*. Princeton: Bollingen Foundation, 1959: 52–54.

37. Barnard, *op. cit.*, 114–123.

38. Herbert Spencer, *Principles of Sociology*. London, 1910: 430 *ff*.

39. E. Shannon and W. Weaver, *The Mathematical Theory of Communication*. Urbana, Ill., 1949. In this view it is tempting but fallacious to postulate an analogue between negentropic information and intelligence, an error to which the proponents of AI, artificial intelligence, whose ranks include H. A. Simon, are especially susceptible. However, to the question posed by the hypothetical Türing machine that could indistinguishably replicate human mental functions the philosopher is obliged to respond that, if such were the case, then the machine *would* be human.

40. Daniel Katz and Robert L. Kahn, *The Social Psychology of Organizations*. New York: Wiley, 1966: 453–454. The point is confirmed in the 2nd edn, 1978.

41. T. B. Greenfield, 'Theory in the Study of Organizations and Administrative Structures.' Cited in *Educational Administration: International Challenges*. G. Baron, ed. London: Athlone Press, 1975.

42. Greenfield, 1993, *op. cit.*

43. Jacob W. Getzels and Egon Guba, 'Social Behavior and the Administrative Process.' *School Review*, 1957, Winter: 423. The model has been particularly popular within the subset of educational administration. The reasons for this are not entirely clear.

44. P. Georgiu, 'The Goal Paradigm and Notes towards a Counter Paradigm.' *Administrative Science Quarterly*, 1973, Vol. 18: 291; Michael D. Cohen, James G. March, Johann P. Olsen, 'A Garbage Can Model of Organizational Choice.' *Administrative Science Quarterly*, 1972, March, Vol. 17: 1–25.

45. Friedrich Hayek, 'The Use of Knowledge in Society.' *American Economic Review*, 1965, Sept., Vol. 35: 526–528.

46. John McGowan, *Postmodernism and Its Critics*. London: Cornell University Press, 1991: 254.

47. See Christopher Hodgkinson, *Educational Leadership: The Moral Art*. State University of New York Press, 1991: 152 *ff*. for a revisitation of this perspective.

CHAPTER 3

1. Herbert A. Simon, *Administrative Behavior*, 2nd edn. New York: Free Press, 1965.

2. G. H. Litchfield, 'Notes on a General Theory of Administration.' *Administrative Science Quarterly*, 1956, Jan., Vol. 1: 1.

3. See also Chapter 2, pp. 34 *ff.* above.

4. Litchfield, *ibid.*

5. We shall return to this question in detail in Part III.

6. J. F. Kennedy.

7. Canadian Prime Minister Brian Mulroney justified an ill-fated constitutional decision by saying, 'We decided to roll the dice.'

8. Simon, *op. cit.*, 83.

9. *Cf.* Kurt Gödel, *über formal entscheidbar Sätze der Principia Mathematica und verwandte Systeme. Monatshefte für Mathematik und Physik*. 1931, 38: 173–198. Also in English, Roger Penrose, *The Emperor's New Mind*. New York: Oxford University Press, 1990: 132–133, 138–141.

10. Simon, *op. cit.*

11. Ludwig Wittgenstein, *Tractatus Logico-Philosophicus*. London: Routledge and Kegan Paul, 1976: Proposition 7; 74.

12. Abraham Kaplan, *The Conduct of Inquiry*. San Francisco: Chandler, 1964: 6–11.

13. Colin W. Evers and Gabriele Lakomski, *Knowing Educational Administration*. Oxford: Pergamon, 1991: 167–177, 189.

14. Including the phenomenon of catalytic participants to the decision process who affect outcomes passively without overt active participation. Again, as we shall see, in group processes it may not be at all clear who provides the ultimate dynamic in decision closure.

15. Simon, *op. cit.*, 33, 111, 272.

16. G. E. Moore, *Principia Ethica*. Cambridge University Press, 1903: 10, 13–14.

17. D. L. Stufflebeam *et al.*, *Educational Evaluation and Decision Making*. Itasca, Ill.: Peacock, 1971: 43, 297–307.

18. This can, however, take a quasi-executive turn when the policy analyst conceives of himself as 'counsellor.' *Cf.* Jannings, B. 'Policy Analysis: Science, Advocacy, or Counsel.' In S. Nagel, ed., *Research in Public Policy Analysis and Management*. Greenwich, Conn.: JAI Press, 1987 and Aaron Wildavsky, *Speaking Truth to Power: The Art and Craft of Policy Analysis*. Boston: Little, Brown, 1979.

19. H. Simon, D. Smithburg, and V. Thompson, *Public Administration*. New York: Knopf, 1950: 567. This reference is a classic and standard text.

20. As long ago as the 1960s Abraham Kaplan formulated the 'law of the hammer' and applied it to computerology. The law states that when a small boy discovers the use of a hammer he suddenly finds that all objects need hammering. Abraham Kaplan, *op. cit.*, 28.

21. For further discussion see bureaupathologies below, Chapter 10.

22. Lawrence H. Tribe, 'Policy Science: Analysis or Ideology.' *Philosophy and Public Affairs*, 1972, Fall: 66–110.

23. Geoffrey Vickers, *The Art of Judgment*. New York: Basic Books, 1970: 31.

24. D. Lerner and B. Lasswell, eds., *The Policy Sciences*. Palo Alto, 1951: ix.

25. Lorne W. Downey, *Policy Analysis in Education*. Calgary: Detselig, 1988: 10.

26. Daniel Katz and Robert L. Kahn, *The Social Psychology of Organizations*, 2nd edn. New York: Wiley, 1978: 475 *ff.*

27. *Ibid.*

28. The specification of term does not preclude them from spending all, or nearly all, of their career in administrative office.

29. The sociologist Alvin Gouldner drew a famous distinction between 'cosmopolitans' and 'locals', the former being professional organization members who identified with their profession at large in contrast to colleagues who chose a career path within the organization itself. Alvin Gouldner, 'Cosmopolitans and Locals: Toward an Analysis of Latent Social Roles,' *Administrative Science Quarterly*, 1957/8, 2: 281–306, 440–480.

30. C. Hodgkinson, 'Philosophy, Politics, and Planning. An extended Rationale for Synthesis.' *Educational Administration Quarterly*, 1975, Winter, 11: 11.

31. The classical exposition of policy strategies has been presented in David Braybrooke and Charles E. Lindblom, *A Strategy of Decision*. New York: Free Press, 1963. See also Herbert A. Simon, 'Theories of Decision-Making in Economic and Behavioral Science.' *American Economic Review*, XLIX, 1959: 255. For an interesting and suggestive modification of the Braybrooke–Lindblom cross-break analysis see D. L. Stufflebeam, *op. cit.*

32. Amitai Etzioni, 'Mixed-Scanning: A 'Third' Approach to Decision Making.' *Public Administration Review* XXVII, 1967, Dec.: 385.

33. Charles E. Lindblom, *The Policy Making Process*. Englewood Cliffs, NJ: Prentice Hall, 1968.

34. Charles E. Lindblom, 'The Science of Muddling Through.' *Public Administration Review*, 1959, Spring: 155–169. This article was reviewed by the author twenty years later in 'Still Muddling: Not Yet Through.' *Public Administration Review*, 39: 517–526. His conclusions left the original conceptions intact.

35. J. J. Bailey and R. J. O'Connor, 'Operationalizing Incrementalism: Measuring the Muddles.' *Public Administration Review*, 1975, 35: 60.

36. William N. Dunn, *Public Policy Analysis*. Englewood Cliffs, NJ: Prentice Hall, 1981: 60.

37. *Ibid.*, 30.

38. B. Jennings, 'Interpretive Social Science and Policy Analysis.' In D. Callahan and B. Jennings, eds., *Ethics, The Social Sciences, and Policy Analysis*. New York: Plenum, 1987.

39. Aaron Wildawsky, *Speaking Truth to Power: The Art and Craft of Policy Analysis*. Boston: Little, Brown, 1979.

40. The diagram is inspired by and *pace* Lorne W. Downey, *Policy Analysis in Education*. Calgary: Detselig, 1988: 19.

41. Peter Collier, 'Blood on the Charles', *Vanity Fair*, 1992, Oct.: 144–164.

42. See, however, Victor A. Thompson, *Without Sympathy or Compassion* for an insightful treatment of bureaucratic/organizational responses to some of these psycho-structural problems.

43. *Cf.* Eugénie Samier. 'A Study of the Relevance of Max Weber's Work to Educational Administration Theory' (*Nach eine verstehende Erziehungsverwalthungswissenschaft*), unpublished Ph.D. dissertation, University of Victoria, 1993.

44. Daniel Katz and Robert L. Kahn, *The Social Psychology of Organizations*. New York: Wiley, 1966: 298. The general tenor of this passage is supported in the 2nd edn of this work, 1978. *Cf.* pp. 502–506.

45. Daniel Bell, *The Coming of Post-Industrial Society*. New York: Basic Books, 1976.

46. William N. Dunn, *op. cit.*, 25.
47. Allen Schick, 'Beyond Analysis.' *Public Administration Review*, 1977, 37, 3: 258–263.
48. Jennings and Wildawsky, *ibid.*
49. Schick, *loc. cit.* 258 and for a careful treatment see Dunn, *op. cit.*, 8–33.
50. Peter Coveney and Roger Highfield, *The Arrow of Time*. London: Flamingo, 1991: 272–277.
51. *Ibid.*, 346 n.2.
52. Or, conceivably, several well-documented instances of Hitler's successful generalship in the face of unanimous opposition from his General Staff.
53. Coveney and Highfield, *op. cit.*, 210.
54. Lawrence H. Tribe, 'Policy Science: Analysis or Ideology.' *Philosophy and Public Affairs*, 1972, Fall: 106.

CHAPTER 4

1. Chin-ning Chu, *Thick Face Black Heart*. Beaverton, Oregon: AMC Publishing, 1992.
2. Michel Foucault, *Power/Knowledge*. New York: Pantheon, 1980.
3. Michael Power, 'Modernism, Postmodernism and Organization.' In John Hassard and Denis Pym, *The Theory and Philosophy of Organizations*. London: Routledge, 1990. Chapter 7.
4. The language is implicitly inclusive.
5. Lord Acton (1836–1902), *Historical Essays and Studies*.
6. H. A. Simon; C. I. Barnard, *op. cit. q.v.*
7. R. L. Ackoff and F. E. Emery, *Purposive Systems*. Tavistock Institute: London: 1972.
8. *Cf.* Camille Paglia, *Sexual Personae*. Yale University Press, 1990, Chapter 3.
9. See n. 3 above.
10. Paglia, *op. cit.*, 555.
11. Chris Argyris, *Personality and Organization*. New York: Harper, 1957. Argyris' work is endorsed by the later research and themes of F. Fiedler, *cf.* Fiedler *et al.*, *Improving Leadership Effectiveness*. New York: Wiley, 1976.
12. Herbert Goldhamer and Ed A. Shils, 'Types of Power and Status.' *American Journal of Sociology* XIV, 1939: 172.
13. Burkhard Sievers, 'The Diabolization of Death. Some Thoughts on the Obsolescence of Mortality in Organization Theory and Practice.' In J. Hassard and D. Pym, eds., *The Theory and Philosophy of Organizations*. London: Routledge, 1990: 135 *ff.*
14. Ludwig Wittgenstein, *Philosophical Investigations*. Oxford: Basil Blackwell, 1953: 23; *On Certainty*. Oxford: Basil Blackwell, 1969: 65.
15. Chester Barnard, *The Functions of the Executive*. Cambridge, Mass.: Harvard University Press, 1972: 164.
16. Stanley Milgram, *Obedience to Authority*. New York: Harper and Row, 1974.
17. Or H. A. Simon's equivalent 'zone of acceptance.'
18. Barnard, *ibid.*, 163.
19. *Ibid.*, 165.
20. Hannah Arendt, *Eichmann in Jerusalem: The Banality of Evil*. New York: Viking, 1963.
21. See Francis Wilkinson, *Police Leadership*. New York: Gower, 1993, for a possible exemption to this generalization in police forces that promote all administrators from the entry rank of constable.

22. Victor A. Thompson, *Modern Organization*. New York: Knopf, 1961: 138–178, provides the most lucid exposition but Goffman's earlier classic, *The Presentation of Self in Everyday Life*. Harmondsworth: Penguin, 1959, is also insightful and relevant. More recently *cf.* Peter Gronn, 'Talk as the Work: The Accomplishment of School Administration.' *Administrative Science Quarterly*, 1983, 28, 1: 1–21.

23. Although we have cast this argument in contemporary terms it is at least as ancient as Socrates and Plato who both would assign leadership to the 'one who knows,' Socrates giving the example of the master of a ship to whom all, including the owners defer. See Xenophon, *Memorabilia*. Loeb Classical Library 1918–1925: 3, 8, 10–11 (4: 229) and also *cf.* I. F. Stone, *The Trial of Socrates*. New York: Anchor, 1989: 13.

24. *Cf.* J. Lyons, *Chomsky*, 2nd edn. London, 1972.

25. Simon, *ibid.*; Barnard, *ibid.*; D. Katz and R. Kahn, *The Social Psychology of Organizations*, 2nd edn. New York: Wiley, 1978.

26. John McGowan, *Postmodernism and its Critics*. Cornell University Press, 1991: 60.

27. *Ibid.*, 254.

28. Richard Tarnas, *The Passion of the Western Mind*. New York: Crown, 1991: 492–493.

29. Paglia, *ibid.*, 42 *ff.*

30. The German poet Heinz Johst (*not* Hermann Goering) is to be credited with the expression 'When I hear the word culture I reach for my gun.' Similar sentiments might be evinced with the notion of leadership.

31. *Cf.* William E. Rosenbach and Robert L. Taylor, *Contemporary Issues in Leadership*, 2nd edn. London: Westview Press, 1989.

32. David D. Van Fleet and Gary A. Yukl, 'A Century of Leadership Research.' *Papers Dedicated to the Development of Modern Management*. US Academy of Management, 1986: 12–23.

33. F. E. Fiedler and M. M. Chemers, *Leadership and Effective Management*. Glenview, Ill.: Scott, Foresman, 1974. Professor Fiedler is the pre-eminent exponent of an empirical–analytical approach to leadership research.

34. Max Weber, *Economy and Society: An Outline of Interpretive Sociology*. Vol. I. Berkeley, Calif.: University of California Press, 1978: 215–216. The reference is to the three pure types of legitimate authority rather than leadership. Weber might not accept them as synonymous but would agree that some forms of leadership are derived from legitimate authority.

35. J. M. Burns, *Leadership*. New York: Harper and Row, 1978. It should be noted, however, that transformational leadership appears to be confined to a benevolent sense and would therefore be subsumed under our own larger interpretation of charismatic leadership.

36. *Op. cit.*

37. Barnard, *op. cit.*, 260.

38. *Ibid*.

39. *Ibid.*, 259.

40. *Ibid.*, 288.

CHAPTER 5

1. Benjamin DeMott, 'Inside the Leadership Studies Racket.' *Harper's*, Dec. 1993: 61.

2. K. Matsushita, *Not for Bread Alone. A Business Ethos. A Management Ethos.* Osaka: PHP Institute, 1988. Christopher Hodgkinson, 'Japanese Management and Leadership.' Department of Educational Administration, University of Alberta, January 1989.

3. Christopher Hodgkinson, 'Towards an Axiology of Leadership.' *American Educational Research Association.* New Orleans, April 1994.

4. *Cf.* R. J. House, 'A Path–Goal Theory of Leader Effectiveness.' *Administrative Science Quarterly*, 1971, 16: 321; R. M. Stogdill, 'The Evolution of Leadership Theory.' *Proceedings of the Academy of Management*, 1975: 4; Fred Fiedler, *A Theory of Leadership Effectiveness.* New York: McGraw-Hill, 1967; Fred Fiedler, 'The Contingency Model and the Dynamics of the Leadership Process.' In L. Berkowitz, ed., *Advances in Experimental Social Psychology*, Vol. II. New York: Academic Press, 1978.

5. *Cf.* Fred Fiedler, *op. cit.* fn 4 and C. A. Schriesheim and B. J. Bird, 'Contributions of the Ohio State Studies to the Field of Leadership.' *Journal of Management*, 1979, 5: 135.

6. Personal communication with Professor Fiedler. It should be noted this multivariate R^2 statistic is a maximal or optimal estimate.

7. J. P. Campbell, 'On the Nature of Organizational Effectiveness.' In P. S. Goodman and J. M. Pennings, eds., *New Perspectives in Organizational Effectiveness.* San Francisco: Jossey-Bass, 1977: 18.

8. Thomas B. Greenfield, 'Organizations as Talk, Chance, Action, and Experience.' In A. Heigl-Evers and V. Streeck, eds., *Die Psychologie des 20 Jahrhunderts.* Band VIII, Zürich: Kindler Verlag, 1978; Thomas B. Greenfield, 'Reflections on Organization Theory and the Truths of Irreconcilable Realities.' *Educational Administration Quarterly*, 1978, 14, 2: 1–23; Thomas B. Greenfield and Peter Ribbins, eds., *Greenfield on Educational Administration: Towards a Humane Science.* London: Routledge, 1993.

9. Don Lang, 'Values and Commitment: An Empirical Verification of Hodgkinson's Value Paradigm as Applied to the Commitment of Individuals to Organizations.' Unpublished dissertation, University of Victoria, 1976.

10. David D. Van Fleet and Gary A. Yukl, 'A Century of Leadership Research.' *Papers Dedicated to the Development of Modern Management.* New York: Academy of Management, 1986: 12 reprinted in William E. Rosenbach and Robert L. Taylor, *Contemporary Issues in Leadership*, 2nd edn. San Francisco: Westview Press, 1989.

11. J. A. Wheeler, 'Genesis and Observership.' In Batts and Hintikka, eds., *Foundational Problems in the Social Sciences.* Dordrecht: Reidel, 1977: 3.

12. For a sophisticated treatment of Weberian theory of types see Eugénie Samier, 'A Study of the Relevance of Max Weber's Work to Educational Administration Theory.' Unpublished dissertation, University of Victoria, 1993.

13. Ludwig Wittgenstein, *Philosophical Investigations.* G. E. M. Anscombe tr. Oxford: Basil Blackwell, 1976: 7.

14. W. J. Reddin, *Managerial Effectiveness.* New York: McGraw-Hill, 1970.

15. John G. Bennett, *Enneagram Studies.* York Beach, ME: Samuel Wiser, 1983; Don Richard Riso, *Personality Types: Using the Enneagram for Self-Discovery*, Boston: Houghton Mifflin, 1987; Kathleen V. Hurley and Theodore G. Dobson, *What's My Type?* San Francisco: Harper, 1991.

16. Derek Allison, 'Weberian Bureaucracy and the Public School System.' Unpublished dissertation, University of Alberta, 1980.

17. Max Weber, *ibid*.

18. See Part III.

19. *Cf.* Francis Wilkinson, *Police Leadership*. London: Gower, 1993. In correspondence with the author it was agreed by Birmingham Asst. Chief Constable Wilkinson that the remarkable hierarchy of ranks could be considered as a reward system conducive to 'leadership,' *q.v.*

20. See above, Chapters 4, 6 and 7, also *Journal of Business Ethics*, 1996, 15: 415.

21. Mary Midgley, *Beast and Man: The Roots of Human Nature*. Ithaca, NY: Cornell University Press, 1978: 330.

22. In either case these could be construed as Eastern and Western versions of the 'Mandate of Heaven.'

23. See below, Chapter 6, for definition of this concept.

24. Chester I. Barnard, *The Functions of the Executive*. London: Harvard University Press, 1968: 56–59 and passim.

25. Daniel Katz and Robert L. Kahn, *The Social Psychology of Organizations*, 2nd edn. New York: Wiley, 1978: 550–561; E. A. Fleishmann and D. R. Peters, 'Interpersonal Values, Leadership Attitudes and Managerial Success,' *Personnel Psychology*, 1962, 15: 127–143.

26. Alexander Pope, *An Essay on Criticism*.

27. Adam Smith, *The Wealth of Nations*. London, 1776.

28. Albert Speer, *Inside the Third Reich: Memoirs*. New York: Macmillan, 1970: 19–20.

29. Victor A. Thompson, *Modern Organization*. New York: Knopf, 1961; *Bureaucracy and the Modern World*. Morristown, NJ: General Learning Press, 1976; *Without Sympathy or Enthusiasm: The Problem of Administrative Compassion*. New York: Macmillan, 1975.

30. George Orwell, *1984*. Harmondsworth: Penguin, 1949.

31. J. L. Mackie, *Ethics*. Harmondsworth: Penguin, 1977; Edward O. Wilson, *Sociobiology: The New Synthesis*. Cambridge, Mass.: Harvard University Press, 1975.

32. This can be considered the central theme of Barnard's text, *op. cit.* as decision-making is the central theme of his protégé H. A. Simon.

33. Edward O. Wilson, *op. cit.*, 10.

34. *Op. cit.*, 176.

35. *Ibid*.

CHAPTER 6

1. Arguments and analyses in this chapter are in part elaborations of material in my *Educational Leadership: The Moral Art*. Albany: SUNY, 1991: 49–67.

2. Ludwig Wittgenstein, *Tractatus logico-philosophicus*. London: Routledge and Kegan Paul, 1961: 5, Props. 1, 1.1.

3. Daniel C. Dennett, *Consciousness Explained*. Boston: Little, Brown, 1991: 66 *ff*.

4. Lewis Carroll, *Through the Looking-Glass*. New York: New American Library, 1962: 158.

5. *Time*, June 13, 1994.

6. *Cf.* my *Towards a Philosophy of Administration*. Oxford: Blackwell, 1978: 104 *et. seq.* The ontological status of the concept remains disputatious.

7. Heinrich Zimmer, *Philosophies of India*. New York: Bollingen, 1951.

8. Sun-Tzu's *The Art of War* falls within this category.

9. Maurice Nicoll, *Psychological Commentators on the Teachings of Gurdieff and Ouspensky*. London: Shambala, 1984: 469.

10. Clyde Kluckhohn in Talcott Parsons and Edward Shils, eds., *Toward a General Theory of Action*. New York: Harper, 1962: 395.

11. Abraham Maslow's classic *Toward a Psychology of Being*, 2nd edn. New York: Van Nostrand, 1968 and his sortie into administrative philosophy, *Eupsychian Management*. Irwin, Ill: Homewood, 1965 both avoid the use of the term 'value.'

12. Daniel C. Ennett, *Consciousness Explained*. Boston: Little, Brown, 1991: 386.

13. Dennett, *op. cit.*

14. Ludwig Wittgenstein, *Tractatus Logico-Philosophicus*. London: Routledge and Kegan Paul, 1961, Prop. 7.

15. Immanual Kant, *Critique of Pure Reason*. New York: Liberal Arts Press, 1909, 1956: 285.

16. Actually the cap badge of the 17th/21st Lancers who participated in the famous Charge of the Light Brigade at Balaclava.

17. See J. O. Urmson, *The Emotive Theory of Ethics*. London, 1968 and, more especially, the positivist view expounded by A. J. Ayer in *Language, Truth and Logic*. London: Gollancz, 1946.

18. Ayer, *ibid.*, 103–110.

19. H. A. Simon, *Administrative Behavior*, 2nd edn. New York: Free Press, 1965, Introduction.

20. Christopher Lasch, *The Culture of Narcissism*. New York: W. W. Norton, 1979.

21. Chester Barnard, *The Functions of the Executive. Op. cit.* 272–278.

22. *Cf.* H. S. Broudy, 'Conflicts in Values.' In R. E. Ohm and W. Monahan, eds., *Educational Administration: Philosophy in Action*. Oklahoma City: University of Oklahoma Press, 1965: 42–58.

23. Sir Karl Popper, 'What can Logic do for Philosophy?' *Proceedings of the Aristotelian Society* 1948: 154.

24. Attempts have been made to deny the logical validity of the value-fact separation (see C. W. Evers and G. Lakomski, *Knowing Educational Administration Research*. Oxford: Pergamon, 1991: 104) but see C. Hodgkinson, 'The Epistemological Axiology of Evers and Lakomski: Some un-Quinean Quibblings.' *Journal of Educational Management and Administration*, 1993, Spring, for a refutation of these attempts.

25. James G. March and H. A. Simon, *Organizations*. New York: Wiley, 1958: 130, 169.

26. D. Katz and R. Kahn, *The Social Psychology of Organizations*. New York: Wiley, 1978: 165, 266.

27. Chester Barnard, *op. cit.*, 159.

28. Richard M. Steers and Lyman W. Porter, *Motivation and Work Behavior*. New York: McGraw-Hill, 1975; Katz and Kahn, *op. cit.*; R. S. Peters, *The Concept of Motivation*. London: Routledge and Kegan Paul, 1960 provides a definitive analysis.

29. Barnard, *op. cit.* 93; P. Georgiu, 'The Goal Paradigm and Notes towards a Counter Paradigm.' *Administrative Science Quarterly*, 1973, 18: 291.

30. William Barrett, *The Illusion of Technique*. New York: Doubleday, 1979: 293.

31. F. Herzberg, *Work and the Nature of Man*. Cleveland: World Publishing, 1966; Abraham Maslow, *Motivation and Personality*. New York: Harper, 1956; *Toward a Psychology of Being*. New York: Van Nostrand, 1968.

32. *Cf.* Nietzsche, *Beyond Good and Evil.* Walter Kaufmann tr. New York: Modern Library, 1968: 211.
33. Albert Speer, *Inside the Third Reich.* New York: Macmillan, 1980.
34. I am indebted to a paper by Carol Harris entitled, 'The Naked Participant: Balancing Personal Perspectives with the Concept of Verstehen in Interpretive Inquiry.' *Commonwealth Society for the Study of Educational Administration*, Toronto, 1989 for an explication of Weber's value analysis and its paradigmatic correspondences.

CHAPTER 7

1. The remark is attributed to Henry James. *loc. incog.*
2. Chris Argyris, *Personality and Organization.* New York: Harper, 1957; *Integrating the Individual and the Organization.* New York: Wiley, 1964; 'Personality and Organization Theory Revisited,' *Administrative Science Quarterly*, 1973 October: 141.
3. *Cf.* D. Katz and R. Kahn, *The Social Psychology of Organizations.* New York: Wiley, 1978.
4. Simone Weil, 'Human Possibility.' In *Selected Essays.* R. Rees tr. New York, 1962: 508.
5. Victor A. Thompson. *Modern Organization.* New York: Knopf, 1961: 170 *ff.*
6. John Ladd, 'Morality and the Ideal of Rationalization in Formal Organizations.' *The Monist*, 1970, 54: 488.
7. William G. Scott and David K. Hart. *Organizational America.* Boston: Houghton Mifflin, 1979: 43–46.
8. Donald J. Willower, 'Dewey's Theory of Inquiry and Reflective Administration.' *Journal of Educational Administration*, 1994, 32, 1: 5 *ff.*
9. S. Milgram. 'Behavioral Study of Obedience.' *Journal of Abnormal and Social Psychology*, 1963, 67: 37; 'Some Conditions of Obedience and Disobedience to Authority.' *Human Relations*, 1965, 18: 57–76; *Obedience to Authority.* New York: Harper and Row, 1974.
10. On the relation between organization and environment see Mary Meride in D. Katz, R. L. Kahn, and J. S. Adams, eds. *The Study of Organizations.* San Francisco: Jossey-Bass, 1980: 59; also *ibid.* Barry M. Staw and E. Szwajkowski, 65; and W. Richard Scott, *Organizations: Rational, Natural and Open Systems.* Englewood Cliffs, NJ: Prentice Hall, 1981.
11. Friedrich Nietzsche, *Human, All Too Human*, 2nd edn. 1886.
12. Fn. 4 *q.v.*
13. H. Mintzberg, *The Nature of Managerial Work.* New York: Harper Row, 1973: 28–38.
14. Friedrich Nietzsche, *Daybreak.* 1980: Preface (1886).
15. Peter Self, *Administrative Theories and Politics.* London: Allen and Unwin, 1972: 234–235.
16. Simone Weil, *Oppression and Liberty.* London: Routledge and Kegan Paul, 1965: 508.
17. Evers and Lakomski may be taken as representative of the former (C. W. Evers and G. Lakomski, *Knowing Educational Administration: Contemporary Methodological Controversies in Educational Administration Research.* Oxford: Pergamon, 1991) while T. B. Greenfield is a major proponent of the latter (Thomas B. Greenfield and Peter Ribbins, eds., *Greenfield on Educational Administration: Towards a Humane Science.* London: Routledge, 1993). The entire spectrum, regardless of administrative subset, is objectively described by Gareth Morgan (*Images of Organization.* London: Sage, 1986).

18. Within the subset of educational administration this position is most persuasively represented by Donald J. Willower, *cf.* 'Dewey's Theory of Inquiry and Reflective Administration,' *Journal of Educational Administration*, 1994, 32, 1: 5.

19. Katz and Kahn, n. 3 *q.v.*; Simon, *op. cit.*; R. M. Cyert and J. G. March, 'The Behavioral Theory of the Firm: A Behavioral Science-Economics Amalgam.' In W. W. Cooper *et al.*, eds., *New Perspectives in Organizational Research*. New York: Wiley, 1964: 289 epitomize the former while Greenfield n. 17 *q.v.*; Richard J. Bates 'Educational Administration, the Sociology of Science, and the Management of Knowledge.' *Educational Administration Quarterly*, 1980, 16: 1; and Alberto G. Ramos, *The New Science of Organizations: A Reconstruction of the Wealth of Nations*. Toronto: University of Toronto Press, 1981 are epigones of the latter. Middle ground is maintained by J. D. Thompson, *Organizations in Action*. New York: McGraw-Hill, 1967 and Philip Selznick, 'Foundations of the Theory of Organization.' In Amitai Etzioni, ed., *Complex Organization: A Sociological Reader*. New York: Holt, Rinehart and Winston, 1962: 29.

20. Thomas B. Greenfield, 'Environment as Subjective Reality: A Retrospective View of Modern Organization Theory and its Failure as Administrative Theory in Education and Elsewhere.' Conference paper, *American Educational Research Association* Montreal, April 1983: 3.

21. *Ibid.*, 5.

22. Gilbert Ryle, *The Concept of Mind*. New York: Barnes and Noble, 1949: 15–16, 22–23.

23. Greenfield, *op. cit.*, n. 20: 9.

CHAPTER 8

1. G. Hardin, *Exploring New Ethics for Survival*. New York: Penguin, 1968. See also M. Pastin, *The Hard Problems of Management*. San Francisco: Jossey-Bass, 1986.

2. Diane Berreth and Maize Scherer, 'A Conversation with Amitai Etzioni.' *Educational Leadership*, 1993, 6, 3: 15.

3. Note the etymology of 'id' in the term idiographic. The connotations and resonances are both Freudian and Jungian.

4. Gareth Morgan, *Images of Organization*. London: Sage, 1986.

5. The author is aware of instances of 'go-slow' and 'soldiering' practices in heavy industry in World War II on the Allied side. Enemy equivalents are undocumented but comparison is complicated by the employment of drafted and forced labour.

6. T. B. Greenfield, 'The Man who comes Back through the Door in the Wall: Discovering Truth, Discovering Self, Discovering Organizations.' *Educational Administration Quarterly*, 1980, 16: 3: 26–59; 'Against Group Mind: An Anarchistic Theory of Organization.' In *Reflective Readings in Educational Administration*. Victoria, Australia: Deakin University Press, 1983: 293–301.

7. A. Bloom, *The Closing of the American Mind*. New York: Simon and Schuster, 1987: 172.

8. D. McGregor, *The Human Side of Enterprise*. New York: McGraw-Hill, 1960: 33–57.

9. The term has been elucidated by R. J. S. MacPherson in Australia and was defined in the Picot Royal Commission on Education in New Zealand, 1985. It refers to the state of affairs where the providers of a public service have effectively gained control of (captured) the terms of their own services. In the same way regulatory authorities

often become servants of the bodies they are supposed to be regulating in the larger public interest. George J. Stigler, 'The Theory of Economic Regulation.' In *The Bell Journal of Economics and Management Science*, 1971, Spring, 2: 3–21.

10. *Cf.* S. S. Ker, 'Substitutes for Leadership: Some Implications for Organizational Design.' *Organization and Administrative Sciences*, 1977, 8: 135–146 and S. S. Ker.

11. Jean-Jacques Rousseau. *Le Contract Sociale*. Paris: 1762: 7. 11.

12. J. M. Burns, *Leadership*. New York: Harper and Row, 1978.

13. The human relations development has been documented above (*cf.* Chapter 2). Morgan presents a good summative bibliography of the general scientific approach in *Images of Organization* at 366–351 *q.v.*.

14. Sir Geoffrey Vickers, *Human Systems are Different*. London: Harper and Row, 1983: xxvii.

15. Hannah Arendt, *Eichmann in Jerusalem: The Banality of Evil*. New York: Viking, 1963; Vasily Grossman, *Life and Fate*. London: Collins, 1987; and Alexander Solzhenitsyn's *oeuvre* in general.

16. Kurt Lewin, *The Conceptual Representation and Measurement of Psychological Forces*. Durham, NC: Duke University Press, 1939.

17. Gareth Morgan, *op. cit.*, 190–191; 201–202, 366–367; I. L. Janis, *Victims of Groupthink*. Boston: Houghton Mifflin, 1972.

18. William A. Henry, *In Defense of Elitism*. New York: Doubleday, 1994 provides a polemical but persuasive account.

19. S. Milgram, *Obedience to Authority*. New York: Harper and Row, 1974.

20. E. Schein, *Organizational Culture and Leadership*. San Francisco: Jossey-Bass, 1985.

21. Whyte's *The Organization Man*, *q.v.* provides the classic statement.

22. Peters and Waterman recommend the technique of 'management by walking around' for the latter obligation. T. J. Peters and R. B. Waterman, *In Search of Excellence*. New York: Harper and Row, 1982.

23. Mikhail Gorbachev, *Perestroika*. New York: Harper and Row, 1987.

24. Barnard, *op. cit.*, 23.

25. Karl Popper, *The Open Society and its Enemies*. London: Routledge and Kegan Paul, 1945.

26. *Cf.* Noel Annan, *Our Age*. London: Fontana, 1991 for a biographical account of the problems of group interest from the standpoint of a political and academic leader. Also Philip Selznick, *The Moral Commonwealth: Social Theory and the Promise of Community*. Berkeley, Calif.: University of California Press, 1992.

27. Swami Vividishananda, *A Man of God*. Madras: Sri Ramakrishna Math, 1957: 188.

CHAPTER 9

1. Thomas B. Greenfield and Peter Ribbins, eds., *Greenfield on Educational Administration: Towards a Humane Science*. London: Routledge, 1993: 217.

2. It must be allowed that, strictly speaking, this is *not* the sense of Greenfield's interpretation since it implies that the whole is more than the sum of its parts. But see Thomas B. Greenfield, 'Environment as Subjective Reality: A Retrospective View of Modern Organization Theory and its Failure as Administrative Theory in Education and Elsewhere.' Conference paper, *American Educational Research Association* Montreal, April 1983 for an acknowledgement of the Hodgkinson perspective.

3. James G. March and H. A. Simon, *Organizations*. New York: Wiley, 1958.

4. Such is the case, for example, in the University of Victoria, Canada, where the tenure document declares teaching to be of *paramount* importance and this example is not isolated in the Canadian system of higher education.

5. Chester I. Barnard, *The Functions of the Executive*. London: Harvard University Press, 1968: 233.

6. *Ibid*.

7. *Op. cit.*, 138.

8. H. A. Simon, *Administrative Behavior*, 2nd edn. New York: Free Press, 1965: 140.

9. Barnard, *op. cit.*, 141.

10. Simon, *op. cit.*, 144.

11. Iris Murdoch, *Metaphysics as a Guide to Morals*. London: Penguin, 1992: 492.

12. The disbanding of the Canadian Airborne Regiment by politicians on the grounds that its hazing practices offended political correctness provides an instructive case study for administrative philosophy.

13. Philip Selznick, *Leadership in Administration*. Evanston, Ill.: Row, Peterson, 1957: 17.

14. D. Katz and R. Kahn, *The Social Psychology of Organizations*. New York: Wiley, 1978: 341.

15. John Ladd, 'Morality and the Ideal of Rationalization in Formal Organizations.' *The Monist*, 1970, 54: 488–516.

16. Barnard, *op. cit.*, 203.

17. Simon, *op. cit.*, 29.

18. Ladd, *op. cit.*

19. Murdoch, *op. cit.*, 426.

20. It is interesting that in a different V_5 ethos the Chairman of Japan Airlines *did* hold himself personally responsible for a pilot-error accident and resigned his office.

21. R. Michels, *Political Parties: A Sociological Study of the Oligarchical Tendencies of Modern Democracy*. New York: 1962; T. B. Bottomore, *Elites and Society*. Harmondsworth: Penguin, 1966.

22. Barnard, *op. cit.*, 261.

23. *Ibid*.

24. Barnard, *op. cit.*, 266–267.

25. Gareth Morgan, *Images of Organization*. London: Sage, 1986.

26. *Ibid*., 382.

27. *Ibid*., 383.

28. Christopher Hodgkinson, *Educational Leadership: The Moral Art*. Albany: SUNY, 1991. Chapter 1 gives an illustration with respect to educational organizations.

29. W. H. Whyte analysed this so-called ethic in *The Organization Man* (1956) and concluded that it was essentially a 'utopian faith'. We have referred to it in its contemporary form in the text as the 'organizational imperative' *q.v.*

CHAPTER 10

1. The philosopher Kant, although an idealist, subscribed to the concept of radical evil in the human condition from which it is but a step to the notion of ineradicable evil.

2. It may be of some interest that the latest translation of this book by Sir Desmond Lee has sold over nine million copies worldwide and continues in strong demand. *Letter*

of the Corpus Association. Cambridge: Michaelmas, 1966, 73: 27. (See also p. 162 *ff* above.)

3. Bertrand Russell, *Power*. London: Unwin, 1975: 19.

4. Plato, *The Republic*, 2nd edn. Harmondsworth: Penguin, 1974: 16.

5. *Cf.* Erich Fromm, *The Anatomy of Human Destructiveness*. Greenwich, Conn.: Fawcett, 1973: 75.

6. Victor A. Thompson. *Modern Organization*. New York: Knopf, 1961: 152.

7. Chapter 2 above.

8. William G. Scott and David K. Hart. *Organizational America*. Boston: Houghton Mifflin, 1979: 95 *ff*.

9. Alvin Gouldner's distinction in the classic article 'Cosmopolitans and Locals: Toward an Analysis of Latent Social Roles,' *Administrative Science Quarterly*, 1957/8, 2: 281.

10. Thompson, *op. cit.* 58 *ff*., 138.

11. Robert S. McNamara, *In Retrospect: The Tragedy and Lessons of Vietnam*. New York: Random House, 1995.

12. The eminent management authority Peter Drucker has been said to have considered the essential prerequisite to an administrative career should be *not* having an MBA.

13. H. Mintzberg, *The Nature of Managerial Work*. New York: Harper Row, 1973.

14. H. Simon, D. Smithburg, and V. Thompson, *Public Administration*. New York: Knopf, 1950: 533.

15. In the introduction to his *Administrative Behavior q.v.*

16. A response editorial in the *New York Times* (10 April 1995) points out, however, that while three million Vietnamese and fifty-eight thousand Americans died in the war, McNamara himself 'got a sinecure at the World Bank and summers at the Vineyard'.

17. Exceptions to this are delineated in the section on the arthasastra below, *q.v.*.

18. Lord Thomson, *The Times*, 2 January 1976.

19. Swami Satprakashananda, *Methods of Knowledge*. London: Allen and Unwin, 1965: 208.

20. But not between the genders. See S. Goldberg, *The Inevitability of Patriarchy*. London: Temple Smith, 1977.

21. S. Milgram, *Obedience to Authority*. New York: Harper and Row, 1974.

22. S. Cohen and L. Taylor, *Escape Attempts: The Theory and Practice of Resistance to Everyday Life*. Harmondsworth: Penguin, 1978. See also Peter L. Berger and Thomas Luckmann, *The Social Construction of Everyday Life*. Harmondsworth: Penguin, 1972.

23. Cohen and Taylor, *op. cit.*, 19.

24. P. Laslett and W. G. Runciman, eds., *Philosophy, Politics and Society*. 3rd series. Oxford: Basil Blackwell, 1967: 134–156.

25. Emile Durkheim, *Professional Ethics and Civil Morals*. C. Brookfield tr. London, 1957: 12.

26. Roger Beehler and Alan Drengson, *The Philosophy of Society*. London: Methuen, 1978: 404.

27. I am indebted to Professor Heinrich Zimmer for his treatment of this subject in *Philosophies of India*. New York: Bollingen Foundation, 1951.

28. *Cf.* ref. to Hitler p. 193 above.

29. M. Wright, 'The Professional Conduct of Civil Servants.' *Public Administration*, 1973, 51: 1–16.

30. L. J. Peters, *The Peter Principle*. New York: Morrow, 1969.
31. E. Goffman, *The Presentation of Self in Everyday Life*. New York: Doubleday, 1959 expounds the general principles.

CHAPTER 11

1. *Cf.* G. Lichtheim, *The Concept of Ideology and Other Essays*. New York, 1967; K. Thompson, *Beliefs and Ideology*. London, 1986; also Marx's *The German Ideology*; K. Mannheim's *Ideology and Utopia*. London: 1956.
2. The Kantian notion of the 'sublime' is lucidly (and concisely) presented in Iris Murdoch, *Metaphysics as a Guide to Morals*. London: Penguin, 1992: 108.
3. It has, however, contributed to postmodern relativism (see Chapter 13).
4. McNamara (1995), *op. cit.*; Richard A. Gabriel and Paul L. Savage, *Crisis in Command*. New York: Hill and Wong, 1978.
5. Arthur E. Wise, 'Why Educational Policies often Fail: The Hyperrationalization Hypothesis.' *Curriculum Studies* 9, 1: 43–57; J. Culbertson *et al.*, 'Symposium on the Theory of Practice.' *American Educational Research Association*. Los Angeles, 1981.
6. *'Wie schwer fällt mir zu sehen, was vor meinen Augen liegt!'* Ludwig Wittgenstein, *Culture and Value*. Oxford: Basil Blackwell, 1980: 29, 39.
7. Ferdinand Tönnies, *Community and Association*. London: Routledge and Kegan Paul, 1955; Max Weber, *Economy and Society: An Outline of Interpretive Sociology*. Berkeley, Calif.: University of California Press, 1978.
8. William Barrett, *The Illusion of Technique*. New York: Doubleday, 1979: 247. It may also be noted that Heidegger served as Rector of his university (Freiburg) and proclaimed a conversion to National Socialism in 1933 in his famous *Rektoratsrede* thus combining administration and ideology with a formal background in philosophy.
9. *Cf.* J. M. Burns, *Leadership*. New York: Harper and Row, 1978 for a classic statement on 'transformational' leadership.
10. Robert House, address on charismatic leadership, University of Victoria, 27 July 1993. See also R. J. House, 'Theory of Charismatic Leadership.' In J. G. Hunt and L. L. Largen, eds., *Leadership: The Cutting Edge*. Southern Illinois University Press, 1977; Max Weber, *On Charisma and Institution Building*. S. N. Eisenstadt, ed., Chicago: Chicago University Press, 1922.
11. The 'unspeakable' which lies beyond the limits of our language but nevertheless informs our efforts to express it.
12. An interesting paper by Colin W. Evers and Gabriele Lakomski, 'Science in Educational Administration: A Postpositivist Conception.' *American Educational Research Association*, San Francisco.' April, 1995 delineates the evolution of administrative theories and their epistemological bases. While it reinforces the rationalist and naturalistic roots of administrative ideology it does, however, elide the problem of charisma.
13. The Leni Riefenstahl documentary of a Nazi rally in Nürnberg in the 1930s, *Triumph of the Will* portrays vividly the poetic orchestration of charisma and has been rightly acknowledged as a cinematic classic.

14. Ron Rosenbaum, 'Explaining Hitler.' *New Yorker*. 1 May 1995: 50; Hugh Trevor Roper, *The Last Days of Hitler*, 1947; Alan Bullock, *Hitler: A Study in Tyranny*, 1952.
15. Rosenbaum, *ibid.*, 60.
16. *Ibid*, 61; Adolf Hitler, *Mein Kampf*. New York: Reynal and Hitchcock, 1939.
17. Friedrich Nietzsche, *Human, All too Human*. 1886: 52.
18. Rosenbaum, *loc. cit.* 67.
19. Explicated in Iris Murdoch, *Metaphysics as a Guide to Morals*. London: Penguin, 1992: 124; Søren Kierkegaard, *Fear and Trembling*.
20. See n. 12 above.
21. The fallacy popular with H. A. Simon and Katz and Kahn, *op. cit.*
22. C. P. (Lord) Snow, *Science and Government*. Cambridge, Mass.: Harvard University Press, 1961; H. E. Dale, *The Higher Civil Service of Great Britain*. Oxford: Clarendon, 1961.
23. I would consider the late Sir Geoffrey Vickers (*Human Systems are Different*. London: Harper and Row, 1983) to have been an exemplar of the type; a judgment based both on his biography and extensive personal correspondence.
24. Milton Rokeach, *The Nature of Human Values*. New York: Free Press, 1973: 215–235, 286–313.

CHAPTER 12

1. William G. Scott and David K. Hart. *Organizational America*. Boston: Houghton Mifflin, 1979: 45–46.
2. Frederick Enns, 'Some Ethical–Moral Concerns in Administration.' *Canadian Administrator*, 1981, 20: 5. See also K. Leithwood and R. Steinbach, *Expert Problem Solving*. Albany: State University of New York Press, 1995 and P. T. Begley and K. Leithwood, 'The Influence of Values on School Administrator Practices.' *Journal of Personnel Evaluation in Education*, 1990, 3: 337–352.
3. Calvin Coolidge's remark that 'The business of America is business' has an ironical resonance and relevance but empirical evidence is nicely presented in the study by H. Mintzberg, *The Nature of Managerial Work*. New York: Harper and Row, 1973.
4. Herbert A. Simon, *Administrative Behavior*, 2nd edn. New York: Free Press, 1965: 20–44.
5. Charles E. Lindblom, 'The Science of Muddling Through.' *Public Administration Review*, 1959, Spring: 155–169 and its revisitation: 'Still Muddling: Not Yet Through.' *Public Administration Review*, 1979: 517–526.
6. Nor can rank-ordered preferences be summed or averaged without encountering the 'voting paradox' and Arrow's impossibility theorem, as discussed *supra*.
7. The terms 'silent majority' and 'moral majority' reflect this distinction.
8. Albert Speer, *Inside the Third Reich: Memoirs*. New York: Macmillan, 1971: 19.
9. This *eo ipso* shows that 'number' in 'the greatest number' utilitarian maxim is not qualitatively neutral. The interest of the citizen voter is not equivalent to that of the elected official.
10. M. Silver and D. Geller, 'On the Irrelevance of Evil: The Organization and Individual Action.' *Journal of Social Issues*, 1978, 34, 4: 125.

11. James Cutt, *Comprehensive Auditing in Canada*. New York: Praeger, 1988. See also A. R. Dobell and D. Zussman, 'An Evaluation System for Government: If Politics is Theatre, then Evaluation is (mostly) Art.' *Canadian Public Administration*, Fall 1981.
12. Friedrich Nietzsche, *Von Nutzen und Nachteil der Historie für das Leben*. (2nd Untimely Meditation), 1874.
13. H. S. Broudy, 'Conflicts in Values.' In R. E. Ohm and W. Monahan, eds., *Educational Administration: Philosophy in Action*. Tulsa: University of Oklahoma Press, 1965: 42–58.
14. A decision which may be simplified or complicated by equity codes of preferential hiring.
15. Literally 'sitting-flesh' or the ability to stay at the table until the opposition defaults through ennui or fatigue.
16. *Cf.* the 'postulate of degeneration' in Chapter 6.
17. Lessing, *Die Erziehung des Menschengeschlechts*. 1780: sections 84, 91.
18. Alexander Pope (1688–1744), *An Essay on Man*. I: 289.
19. Walter Kaufmann in *Nietzsche*, 4th edn. Princeton University Press, 1974: 148.
20. Friedrich Nietzsche, *The Gay Science*. Walter Kaufmann tr. New York: Random House, 1974: 1007.
21. Chester Barnard, *The Functions of the Executive*. Cambridge, Mass.: Harvard University Press, 1972: 282.
22. William Barrett, *The Illusion of Technique*. New York: Doubleday, 1979: 86. The idea of sublimation also enters here. See Walter Kaufmann, *op. cit.* 218–224 for the relationship between Nietzsche and Freud.
23. Even to couch the idea in language is paradoxical for in 'knowing oneself' what knows and what is known?
24. The renowned Matsushita leadership training School of Government and Management is heavily Zen oriented.
25. Iris Murdoch, *Metaphysics as a Guide to Morals*. London: Penguin, 1992: 218.
26. See, however, John Stevens, *The Sword of No-Sword*. Boston: Shambala, 1994 for a biographical example of relevance to Oriental administration which would not (for V_5 reasons) transfer to Western praxis. Christmas Humphries, *The Way of Action*. Harmondsworth: Pelican n.d. is probably the best interpretation for administrative purposes.
27. Simone Weil, 'Human Personality.' In *Selected Essays*. R. Rees tr. New York, 1962: 10.
28. Murdoch, *loc. cit.*
29. B. Buchanan, 'Building Organizational Commitment.' *Administrative Science Quarterly*, 1974, 19: 533.
30. R. T. Mowday, L. W. Porter, and R. M. Steers, *The Psychology of Commitment*. New York: Academic Press, 1982.
31. Donald Lang, 'Organizational Commitment: An Empirial Verification of the Hodgkinson Value Paradigm.' Unpublished dissertation, University of Victoria, 1986.
32. Sir Geoffrey Vickers, *Responsibility—Its Sources and Limits*. Seaside, CA: Intersystems Publishing, 1980: 55.
33. Barrett, *op. cit.*, 253.
34. This is, in fact, an idiosyncratic version of the postulate of degeneracy as applied to value at large.

35. Murdoch *loc. cit.* justifies the use of this terminology on the grounds of deficient ethical theory in a manner analogous to the use of maxims by default in administrative theory.
36. Herbert A. Simon, *Administrative Behavior*, 2nd edn. New York: Free Press, 1965: Introduction.

CHAPTER 13

1. It can be argued that such authorities are too narrowly focused upon administration *per se* to offer any historico-philosophical perspective but all authorities speak implicitly if not explicitly from their intellectual foundations and cultural background.
2. Noel Annan, *Our Age*. London: Fontana, 1991: 337.
3. Only Weber and Heidegger can be truly said to have been practising administrators and many were deliberately antithetical (Schopenhauer, Wittgenstein).
4. *Cf Current Contents*, annual indices of citations.
5. Gareth Morgan, *Images of Organization*. London: Sage, 1986: 257–264.
6. For a specific analysis of Weberian misinterpretation in North America see Eugénie Samier, 'A Study of the Relevance of Max Weber's Work to Educational Administration Theory.' Unpublished dissertation, University of Victoria, 1993.
7. Walter Kaufmann in *Nietzsche*, 4th edn. Princeton University Press, 1974: 161.
8. *Ibid.* for complete refutation of such charges.
9. *Ibid.*, 175.
10. Friedrich Nietzsche, *The Will to Power*. W. Kaufmann and R. J. Hollingdale trs. New York: Random House, 1968: 983.
11. Friedrich Nietzsche, *Twilight of the Idols*. R. J. Hollingdale tr. Harmondsworth: Penguin, 1969: 49.
12. Friedrich Nietzsche, *The Will to Power, op. cit.*, 1026.
13. *Scherz, List, und Rache*: cf. Proem to *The Will to Power*.
14. Greenfield became aware of Nietzsche only in the last months of his life and was unable to incorporate his insights into his compatible work, but see Thomas B. Greenfield and Peter Ribbins, eds., *Greenfield on Educational Administration: Towards a Humane Science*. London: Routledge, 1993: 270.
15. *The Will to Power, op. cit.*, 1007.
16. Friedrich Nietzsche, *Beyond Good and Evil*. W. Kaufmann tr. In *Basic Writings of Nietzsche*. New York: Modern Library Giants, 1968: 212.
17. Kaufmann, *op. cit.*, 255.
18. *Ibid.*, 412 and Gottfried Benn, 'Nietzsche nach 50 Jahren (1950).' *Frühe Prosa und Reden*. Wiesbaden: Limes Verlag, 1950: 253–268.
19. Iris Murdoch, *Metaphysics as a Guide to Morals*. London: Penguin, 1992: 354.
20. Malcolm Bradbury in Alan Bullock, Oliver Stallybrass, and Stephen Trembley, eds., *Modern Thought*. London: Fontana, 1988: 672.
21. John McGowan, *Postmodernism and its Critics*. Cornell University Press, 1991.
22. Pierre Bourdieu, *Outline of a Theory of Practice*. R. Nice tr. Cambridge University Press, 1977.
23. Gilles Deleuze, *Nietzsche and Philosophy*. Hugh Tomlinson, tr. Columbia University Press, 1983.
24. Paul de Man, *Allegories of Reading*. Yale University Press, 1979.

25. Jacques Derrida, *Of Grammatology*. G. C. Spivak tr. Johns Hopkins University Press, 1976.

26. Michel Foucault, *Power/Knowledge*. Colin Gordon, ed. New York: Pantheon, 1980; *Politics, Philosophy, Culture*. Laurence P. Kritzman, ed. New York: Routledge, 1988.

27. Jean-Francois Lyotard, *The Postmodern Condition*. G. Bennington and B. Massumi trs. University of Minnesota Press, 1984.

28. Notably Jürgen Habermas, e.g. *The Philosophical Discourse of Modernity*. F. Lawrence tr. Cambridge, Mass.: MIT Press, 1987.

29. Fns. 21–28 above reveal the commitment of the American academy to the French influence. This has been the subject of polemical and analytical critique by the feminist scholar Camille Paglia, *Sex, Art, and American Culture*. New York: Random House, 1992.

30. Important American contributors include e.g. Richard Rorty, *Contingency, Irony, and Solidarity*. Cambridge University Press, 1989; Edward Said, *The World of the Text, and the Critics*. Harvard University Press, 1986. The former is essentially a naturalistic pragmatist, the latter a Marxist.

31. Murdoch, *op. cit.* for analysis and critique, especially 185 *ff.*

32. *Ibid.*, 194.

33. Annan, *op. cit.*, 352.

34. Lyotard, *op. cit.* Charles Newman, *The Postmodern Aura*. Evanston, Ill., 1985.

35. *Cf. The Essential McLuhan*. Don Mills: General Publishing, 1995.

36. Allan Bloom, *The Closing of the American Mind*. New York: Simon and Schuster, 1987.

37. See Camille Paglia for a general critique of American feminism and in particular for polemics against postmodern influences in the academy: *Sex, Art, and American Culture, op. cit.*, especially 'Junk Bonds and Corporate Raiders: Academe in the Hour of the Wolf; *loc cit.* 170 and 1991 MIT lecture 'Crisis in the American Universities.'

38. Richard Tarnas, *The Passion of the Western Mind*. New York: Ballantine, 1991 but see any of the scientific reviews of research such as Anne Moir and David Jessel, *Brainsex*. London: Mandarin, 1994 for a convincing refutation from the biological standpoint.

39. Christopher Lasch, *The Culture of Narcissism*. New York: W. W. Norton, 1979.

40. Whitehead's remark that the history of Western philosophy is but a footnote to Plato is apropos.

41. Nietzsche's aphorism on the political correctness of his day is cutting, '... the shameful moralized manner of speaking which makes all modern judgments about men and things slimy.' *Genealogy of Morals* III. 19.

42. The Matsushita School of Government and Management, for example, is strongly Zen-oriented and *cf.* K. Matsushita, *Not for Bread Alone: A Business Ethos, a Management Ethic*. Osaka: PHP Institute, 1988.

43. H. G. Frederickson, 'Symposium on Social Equity and Public Administration,' *Public Administration Review*, 1974, 34: 1–51.

44. Marcus Aurelius, *Meditations*. M. Staniforth trs. Harmondsworth: Penguin Classics. 1964: VI: 15.

45. One assumes that Barnard's 'breadth' (*op. cit.* 282) subsumes depth, even as his morality encompasses ethics.

46. Thomas B. Greenfield, 'Environment as Subjective Reality.' *Canadian Society for the Study of Education*. Montreal, 1983 revised but unpublished, Toronto, 1987.

47. Konosake Matsushita, *Portrait of an Industrialist*. Osaka: PHP Institute, 1988.
48. Ludwig Wittgenstein, *Tractatus logico-philosophicus*. London: Routledge and Kegan Paul, 1961: Proposition 5.6.
49. *Ibid*. Proposition 6.522.

References

Ackoff, R. L. and Emery, F. E. *Purposive Systems*. Tavistock Institute: London, 1972.

Lord Acton. *Historical Essays and Studies*.

Allison, Derek. 'Weberian Bureaucracy and the Public School System.' Unpublished dissertation, University of Alberta, 1980.

Annan, Noel. *Our Age*. London: Fontana, 1991.

Arendt, Hannah. *Eichmann in Jerusalem: The Banality of Evil*. New York: Viking, 1963.

Argyris, Chris. *Personality and Organization*. New York: Harper, 1957.

Argyris, Chris. 'Personality and Organization Theory Revisited.' *Administrative Science Quarterly*, Oct. 1973.

Aurelius, Marcus. *Meditations*. M. Staniforth trs. Harmondsworth: Penguin Classics, 1964, VI: 15.

Ayer, A. J. *Language, Truth and Logic*. London: Gollancz, 1946.

Bailey, J. J. and O'Connor, R. J. 'Operationalizing Incrementalism: Measuring the Muddles.' *Public Administration Review*, 1975, 35.

Barnard, Chester I. *The Functions of the Executive*. Cambridge, Mass.: Harvard University Press, 1972.

Barrett, William. *The Illusion of Technique*. New York: Doubleday, 1979.

Bates, Richard J. 'Educational Administration, the Sociology of Science, and the Management of Knowledge.' *Educational Administration Quarterly*, 1980, 16.

Beehler, Roger and Drengson, Alan. *The Philosophy of Society*. London: Methuen, 1978: 404.

Begley, P. T. and Leithwood, K. 'The Influence of Values on School Administrator Practices.' *Journal of Personnel Evaluation in Education*, 1990, 3: 337–352.

Bell, Daniel. *The Coming of Post-Industrial Society*. New York: Basic Books, 1976.

Bendix, R. *Max Weber: An Intellectual Portrait*. New York: Doubleday, 1962.

Benn, Gottfried. 'Nietzsche nach 50 Jahren (1950).' *Frühe Prosa und Reden*. Wiesbaden: Limes Verlag, 1950: 253–268.

Bennett, John G. *Enneagram Studies*. York Beach, ME: Samuel Wiser, 1983.

Berger, Peter L. and Luckmann, Thomas. *The Social Construction of Everyday Life*. Harmondsworth: Penguin, 1972.

Berreth, Diane and Scherer Maize. 'A Conversation with Amitai Etzioni.' *Educational Leadership*, 1993, 6, 3.

Bertalanffy, Ludwig von. 'The Theory of Open Systems in Physics and Biology,' *Science* 1950, III: 23–28.

Bertalanffy, Ludwig von. *General Systems Theory*. New York: 1968.

Bertalanffy, Ludwig von and Rapoport, A. eds., *General Systems Yearbook*. Society for General Systems Research, 1960.

Bloom, Allan. *The Closing of the American Mind.* New York: Simon and Schuster, 1987.

Bottomore, T. B. *Elites and Society.* Harmondsworth: Penguin, 1966.

Bourdieu, Pierre. *Outline of a Theory of Practice.* R. Nice tr. Cambridge University Press, 1977.

Braybooke, David and Lindblom, Charles E. *A Strategy of Decision.* New York: Free Press, 1963.

Broudy, H. S. 'Conflicts in Values.' In R. E. Ohm and W. Monahan, eds., *Educational Administration: Philosophy in Action.* Oklahoma City: University of Oklahoma Press, 1965.

Buchanan, B. 'Building Organizational Commitment.' *Administrative Science Quarterly,* 1974, 19.

Bullock, Alan. *Hitler: A Study in Tyranny,* 1952.

Bullock, Alan, Stallybrass, Oliver and Trembley, Stephen, eds. *Modern Thought.* London: Fontana, 1988.

Burnham, James. *The Machiavellians, Defenders of Freedom.* New York: Day, 1963.

Burns, J. M. *Leadership.* New York: Harper and Row, 1978.

Campbell, J. P. 'On the Nature of Organizational Effectiveness.' In Goodman, P. S. and Pennings, J. M., eds., *New Perspectives in Organizational Effectiveness.* San Francisco: Jossey-Bass, 1977.

Carey, Alex. 'The Hawthorne Studies: A Radical Criticism.' *American Sociological Review,* Vol. 32: 403–416.

Castiglione. *The Courtier.* Harmondsworth: Penguin, 1981.

Chu, Chin-ning. *Thick Face Black Heart.* Beaverton, Oregon: AMC Publishing, 1992.

Cohen, Michael D., March, James G., Olsen, Johann P. 'A Garbage Can Model of Organizational Choice.' *Administrative Science Quarterly,* 1972, 17: 1–25.

Cohen, S. and Taylor, L. *Escape Attempts: The Theory and Practice of Resistance to Everyday Life.* Harmondsworth: Penguin, 1978.

Collier, Peter. 'Blood on the Charles,' *Vanity Fair,* Oct. 1992, 144–164.

Connerton, P., ed. *Critical Sociology.* Harmondsworth: Penguin, 1976.

Carroll, Lewis. *Through the Looking-Glass.* New York: New American Library, 1962.

Coveney, Peter and Highfield, Roger. *The Arrow of Time.* London: Flamingo, 1991, 272–277.

Culbertson, J. *et al.* 'Symposium on the Theory of Practice.' *American Educational Research Association,* Los Angeles, 1981.

Cutt, James. *Comprehensive Auditing in Canada.* New York: Praeger, 1988.

Cyert, R. M. and March, J. G. 'The Behavioral Theory of the Firm: A Behavioral Science–Economics Amalgam.' In W. W. Cooper *et al.,* eds., *New Perspectives in Organizational Research.* New York: Wiley, 1964.

Dale, H. E. *The Higher Civil Service of Great Britain.* Oxford: Clarendon, 1961.

Deleuze, Gilles. *Nietzsche and Philosophy.* Hugh Tomlinson tr. Columbia University Press, 1983.

de Man, Paul. *Allegories of Reading.* Yale University Press, 1979.

DeMott, Benjamin. 'Inside the Leadership Studies Racket.' *Harper's,* Dec. 1993, 61.

Dennett, Daniel C. *Consciousness Explained.* Boston: Little, Brown, 1991.

Derrida, Jacques. *Of Grammatology.* G. C. Spivak tr. Johns Hopkins University Press, 1976.

Derrida, Jacques. *L'écriture et la Différence*. Paris: Editions du Seuil, 1967.

Dimock, M. *A Philosophy of Administration*. New York: Harper, 1958.

Dobell, A. R. and Zussman, D. 'An Evaluation System for Government: If Politics is Theatre, then Evaluation is (mostly) Art.' *Canadian Public Administration*, Fall 1981.

Downey, Lorne W. *Policy Analysis in Education*. Calgary: Detselig, 1988.

Drucker, Peter. *The Future of Industrial Man*. New York: John Day, 1962.

Dunn, William N. *Public Policy Analysis*. Englewood Cliffs, NJ: Prentice Hall, 1981.

Dunsire, Andrew. *Administration, the Word and the Science*. London: Martin Robertson, 1953.

Durkheim, Emile. *Professional Ethics and Civil Morals*. C. Brookfield tr. London, 1957.

Enns, Frederick. 'Some Ethical-Moral Concerns in Administration.' *Canadian Administrator*, 1981, 20.

Etzioni, Amitai. 'Mixed-Scanning: A 'Third' Approach to Decision Making.' *Public Administration Review* XXVII, Dec. 1967.

Evers, Colin E. and Lakomski, Gabriele. 'Science in Educational Administration: A Postpositivist Conception.' *American Educational Research Association*, San Francisco, April, 1995.

Fayol, Henri. *Administration, industrielle et générale*. Paris 1916. Tr. J. Coubrough, London: Putman, 1929.

Fielder, Fred. 'The Contingency Model and the Dynamics of the Leadership Process.' In L. Berkowitz, ed., *Advances in Experimental Social Psychology*, Vol. II. New York: Academic Press, 1978.

Fielder, F. *A Theory of Leadership Effectiveness*. New York: McGraw-Hill, 1967.

Fielder, F. E. *et al. Improving Leadership Effectiveness*. New York: Wiley, 1976.

Fielder, F. E. and Chemers, M. M. *Leadership and Effective Management*. Glenview, Ill.: Scott, Foresman, 1974.

Fleishmann, E. A. and Peters, D. R. 'Interpersonal Values, Leadership Attitudes and Managerial Success,' *Personnel Psychology*, 1962, 15: 127–143.

Follett, Mary Parker. *Creative Experience*. London: Longmans, 1924.

Foucault, Michael. *Politics, Philosophy, Culture*. Laurence P. Kritzman, ed. New York: Routledge, 1988.

Foucault, Michael. *Power/Knowledge*. New York: Pantheon, 1980.

Frederickson, H. G. 'Symposium on Social Equity and Public Administration.' *Public Administration Review*, 1974, 34: 1–51.

Gabriel, Richard A. and Savage, Paul L. *Crisis in Command*. New York: Hill and Wong, 1978.

Gardner, James C. 'Organization and Methods Development in the Government of Canada.' *Public Administration*, U.K., Autumn 1976.

Geertz, C. *The Interpretation of Cultures*. New York: Basic Books, 1973.

Georgiu, P. 'The Goal Paradigm and Notes towards a Counter Paradigm.' *Administrative Science Quarterly*, 1973, 18: 291.

Getzels, Jacob W. and Egon Guba. 'Social Behavior and the Administrative Process.' *School Review*, Winter 1957.

Giddens, A. *New Rules of Sociological Method*. London: Hutchinson, 1977.

Gödel, Kurt. *Über formal entscheidbar Sätze der Principia Mathematica und Verwandte Systeme. Monatsheft für Mathematik und Physik*. 1931.

Goffman, E. *The Presentation of Self in Everyday Life*. Harmondsworth: Penguin, 1959.

Goldberg, S. *The Inevitability of Patriarchy*. London: Temple Smith, 1977.

Goldhamer, Herbert and Shils Edward A. 'Types of Power and Status.' *American Journal of Sociology* XIV, 1939.

Gorbachev, Mikhail. *Perestroika*. New York: Harper and Row, 1987.

Gouldner, Alvin. 'Cosmopolitans and Locals: Toward an Analysis of Latent Social Roles,' *Administrative Science Quarterly*, 1957/8, 2: 281–306, 440–480.

Gouldner, Alvin. *The Future of Intellectuals and the Rise of the New Class*. New York: Oxford University Press, 1982.

Gowen, Herbert H. *A History of Indian Literature*. New York: Appleton, 1931.

Greenfield, Thomas B. 'Organizations as Talk, Chance, Action, and Experience.' In A. Heigl-Evers and V. Streeck, eds., *Die Psychologie des 20 Jahrhunderts*. Band VILL, Zürich: Kindler Verlag, 1978.

Greenfield, Thomas B. 'Reflections on Organization Theory and the Truths of Irreconcilable Realities,' *Educational Administration Quarterly*, 1978, 14, 2.

Greenfield, Thomas B. 'Theory in the Study of Organizations and Administrative Structures.' Cited in *Educational Administration: International Challenges*. G. Baron, ed. London: Athlone Press, 1975.

Greenfield, Thomas B. 'Environment as Subjective Reality: A Retrospective View of Modern Organization Theory and its Failure as Administrative Theory in Education and Elsewhere.' Conference paper, *American Educational Research Association*, Montreal, April 1983.

Greenfield, Thomas B. 'The Man who comes Back through the Door in the Wall: Discovering Truth, Discovering Self, Discovering Organizations.' *Educational Administration Quarterly*, 1980, 16, 3: 26–59.

Greenfield, Thomas B. 'Against Group Mind: An Anarchistic Theory of Organization.' In *Reflective Readings in Educational Administration*. Victoria, Australia: Deakin University Press, 1983, 293–301.

Greenfield, Thomas B. and Peter Ribbins ed., *Greenfield on Administration. Towards a Humane Science*. London: Routledge, 1992.

Gronn, Peter. 'Talk as the Work: The Accomplishment of School Administration.' *Administrative Science Quarterly*, 1983, 28, 1: 1–21.

Grossman, Vasily. *Life and Fate*. London: Collins, 1987.

Gulick, Luther and L. Urwick, eds. *Papers on the Science of Administration*. New York: Columbia University Press, 1937.

Habermas, Jürgen. *Knowledge and Human Interests*. Tr. J. Shapiro. London: Heinemann, 1972.

Habermas, Jürgen. *The Philosophical Discourse of Modernity*. F. Lawrence tr. Cambridge, Mass.: MIT Press, 1987.

Hardin, G. *Exploring New Ethics for Survival*. New York: Penguin, 1968.

Harris, Carol. 'The Naked Participant: Balancing Personal Perspectives with the Concept of Verstehen in Interpretive Inquiry.' *Commonwealth Society for the Study of Educational Administration*, Toronto, 1994.

Hayek, Friedrich. 'The Use of Knowledge in Society.' *American Economic Review*, 1965 Sept., 35: 526–528.

Henry, William A. *In Defense of Elitism*. New York: Doubleday, 1994.

Herzberg, Fred. *Work and the Nature of Man*. Cleveland: World Publications, 1966.

Hitler, Adolf. *Mein Kampf*. New York: Reynal and Hitchcock, 1939.

Hodgkinson, Christopher. 'Philosophy, Politics, and Planning. An extended Rationale for Synthesis.' *Educational Administration Quarterly* II, 1975.

Hodgkinson, Christopher. *Towards a Philosophy of Administration*. Oxford: Blackwell, 1978.

Hodgkinson, Christopher. 'Japanese Management and Leadership.' Department of Educational Administration, University of Alberta, January 1989.

Hodgkinson, Christopher. *Educational Leadership: The Moral Art*. State University of New York Press, 1991.

Hodgkinson, Christopher. 'The Epistemological Axiology of Evers and Lakomski: Some un-Quinean Quibblings.' *Journal of Educational Management and Administration*, Spring 1993.

House, R. J. 'Theory of Charismatic Leadership.' In J. G. Hunt and L. L. Largen, eds., *Leadership: The Cutting Edge*. Southern Illinois University Press, 1977.

House, R. J. 'A Path-Goal Theory of Leader Effectiveness.' *Administrative Science Quarterly*, 1971, 16.

Hurley, Kathleen V. and Dobson, Theodore G. *What's My Type?* San Francisco: Harper, 1991.

Introduction to the Matsushita School of Government and Management. Kanagawa: Matsushita Corporation, 1980.

Janis, I. L. *Victims of Groupthink*. Boston: Houghton Mifflin, 1972.

Jannings, B. 'Policy Analysis: Science, Advocacy, or Counsel.' In S. Nagel, ed. *Research in Public Policy Analysis and Management*. Greenwich, Conn.: JAI Press, 1987.

Jennings, B. 'Interpretive Social Science and Policy Analysis.' In D. Callahan and B. Jennings, eds. *Ethics, The Social Sciences, and Policy Analysis*. New York: Plenum, 1987.

Kant, Immanuel. *Critique of Pure Reason*. New York: Liberal Arts Press, 1909, 1956.

Kaplan, Abraham. *The Conduct of Inquiry*. San Francisco: Chandler, 1964.

Katz, Daniel and Robert L. Kahn. *The Social Psychology of Organizations*. New York: Wiley, 1966.

Katz, D., R. L. Kahn and J. S. Adams, eds. *The Study of Organizations*. San Francisco: Jossey-Bass, 1980.

Kaufmann, Walter. *Nietzsche*, 4th edn. Princeton University Press, 1974.

Ker, S. S. 'Substitutes for Leadership: Some Implications for Organizational Design.' *Organization and Administrative Sciences*, 1977, 8: 135–146.

Ker, S. S., Ker J. Jermier. 'Substitutes for Leadership: Their Meaning and Measurement.' *Organizational Behavior and Human Performance*, 1978, 22: 375–403.

Kierkegaard, Søren. *Fear and Trembling*.

Kinsey, Alfred C. *et al. Sexual Behavior in the Human Male*. W. B. Saunders, 1969.

Kinsey, Alfred C. *et al. Sexual Behavior in the Human Female*, W. B. Saunders, 1953.

Ladd, John. 'Morality and the Ideal of Rationalization in Formal Organizations.' *The Monist*, 1970, 54.

Lang, Don. 'Values and Commitment: An Empirical Verification of Hodgkinson's Value Paradigm as Applied to the Commitment of Individuals to Organizations.' Unpublished dissertation, University of Victoria, 1976.

Lasch, Christopher. *The Culture of Narcissism*. New York: W. W. Norton, 1979.

Laslett, P. and W. G. Runciman, eds. *Philosophy, Politics and Society*, 3rd series. Oxford: Basil Blackwell, 1967.

Leithwood, K. and Steinbach, R. *Expert Problem Solving*. Albany: State University of New York Press, 1995.

Lerner, D. and H. Lasswell, eds. *The Policy Sciences*. Palo Alto, 1951.

Lessing. *Die Erziehung des Menschengeschlechts*. 1780.

Lewin, Kurt. *The Conceptual Representation and Measurement of Psychological Forces*. Durham, NC: Duke University Press, 1939.

Lichtheim, G. *The Concept of Ideology and Other Essays*. New York, 1967.

Lindblom, Charles E. *The Policy Making Process*. Englewood Cliffs, NJ: Prentice Hall, 1968.

Lindblom, Charles E. 'The Science of Muddling Through.' *Public Administration Review*, 1959 Spring: 155–169.

Lindblom, Charles E. 'Still Muddling: Not Yet Through.' *Public Administration Review*, 39: 517–526.

Litchfield, G. H. 'Notes on a General Theory of Administration.' *Administrative Science Quarterly*, 1956, 1.

Lyotard, Jean-Rancois. *The Postmodern Condition*. G. Bennington and B. Massumi, trs. Minneapolis: University of Minnesota Press, 1986.

McGowan, John. *Postmodernism and Its Critics*. London: Cornell University Press, 1991.

McGregor, D. *The Human Side of Enterprise*. New York: McGraw-Hill, 1960.

McGregor, D. and W. G. Bennis, eds. *The Professional Manager*. New York: McGraw-Hill, 1967.

The Essential McLuhan. Don Mills: General Publishing, 1995.

McNamara, Robert S. *In Retrospect: The Tragedy and Lessons of Vietnam*. New York: Random House, 1995.

Machiavelli, Nicolo. *The Prince*. London: Routledge, 1886.

Mackie, J. L. *Ethics*. Harmondsworth: Penguin, 1977.

Magee, Bryan. *Modern British Philosophy*. St. Alban's: Paladin, 1973.

Mannheim, K. *Ideology and Utopia*. London: 1956.

March, James G. and Simon, H. A. *Organizations*. New York: Wiley, 1958.

Marini, E., ed. *Toward A New Public Administration*. New York: Chandler, 20.

Marx, Karl. *The German Ideology*.

Maslow, Abraham. *Eupsychian Management*. Irwin, Ill.: Homewood, 1965.

Maslow, Abraham. *Toward a Psychology of Being*, 2nd edn. New York: Van Nostrand, 1968.

Maslow, Abraham. *Motivation and Personality*. New York: Harper, 1956.

Matsushita, K. *Portrait on an Industrialist*. Osaka: PHP Institute, 1988.

Matsushita, K. *Not for Bread Alone. A Business Ethos. A Management Ethos*. Osaka: PHP Institute, 1988.

Mayo, Elton. *The Human Problems of an Industrial Civilization*. London: Routledge and Kegan Paul, 1969.

Michels, R. *Political Parties: A Sociological Study of the Oligarchical Tendencies of Modern Democracy*. New York, 1962.

Midgley, Mary. *Beast and Man: The Roots of Human Nature*. Ithaca, NY: Cornell University Press, 1978.

Milgram, S. 'Behavioral Study of Obedience.' *Journal of Abnormal and Social Psychology*, 1963, 67.

Milgram, S. 'Some Conditions of Obedience and Disobedience to Authority.' *Human Relations*, 1965, 18.

Milgram, Stanley. *Obedience to Authority*. New York: Harper and Row, 1974.

Mintzberg, Herbert. *The Nature of Managerial Work*. New York: Harper and Row, 1973.

Moir, Anne and David Jessel. *Brainsex*. London: Mandarin, 1994.

Mooney, J. D. *The Principles of Organization*. New York: Harper, 1937.

Moore, G. E. *Principa Ethica*. University Press, 1903.

Morgan, Gareth. *Images of Organization*. London: Sage, 1986.

Murdoch, Iris. *Metaphysics as a Guide to Morals*. London: Penguin, 1992.

Charles Newman, *The Postmodern Aura*. Evanston, Ill., 1985.

Nicoll, Maurice. *Psychological Commentators on the Teachings of Gurdieff and Ouspensky*. London: Shambala, 1984.

Nietzsche, Friedrich. *Beyond Good and Evil*. Walter Kaufmann tr. New York: Modern Library, 1968.

Nietzsche, Friedrich. *The Will to Power*. W. Kaufmann and R. J. Hollingdale trs. New York: Random House, 1968.

Nietzsche, Friedrich. *Twilight of the Idols*. R. J. Hollingdale tr. Harmondsworth: Penguin, 1969.

Nietzsche, Friedrich. *The Gay Science*. Walter Kaufmann tr. New York: Random House, 1974.

Nietzsche, Friedrich. *Human, All Too Human*, 2nd edn. 1886.

Nietzsche, Friedrich. *Daybreak*. 1980: Preface (1886).

Nietzsche, Friedrich. *Von Nutzen and Nachteil der Historie für das Leben*. (2nd Untimely Meditation), 1874.

Orwell, George. *1984*. Harmondsworth: Penguin, 1949.

Paglia, Camille. *Sexual Personae*. Yale University Press, 1990.

Paglia, Camille. *Sex, Art, and American Culture*. New York: Random House, 1992.

Parsons, Talcott and Edward Shils, eds. *Toward a General Theory of Action*. New York: Harper, 1962.

Pastin, M. *The Hard Problems of Management*. San Francisco: Jossey-Bass, 1986.

Penrose, Roger. *The Emperor's New Mind*. New York: Oxford University Press, 1990.

Peters, L. J. *The Peter Principle*. New York: Morrow, 1969.

Peters, R. S. *The Concept of Motivation*. London: Routledge and Kegan Paul, 1960.

Peters, T. J. and Waterman, R. H. *In Search of Excellence*. New York: Harper and Row, 1982.

Plato. *The Republic*, 2nd edn. Harmondsworth: Penguin, 1974.

Pollard, Harold R. *Developments in Management Thought*. London: Heinemann, 1976.

Pope, Alexander. *An Essay on Criticism*.

Pope, Alexander. *An Essay on Man*.

Popper, Karl. *The Open Society and its Enemies*. London: Routledge and Kegan Paul, 1966.

Popper, Karl. 'What can Logic do for Philosophy?' *Proceedings of the Aristotelian Society*, 1948.

Power, Michael. 'Modernism, Postmodernism and Organization.' In John Hassard and Denis Pym, *The Theory and Philosophy of Organizations*. London: Routledge, 1990.

Prabhavananda, Swami and Christopher Isherwood tr. *Bhagavad-Gita*. New York: Mentor, 1982.

Ramos, Alberto G. *The New Science of Organizations: A Reconstruction of the Wealth of Nations*. Toronto: University of Toronto Press, 1981.

Reddin, W. J. *Managerial Effectiveness*. New York: McGraw-Hill, 1970.

Riso, Don Richard. *Personality Types: Using the Enneagram for Self-Discovery.* Boston: Houghton Mifflin, 1987.

Roethlisberger, F. J. and Dickson, W. J. *Management and the Worker.* Cambridge, Mass.: Harvard University Press, 1939.

Rokeach, Milton. *The Nature of Human Values.* New York: Free Press, 1973.

Roper, Hugh Trevor. *The Last Days of Hitler.* 1947.

Rorty, Richard. *Contingency, Irony, and Solidarity.* Cambridge University Press, 1989.

Rosenbaum, Ron. 'Explaining Hitler.' *New Yorker*, 1 May 1995: 50.

Rosenbach, William E. and Taylor, Robert L. *Contemporary Issues in Leadership*, 2nd edn. London: Westview Press, 1989.

Russell, Bertrand. *Power.* London: Unwin, 1975.

Ryle, Gilbert. *The Concept of Mind.* New York: Barnes and Noble, 1949.

Rousseau, Jean-Jacques. *Le Contract Sociale.* Paris: 1762.

Said, Edward. *The World, the Text, and the Critics.* Harvard University Press, 1986.

Samier, Eugénie. 'A Study of the Relevance of Max Weber's Work to Educational Administration Theory' (*Nach eine verstehende Erziehungsverwaltungswissenschaft*), unpublished Ph.D. dissertation, University of Victoria, 1993.

Satprakashananda, Swami. *Methods of Knowledge.* London: Allen and Unwin, 1965.

Schein, E. *Organizational Culture and Leadership.* San Francisco: Jossey-Bass, 1985.

Schick, Allen. 'Beyond Analysis.' *Public Administration Review*, 1977, 37, 3: 258–263.

Schuhmacher, E. F. *A Guide for the Perplexed.* New York: Harper and Row, 1977.

Scott, W. Richard. *Organizations: Rational, Natural and Open Systems.* Englewood Cliffs, NJ: Prentice Hall, 1981.

Scott, William G. and Hart, David K. *Organizational America.* Boston: Houghton Mifflin, 1979.

Self, Peter. *Administrative Theories and Politics.* London: Allen and Unwin, 1972.

Selznick, Philip. 'Foundations of the Theory of Organization.' In Amitai Etzioni, ed. *Complex Organizations: A Sociological Reader.* New York: Holt, Rinehart and Winston, 1962.

Selznick, Philip. *Leadership in Administration.* Evanston, Ill.: Row, Peterson, 1957.

Selznick, Philip. *The Moral Commonwealth: Social Theory and the Promise of the Community.* Berkeley, Calif.: University of California Press, 1992.

Sergiovanni, T. J. and J. E. Corbally, eds. *Leadership and Organizational Culture.* Urbana, Ill.: University of Illinois Press, 1986.

Shannon, E. and Weaver, W. *The Mathematical Theory of Communication.* Urbana, Ill., 1949.

Sievers, Burkhard. 'The Diabolization of Death. Some Thoughts on the Obsolescence of Mortality in Organization Theory and Practice.' In J. Bassard and D. Pym, eds., *The Theory and Philosophy of Organizations.* London: Routledge, 1990.

Silver, M. and Geller, D. 'On the Irrelevance of Evil: The Organization and Individual Action.' *Journal of Social Issues*, 1978, 34, 4.

Simon, Herbert, A. 'Theories of Decision-Making in Economic and Behavioral Science.' *American Economic Review* XLIX, 1959.

Simon, Herbert. *Principles of Sociology.* London, 1910.

Simon, Herbert A. *Administrative Behavior.* New York: Free Press, 1965.

Simon, H., Smithburg, V. and Thompson, V. *Public Administration.* New York: Knopf, 1950.

Skinner, B. F. *Beyond Freedom and Dignity*. New York: Knopf, 1971.

Smith, Adam. *The Wealth of Nations*. London, 1776.

Snow, C. P. (Lord). *Science and Government*. Cambridge, Mass.: Harvard University Press, 1961.

Speer, Albert. *Inside the Third Reich: Memoirs*. New York: Macmillan, 1970.

Steers, Richard M. and Porter, Lyman W. *Motivation and Work Behavior*. New York: McGraw-Hill, 1975.

Stevens, John. *The Sword of No-Sword*. Boston: Shambala, 1994.

Stigler, George J. 'The Theory of Economic Regulation.' In *The Bell Journal of Economics and Management Science*, Spring 1971, 2: 3–21.

Stogdill, R. M. 'The Evolution of Leadership Theory.' *Proceedings of the Academy of Management*, 1975.

Stone, I. F. *The Trial of Socrates*. New York: Anchor, 1989.

Stufflebeam, D. L. *et al*. *Educational Evaluation and Decision Making*. Itasca, Ill.: Peacock, 1971.

Suzuki, Daisetz. *Zen and Japanese Culture*. Princeton: Bollingen Foundation, 1959.

Tarnas, Richard. *The Passion of the Western Mind*. New York: Ballantine, 1991.

Taylor, Frederick W. *The Principles of Scientific Management*. New York: Harper, 1915.

Taylor, Frederick W. *Scientific Management*. London: Harper, 1966.

Thomas, Rosamund. *The British Philosophy of Administration*. London: Longmans, 1978.

Thompson, J. D. *Organizations in Action*. New York: McGraw-Hill, 1967.

Thompson, K. *Beliefs and Ideology*. London, 1986.

Thompson, Victor A. *Modern Organization*. New York: Knopf, 1961.

Thompson, Victor A. *Bureaucracy and the Modern World*. Morristown, NJ: General Learning Press, 1976.

Thompson, Victor A. *Without Sympathy or Enthusiasm: The Problem of Administrative Compassion*. New York: Macmillan, 1975.

Ferdinand Tönnies. *Community and Association*. London: Routledge and Kegan Paul, 1955.

Tribe, Lawrence H. 'Policy Science: Analysis or Ideology.' *Philosophy and Public Affairs*, Fall 1972.

Urmson, J. O. *The Emotive Theory of Ethics*. London, 1968.

Van Fleet, David and Yukl, Gary. 'A Century of Leadership Research.' *Papers Dedicated to the Development of Modern Management*. U.S. Academy of Management, 1986: 12–23.

Vickers, Geoffrey. *The Art of Judgment*. New York: Basic Books, 1970.

Vickers, Sir Geoffrey. *Human Systems are Different*. London: Harper and Row, 1983.

Vickers, Sir Geoffrey. *Freedom in a Rocking Boat*. Harmondsworth: Penguin, 1972.

Vickers, Sir Geoffrey. *Responsibility—Its Sources and Limits*. Seaside, CA: Intersystems Publishing, 1980: 55.

Vividishananda, Swami. *A Man of God*. Madras: Sri Ramakrishna Math, 1957.

Waldo, Dwight. *The Enterprise of Public Administration*. Novato, Calif.: Chandler and Sharp, 1980.

Weber, Max. *The Theory of Social and Economic Organization*. A. Henderson and T. Parsons trs. London: Oxford University Press, 1969.

Weber, Max. *On Charisma and Institution Building*. S. N. Eisenstadt, ed. Chicago: Chicago University Press, 1922.

Weber, Max. *Economy and Society: An Outline of Interpretive Sociology*. Berkeley, Calif.: University of California Press, 1978.

Weber, Max. *Staatssoziologie*. Berlin: Duncker u. Humblot, 1956.

Weil, Simone. *Selected Essays*. R. Rees tr. New York, 1962.

Weil, Simone. *Oppression and Liberty*. London: Routledge and Kegan Paul, 1965.

Wheeler, J. A. 'Genesis and Observership.' In Batts and Hintikka, eds., *Foundational Problems in the Social Sciences*. Dordrecht: Reidel, 1977.

Whyte, W. H. *The Organization Man*. 1956.

Wilson, Edward O. *Sociobiology: The New Synthesis*. Cambridge, Mass: Harvard University Press, 1975.

Wildawsky, Aaron. *Speaking Truth to Power: The Art and Craft of Policy Analysis*. Boston: Little, Brown, 1979.

Willower, Donald J. 'Dewey's Theory of Inquiry and Reflective Administration.' *Journal of Educational Administration*, 1994, 32: 1.

Wilkinson, Francis. *Police Leadership*. New York: Gower, 1993.

Wise, Arthur E. 'Why Educational Policies often Fail: The Hyperrationalization Hypothesis.' *Curriculum Studies* 9, 1: 43–57.

Wittgenstein, Ludwig. *Tractatus Logico-Philosophicus*. London: Routledge and Kegan Paul, 1976.

Wittgenstein, Ludwig. *Culture and Value*. Oxford: Basil Blackwell, 1980.

Wittgenstein, Ludwig. *On Certainty*. Oxford: Basil Blackwell, 1969.

Wright, M. 'The Professional Conduct of Civil Servants.' *Public Administration*, 1973, 51: 1–16.

Xenophon. *Memorabilia*. Loeb Classical Library, 1918–1925.

Zimmer, Heinrich. *Philosophies of India*. New York: Bollingen Foundation, 1956.

Author Index

Subject Index